Colonial Blackness

Colonial Blackness

A HISTORY OF AFRO-MEXICO

Herman L. Bennett

Indiana University Press

BLOOMINGTON AND INDIANAPOLIS

This book is a publication of

Indiana University Press

601 North Morton Street
Bloomington, IN 47404-3797 USA

http://iupress.indiana.edu

Telephone orders	800-842-6796
Fax orders	812-855-7931
Orders by e-mail	iuporder@indiana.edu

The paper used in this publication meets the minimum
requirements of American National Standard for
Information Sciences—Permanence of Paper for Printed
Library Materials, ANSI Z39.48-1984.

MANUFACTURED IN THE UNITED STATES OF AMERICA

Library of Congress Cataloging-in-Publication Data

Bennett, Herman L. (Herman Lee), date-
  Colonial blackness : a history of Afro-Mexico / Herman L. Bennett.
    p. cm. — (Blacks in the diaspora)
  Includes bibliographical references and index.
  ISBN 978-0-253-35338-2 (cloth : alk. paper) 1. Blacks—Mexico—History—
17th century. 2. Mexico—Race relations—History—17th century. I. Title.
  F1392.B55B467 2009
  972'.00496—dc22
                          2009001520

1 2 3 4 5 14 13 12 11 10 09

Dedicated to Jennifer Lyle Morgan and the beloved
memory of her parents Claudia Burghardt Morgan
and John Paul Morgan, M.D.

He had planned to return to his parish after the wedding, but he was appalled at the hardness of the inhabitants of Macondo, who were prospering in the midst of scandal, subject to the natural law, without baptizing their children or sanctifying their festivals. Thinking that no land needed the seed of God so much he decided to stay on for another week to Christianize both circumcised and gentile, legalize concubinage, and give the sacraments to the dying. But no one paid any attention to him. They would answer him that they had been many years without a priest, arranging the business of their souls directly with God, and that they had lost the evil of original sin.

Gabriel García Márquez, *One Hundred Years of Solitude*

Contents

Tables

Preface

The ideas for *Colonial Blackness* crystallized in the postcolonial aura flourishing in and around the Curriculum in African and Afro-American Studies at the University of North Carolina at Chapel Hill. For much of the eighties, Chapel Hill (both the university and the town) constituted a *palenque* where a diverse assortment of exiles and expatriates from Africa, the Caribbean, Europe, Latin America, and the United States found refuge. Whether they were temporary or long-term residents, members of the gathering of sojourners created overlapping public spheres in which diverse global realities were made manifest, vigorously debated, and acted upon. At the same time, the realities of a Reagan-dominated America reinforced local and global concerns. In what seemed like never-ending conversations, debates, arguments, and lectures featuring Afro-Germans, Black Americans, Black British, Central Americans, Chicanos, Jamaicans, Nigerians, Tanzanians, South Africans, and southern White liberals and radicals, we engaged the global manifestations of blackness through our differences.

Since those days in North Carolina, during sojourns in Durham, Mexico City, London, Baltimore, and New York, I have pressed on my initial concern with blackness. Lately, a group of law professors, anthropologists, literary and performance theorists, and historians interested in deepening the critique of the political present have turned to the study of slavery and its legacies. In these interdisciplinary conversations, I perceive a deep commitment to discerning the shifting logics of power and agency and domination and resistance that shape modern life. Skeptical of the orthodoxy that informs the politics of knowledge, these intellectuals consistently raise issues about the political present and seek to re-map our political future. Through our conversations, I have been affirmed in the belief that studying the slave constitutes an engagement with the present, the past, and the future.

Our concerns with the present are linked to the past through the following question: In what ways did African survivors of the Middle Passage experience the New World? Each generation of black intellectuals contends with this ontological question. But now another more politically charged refrain accompanies this cultural-philosophical question: When was freedom? How did that freedom enable this present? Through our many differences some of us turn to the African presence, particularly the slave experience, to engage the elusive quest to know and understand the black present. Far from representing a quixotic quest for black authenticity and historical truth, our concerns with the formation of blackness reflect a deep interest in the cultural logic of the modern. For this reason, my interlocutors and I engage the concepts of modernity that are imbued with the burden of European political thought: state formation, political economy, labor, slavery, race, religion, and freedom.

Colonial Blackness examines the making of cultures and identities in an early modern society, thereby confronting a set of questions related to the meaning and representation of blackness, still a reigning problem of my intellectual generation in the Anglophone world. Recent invocations of identities as hybrid, performed, situational, contingent, context specific, fluid, or oppositional have transformed studies of race and slavery. However, similar efforts in Latin American scholarship that have occurred alongside attempts to engage the contemporary Afro-Latin American condition have done little to change the hegemonic representation of the slave past and racial present. Indeed, the persistence with which contemporary Afro-Latin American experiences continue to be based on a monolithic past despite attempts to grapple with the social dynamic of *mestizaje* reflects a pre-configured historical imagination, especially with regard to the foundational category of slavery. At its most elemental level, this structuring associates, then and now, specific persons and places with the institution of slavery.

In scope, these images determine both the authentic sites of the slave experience and the contours of cultural memory. The problem of slavery influences how scholars and nonscholars alike approach the past, the present, and possibly even the future. The emphasis on experience—with the slave experience constituting the master trope—structures the historical imagination. As a result, experiences that underscore the context-specific aspects of consciousness and identity are simply absorbed or rendered as exceptions. By extension of this same logic, scholars have long asserted that universal memories and experiences produce a universal consciousness rooted in the black community. As a commonplace assertion, this idea reinforces the prevailing depiction of a timeless and ahistorical black cultural experience—an essentialized representation that can only be identified as "black structuralism." In its standard formulation, black structuralism rests on the idea of a singular slave subject with a generic African past and predictable racial consciousness. In turn, contemporary cultural memory can be traced to the particular inscription of New World slavery that writers, then and now, configured as the ultimate source of what it means to be black.

In the modern imagination, the black figure still conjures up slavery. Slavery invokes images of structural continuity and cultural stasis. Despite the discursive emphasis on process, dynamism, and contingency—temporal, spatial and juridical—discussions about human bondage still seem lodged in a quest to discern the social logic of master-slave relationships and efforts to excavate the institutional manifestations of a particular slave regime. Intent notwithstanding, this quest magnifies structuralism's hold over social theories that inform the study of slave societies and black cultural formation. Yet what happens to our understanding of black identity when its foundational trope, the slave, is no longer conceived of as a stable subject? Posed differently, how does our understanding of the black present change when we configure complexity into the slave past? Complicating these questions are issues directed specifically at Mexican history and its historians. In what ways is our image of the slave past transformed by an engagement with African history? How does an awareness of African ethnicity trouble existing notions of the black community? In light of *mestizaje*—the process of physical and cultural mixing—can we even speak of a black community, especially when most of its alleged members embraced the label mulatto? Among individuals who acquired their freedom, did the formation of black culture cease? Should we assume a seamless shift from slave to *casta* status whereby freedom signified the end of blackness? At its core, *Colonial Blackness* attends to these questions which are pertinent to the contemporary black world though a re-imaging of its early modern past.

Acknowledgments

A lot of labor and love—not all mine—went into the making of this book, a reality that I gladly acknowledge. Having spent years deliberating over the multi-faceted aspects of black domesticity and interiority, it seems only fitting that I begin by thanking my family. My children, Carl and Emma, supremely confident cultural critics, asked to hear about the storied lives that grace this book, often pressing beyond my interpretations to make connections of their own. I thank their mother, Jennifer Lyle Morgan, for her unconditional love and intellectual labor. Even in the wake of losing her parents, my beloved in-laws, Jennifer continues to exhibit a soulful resilience that envelops us all. In thanking Jennifer and invoking John Paul and Claudia, I want to affirm how central the domesticity that they offered has been to all of us and my intellectual creativity. I am deeply appreciative of my parents, Mutti and Pops, whose emotional support over the years has been a constant source of comfort. My in-laws, Cynthia Young and Zachary Morgan, constantly remind me that the world of ideas and a rich family life need not exist in conflict with one another. I also wish to acknowledge Ethel 'Maymette' Carter's contribution to the book's completion. She honored me in asking to read an early draft of this book.

The various intellectual circles through which I ventured and now travel have been a steady source of inspiration. Most of the individuals listed below did not read a single word of what I wrote here, but they did challenge me with their own ideas and writings. Their engagement represented the highest form of camaraderie. I will never be able to repay the intellectual and emotional debts to the following individuals: Colin A. Palmer, Ann Dunbar, Marty Leary, Myron Dunston, Burly Page, Carlton Wilson, Reginald Hildebrand, Lydia Lindsay, Julius Nyang'oro, J. Lee Greene, Lillian Edwards, Darnell Hawkins, Sherman James, Robert Magubane, and Trudier Harris. If I can claim to be a black intellectual the aforementioned bear significant responsibility for that feat. Writings and talks matter. We are often engaged months and years after reading a compelling essay or book, or hearing a provocative talk. In acknowledging: Rex Nettleford, Orlando Patterson, Colin Palmer, Monica Schuler, Robert (Bobby) Hill, Mary Karasch, Lansiné Kaba, Franklin Knight, David Barry Gaspar, Raymond Gavins, Peter H. Wood, the late John J. TePaske, Julius Scott, Charles Bergquist, and A. J. R. Russell-Wood I bring into relief the disparate genealogies shaping this project. Among my numerous interlocutors I would include Barbara Balliet, Stephen Best, Antoinette Burton, Kim

Butler, Vincent Brown, Alex Byrd, Stephanie Camp, Cheryl Clarke, Mary Ellen Curtin, Belinda Edmondson, Brent Edwards, Kim Hall, Cheryl Harris, Saidiya Hartman, Tera Hunter, Judith Jackson-Fossett, Walter Johnson, Will Jones, Steven Kantrowitz, David Kazanjian, Axel Körner, Julie Livingston, Harry Marks, Yolanda Martinez-San Miguel, Genna Rae McNeil, Fred Moten, Dylan Penningroth, Robert Reid-Pharr, Josie Saldaña, Ben Sifuentes Jarequi, Karl Shoemaker, Faith Smith, Tim Tyson, Eve Trout-Powell, and Ben Vinson, III. Thank you for the small and big things that went into making this book. Among those who made this a better book I gladly acknowledge the heroic efforts of Kate Babbitt, Sherwin Byrant, Jon Sensbach, Ben Vinson, III, Barbara Weinstein, Jeremy Adelman, and Aline Helg. Ann Fabian and Julie Livingston deserve special thanks for being two fabulous readers of a small but critical writing group.

Annalee Davis and Steven Amsterdam are independently responsible for the creative appearance of the book. Years ago, I knew that Annalee Davis's brilliant print entitled, "Putting on My Blackness," spoke to the political and cultural concerns at the heart of *Colonial Blackness*. Our separate engagements with the Middle Passage, its consequences, and legacies bring our disparate projects into conversation with each other. Steven Amsterdam pressed on these concerns with his keen questions and his creative vision thus resulting in the cover jacket. I am deeply indebted to Annalee and Steven.

Institutional support and collegiality have been central throughout the life of this project. Among my colleagues, I would like to thank Indrani Chatterjee, Ann Fabian, Nancy Hewitt, Allen Howard, Temma Kaplan, Steven Lawson, Julie Livingston, and Keith Wailoo. Numerous colleagues at The Johns Hopkins University and Rutgers University were instrumental in molding my thoughts in countless ways. At various institutions the administrative staffs have offered more emotional sustenance than a person could expect in a lifetime. Saying thank you is truly an understatement. I am grateful to the American Council of Learned Societies, the National Endowment for the Humanities, and the Institute of Advanced Study for their fellowship support. Bob Sloan and his colleagues at Indiana University Press have ushered the book through the production process in ways that continue to elicit marvel and deep appreciation. Kate Babbitt has been a rock and a friend I look forward to working with in the future.

I am deeply saddened that Claudia Burghardt Morgan and John Paul Morgan cannot witness the publication of this book. The family life that John and Claudia forged sustained many of the ideas contained in this work. It is to them and their devoted daughter, Jennifer, that I dedicate *Colonial Blackness*. In doing so, I acknowledge the centrality of lovers, family, and friends in the shaping and writing of the past.

Colonial Blackness

Writing Afro-Mexican History

This book examines how Africans, blacks, and mulattos—slave and free—forged communities in colonial Mexico over the course of the seventeenth century. In subjecting converted Africans, blacks, and mulattos to ecclesiastical law (canon law), the Catholic Church authorized certain forms of private life among slaves. In the early years of Spanish rule, particularly in urban centers where Catholic authority prevailed, Africans and blacks exhibited private lives framed around their legally recognized identities as husbands, wives, parents, and legal minors. Of course, these terms and the experiences associated with them stood at odds with the master's will and definitions of slavery based on civil (Roman) law. Writers in the past and the present have asserted that as the master's property (*res*), slaves did not have a legally sanctioned existence independent of their owners. If slaves manifested a private life, the argument went, masters willed it.[1] But now a more careful examination of slavery calls this assertion into question. Even as civil law sanctioned the master's dominion over chattel, canon law simultaneously upheld the slave's personhood.

In my exploration of the concept of a private life in an early modern society, my study privileges Christianity and the workings of the Catholic Church. This approach stands at odds with those slavery scholars who find that Christianity occupied a more distanced role than previously claimed, leading some to argue against its centrality in the formation of black life in the Americas. I illustrate how

---

1. Herbert S. Klein, *Slavery in the Americas: A Comparative Study of Virginia and Cuba* (Chicago: Elephant Paperbacks, 1989), 1–2 and passim; Ira Berlin, *Many Thousands Gone: The First Two Centuries of Slavery in North America* (Cambridge, Mass.: Belknap Press of Harvard University Press, 1998); Ira Berlin, *Generations of Captivity: A History of African-American Slaves* (Cambridge, Mass.: Belknap Press of Harvard University Press, 2003); Herman L. Bennett, *Africans in Colonial Mexico: Absolutism, Christianity, and Afro-Creole Consciousness, 1570–1640* (Bloomington: Indiana University Press, 2003), 33–78; Jennifer L. Morgan, *Laboring Women: Reproduction and Gender in New World Slavery* (Philadelphia: University of Pennsylvania Press, 2004), 69–143.

the Catholic Church in colonial Mexico played an instrumental role in the lives Africans, blacks, and mulattos. It sanctioned the private lives of slaves, enabling Africans, blacks, and mulattos to forge far more specific communities than ever realized. As I have demonstrated in a previous study, a contest ensued between patricians on the one hand and ecclesiastical authorities, royal officials, and enslaved persons on the other. The proliferation of mothers and fathers, aunts and uncles, brothers and sisters, and eventually grandparents and cousins hints at which side prevailed.

In the wake of early modern European expansion and its cultural-political encounters between sovereign and subject, Spaniard and African, master and slave, two novel social phenomena—"the individual" and "liberty"—arose among the diasporic African population, which, along with private life, receives considerable attention in this study. A novelty in early modern Europe, "the individual" evinced "liberty," a nascent social state that in the colonial slave societies of Spanish America arose from the lived experiences of slaves. Conceived through hierarchical relations (patriarch and servant, man and woman, father and son), liberty was forged through the dualities engendered by a black private life. This early modern expression of liberty—one of several that prevailed in that era— materialized among persons of African descent who in the absolutist legal matrix simultaneously constituted chattel, vassals of the Spanish king, and persons with souls.[2] Liberty, like the individual and private life, was the result of the complex legal regime imported by Spaniards in which power was largely—if not exclusively—vested in the sovereign rather than the feudal nobility.[3] Eventually grafted to bodies that Catholic theologians and jurists viewed as without sovereignty, liberty arose as a customary practice.

A previous generation of historians has demonstrated that for British North America, the slave experience brought liberty into relief for English subjects.[4] Just

2. Frank Tannenbaum, *Slave and Citizen: The Negro in America* (New York: Alfred A. Knopf, 1946); Klein, *Slavery in the Americas*; Bennett, *Africans in Colonial Mexico.*

3. Norbert Elias, *The Civilizing Process: Sociogenetic and Psychogenetic Investigations,* trans. Edmund Jephcott (1939; repr., Oxford: Blackwell, 1994).

4. Paul Gilroy's concern that "a quiet cultural nationalism" informs even the best tradition of "some radical thinkers" holds true despite the depth of scholarship on British North America and the more recent studies of the British Atlantic. Gilroy rightly observed that "this crypto-nationalism means that [scholars] are often disinclined to consider the cross catalytic or transverse dynamics of racial politics as a significant element in the formation and reproduction of English national identities." Gilroy, *The Black Atlantic: Modernity and Double Consciousness* (Cambridge, Mass.: Harvard University Press, 1993), 4. Gilroy directed his critique at such brilliant works as Christopher Hill's *The World Turned Upside Down: Radical Ideas during the English Revolution* (New York: Penguin Books, 1972). Gilroy's critique still prevails among studies of the British Atlantic with the notable exception of the work of Peter Linebaugh and Marcus Rediker, which tacks in the wake of English revisionist social and political history but is attuned to the wider context in which social formations operate. Few works rival the scope and breadth of their *The Many-Headed Hydra: Sailors, Slaves, Commoners and the Hidden History of the Revolutionary Atlantic* (Boston: Beacon, 2000).

so, the preponderance of slaves in the Spanish Indies defined the nature of liberty and the related concepts of authority, honor, race, and status in the Castilian world.[5] But in contrast to scholarship in British North America, where the history of freedom delineates the emergence of whiteness and the story of the white republic, I situate the overlapping histories of the individual, liberty, and private lives in the process of black community formation—only in passing do I identify their impact on the commonwealth of Spaniards (*la república de los Españoles*).[6] The African presence, black slavery, and the proliferation of mixed-race populations influenced the workings of the Spanish commonwealth (*república*), including the ways that Spaniards and Indians imagined difference, value, and honor.[7] But my interest in these social phenomena lies in the meaning they had for Africans, black slaves, and the growing free black population. Discerning how persons of African descent perceived and acted on liberty—by definition an engagement with their social practices as individuals wielding private lives rather than an engagement with consciousness—is a principal aim of this study.

In what follows we will track community formation in the course of the seventeenth century, embodied in the shifting claims of family and friends, neighbors and kinfolk. In writing about community life, I do not intend to revisit the intellectual terrain of resilience and cultural survival that was brilliantly framed by an earlier generation of scholars of slave and free black life. An examination of community formation produces more than the story of survival and resistance. It also illuminates how individuals mediated their social experiences through friends and family, sex and marriage, orthodoxy and sin, thereby affording us a new horizon from which we can conceive of and write about the earliest black experience.

*   *   *

5. Verena Martinez-Alier, *Marriage, Class and Colour in Nineteenth-Century Cuba: A Study of Racial Attitudes and Sexual Values in a Slave Society* (New York: Cambridge University Press, 1974); Patricia Seed, *To Love, Honor, and Obey in Colonial Mexico: Conflicts over Marriage Choice, 1574–1821* (Stanford, Calif.: Stanford University Press, 1988); Ramón A. Gutierrez, *When Jesus Came, the Corn Mothers Went Away: Marriage, Sexuality, and Power in New Mexico, 1500–1846* (Stanford, Calif.: Stanford University Press, 1991); R. Douglas Cope, *The Limits of Racial Domination: Plebeian Society in Colonial Mexico City, 1660–1720* (Madison: University of Wisconsin Press, 1994); Ann Twinam, *Public Lives, Private Secrets: Gender, Honor, Sexuality, and Illegitimacy in Colonial Spanish America* (Stanford, Calif.: Stanford University Press, 1999).

6. For the story of freedom and the history of whiteness, see David S. Lovejoy, *The Glorious Revolution in America* (Middletown, Conn.: Wesleyan University Press, 1972); Winthrop D. Jordan, *White over Black: American Attitudes toward the Negro, 1550–1812* (Chapel Hill: University of North Carolina Press, 1968); Edmund S. Morgan, *American Slavery, American Freedom: The Ordeal of Colonial Virginia* (New York: W. W. Norton & Co. 1975); and David R. Roediger, *The Wages of Whiteness: Race and the Making of the American Working Class* (New York: Verso, 1991). An important exception to the historiography of freedom that privileges whiteness and the ascendance of the white republic is Ira Berlin, *Slaves without Masters: The Free Negro in the Antebellum South* (New York: Free Press, 1974).

7. Laura A. Lewis, *Hall of Mirrors: Power, Witchcraft, and Caste in Colonial Mexico* (Durham, N.C.: Duke University Press, 2003).

After the Spanish conquest of Tenochitlán (1519–1521), a steady trickle of Africans augmented central Mexico's initial black population. Fifty years later, the African population outnumbered the Spanish population. Most of the arrivals in the sixteenth century originated in West Africa, but in the forepart of the seventeenth century (1595–1640), West-Central Africans prevailed. By 1640, Spaniards had imported nearly 275,000 West and West-Central Africans into New Spain. The survivors of the dreaded Middle Passage were a subject of much concern. As the Spanish community, which was composed of royal officials, ecclesiastics, and Spaniards of various means, engaged in a protracted struggle to put into practice their competing social visions, which were largely formulated around labor and land, the institution of African slavery occupied a prominent role in their thinking. In the sixteenth century, Africans were at first located in New Spain's urban domestic economy, where they worked as servants attending to the needs of Spaniards, but a growing number found themselves in the countryside employed in the expanding commercial economy. In rural areas, most Africans and their descendants staffed Spanish agricultural and livestock estates of different scales. Spaniards employed a sizeable number of Africans in other commercial activities, most notably mining, that sprang up throughout the sixteenth-century countryside. Finally, the Spaniards relied on the African-descended as vital cogs in the commercial economy; peoples of African descent guided beasts of burden in transporting goods to local and regional markets. Even as the Spaniards formulated new land and labor practices, they tied the African presence to the expanding commercial economy. As slaves, Africans were the vanguard of an increasingly extensive commercial economy that revolved around commodification of goods and people.

Scholars of New World slavery have usually presented Africans and their descendants as laborers on commercial estates located in rural areas. The countryside has emerged as the social site for conceptualizing African and black cultural formation in the Americas. The survivors of the Middle Passage allegedly re-established their connections to Africa in rural areas by forging a semblance of a culture in the Americas that in subsequent generations resulted in the emergence of blackness, defined as the collective experiences of Africans, black creoles, and mulattos. On the basis of this assumption, rural areas have emerged in the scholarship as the *locus classicus* of African ethnicity and black life in the New World.[8]

This perspective does not attend to the full reality of early Spanish America. By 1570, Mexico City was home to the largest African population in the Americas.

8. "These highly developed centers of plantation-based export production," writes historian George Reid Andrews, "became the largest importers of African slaves, and thus the heartlands of Afro-Latin America." George Reid Andrews, *Afro-Latin America: 1800–2000* (New York: Oxford University Press, 2004), 17.

In Mexico City, 9,000 persons of African descent (8,000 African and black slaves alongside 1,000 mulattos) outnumbered the 8,000 Spanish residents. The disparity between the number of Africans and the number of Spaniards increased over the course of the seventeenth century as thousands of Angolans arrived in the capital, augmenting a steadily growing creole population of blacks and mulattos. By 1646, creoles constituted 70 percent of New Spain's black population (having surpassed the African presence), a pattern that was in all likelihood exhibited in Mexico City. In that year, approximately 62,814 of Mexico's combined total of 151,618 persons of African descent lived in the archdiocese of Mexico; put another way, nearly half of the colony's black population lived in or near the viceregal capital.[9] As enslaved Africans, blacks, and mulattos worked in Mexico City's commercial sector and domestic households, their patterns of interaction assumed an urban cultural expression that shaped slavery, eventually engendering novel manifestations of community formation and freedom.

Even though the Crown conceived of the slave trade as a way augment the slave population, the trade in slaves actually facilitated the growth of the free colored population. As the slave population increased in the first half of the seventeenth century, a period when the colony of New Spain introduced 104,205 enslaved Africans, the size of the free black population grew and then rivaled the slave population, which it finally surpassed in the second half of the century.

The rapid emergence of free coloreds in sixteenth-century Spanish America is an astonishing phenomenon that most historians have overlooked in the absence of early colonial census material on the black population. Clearly, Africans did not manifest a natural rate of increase capable of reproducing the slave population, but the enslaved did produce slaves, freed, and free persons, yet this did not mean that Africans, blacks, and mulattos—all of whom were present at the conquest of Mexico—failed to generate offspring. Of course they did. As enslaved African men sired children with Indian women in the early years after the conquest they established the nucleus of the free black population. As free people, their offspring were also free. By the end of the sixteenth century births among the black free began to rival deaths, resulting in a sizeable free population. In our focus on the absence of a natural rate of increase among the slave population, we have overlooked a century of black births involving African men and Mexican women and then among the survivors of these unions. These unions generated the earliest and one of the largest free black populations in the New World.

In light of this phenomenon, one must question why the analytical category of slavery is the defining lens through which scholars examine the experiences and

9. Bennett, *Africans in Colonial Mexico*, 23.

lives of free coloreds.[10] I view slavery—as an institution and as an analytical category—as the foundational ontology that shaped the emergent social and cultural forms manifest among Africans and their descendants. But I am dubious about whether conceptual assumptions derived from the so-called slave experience (which is invariably rooted in the African-American culture of the nineteenth-century United States) apply to the population of free people that emerged a generation after their African parents landed in New Spain. The political context in which Spanish American slavery emerged is very different from that of the British colony that later became the United States. In the Spanish Indies the institution of slavery—a juridical category that defined enslaved Africans as property—had to contend with the competing institutional mechanisms that accorded slaves rights as Christian beings (persons), a process that precipitated the growth of a population of free blacks and coloreds. As Africans, black creoles, and mulattos asserted claims as Christians, first as husbands and wives and later as individuals with free will, they steadily enhanced their personal liberty, which became the vehicle for pressing for freedom.

*   *   *

Contemporary writings on the Afro-Mexican experience are deeply engaged with the project of recovering and inserting the histories of Africans and their descendants into the narrative of New Spain.[11] But this revisionist impulse, despite its most noble efforts, rests on the assumption that Afro-Mexicans presented an epistemological problem because they occupied an intermediate status between conquerors and conquered. Consequently, the conventional approach for examining the lives and experiences of Africans and their descendants focuses on the slave trade and the African past, slavery and the resulting labor arrangements, racial formation, and the ensuing elaboration of status in a shifting colonial polity. Thus, studies of the Afro-Mexican experience tend to focus on the sixteenth or eighteenth century and Afro-Mexican history appears as either the story of slavery or

---

10. Aline Helg has observed that "historians have often neglected the Afro-Colombian experience except in relation to colonial slavery." Helg, *Liberty & Equality in the Caribbean Colombia, 1770–1835* (Chapel Hill: University of North Carolina Press, 2004), 13.

11. Joan Bristol, *Christians, Blasphemers, and Witches: Afro-Mexican Ritual Practices in the Seventeenth Century* (Albuquerque: University of New Mexico Press, 2008); Nicole von Germeten, *Black Blood Brothers: Confraternities and Social Mobility for Afro-Mexicans* (Gainesville: University Press of Florida, 2006); Frank T. Proctor III, "Slavery, Identity, and Culture: An Afro-Mexican Counterpoint, 1640–1763" (Ph.D. diss., Emory University, 2003); Ben Vinson, *Bearing Arms for His Majesty: The Free-Colored Militia in Colonial Mexico* (Stanford, Calif.: Stanford University Press, 2001); Luz Ma. Martínez Montiel y Juan Carlos Reyes G., eds., *Memoria del III Encuentro Nacional de Afromexicanistas* (México: Gobierno del Estado de Colima, 1993); Luz María Martínez Montiel, coordinora, *Presencia africana en México* (México: Consejo Nacional para la Cultura y las Artes, 1994).

the story of the upward social mobility of free blacks.[12] As a result of this narrative strategy, Africans and their progeny emerge as objects but rarely as subjects of the historical plot. While the historiography affords an invaluable glimpse of the foundational experiences of Africans and creoles, thereby offering a corrective to most studies of New World slavery and the formation of black societies in the Americas (which tend to focus on the eighteenth century and beyond), it does little to address the themes that informed the lives of subsequent generations of creoles beyond debating whether race or class was more prevalent in shaping the lives of Afro-Mexicans. The history of the formation of Afro-Mexican culture, especially among the free, languishes in a tradition of neglect and indifference.

A comparative social science paradigm that anchors the free black experience to a history of oppression was initially framed by the historian Frank Tannenbaum in 1946. As news of the German extermination camps of World War II entered public awareness, modernists and proponents of modernization ascribed even greater urgency to concepts of race and culture. Written in the wake of the Holocaust, Tannenbaum's *Slave and Citizen* explicitly delineated a link between racial thinking and modern civil society. Tannenbaum brought the discussion on slavery, colonial racism, and the free black experience to the forefront of scholarly debate.[13] He positioned the study of free blacks in relationship to slavery, thus locating Latin American free blacks in a dual comparative context—a contrast between the black experience in Anglo and Iberian America and the juxtaposition

12. Colin A. Palmer, *Slaves of the White God: Blacks in Mexico, 1570–1650* (Cambridge, Mass.: Harvard University Press, 1976); Patrick J. Carroll, *Blacks in Colonial Veracruz: Race, Ethnicity, and Regional Development* (Austin: University of Texas Press, 1991); Seed, *To Love, Honor and Obey in Colonial Mexico*; Cope, *The Limits of Racial Domination*; Lewis, *Hall of Mirrors*.

13. Frank Tannenbaum acknowledged his conceptual debt to Brazilian sociologist Gilberto Freyre; see Tannenbaum, *Slave and Citizen*, 3–4. We need to remind ourselves that they both, Freyre and Tannenbaum, were interested in the issue of comparative development. Freyre's social science imperative is underscored in the subtitle of his most notable work, *The Masters and the Slaves: A Study in the Development of Brazilian Civilization* (New York: Alfred A. Knopf, 1946). In the subsequent thicket of historiography, the political urgency that informed the writing of *Slave and Citizen* has been tempered. As an Austrian émigré, erstwhile labor leader, and advisor to Mexican revolutionaries, historian Frank Tannenbaum consciously framed *Slave and Citizen* in the wake of news about the Holocaust, thereby sharing the same political imperative and discursive space as Theodore Adorno and Max Hokheimer's *Dialectics of Enlightenment* and Hannah Arendt's *The Origins of Totalitarianism*. In the aftermath of Nazi terror, Tannenbaum challenged the belief that irrational ideologies and practices, including racism, were incompatible with a modern capitalist society. Progressive evolutionary thinking, mediated through the language of civilization, held steadfastly to the belief that race and racism as manifestations of the archaic would eventually succumb in the modern world. But the modern terror that defined the first half of the twentieth century suggested otherwise. It is in this larger context that Tannenbaum framed his comparative examination of race and slavery in the Americas. Instead of simply wanting to vindicate Latin American race relations, Tannenbaum sought to underscore the specious nature of thinking that equated modern society with civil rights. In the ensuing debate, scholars have lost sight of the political horizon that informed Tannenbaum's engagement with the past. And in so doing, they also have dislodged an awareness of his argument that slavery and racism played constitutive roles in the formation of our modernity. In fact, until very recently, most scholars have framed slavery and race in quite narrow terms, rarely situating these phenomena in the history of the West.

of the experience of free blacks against that of chattel. Historian Herbert Klein observed that "for many years social scientist have recognized that the place of the Negro in contemporary North American society was molded by the historical experience of chattel slavery."[14] But Tannenbaum noted "that the political and social environment in Latin America has proved different. Not only was the Negro encouraged to secure his freedom, but once he was free, no obstacles were placed to his incorporation into the community, insofar as his skills and abilities made that possible."[15] Subsequent scholars of Latin America's free blacks adopted the framework of comparative race relations in their efforts to understand the experience of free blacks.[16] As a result, Tannenbaum and his supporters and detractors have implicitly precluded the examination of the Latin American free black experience on its own terms. As anthropologist Peter Wade remarked, "There never really emerged a tradition, functionalist or otherwise, of doing intensive ethnographies that had as their object the explication of the internal characteristics of particular black communities."[17]

To this day, comparative social science, conceived as race relations, frames the Latin American narrative of free blacks. In the introduction to his study on Puerto Rican free coloreds, for example, historian Jay Kinsbrunner defined intellectual success as work that leads "some readers to desire more knowledge about the origins and mechanisms of Spanish American racial prejudice."[18] In her study on free blacks in Spanish New Orleans, historian Kimberly Hanger positioned her concerns in the following terms: "Within the debate over the comparative characteristics of slave societies, my own work discerns a combination of cultural-legal traditions and material conditions, with the latter having greater influence, in assessing the role of *libres* in Spanish New Orleans."[19] Historian Jane Landers also situated her impressive study of free blacks and slaves in Spanish Florida in the race relations paradigm. "This is not to suggest that Spain and its colonies were free of racial prejudice," wrote Landers, "however, acknowledgement of a slave's humanity and rights and a liberal manumission policy eased the transition from slave to citizen and allowed the formation of a significant free black society throughout the Spanish world."[20] Landers is right, of course, but among Latin Americanists, race relations in the form of freedom, access to material resources, upward mobility,

---

14. Klein, *Slavery in the Americas,* vii.
15. Tannenbaum, *Slave and Citizen,* 91.
16. Peter Wade, *Race and Ethnicity in Latin America* (Chicago: Pluto, 1997), 37.
17. Ibid., 51.
18. Jay Kinsbrunner, *Not of Pure Blood: The Free People of Color and Racial Prejudice in Nineteenth-Century Puerto Rico* (Durham, N.C.: Duke University Press, 1996), xi.
19. Kimberly S. Hanger, *Bounded Lives, Bounded Places: Free Black Society in Colonial New Orleans, 1769–1803* (Durham, N.C.: Duke University Press, 1997), 5.
20. Jane Landers, *Black Society in Spanish Florida* (Urbana: University of Illinois Press, 1999), 2.

and patterns of discrimination (all concerns that emanate from a focus on Spanish colonial values) assume primacy over the social and cultural dynamics persons of African descent created for themselves.

Ironically, scholarship on Anglo America—one of the paradigms through which most Latin Americanists still frame their discussion of the black experience—discerns a difference between race relations and black community formation. Historian Gary B. Nash, for example, sees race relations and "the history of the developing black community" as two separate yet interrelated categories of historical analysis.[21] For scholars of Anglo America, the social and cultural practices among blacks shaped "the history of racial relations" as much as such practices were determined by external forces.[22]

Latin Americanists, however, seem content to privilege Spanish "cultural-legal traditions" in determining how free blacks related to whites and the society at large. In short, the prevailing scholarly perspective assumes that social mobility took priority over community formation. Among Mexicanists, notes historian Ben Vinson, this model has been narrowly framed as the "caste versus class debate."[23] In Latin American studies, in other words, the black experience largely arises only as a question of upward social mobility—what rung blacks occupied on the ladder of the colonial and republican social order. "The study of blacks," notes observer Peter Wade, "is one of racism and race relations."[24] But this framework is not confined to the historical study of the black presence. It remains organic to the ways that comparative social science has configured and still configures specific populations in Latin America. Critical of this analytical dilemma, political scientist Michael Hanchard laments how "in some crucial respects, Latin American studies—unlike regional studies literatures of Southeast Asia, Eastern and Western Europe, and Africa—have not incorporated recent developments in conceptualizing racial and ethnic politics."[25] For Hanchard, the problem lies with analysts, politicians, and activists who equate the black experience with race relations, thereby refusing to see the black experience as part of the "political totality." Yet Hanchard reproduces the disciplinary limits of Western social sciences by insisting on the need for "macrolevel theorizing about the power relations between white and black Brazilians."[26]

21. Gary B. Nash, *Forging Freedom: The Formation of Philadelphia's Black Community, 1720–1840* (Cambridge, Mass.: Harvard University Press, 1988), 6.
22. Melvin Patrick Ely, *Israel on the Appomattox: A Southern Experiment in Black Freedom from the 1790s through the Civil War* (New York: Alfred A. Knopf, 2004).
23. Vinson, *Bearing Arms for His Majesty*, 4.
24. Wade, *Race and Ethnicity in Latin America*, 37.
25. Michael Hanchard, *Orpheus and Power: The Movimento Negro of Rio de Janiero and São Paulo, Brazil, 1945–1988* (Princeton, N.J.: Princeton University Press, 1994), 13.
26. Ibid., 7.

He perceives the effects of hegemony as the salient issue, a perspective that renders contemporary black Brazilians bereft of agency, interiority, and lived experience beyond the parameters of political economy. Such views are by far the most preponderant in the study of Latin Americans of African descent.

In Latin American studies, the focus on the exteriority of the black experience has come at the expense of any serious examination of community formation. The most elementary questions still need to be posed. Can we use the concept of "family" in relation to the African experience? If so, what was the family structure of enslaved Africans and how did it vary in the generations after slavery? In what ways did free black family formation differ from that of African arrivals? If indeed it did, when and how did that cultural transformation occur? Given the wealth of archival material, these questions can be addressed in a manner that has proven to be difficult for other regions of the Americas. This scholarly neglect of the elemental level of the lives of African arrivals and their descendants underscores how little we actually know about the enslaved and the culture they created and were allowed to forge. Despite important scholarly contributions that have enriched our understanding of the early African experience in the viceroyalty of New Spain, more than a half-century after the publication of Gonzalo Aguirre Beltrán's foundational *La población negra de Mexico: Estudio ethnohistorico,* the study of persons of African descent, remains trapped in an intellectual framework that privileges slavery.[27] We now have an understanding of New Spain's formative experience with enslaved Africans, a reliable estimate of slave imports and the size of the slave population from inception to its seventeenth-century numerical ascendancy, the distribution of the slave population through time and space, the general pattern of slaveholding, and the role of slaves in the colonial economy. These themes are predicated on a social-theoretical assumption that links Spanish labor needs to the demographics of African slavery, thus offering an explanation for racial slavery in colonial Mexico. The need for labor, rather than an immutable and growing perception of difference among members of Spain's social hierarchy, explains the decision to enslave Africans. In light of Mexico's historical amnesia on the subject of the African presence and the silence of social and cultural historians on the topic, an emphasis on sociocultural themes in the history of Mexico's blacks seems necessary.

*   *   *

A study of freedom naturally begins by conveying the story of slavery but should not be unduly concerned with an institutional history of bondage. Similarly, it is

27. Gonzalo Aguirre Beltrán, *La población negra de México: Estudio ethnohistorico* (Mexico: Fondo de Cultura Económica, 1946).

critical not to represent slavery as a timeless institution. Temporality shaped slavery. In this project, we begin with the seventeenth century, when slavery in New Spain was at its apogee and (paradoxically) when free blacks already outnumbered slaves. The ascendancy of freedom in the seventeenth century requires us to reexamine New Spain's neglected century. In the absence of a history that tracks the legal opportunities and restrictions Africans and their descendants confronted in trying to achieve freedom, the stories that follow center on the private lives of peoples of African descent. By focusing on social and cultural practices forged under absolutism—because they appear, are contested, and are narrated through the colonial archive—we glimpse the relations that defined freedom.

"Freedom" is a much-written-about subject, but most of this work privileges Enlightenment thought and its focus on commercialization, possessive individualism, and the contract. A growing body of writings on the postemancipation era in the Americas engages these themes in order to delineate the realm of the social. Much of this work focuses on the eighteenth century and beyond. But freedom, like slavery, has a genealogy that precedes the consumer society and bourgeois subjectivity. The peculiar incarnations of early modern liberty anticipated subsequent forms of freedom manifest in centers of the Enlightenment and the nascent hubs of bourgeois democracy.[28] This narrative of liberty tells the stories of individual Africans and their descendants who exploited the legal opportunities within absolutism to make claims to their social selves.

Questioning the assumption that colonial and national elites had an unrestricted ability to define the historical icons of colonial and national culture, my intent represents more than a conceptual shift. Herein is a story (or stories) that Mexico's nationalist historians have defined as a non-event (or a sequence of non-events) thereby confining it (or them) to historical invisibility. Even the few historians who object to characterizing these stories as irrelevant agree that including the subjects of these stories in colonial Mexican historiography can be justified only by illustrating the ways that the workings of the state and economy shaped these colonial lives. Blackness cannot be the subject of inquiry as such. This formulation raises several questions. Whose story is being told? Is the story of upward social mobility the entire story of a peoples' history? In what ways can we really understand race relations if there is no understanding of what the historical subjects bring to their encounters with the dominant power and with those who are also subject to dominance? Rather than ask in what ways developments among peoples of African descent were relevant to the political and economic epic of colonial Mexican history, we might want to privilege questions that center Africans and creoles. Posed another way, can there actually be a complex understanding

28. For an earlier example, see Helen Nader, *Liberty in Absolutist Spain: The Habsburg Sale of Towns, 1516–1700* (Baltimore: Johns Hopkins University Press, 1990).

of race and class in colonial Mexican history if our social and cultural histories examine only the Spanish elite and indigenous communities? The relationship between Spaniards and Indians is comprehensible because numerous social and cultural histories of those communities exist that enable historians to discern how members of these collectives molded colonial rule.[29] Histories of the experiences of Africans and their descendants that address similar issues need to be written.

What forms did Afro-Mexican life assume beyond slavery and racial oppression? Can the experiences of Afro-Mexicans in the seventeenth and eighteenth centuries be limited to issues of bondage and status? How might one conceive of the history of Afro-Mexicans in light of abundant archival evidence that alludes to a variety of social and cultural experiences that transcend conventional wisdom about slavery and freedom in distinct places and periods in the New World? How might one write a history of Afro-Mexicans that centers on their concerns, interests, opportunities, and actions? In crafting such a narrative, are the experiences of Afro-Mexicans reconcilable with the conventional epic that defines colonial Mexican history? Prompted by these and related questions, this book offers both a rewriting and an original conceptualization of Afro-Mexican social and cultural history for the seventeenth century and beyond. I privilege the social and cultural experiences of early modern Afro-Mexicans at the expense of a narrative that centers on the colonial dynamic configured around the economy, elite and metropolitan politics, and colonial culture. The colonial dynamic constituted the social field through which Afro-Mexicans channeled much of their lived experiences. However, the limits of early modern absolutism, especially during the second half of the seventeenth through the first half of the eighteenth century, ensured that slavery and freedom were far from hegemonic.

The subjects described in the fragments that follow should be recognized as beings whose actions and experiences are uncovered from documents in an absolutist archive—a domain that recorded their cultural selves in absolutist terms. The stories and narratives that are privileged are always-already enmeshed in a representational discourse that preceded Enlightenment forms of the self, culture, and experience. This study thus engages the vexed terrain of inscribing culture during the absolutist era. Anthropologist David Scott alerts us to the difficulties involved in this process of writing culture. Writing in the wake of the crisis of

29. Charles Gibson, *The Aztecs under Spanish Rule: A History of the Indians of the Valley of Mexico, 1519–1810* (Stanford, Calif.: Stanford University Press, 1964); Karen Spalding, *Huarochirí: An Andean Society under Inca and Spanish Rule* (Stanford, Calif.: Stanford University Press, 1984); Brooke Larson, *Cochabamba, 1550–1900: Colonialism and Agrarian Transformation in Bolivia* (Princeton, N.J.: Princeton University Press, 1988); James Lockhart, *The Nahuas after the Conquest: A Social and Cultural History of the Indians of Central Mexico, Sixteenth through Eighteenth Centuries* (Stanford, Calif.: Stanford University Press, 1992); Rebecca Horn, *Postconquest Coyoacan: Nahua-Spanish Relations in Central Mexico, 1519–1650* (Stanford, Calif.: Stanford University Press, 1997).

representation that gripped anthropology in the 1980s and 1990s, Scott noted that "it has become clear—or clearer, anyway—not only that it will not do to treat non-Western cultures as though they were historyless, but also that 'other' pasts, so to call them, have their own distinctive narrative conventions, forms, and modalities of constituting the past which are irreducible to those of the historical imaginary of the West."[30] Scott understandably restricts himself to a binary formulation of culture—Western and non-Western. This is only part of the picture, since in the case of seventeenth-century Mexico and the Afro-Creole experience, we encounter an absolutist world juxtaposed with the social worlds created by a complex community of uprooted Africans and New World creoles. Collectively these histories preceded the "narrative conventions, forms and modalities" that characterized the Enlightenment imaginary. In short, the ensemble of experiences that proliferated in the era of absolutism denies the claims of singularity attributed here to the "historical imaginary of the West." Still, Scott's engagement is an important starting point as we take up the issue of cultural representation in the era of absolutism.[31]

In light of both a tradition of neglect and a representational strategy for the black experience that has thus far privileged the history of Europe, proposing to write a history of seventeenth-century Afro-Mexicans is fraught with challenge. Even as a critique, this strategy of writing shares the problem of conventional histories: the belief in the transformative power of the archive to uncover hidden truths. I believe that mining the colonial archive produces a far richer narrative than we currently have of the lives Afro-Mexicans. My claims simply embellish the story line of the colonial past; they do not transform it. This fact, however, does not determine my interpretation of my archival findings. Although Afro-Mexican histories may be influenced by the economic and political trajectory of the colonial narrative, attempts to reconcile them with the dominant discourse risk overshadowing their distinctive social logic. Indeed, efforts to recover the Afro-Mexican past can be understood as being related to but not subservient to the epic of colonial Mexican history as it is currently conceived. I suggest that the cultural experiences of Afro-Mexicans should be configured in relation to what it meant for Africans and their progeny as opposed to how those experiences can be interpreted as being meaningful to the narrative of colonial Mexico. It may not

30. David Scott, *Formations of Ritual: Colonial and Anthropological Discourses on the Sinhala Yaktovil* (Minneapolis: University of Minnesota Press, 1994), xv.

31. Given his specific concerns, Scott's observation is understandable. In fact, by employing the concept of "historicity," Scott offers a means for those concerned with "narrative conventions, forms and modalities" prior to the Enlightenment. "Even so," he notes, "the way in which this relation has been thought has varied considerably from anthropologist to anthropologist, and it may well be time to argue not so much for anthropology to be more historical as for certain kinds of historicity and against others." Scott, *Formations of Ritual*, xv. See also John and Jean Comaroff, *Ethnography and the Historical Imagination* (Boulder, Colo.: Westview, 1992), 13–18.

be possible to reconcile Afro-Mexican cultural history with the "national narrative" without simultaneously reducing it to the dominant economic and political narrative. As cultural historians, our goal should be to determine the meaning of experience for our subjects instead of trying to make those experiences meaningful within the dominant colonial narrative.[32]

In light of the cultural dislocation and natal alienation the slave trade introduced—a process that sociologist Orlando Patterson has characterized as social death—the social logic that informed the behavior and consciousness of descendents of Africans may have sought to overcome the dread of the slave experience rather than focusing on how their lives could or should be reconciled with the hegemony of colonial Mexico.[33] Though Afro-Mexican ethnohistory constitutes a feature of colonial Mexican history by definition, we need to be mindful that they were not synonymous. In attending to Afro-Mexican history, we must venture in new directions in the hope of understanding the meaning of experiences of Afro-Mexicans. Such efforts, as we shall see, implicitly amount to a critique of and a challenge to Mexican history.

In his study on national cultural formation, anthropologist Claudio Lomnitz-Adler observed that "Mexican historian Edmundo O'Gorman has argued that politics in Mexico's nineteenth century were riddled by an irresolvable paradox: Conservatives wanted to adopt the economic system of Europe and the United States without substantially changing the colonial social order, while liberals wanted to adopt the United States' economic and political system while retaining Mexico's own cultural traditions. In both cases the issue was how to modernize without giving up valued aspects of Mexican culture and, conversely, how to change the negative aspects of Mexican culture in order to modernize."[34] Though their differences resulted in armed conflict and incessant political turmoil, the political elite shared an exclusive definition of Mexican culture that they insisted was embodied in the Mexican nation. Paul Gilroy refers to "the fatal junction of the concept of nationality with the concept of culture."[35] For the same reasons that the black past was silenced and rendered invisible in the colonial epic that sustains nationalists' renditions of Mexican history, invoking and insisting on the inscription of that past involves far more than a historiographical intervention. As Gilroy notes, "Where racist, nationalist, or ethnically absolutist discourses orchestrate

32. For a formulation that argues on epistemological grounds for the critical importance of "context," see John and Jean Comaroff, *Ethnography and the Historical Imagination,* 11, 16–17.

33. Orlando Patterson, *Slavery and Social Death: A Comparative Study* (Cambridge, Mass.: Harvard University Press, 1982).

34. Claudio Lomnitz-Adler, *Exits from the Labyrinth: Culture and Ideology in the Mexican National Space* (Berkeley: University of California Press, 1992), 1.

35. Gilroy, *The Black Atlantic,* 2.

political relationships so that these identities appear to be mutually exclusive . . . occupying the space between them or trying to demonstrate their continuity has been viewed as a provocative and even oppositional act of political insubordination."[36] Representing the formation of colonial Mexico's black culture disrupts the hegemonic and ideological conceit of national culture. In a discursive domain defined by nationalism, writing about the black presence is a provocation aimed at redefining the terrain of culture and nation.

Before my insistence is misconstrued as a blanket critique of all forms of nationalism, I hasten to note that the ideology of nineteenth-century Mexican political elites confronted, if not challenged, Western imperial claims to economic sovereignty on the grounds that Mexicans lacked a discernible culture and therefore the basis for a nation. Though the political elite once claimed a unique national cultural tradition while purposefully denying the existence of a black presence, such strategic political practices can no longer be justified. The demands of a previous political moment should no longer sanction the ideological practices that historically excluded the black past and presently confines it to the margins of history. In our political present, excluding blacks from the colonial past and from histories of the early republic is an act of ethnic cleansing. Indeed, our present political moment requires us to uncover the Afro-Mexican past in order to arrive at a deeper understanding of the colonial and republican cultures that now demand a rewriting of Mexican history. Endeavoring to write the Afro-Mexican past engages the politics of modernization and modernity; what is at stake is the meaning of nationhood, national culture, and political representation. "Though largely ignored by recent debates over modernity and its discontents," Paul Gilroy writes, "these ideas about nationality, ethnicity, authenticity, and cultural integrity are characteristically modern phenomena that have profound implications for cultural criticism and cultural history."[37]

Intent on conceiving liberty as a social relationship that emerged through the European encounter with Africans, I view the resulting subjectivities—African, slave, black, creole, and mulatto—and their associated experiences as constitutive of modernity. Successive generations of writers, who have often been critics of modernity and prominent theorists of the black condition, have tackled the relationships between slavery, freedom, and modernity.[38] In formulating this trin-

---

36. Ibid., 1.
37. Ibid., 2.
38. C. L. R. James, *The Black Jacobins: Toussaint L'Ouverture and the San Domingo Revolution,* 2nd rev. ed. (New York: Vintage, 1989); Eric E. Williams, *Capitalism & Slavery* (Chapel Hill: University of North Carolina Press, 1944); Aime Cesaire, *A Discourse on Colonialism* (New York: Monthly Review Press, 2001); Walter Rodney, *How Europe Underdeveloped Africa,* rev. ed. (Washington, D.C.: Howard University Press, 1981).

ity and its consequences, these writers have privileged the period that ended with the ascendancy of eighteenth-century England and France; they have rarely privileged sixteenth- and seventeenth-century Spain. This perspective, which can be described as both an ahistorical rendering of modernity and a denial of Spain's experience with slavery and freedom, supplants an earlier and equally vibrant history from which contemporary notions of liberty were only gradually untangled. In delineating this older political tradition, I am conscious of writing the neglected story of the New World's first culture of freedom.

This neglect underscores more than a focus on the slave experience. It magnifies how recording often reflected how the chronicler (and now historians) defined an event as the strategy whereby History, with a capital H, would be plotted. In other words, the growth of the freed and free population in the seventeenth century was not a collective event—a cataclysmic moment, a break, a rupture that shaped or altered the course of History.[39] The inability to conceptualize the presence of the free population of African descent is far more than a problem of knowledge production. In the nationalist context, the problem is additionally complicated by what anthropologist Liisa Malkki, building on the work of Victor Turner, defines as liminality. Malkki notes how "most of us see only what we expect to see, and what we expect to see is what we are conditioned to see when we have learned the definitions and classifications of our culture. . . . The structural 'invisibility' of liminal personae has a twofold character. They are at once no longer classified and not yet classified."[40]

The dearth of social historical inquiries on the nature of freedom is linked to the ways that nationalist hegemony—in the form of the historiographical priorities—has predetermined the discussion about race and the black subject. Sources are not the problem. I disagree with historian Frederick Bowser, who remarked that "the African in bondage is both more dramatic and easier to study than his free and often racially mixed brother." Noting how freedom represents "a more elusive subject for study," Bowser observed that the free person "frequently at the bottom of the social and economic scale . . . aroused only intermittent government concern, was often mentioned only in the most general terms in the accounts of travelers, and rarely participated in the types of activities that generated official records. His very existence, not to mention his individuality, is difficult for the historian to uncover."[41] In making this observation, Bowser restricted himself to a secu-

39. Ira Berlin underscores how the transition from British colony to American republic marked a defining moment in the history of antebellum free blacks. Berlin, *Slaves without Masters*, 15–50.

40. Liisa H. Malkki, *Purity and Exile: Violence, Memory, and National Cosmology among the Hutu Refugees in Tanzania* (Chicago: University of Chicago Press, 1995).

41. Frederick P. Bowser, *The African Slave in Colonial Peru, 1524–1650* (Stanford, Calif.: Stanford University Press, 1974), 272.

lar archive in which the sources confined slaves to the status of commodities—bills of sale, wills, and acts of manumission. Ecclesiastical sources, from which we can glean the most extensive testimony about the ways Afro-Mexicans organized their lives and therefore constructed their histories, demand more than discussions of commodities and the race-class continuum.

Recovering the narratives of Afro-Mexican freedom relies on an unconventional approach that juxtaposes ethnohistory, anthropology, sociology, and literary criticism and privileges the tales, anecdotes, and fragments that Afro-Mexicans left to posterity, even though in their minutiae they detract from the existing colonial epic.[42] This is often labeled a cultural approach, and its finest embodiment has enhanced an understanding of the past that does not privilege conventional views of structure, power, and agency. By connecting heretofore disparate intellectual traditions, I endeavor to bring conventional Latin American history into conversation with studies of Asia, Africa, the Caribbean, Afro-America, and the African diaspora.

My reformulation of slavery and freedom argues that there are conceptual spaces and practices in which the complex calculus of experience is not overdetermined. How else can we explain the decision by seventeenth-century slaves and free people to select individuals of African descent as spouses, as matrimonial sponsors, as godparents and character witnesses? Even though a desire for social mobility sometimes influenced choices, greater consideration should be given to choices made within the realm of familiarity and intimacy; these choices should not be dismissed as forms of bourgeois subjectivity.[43] Social theorist W. E. B. Du Bois wrote, "Leaving, then, the world of the white man, I have stepped within the Veil, raising it that you may view faintly its deeper recesses,—the meaning of its religion, the passion of its human sorrow, and the struggle of its greater souls."[44] For Du Bois, cultural practices, not social striving, defined the black interior. Mexico did not have a "veil" as finely woven as that of the nineteenth-century United States, but the divide it marked was configured in the language of blood (*mala raza*) and the immutable differences of *castas*. In venturing beyond the colonial Mexican racial divide, this book offers a story of slavery and freedom that privileges the social practices of Africans and their descendants.

---

42. Recent studies that use this insurgent representative strategy include Edmund T. Gordon, *Disparate Diasporas: Identity and Politics in an African-Nicaraguan Community* (Austin: University of Texas Press, 1998); and Tina M. Campt, *Other Germans: Black Germans and the Politics of Race, Gender, and Memory in the Third Reich* (Ann Arbor: University of Michigan Press, 2004).

43. For a recent and instructive intervention on this issue that moves beyond the domain of cultural relevance, see Saba Mahmood, *Politics of Piety: The Islamic Revival and the Feminist Subject* (Princeton, N.J.: Princeton University Press, 2005).

44. W. E. Burghardt Du Bois, *The Souls of Black Folk,* intro. Nathan Hare and Alvin F. Poussaint (New York: Signet Classic, 1982), xi–xii.

Time

The scope of the book covers the seventeenth century, especially the period after 1622, a date that does not figure prominently in the conventional histories of colonial Mexico. But it is an important date for scholars of black colonial Mexico: It was the midpoint of the seventeenth-century slave trade. Though the slave trade continued for another eighteen years, by 1622, a century after the inauguration of the slave, slave traders (*asientistas*) had already introduced most of the slaves who would be brought to Mexico in the seventeenth century.[45] After 1622, the structure of the slave trade was less organized and Africans were shipped only sporadically until 1640, the year the universal Catholic monarchy was dissolved and the independence of the Portuguese Crown restored. These events culminated in the cessation of the monopoly (*asiento*) contract and the end of the regular slave trade to New Spain. "The year 1640 marked the end of the regular slave trade to New Spain (colonial Mexico)," writes historian Frank Proctor, which inaugurated "a series of transformations within and for the population of African descent in the colony."[46]

My emphasis on 1622 builds on Proctor's efforts to delineate the dynamics of Afro-Mexico that royal and institutional chronologies have overshadowed.[47] The fact that creoles and mulattos were a discernable presence by 1600 suggests that the West-Central African survivors of the seventeenth-century slave trade entered a dynamic social field composed of more than Spaniards and Indians. Since the slave traders mostly introduced persons identified as being "from the land of Angola" as slaves, Angolans heavily influenced the slave culture of the seventeenth century New Spain. In the process Angolans overlapped with successive generations of creoles. In short, a vibrant cultural dynamic informed black life before the seventeenth-century slave trade ended.[48] "Angolans" were central in the reconfiguration of African culture in New Spain; this explains why I pay relatively little attention to sixteenth-century West Africans. Angolans fundamentally reconfigured New Spain's African presence while layering the creole cultural complex derived from an earlier West African presence. Colin Palmer has identified 1606, 1608, 1609, 1610, and the period from 1616 to 1621 as the peak years of the seventeenth-century slave trade, supporting my argument that by 1622 peoples and cultures "from the land of Angola" predominated among the African popula-

45. Palmer, *Slaves of the White God,* 2, 15, 16, 18.

46. Proctor, "Slavery, Identity, and Culture," 1.

47. Here Proctor elaborates on Colin Palmer and Patrick J. Carroll's pioneering efforts at periodization. See Palmer, *Slaves of the White God,* 2–3; and Carroll, *Blacks in Colonial Veracruz,* 28–37.

48. As von Germeten illustrates, the numerical ascendancy of mulattos in Valladolid by the early 1600s suggests that an Afro-Mexican cultural pattern that was derived from the presence of West Africans preceded the arrival of West Central Africans and was not peculiar to Mexico City. Von Germeten, *Black Blood Brothers,* 129.

tion and complemented black creoles.[49] It is doubtful that Angolans, blacks, or mulattos—slave and free—were aware of 1622 as a distinctive moment in time. But the Angolan majority's social practices accompanied by the creole population's numerical ascendancy—a population whose free members were increasing and creating strong kinship ties—marked a key moment in black life and culture.

Beyond the focus on the seventeenth century, I offer a brief glimpse of the middle decades of the eighteenth century, concluding around 1778. In that year, officials implemented the Real Pragmática (Royal Pragmatic) that Bourbon sovereign Charles III (1759–1788) had issued two years earlier in Spain. With the Pragmatic, the Bourbon state intervened and sought to regulate marriage practices. Designed to stave off "unequal" unions among distinct castes, the Pragmatic granted parents the authority to challenge the marital selection of their children. Youth, which the Pragmatic defined as individuals twenty-five and younger, now needed parental consent to contract a marriage. By instilling this decree, Bourbon policymakers signaled their concurrence with the sentiments of elite Spanish settlers that unbridled freedom constituted a threat to the social order. In order to shore up racial boundaries around white Spaniards, the Pragmatic vilified nonwhites, *castas,* as pervasive social climbers intent on racial exogamy. But since most *castas* opted for endogamous marriages, the concerns expressed in the Pragmatic were white racial fantasies with little basis in social reality.

Space

Seventeenth-century New Spain was home to the most diverse black population in the Americas. Mexico, as the principal center of slaves and free blacks, was an urban mosaic that defied characterization. Seventeenth-century Mexico, like Lima, resembled the present-day cosmopolitan centers of Rio de Janeiro and Salvador da Bahia but anticipated those cultural mosaics by several centuries. With two notable exceptions—chapters 4 and 7—the spatial focus of *Colonial Blackness* is confined to Mexico City.

In an evocative study of the human landscape in nineteenth-century Salvador da Bahia, historian Rachel Harding illustrates the difficulty of characterizing a social landscape.[50] As the former colonial capital of Brazil and one of the most discernible sites of Africa in the Americas, Salvador was a city of contrasts: *escravos* (slave) and *libertos* (free), Africans and creoles, *brancos* (white) and *pretos* (black), Jejes and Nagôs. Harding underscores how the faithful of Candomblé *terreiros*

---

49. Palmer, *Slaves of the White God,* 14–16.
50. Rachel Harding, *A Refuge in Thunder: Candomblé and Alternative Spaces of Blackness* (Bloomington: Indiana University Press, 2000).

(houses) manifested culturally specific understandings of space, topography, and nature—the rudiments of human geography—that defined how they perceived and interacted with Salvador and its diverse inhabitants. For Mexico's inhabitants, similarly privileged sites and distinct routes traversed the capital. In the seventeenth century there were many Mexicos.

In delineating the social geography of seventeenth-century Mexico, we chart the overlapping cultural histories lodged there. To study Angolans and creoles at a specific moment, as I do in the initial chapters, highlights the variegated forms of cultural formation among "blacks." Within the monumental landscape that *conquistadores* layered with Spanish and Christian forms, Angolans and black creoles, as slaves and servants, lived near each other and their masters. By the seventeenth century, Spanish households were established in close proximity to the *plaza mayor,* the cathedral, the *cabildo* (town council), and the viceregal palace. Angolans, along with the descendants of earlier arrivals from West Africa, inhabited the same space as the Spanish elite. Collectively, they lived and worshiped in close proximity to each other. But slaves and servants with access to street life by virtue of their work also shaped recreational worlds that were not frequented by their owners and employers. In these sites—the very interstices of the city—Angolans and creoles found specific *plazas,* parishes, *barrios,* markets (*tianguis*), and residences that they associated with persons like themselves. A site acquired its ethnic or cultural character from the configuration of people gathered there and because those defining themselves as a distinct group identified it as a privileged site.

Specific markets, squares (*trazas*), and streets emerged as playgrounds for ethnic dances, coronations, and festivities. The various parish churches in which baptisms, weddings, funerals, and the activities of conformations took place served as locations of ethnic, cultural, and community gatherings that complemented these other, more private neighborhood sites. When authorities enacted ordinances against collective gatherings, new sites had to be found. Mexico's diverse black core could occupy but never own a location outright. For private dalliances beyond courtship, individuals had to find refuge in the homes of their owners and employers or the isolated shacks (*jacales*) rented by a companion or friends. Privacy was always fleeting, always compromised, and yet sufficient for slaves and free blacks to use their leisure time to forge private lives.

Organization

Social and cultural themes permeate this history. Beginning in chapter 1, "Discipline and Culture," I focus on social discipline as a way to access the cultural practices that informed the lives of free blacks, mulattos, and enslaved Africans. I intentionally focus on the free to underscore the rich cultural dynamic that thrived in the first half of the seventeenth century. This dynamic proliferation of free mulattos alerts us to the existing black presence—slave and free—that preceded the arrival of West Central Africans. In chapter 2, "Genealogies of a Past," I describe the nature of African social practices during the first half of the seventeenth century and reference Mexico's specific African past. I offer a speculative narrative of New Spain's African history and cultural formation among West-Central Africans. Chapter 3, "Creoles," focuses on creole marriage patterns and cultural appropriation for the period 1600–1640. Although the cultural processes of ethnic Africans and creoles were simultaneous, the contrast in a specific place and time illustrates how creoles began to exhibit different cultural forms.

Chapter 4, "Provincial Black Life," takes the story beyond the confines of Mexico City to offer a tentative glimpse of cultural formation in diverse rural areas. Chapter 5, "Local Blackness," concerns itself with how the *casta* framework determines our approach to the black and mulatto experience and looks at subsequent generations of creoles whose ties were profoundly local. Chapter 6, "Narrating Freedom," discusses the role that black private lives played in the history of early modern freedom. Chapter 7, "Sin," attends to the diversity of stories of a society within a society by offering a provisional yet transforming glimpse of important dimensions of the New World black experience—premarital sex, virtue, and a culture of honor among blacks.

The stories that emerge about Afro-Mexican domesticity, desire, and deviance underscore the need for a reassessment of slavery's legacy, which is typically framed by four themes: social death, the creolization interlude, the use of *casta* to identify New Spain's subaltern formation, and the nationalist fiction that blackness was exorcised from the polity during the mid-colonial period. Even as the ethos and practices of a slave society prevailed in key regions of New Spain—Guerrero, Michoácan, Morelos, and Veracruz—many, if not most, blacks were no longer slaves. For most eighteenth-century Afro-Mexicans, slavery's legacy—still framed as a form of social death—had little influence on their kinship practices and the ways they defined community. But legal freedom did not render blackness meaningless as the basis for constituting the self, identifying a desirable spouse, and maintaining community boundaries. As a profoundly localized expression of subjectivity, blackness was manifest in community formation, in which spouse and sponsor selection constituted the cornerstones. As the embodiment of a localized subjectivity, blackness was the antithesis of racial consciousness with its emphasis on some transcendent identity that purportedly linked all persons of African descent. In forging family and kinship ties, in sustaining lifelong relationships and friendships, in establishing contact with specific individuals as they traversed New Spain's commercial landscape, variously defined persons of African descent interacted with persons similarly identified. Such patterns of interaction were far from random. And in their specificity, they magnify the critical importance of blackness. Blackness played a prominent role in the process by which day laborers, hacienda residents, and especially *rancheros* selected spouses and sponsors and thereby in forming the boundaries of their communities.

In the final analysis, remapping the entangled story of cultural formation and freedom demands a fundamental rethinking of how we approach, write about, and locate the rich evidence of African and creole sociocultural formation in the early modern Americas. What follows is an examination of how blacks—the erstwhile descendants of slaves and collective representatives of colonial subjects—forged lives under colonial rule.

ONE

Discipline and Culture

Seventeenth-century Mexico City was a turbulent cosmopolitan center. As the principal site of Spanish power, Mexico City emerged from the remnants of the Mexicas' destroyed capital, Tenochtitlán. Beginning with its reconstruction in the sixteenth century, Mexico housed a diverse population of impoverished Spaniards, conquered but differentiated Indians, enslaved Africans (*ladinos,* individuals who were linguistically conversant in Castilian, and *bozales,* individuals directly from Guinea, or Africa, who were unable to speak Castilian), and the new hybrid populations (*mestizos, mulatos,* and *zambos,* persons with both Indian and African heritage). This diverse group filled the labor needs of the elite as artisans, domestic servants, day laborers, and slaves. As they attended to patrician needs, real and imagined, urban workers of various hues forged a world that soon transcended mere subsistence.[1] Even as finding the balance between life and death posed a daily challenge, the plebeian social world manifested signs of social reproduction and cultural vitality.

In 1609, Portuguese slave traders and Spanish buyers imported over 6,000 enslaved Africans into New Spain. As the Angolans made their way into the vice-regal capital, they entered a social landscape already in the process of formation. Arriving in the midst of New Spain's Catholic renewal, the Angolans landed in a very dynamic cultural arena. In 1609, for instance, the ecclesiastical judge (*provisor*) of Mexico's archdiocese ordered his prosecutor (*fiscal*) to stage periodic raids against alleged sinners. Intent on curtailing the sexual offenses "causing notoriety

---

1. In the historiography of colonial Latin America the term plebeian has long been used to refer to artisans, day laborers, servants, and slaves who lived and worked in cities and towns where they composed the lower order. See Cope, *The Limits of Racial Domination*; John Leddy Phelan, *The People and the King: The Comunero Revolution in Colombia, 1781* (Madison: University of Wisconsin Press, 1978).

and scandal in the neighborhood," the ecclesiastical raids, which were followed by judicial proceedings, brought Catholic discipline into stark relief. Focused on couples who "were publicly concubines" (*están publicamente amancebados*), the raids and the subsequent criminal procedures aimed at quelling the "murmur in the barrio where the [culprits] lived." As the topic of conversation—referred to as "notoriety," "scandal," and "murmur" in the ecclesiastical record—illicit sex constituted both a perennial problem and a threat to the fragile social order with which Catholic authorities had to contend.[2]

At their core, the ecclesiastical proceedings highlight how the Catholic clergy regulated gender and conjugal norms that persons of African descent could assume in the Christian commonwealth (*república*). As Christian regulation structured the experiences of previous arrivals from Africa and the social practices of blacks and mulattos, the clergy signified to the new arrivals what could be publicly practiced. Ecclesiastical discipline among the creole population offers glimpses of both the existence of black private lives as a phenomenon the clergy hoped to control and the pervasive role Christianity assumed in the urban social landscape.

Intent on punishment and regulation, each ecclesiastical raid—whose history in New Spain can be dated to the era of Catholic renewal (1569)—was prompted by the *fiscal's* charge (*denuncia*) and corroborating testimony (*información*) from two witnesses.[3] At this point the *fiscal,* escorted by a royal constable (*alguacil*) and his assistants, would launch a surprise visit to the homes of the alleged sinners,

2. Archivo General del Nación, México City, México (hereafter AGN), Bienes Nacionales 442, expediente 33, 1609, "Proceso del Fiscal del Arzobispado contra Diego de Salinas, sombrero y Catalina, mulata, por Amancebados"; AGN, Bienes Nacionales 442, expediente 8, 1609, "Proceso del Fiscal del Arzobispado contra Gaspar Trejo y Beatriz, mulata, por Amancebados"; AGN, Bienes Nacionales 442, expediente 35, 1609, "Proceso del Fiscal del Arzobispado contra Francisco, español, panadero y Francisca, negra, por Amancebados"; AGN, Bienes Nacionales 442, 1609, "Proceso del Fiscal del Arzobispado de México contra Alonso García, tabernero, e Isabel, mulata for haber reincidido en su Amancebamiento"; AGN, Bienes Nacionales 442, expediente 44, 1609, "Proceso del Fiscal del Arzobispado contra Andrés de Oliva, mestizo, zapatero y Leonor, mulata, por Amancebados"; AGN, Bienes Nacionales 442, expediente 20, 1609, "Proceso del Fiscal del Arzobispado contra Bartolomé Chacón, carnicero, y Juana, mulata"; AGN, Bienes Nacionales 442, expediente 41, 1609, "Proceso del Fiscal del Arzobispado contra Agustín de Loya, mulato, y Ana, mulata, por Amancebados"; AGN, Bienes Nacionales 442, December 1609, "Proceso del Fiscal del Arzobispado contra Diego, mulato, carnicero, y Ana Gomez, mulata, soltera, por Amancebados"; AGN, Bienes Nacionales 810, expediente 125, 1609, "Proceso del Fiscal del Arzobispado contra Julepe de Perea, borador, y Leonor, mulata, por Amancebados."

3. AGN, Bienes Nacionales 497, expediente 319, 1569, "Proceso de Pedro Díaz de Aguero, Fiscal deste Arzobispado contra Francisco Pabon y Teresa Carrillo, mulata, por Amancebados"; AGN, Bienes Nacionales 497, expediente 10, 1570, "Proceso Criminal hecho por Hernán Gutiérrez de Bustamante Promotor Fiscal deste Arzobispado contra Cristóbal, mulato sombrerero, e María, india, por Amancebados"; AGN, Sin Referencia, 1570, "Proceso de Hernán Guteriérrez de Bustamante, Fiscal de este Arzobispado de México contra Francisco del Acevedo, español, y Juana, mulata, por Amancebados"; AGN, Bienes Nacionales 497, expediente 29, 1571, "Proceso Criminal de Diego Anaya de Chaves, Fiscal, contra Juan García, español, y Juan de Aviles, mulata, por Amancebados"; AGN, Bienes Nacionales 497, expediente 30, 1572, "Proceso Criminal del Diego Anaya de Chaves, Fiscal, contra Marcos Pérez, tejedor, español, e Isabel López mulata por estar públicamente Amancebados y

often at night, hoping to secure additional evidence of illicit behavior. "Last night while we were nude," recalled the free mulatto Jusepe de la Cruz, "the *fiscal* of the archdiocese and an *alguacil* . . . apprehended me with Melchora."[4] Following a dramatic raid and arrests, the *fiscal* would subject the accused to an interrogation (*confesión*) while the *provisor* sat in judgment. In most instances, the judge simply forbade the couple to interact "in public or in secret" while sentencing them to pay the *fiscal* two pesos of gold "for his work." Since most of Mexico's inhabitants struggled to survive (two pesos was comparable to a month's rent for a one-room ground-floor living quarter), the fine was a substantial imposition.[5] But concubines, both men and women, received a relatively light sentence in comparison to convicted bigamists, who routinely received 200 lashes followed by years of enforced exile. In both cases, as medievalist Jacqueline Murray observed, the disciplinary process "was thoroughly embedded in the medieval understanding of the necessity to control animal appetites and subordinate the desires of the unruly flesh to the discipline of reason. It mattered little whether the discipline was internally or externally imposed, so long as individual behaviour was controlled and modified, and social order thereby preserved."[6]

Fifteen years into New Spain's seventeenth-century slave trade, the Angolan arrivals in 1609 found themselves in the presence of other Angolans along with successive generations of creoles descended from West-Central Africans. What message would they all glean from Christian regulation and discipline? What meanings did Angolans take from the raids, *autos de fe,* and public executions around them? Answers to such questions are elusive, but we can make conjectures about the possible meanings Africans attributed to the dramatic assaults, the inquisitorial proceedings, and the executions, the penultimate expression of royal authority. Indeed, the terms that scholars use to refer to the African experience in the wake of the Middle Passage—"displacement," "intensification," "reorientation," and "modification"—aptly describe how Africans confronted creoles and, as a result of their encounter with the West, became not only slaves and black creoles but also individuals who lived private lives.[7]

As traders and buyers brought coffle after coffle of Angolans into Mexico City, the *fiscal* launched successive proceedings against long-term residents of the

Reunidos"; AGN, Bienes Nacionales 1087, expediente 12, 1572, "Autos hechos contra Alonso y María, mulatos, por Amancebados."

4. AGN, Bienes Nacionales 810, expediente 65, 18 August 1601, "Confesión de Jusepe de la Cruz."

5. Cope, *The Limits of Racial Domination,* 30.

6. Jacqueline Murray, "Introduction," in *Desire and Discipline: Sex and Sexuality in the Premodern West,* ed. Jacqueline Murray and Konrad Eisenbichler (Toronto: University of Toronto Press, 1996), xvii.

7. Melville J. Herskovits, *The Myth of the Negro Past* (Boston: Beacon, 1941); E. Franklin Frazier, *The Negro Family in the United States* (Chicago: University of Chicago Press, 1942).

viceregal capital who stood accused of *amancebamiento*. By focusing on blacks and mulattos, who were mostly free but occasionally were creolized slaves, the reformed clergy signified what would be tolerated in New Spain. The proceedings also offer a glimpse of the customs exhibited by an already dynamic and dense creole population whose social practices served as both example and counterpoint for Angolans.

In the absence of a seventeenth-century colonial census, we know next to nothing about the size and nature of the free black population. Though the social practices—private lives—of free blacks figure prominently in ecclesiastical and inquisitorial records, such sources do not lend themselves to the accounting of a population. But an impressionistic reading of these sources underscores the existence of an extensive free black presence early in the seventeenth century. In a social formation composed of various ways to organize labor and various subjectivities (slave, free, and tributary), the term "private life" raises many questions. If free blacks had private lives, when in the eyes of the Church did Africans acquire such lives? Did private life begin at the point of baptism or conversion to Christianity? How did private life shape the absolute authority of masters, which was conditioned on the slave's alienation from the land of his or her birth? To what extent did concern with individual behavior extend to persons of African descent? What particular form did it assume in seventeenth-century New Spain? After all, most *bozales* were chattel in the eyes of Spanish contemporaries, yet by the time the clergy launched Catholic renewal in New Spain, a vibrant free black population was already in place.

Perhaps private life became possible only with freedom. But if it began earlier than that, were the private lives of slaves defined and adjudicated differently from those of free blacks? What were the implications for African social identities— notions of the self that predated the enslavement process—when the Catholic Church regulated individual behavior of West-Central Africans? And how did the regulatory process vary for creoles, either blacks or mulattos, who were born in a Christian milieu?

In posing these questions, my intent is not to discern if the Catholic Church formulated race-specific disciplinary procedures. I am concerned to know the extent to which the Catholic Church imagined Africans, blacks, and mulattos as part of the laity and the consequences that flowed from this conception of the social order. This focus underscores how the Catholic imaginary shaped and simultaneously was affected by the social practices of variously defined black folks. The social practices among persons of African descent figure prominently in the overall analysis. In identifying the subjectivities (African, black, creole) of individuals, the colonial sources both illustrate the colonial reality of race and delineate the existence of cultural practices within the regime of colonial labor. The clergy's disciplinary efforts were a reaction to the vibrancy of cultural forms among Africans and blacks, slave and free. Mediated through ecclesiastical sources, the social and cultural practices among persons of African descent warrant our attention as the earliest recorded manifestation of black cultural forms in the Americas.

The answer to the question of whether the Catholic Reformation focused on the African population in New Spain is complex and elusive.[8] We do not have texts that indicate what practices the clergy hoped to eradicate among recent arrivals from Guinea (the generic Iberian word for West and West-Central Africa) and what black creole customs the church felt should be stamped out. We know that the confessional literature regarding Indians focused extensively on preexisting customs and worldviews. With this clerical understanding (which was based on missionary and theological ethnographies) of Indian social, spiritual, and onto-logical beliefs in mind, the confessional manuals advised how to proceed against Indian customs.[9] Aside from Alonso de Sandoval's *De instauranda aethiopum salute* and the occasional travel narrative—which was largely written by factors (merchants) and royal chroniclers—no missionary treatise was produced that de-scribed the polities and ethnos of Guinea's peoples with the intent of facilitating African conversion in the Indies.[10]

The question of Catholic renewal takes on added significance in the absence of confessional literature aimed at converting persons of African descent and spe-cific missionary tracts, catechisms, and theological treatises that acknowledged the presence of Africans as a doctrinal matter. We may, nonetheless, pursue this in-quiry in light of the demographic reality that descendants of Africans constituted the majority of non-Indians subject to ecclesiastical discipline. The actions of the clergy, who were intent on disciplining all of the laity into penance and conformity on matters of the flesh, reveal that New Spain's Catholic Reformation concerned itself both with the black creole population in general and with Africans who con-verted to Christianity. In the innumerable proceedings that featured confessional

8. R. Po-Chia Hsia offers a useful etymology; he argues that "Catholic Renewal" may be more historically precise than counterreformation; Hsia, *The World of Catholic Renewal, 1540–1770* (New York: Cambridge University Press, 1998), 1–7. Here, of course, he builds on the work of Wolfgang Reinhard; see Reinhard, "Gegenreformation als Modernisierung? Prolegomena zu einer Theorie des konfessionellen Zeitalters," *Archiv für Reformationsgeschichte* 68 (1977): 226–252.

9. Robert Ricard, *The Spiritual Conquest of Mexico: An Essay on the Apostolate and the Evangelizing Methods of the Mendicant Orders in New Spain, 1523–1572*, trans. Lesley Byrd Simpson (Berkeley: University of California Press, 1966); J. Jorge Klor de Alva, "Spiritual Conflict and Accommodation in New Spain: Toward a Typology of Aztec Responses to Christianity," in *The Inca and Aztec States, 1400–1800: Anthropology and History*, ed. George A. Collier, Renato I. Rosaldo, and John D. Wirth (New York: Academic Press, 1982), 345–366; and Serge Gruzinski, "Individualization and Acculturation: Confession among the Nahuas of Mexico from the Sixteenth to the Eighteenth Century," in *Sexuality and Marriage in Colonial Latin America*, ed. Asunción Lavrín (Omaha: University of Nebraska Press, 1989), 96–117.

10. To date, Joan Bristol has crafted the most layered treatment of European travel writing and African conversion to Christianity that is relevant for scholars of early Spanish America. See *Christians, Blasphemers, and Witches*, 27–47.

moments—the instance in ecclesiastical and inquisitorial proceedings when the clergy formally and under the sacrament of penance questioned an individual in order to discern the truth—the clergy can be said to have displayed a keen interest in certain persons of African descent. In these proceedings several issues stand out: the persecution of concubines (*amancebados*), marriage petitions (*informaciones matrimoniales*), cases documenting conflicts over marriage, and Inquisition proceedings. In the periodic social transactions that brought the laity's private life into view, the clergy scrutinized Christianized Africans and creoles they assumed were Christians.

In an effort to explore the intersection of discipline and cultural formation, we may begin with the following questions: Can the actions of Spain's sovereign and the concerns of the Catholic Church with *policía* be identified as social discipline? If so, what forms did such discipline assume in a social formation composed of overlapping domains defined by colonialism, slavery, and freedom? Our understanding of New Spain's black social formation should begin by acknowledging the complexity and blurry boundaries of a society that was at once free, slave, and colonial. As forms of abstraction, these concepts invite us to embrace a broader understanding of the social world of New Spain than one characterized by the Spanish and Indian divide. In doing so, our analysis of society may become as supple as the lived experiences of our subjects. Acknowledging the social complexity offers a challenge to the existing historiography of social discipline.[11] Similarly, the complexity of the society necessitates a rethinking of the pretense that the historical literature on New Spain is complete.

Of particular relevance for *Colonial Blackness* are the ways that the African encounter with social discipline resulted in the emergence of blackness.[12] How, for instance, did Church and state regulate the private lives of enslaved Africans? Who regulated the life of a free black? How was the slave's private life defined differently

11. Conventional histories have described the institution as a manifestation of labor and racial dominion. Their representations of cultural resilience focus on truculence, insubordination, and rebelliousness of slaves in terms of disorder (drinking, gambling, and theft but also the social disruption caused by unsupervised slaves). The slave—and specifically slave behavior—emerges as the subject of regulation by various civil institutions seeking to maintain or restore order (*policía*). For a comparative perspective on church and state intervention in household authority in Old and New World social formations and in colonial Spanish America in relationship to Anglo America, see Carole Shammas, "Anglo-American Household Government in Comparative Perspective," *William and Mary Quarterly*, 3rd ser., 52 (January 1995): 116, 120.

12. The term "social discipline" derives from German Reformation studies and has long been associated with a Western Europe that did not include Spain. The genealogy of the concept reaches back to Gerhard Oestreich's "Strukturprobleme des europäischen Absolutismus" (in Gerhard Oestreich, *Geist und Gestalt des frühmodernen Staates: Ausgewählte Aufsätze* [Berlin: Duncker & Humblot, 1969], 179–197). But Catholic renewal in Spain and its kingdoms in the Indies, mediated through the term *policía* and the increased vigilance of ecclesiastical authorities, elicited the same results as social discipline: the desire to control private lives. See Sara T. Nalle, *Religious Reform and the People of Cuenca*,

and thereby regulated distinctly from the recently freed and those who were born free? Were distinct mechanisms used in this process? The focus on the politics of the body brings into stark relief the intersection of discipline and cultural formation. The existence of Catholic social discipline raises a question of fundamental concern for colonial, slave, and postcolonial studies: In what ways did the African encounter with the West in the New World precipitate an epic transformation whose result was a distinct black identity? "Traveling through the prodigiously interesting territory that made up the Mexico conquered and ruled by the Spanish from the sixteenth to the nineteenth century," historical anthropologist Serge Gruzinski observed how "one inevitably asks questions such as these."[13] Oddly enough, Gruzinski restricted his wonderment to interactions between Spaniards and Indians, though he referred to the universal subject of "how . . . individuals and groups contrive and experience their relations with the real in a society disrupted by an absolutely unprecedented external domination."[14] Africans do not invite Gruzinski's attention or, for that matter, that of other scholars interested in exploring such lofty concerns as "what the impact of sixteenth-century Western Europe might have meant for America."[15]

As social historians we are invariably disciplined to read within a given document's boundaries rather than approach the content and conditions of its production as mutually constitutive. Intent on discerning the macroperspective and serial patterns, the social historian often loses sight of the fact that such views reflect the colonizer's unfulfilled desire to impose order on the perceived chaos of the human condition. Confessional moments bring this juxtaposition together and offer us a strategy for glimpsing the mechanism whereby persons of African descent confronted their New World experience. "It is true that the relative scarcity of sources hardly permits a reconstruction of an 'ethnic' or 'cultural unconscious,' still less an understanding of its metamorphoses," observed Serge Gruzinski, noting that instead "one must settle for a few modest reports, pointing the way, and follow a

----

1500–1650 (Baltimore: Johns Hopkins University Press, 1992); and Richard L. Kagan, *Urban Images of the Hispanic World, 1493–1793* (New Haven, Conn.: Yale University Press, 2000). The explicit collaboration between royal and ecclesiastical authorities intent on regulating the sovereign's subjects brings into play another concept from Reformation studies—confessionalization—that characterized the workings of absolutism in New Spain against licentiousness and unruly flesh. See Jörg Deventer, "'Confessionalisation'—A Useful Theoretical Concept for the Study of Religion, Politics, and Society in Early Modern East-Central Europe?" *European Review of History/Revue européenne d' Histoire* 11, no. 3 (2004): 403–425.

13. Serge Gruzinski, *The Conquest of Mexico: The Incorporation of Indian Societies into the Western World, 16th-18th Centuries,* trans. Eileen Corrigan (Cambridge, Mass.: Polity, 1993), 1.

14. Ibid.

15. Gruzinski, *The Conquest of Mexico,* 1; Anthony Pagden, *The Fall of Natural Man: The American Indian and the Origins of Comparative Ethnology* (New York: Cambridge University Press, 1982); Tzvetan Todorov, *The Conquest of America: The Question of the Other,* trans. Richard Howard (New York: Harper & Row, 1984).

handful of personalities in their attempts to construct syntheses and fashion compromises between these worlds—which recalls that cultural creation is as much
the task of individuals as of groups."[16]

As an expression both of Catholic reform and social discipline, the ecclesiastical courts should draw our attention to the ways the clergy extended, or attempted
to extend, Christian control over blacks. Accustomed to the spectacle of the brutalized black body, we often overlook less dramatic but just as insidious expressions of social discipline that affected Africans and their descendants. In doing so,
we ignore the multiple sites from which power insinuated itself over a colonial and
slave social formation, thereby underscoring how little we actually know about the
specific nature of colonial Spanish American slavery.[17]

The study of social control in the slave societies of colonial Spanish America
focuses almost exclusively on the violence directed at the slave. As slavery's elemental feature, violence—real and symbolic—defined how slaves processed their
enslavement.[18] Because it permeated the structures and practices that informed
slave life, violence acquired an ontological status. "It was necessary," observed
sociologist Orlando Patterson, "to continually repeat the original, violent act of
transforming the free man into a slave. This act of violence constitutes the prehis-
tory of all stratified societies."[19] In sixteenth- and seventeenth-century New Spain,
a constant resort to violence accompanied the steady influx of enslaved Africans.[20]
Masters used violence to ensure their domination over newly enslaved Africans
and remind both previous arrivals and those born into slavery that domination
daily constructed their debased status. Violence transformed Africans and creoles
into slaves. The enslaved, aware of their humanity, constantly had to be reminded
of their servile status in the evolving social order.

The centrality of violence in the historiography, however, overshadows the

---

16. Gruzinski, *The Conquest of Mexico*, 2–3.
17. Reinhard was one of the first to argue the importance of seeing aspects associated with modernity in Catholic renewal. Reinhard, "Gegenreformation als Modernisierung," 226–252.
18. Patterson, *Slavery and Social Death*, 3, 13 and 38. Patterson's analysis builds on the work of the
French structural anthropologist Claude Meillassoux, whose most recent conclusions on the subject of
violence are detailed in *The Anthropology of Slavery: The Womb of Iron and Gold,* trans. Alide Dasnois
(Chicago: University of Chicago Press, 1991).
19. Patterson, *Slavery and Social Death*, 3. In her stunning ethnography of northeast Brazil, Nancy
Scheper-Hughes implicitly suggests that a former slave society's ontology in violence imposes an enduring cultural logic on contemporary social formation. Though underscoring the colonial and slave
origins of Brazilian violence and their legacy in contemporary life, Scheper-Hughes remains sensitive
to temporal specificity and specific intent. See Scheper-Hughes, *Death without Weeping: The Violence
of Everyday Life in Brazil* (Berkeley: University of California Press, 1992).
20. Evidence of violence abounds in the Spanish colonial archive. But violence and its ultimate
consequence, death, remain seriously undertheorized in the study of colonial Spanish American slavery. For distinct engagements with the cultural meaning of slavery and violence, see Miller, *Way of
Death;* Carolyn E. Fick, *The Making of Haiti: The Saint Domingue Revolution from Below* (Knoxville:
University of Tennessee Press, 1990), 34–39; and Saidiya V. Hartman, *Scenes of Subjection: Terror,
Slavery, and Self-Making in Nineteenth-Century America* (New York: Oxford University Press, 1997).

cultural web of power in which slavery was embedded. Hinged on the series of institutions and practices that constituted the Spanish state, this web of power could mobilize not just violence but also a judicial system and the Catholic Church with all of its constituent bodies and rituals.[21] Since the objective of this web of power was to make Africans and creoles into compliant Christian subjects, it transcended the scope of physical violence. Spanish power involved much more than physical force directed at the African slave.[22]

Scholars of New World slavery have long been aware that the symbolic played a crucial role in enforcing power and regimenting labor; power over slaves rested on more than a resort to violence. But this understanding of the masters' desire for legitimate authority over slaves has restricted the discussion of the symbolic to the terrain of social control. Scholars have unwittingly attributed the process of making and maintaining slaves, if they attend to the process at all, to a construct of slavery divorced from its cultural settings. They imply that slavery and its accompanying ideology stood apart from the reigning dynamics of power in which all master-slave relations were embedded. "The master-slave relationship," writes Patterson, "cannot be divorced from the distribution of power throughout the wider society in which both master and slave find themselves."[23] Yet even this astute student of symbolic manifestations of slavery comes close to representing the cultural logic of slavery as a disembodied ideology: "Slavery is a highly symbolized

21. Richard Morse's "The Heritage of Latin America" is an essential starting point for discerning the meanings of patrimonialism. See Morse, "The Heritage of Latin America," in *The Founding of New Societies: Studies in the History of the United States, Latin America, South Africa, Canada, and Australia*, ed. Louis Hartz (New York: Harcourt Brace Jovanovich, 1964), 151–177. For the enduring legacy of patrimonialism into the late colonial period, see Phelan *The People and the King*. Recent scholarship emphasizes the discursive conflicts that collectives brought to their interpretation of patrimonialism. See Charles F. Walker, *Smoldering Ashes: Cuzco and the Creation of Republican Peru, 1780–1840* (Durham, N.C.: Duke University Press), 16–120. In voicing their grievances, especially against their masters, persons of African descent invariably appealed to the king or his representative to intervene. Rarely did their grievances or demands for freedom imply royal malfeasance. Tactically minded *cimarrones* (runaway slaves) even invoked their services to the monarchy, usually military service, to demonstrate their loyalty to the Catholic sovereign. The emphasis on loyalty to the king suggests that in requesting personal autonomy (in the form of liberty) or collective autonomy (in the form of an administration unit such as a village), persons of African descent did not strive to restore the "African" past or seek to sever royal authority over their lives. AGN, Tierras 3543, 1767, tomo 1–3.

22. My formulation of the ceremonial state is obviously indebted to Clifford Geertz's *Negara: The Theatre State in Nineteenth-Century Bali* (Princeton, N.J.: Princeton University Press, 1980). Geertz's ideas on the relationships between ceremony, ritual, and state practices can also be discerned in his *The Interpretation of Cultures* (New York: Basic Books, 1973), 234–341. As Geertz noted, his work builds on both Africanists working on polities and social structures and European medievalist focused on kinship. See Geertz, "Centers, Kings, and Charisma: Reflections on the Symbolics of Power," in *Rites of Power: Symbolism, Ritual, and Politics since the Middle Ages*, ed. Sean Wilentz (Philadelphia: University of Pennsylvania Press, 1985), 34n5. The anthropological classics have been immensely informative for Africanists; see M. Fortes and E. E. Evans-Pritchard, eds., *African Political Systems* (London: Kegan Paul International, 1940); Max Gluckman, *Custom and Conflict in Africa* (Oxford: Basil Blackwell, 1956); and Victor W. Turner, *Schism and Continuity in an African Society: A Study of Ndembu Village Life* (Oxford: Berg, 1957).

23. Patterson, *Slavery and Social Death*, 35.

domain of human experience. While all aspects of the relationship are symbolized, there is overwhelming concentration on the profound natal alienation of the slave." Oddly enough, Patterson does not locate the idiom of natal alienation in the discursive formations that informed "the distribution of power throughout the wider society." Instead he locates it in a decontextualized ideology of slavery. But in Spanish America, the lexicon, grammar, and tone of natal alienation emerged directly from Christianity, since Christianity configured belonging and order in the polis.[24] In the minds of the Spanish elite, until the enslaved embraced Christianity, they were socially dead. This perceived social death is one of several ontological sites in which Africans became slaves and from which a black identity and a black private life initially emerged.

In discussions of Spanish American slavery, Christianity warrants more analysis as a form of cultural power. Such analysis might begin with the ways the clergy introduced Africans and their descendents to Christianity. Understandably, a significant number of historians of the African diaspora question the centrality of Christianity in black life in the Catholic or Protestant worlds prior to the second half of the nineteenth century.[25] In contrast to those scholars who underscore the limits of Christianization of African-descended people in the Americas, I am interested in Christianity as a mechanism of social discipline and a site through which black culture initially emerged in Spanish America. We can assume that Afro-Christianity was initially superficial at best and competed with the customs and traditions that Africans brought with them or learned in the New World in their interactions with Indians, Europeans, and other Africans.[26] By the seventeenth

24. Patterson notes how "those who exercise power, if they are able to transform it into a 'right,' a norm, a usual part of the order of things, must first control appropriate symbolic instruments. They may do so by exploiting already existing symbols, or they may create new ones relevant to their needs. . . . Symbolic processes, like so many other areas of human experience, have both an intellectual and a social aspect. On the intellectual level, thought attempts to explain, in the language of symbols, a given area of actual experience. It is essentially mythic, similar in intellectual form to the validating concepts and beliefs of religion. The social aspects of symbolic behavior refer to the ritual processes by means of which symbolic ideas are acted out in terms of real human interactions. Such actions invariably are highly formalized and ceremonial. Where the experience being symbolized extends over a long period of time, there is a tendency for a clearly defined symbolic pattern to develop: critical stages in the development process, and especially the transition form one stage to the next, are given special ritual expression." Ibid., 37–38.

25. Sterling Stuckey, *Slave Culture: Nationalist Theory and the Foundations of Black America* (New York: Oxford University Press, 1988); Michael A. Gomez, *Exchanging our Country Marks: The Transformation of African Identities in the Colonial and Antebellum South* (Chapel Hill: University of North Carolina Press, 1998); Philip D. Morgan, *Slave Counterpoint: Black Culture in the Eighteenth-Century Chesapeake and Lowcountry* (Chapel Hill: Published for the Omohundro Institute of Early American History and Culture by the University of North Carolina Press, 1998); James H. Sweet, *Recreating Africa: Culture, Kinship, and Religion in the African-Portuguese World, 1441–1770* (Chapel Hill: University of North Carolina Press, 2003).

26. Roger Bastide, *The African Religions of Brazil: Toward a Sociology of the Interpenetration of Civilizations*, new ed. (Baltimore: Johns Hopkins University Press, 2007); Palmíe, *Wizards and Scientists: Explorations in Afro-Cuban Modernity & Tradition* (Durham N.C.: Duke University Press, 2000); David H. Brown, *Santería Enthroned: Art, Ritual, and Innovation in an Afro-Cuban Religion* (Chicago: University of Chicago Press, 2003).

century, however, Christianity—as a belief, ritual, and practice—was already being internalized by a substantial number of black creoles. While Catholic absolutism intended to control and reproduce the social order, persons of African descent adopted Christian practices in order to shape their lives in a manner meaningful to them. In embracing Christianity, the intent of Africans and creoles may have varied from those of the Church and state. Although its scope was limited, blacks' appropriation of Christian cultural practices had deep implications.[27] It brought individuals into the Church, sanctioned their identities and specific institutional practices, and made them Christians and loyal subjects, though like most nominal Christians, individual behavior and values often deviated from orthodoxy.[28]

As persons born into a Christian social formation, creoles were both insiders and outsiders. Still, they had to be fashioned into slaves. As with enslaved Africans, violence characterized the creoles' journey into slavery. But Catholic customs, which creoles readily appropriated, also played a role in the socialization process, resulting in the growth of a Christian slave population in the second half of the sixteenth century. The Catholic Church vied with the patrimonial state and the violence of masters in the process of creating colonial subjects. As creoles embraced Catholic customs, thereby obliging themselves to accept Christianity's tenets, they also acquired rights. The Christian culture that creoles embraced granted them a social existence beyond the grasp of masters, even though that existence was limited in scope.

As a patriarchal ideology and the dominant disciplinary institution, Christianity delimited a form of personal liberty by determining the appropriate Christian forms of personhood. Christianity enabled the enslaved to stake claims to a social self, but it bound that social existence to the Christian social order.[29] The absolutist state did not exercise control as an all-powerful entity, relying instead on symbolic forms of dominance and (through Christianity) self-regulation.

Rather than ask why patricians allowed practices that undermined their authority—an answer that resides in the will and actions of the Crown—I want to focus our attention on how Catholicism both enabled blacks and mulattos to achieve a modicum of personal autonomy and insinuated itself into their lives. In focusing on trial proceedings, I implicitly address issues of cultural contact and change by highlighting the clergy's expectations. In other words, the structure of the proceedings illuminates a cultural logic. So in the absence of confes-

---

27. Richard Price, *Alabi's World* (Baltimore: Johns Hopkins University Press, 1990).

28. Nalle, *Religious Reform and the People of Cuenca*.

29. According to Shammas, "New England and Pennsylvania colonies set up other mechanisms that circumscribed the powers of the household head in order to pursue community objectives. Some of these mechanisms empowered dependents, giving them more rights. Others designed to bolster a lax or weak household head resulted in more stringent policing of dependents. The ultimate goal in both cases was the encouragement of a more godly community, not individual freedoms." Shammas, "Anglo-American Household Government in Comparative Perspective," 116.

sional literature (i.e., religious manuals with a specific focus on Africans), we can think of the various confessional moments—the moments in ecclesiastical and inquisitorial proceedings when the clergy formally questioned persons of African descent—as indications of the church's effort to conquer Africans' idolatry and bring salvation to blacks and mulattos. In electing to read the ecclesiastical proceedings in this way, I am intent on rendering transparent the clergy's assumption vis-à-vis Africans, blacks, and mulattos. As Gruzinski reminds us, "each trial, each interrogatory yields its share of data, provided one knows how to evaluate what the filter of writing, the aims of the investigator, the questioning of the judge, the intervention of the notary and the *escribano* or the chances of preservation have been able to add to (or subtract from) the original account."[30]

As this chapter underscores, the clergy's actions and the subject of their proceedings call for a nuanced analysis of the culture of Africans and their descendants in colonial Spanish America. In focusing on the intricacies of Christian discipline, I document how the ecclesiastical court proceedings furnish glimpses of cultural agency among blacks and mulattos, thereby underscoring a rarely acknowledged black interiority. In naming this agency "black interiority," I am not arguing for cultural forms that were peculiar or natural to blacks. Obviously this cannot be the case, since many of the proceedings involve interracial sexual encounters. But insofar as this unremarked-upon illicit and unorthodox behavior involves persons identified as blacks, I consciously identify it as constitutive of black interiority. Expressed in the guise of social practices—desire and gender relations—this cultural agency demands a narrative structure based on the cultural logic that governed black life. In a word, the ecclesiastical cases examined in this chapter and throughout the manuscript underscore that black people—as slaves and free people—were not reduced to a category of laborers or an object of the Western imagination. My concern in making this point is not to insist on subaltern contestation or the sovereignty of agency. Instead, I view cultural agency among persons of African descent and the struggle for Christian hegemony as an entangled history. But this entanglement brings into relief both a hegemonic conceit and its limits. Cultural practices that deviated from the design of masters and the clergy remind us that dominance need not be equated with hegemony.

To begin, let us focus on personal autonomy. Delineating autonomy for black Mexicans is a critical historical endeavor. After Africans survived the objectifying experiences of the Middle Passage and enslavement, personal autonomy and the existence of private lives created a divide between master and slave that steadily tempered the effects of social death. "Natal alienation," observed the sociologist Orlando Patterson, "goes directly to the heart of what is critical in the slave's forced

30. Gruzinski, *The Conquest of Mexico*, 4.

alienation, the loss of ties of birth in both ascending and descending generations."[31] If slavery functioned as "the permanent, violent domination of natally alienated and generally dishonored persons," then personal autonomy and existence of private lives staved off the master's totalizing goal of defining the slave as object and as the extension of his/her will.[32] In Spanish America, jurisdictional conflict over the slave's competing status and masterly acts of manumission made possible the growth of a population outside of these totalizing goals as early as the sixteenth century.

In taking issue with scholars who privilege physical force in the making of Christian creoles and scholars who ignore Christianity's role in the lives of people of African descent, I propose an examination of confessional moments that illustrate instances of discipline when we "follow a handful of personalities in their attempts to construct syntheses and fashion compromises."[33] The stakes involve far more than the inscription of a neglected subaltern history, though in the case of Afro-Mexicans that inscription is critical. Instead, my concern focuses on the ways the Catholic Reformation addressed the African presence in New Spain. The ecclesiastical court records and the confessional moments that informed each case illustrate a decidedly modern configuration of power.[34] The concept of confession, as the political philosopher Michel Foucault reminded us, was a principal site of power:

> Since the Middle Ages at least, Western societies have established the confession as one of the main rituals we rely on for the production of truth: the codification of the sacrament of penance by the Lateran Council of 1215, with the resulting development of confessional techniques, the declining importance

31. Patterson, *Slavery and Social Death*, 7.
32. Ibid., 13.
33. Gruzinski, *The Conquest of Mexico*, 2.
34. But the alienation generated by the master-slave relationship was representative of a larger cultural logic that informed the Spanish conquest, the transatlantic slave trade, the Reformation and Catholic reform, and the birth of the Dutch republic, to name some of modernity's obvious benchmarks, and brings into site the structural and cultural forces in which freedom emerged beyond Western Christendom's boundaries. As Patterson reminds us, "There was no word for freedom in most non-Western languages before contact with Western peoples" (Patterson, *Slavery and Social Death*, 27). Locating a genealogy of freedom in the contours of the cataclysmic age brings into relief what sociologist Paul Gilroy called the "primal history of modernity," which he urged us to "[reconstruct] from the slaves' points of view." Gilroy adds that "[the slaves' point of view] emerge[s] in the especially acute consciousness of both life and freedom which is nurtured by the slave's 'mortal terror of his sovereign master' and the continuing 'trial by death' which slavery becomes for the male slave. This primal history offers a unique perspective on many of the key intellectual and political issues in the modernity debates"; Gilroy, *The Black Atlantic*, 55. The earliest incarnation of what Gilroy identified as the counterculture of modernity, the persons who forged this personal autonomy, were some of the first individuals in the New World whom the Spaniards identified as free. As Patterson astutely noted, in the social universe of the New World in which a black body was already synonymous with slave, the individuals subject to ecclesiastical raids literally were the first persons in the modern era marked as free.

of accusatory procedures in criminal justice, the abandonment of tests of guilt (sworn statements, duels, judgments of God) and the development of methods of interrogation and inquest, the increased participation of the royal administration in the prosecution of infractions, at the expense of proceedings leading to private settlements, the setting up of tribunals of Inquisition: all this helped to give the confession a central role in the order of civil and religious powers.[35]

But here, of course, Foucault privileges the West in its most parochial instantiation. Even though the seventeenth century marks a key moment in the overall structure of his argument, "the beginning of an age of repression emblematic of what we call the bourgeois societies, an age which perhaps we still have not completely left behind,"[36] Foucault conceived of the West in the most Eurocentric terms.[37] The confession did, however, travel and came to occupy a ubiquitous role in colonial Latin America and in the lives of Africans and their descendants who lived there.

Yet the issue is not merely that the clergy subjected blacks to the confession—yearly, as part of all ecclesiastical proceedings, and in the course of Inquisition trials. What mattered was the intent behind the procedure. As Africans and creoles encountered the "civil and religious powers," the clergy constantly reminded them that only orthodox Christian behavior would be tolerated. By denying differences born of culture and tradition, the confession sought to produce an individuated Christian being. "The truthful confession," Foucault noted, "was inscribed at the heart of the procedures of individualization by power."[38] In the colonial setting, the confession aspired to more than a disciplined body; it sought to distance Indians and Africans from the collectivities, traditions, and pasts that had sanctioned their former selves. Such distancing was both a stated and implicit objective of masters and colonial authorities.

Illicit sex was at the center of the ecclesiastical proceedings, and the clergy steadfastly focused on discerning the sordid and sinful details. They concerned themselves with more than the souls of the black laity. Foucault located sexuality within the regimes of power: "What is at issue . . . is the over-all 'discursive fact,'

35. Michel Foucault, *The History of Sexuality: An Introduction,* trans. Robert Hurley (New York: Vintage Books, 1978), 58.
36. Ibid., 17.
37. As is often the case, however, when theorists privilege the West as the foundational site of modern power—embodied in capitalism and state formation—they rarely contextualize their works in colonialism or imperialism or acknowledge the ways in which those settings are simultaneously constitutive of Europe and alternate modernities. In fairness to the European theorists, we must acknowledge that only the narrowest configuration of Christendom was included in formulations of "Europe." For an example of such privileging, see Elias, *The Civilizing Process*; Ann Laura Stoler's *Race and the Education of Desire: Foucault's History of Sexuality and the Colonial Order of Things* (Durham, N.C.: Duke University Press, 1995) offers an exemplary critique of Foucault's Eurocentrism.
38. Foucault, *The History of Sexuality,* 58–59.

the way in which sex is 'put into discourse.' Hence . . . my main concern will be to locate the forms of power, the channels it takes and the discourses it permeates in order to reach the most tenuous and individual modes of behavior, the paths that give it access to the rarer or scarcely perceivable forms of desire, how it penetrates and controls everyday pleasure."[39] Clearly, the clergy was intent on blurring the nascent distinctions between the sacred and the secular. Sex, as the archive of confessional moments reveals, involved much more than morality.

Succumbing to desire was common throughout Christendom and no less among persons of African descent, who freely and frankly spoke to the clergy of their sexual relationships. Eight months after the *fiscal* accused 25-year-old furniture maker Spaniard Diego de Salinas and mulatto Catalina de Leon of concubinage, the couple stood before the ecclesiastical judge to answer questions about their relationship.[40] "I have only known her carnally once," declared Diego. The *fiscal* asked 25-year-old Catalina de Leon—on the basis of the testimony of two eyewitnesses—if it was true that she had been Diego's concubine, "knowing him carnally as if she were his wife." Yes, responded Catalina, relating how she "repeatedly interacted and had known the said Salinas carnally." But now, said Catalina, they did not "interact, speak or communicate." Despite the divergent responses— "only . . . once" and "repeatedly"—the *provisor* chose to admonish the couple to stay clear of one another. Beatríz de Cardenas, a 35-year-old freed mulatto, was similarly forthcoming. Aware that her arrest was linked to her illicit affair with the Spaniard Gaspar, she acknowledged knowing him intimately. "It is true," noted Beatríz, that "in fifteen years . . . I repeatedly interacted with him carnally." But asked if they had had a continuous affair, Beatríz said no. "For the last ten years," Beatríz noted, "I have not . . . interacted with him carnally and only returned to . . . wash his cloths since he doesn't have help."[41] Gaspar de Trejo, Beatríz's alleged lover, sounded less than contrite in his confession. "As a man," declared Gaspar, "I was repeatedly with her carnally." But he denied that they had had a steady affair or that he had fathered Beatríz's children.[42] The proceedings delineate the norms that the clergy upheld, but they also reveal that the descendants of Africans, though aware of Christian norms, exhibited alternative social practices with their Spanish lovers. Such practices afford us a glimpse of existing private lives that had taken hold by the seventeenth century.

---

39. Ibid., 11.

40. AGN, Bienes Nacionales 442, expediente 33, México, 21 March 1609, "Proceso del Fiscal del Arzobispado contra Diego de Salinas, sombrerero y Catalina, mulata, por amancebados."

41. México, 21 May 1609, "Confesión de Beatriz, mulata, presa en la carcel arzobispal," in "Proceso del Fiscal del Arzobispado contra Gaspar Trejo y Beatriz, mulata, por amancebados."

42. AGN, Bienes Nacionales 442, expediente 8, México, 21 May 1609, "Confesión de Gaspar Trejo, español, preso en la carcel arzobispal," in "Proceso del Fiscal del Arzobispado contra Gaspar Trejo y Beatriz, mulata, por amancebados."

Although the clergy pursued people of African descent who engaged in extra-marital sexual relations, what stands out among the proceedings is the routine way the clergy regulated blacks and mulattos. In their interrogations, ecclesiastical officials required blacks and mulattos to "put their memory in order" before divulging their sins and engaging in the sacrament of penance. As the clergy extracted confessions from the accused, we hear blacks and mulattos testifying about the existence of their private lives. "I have repeatedly known him carnally," confessed Leonor de la Concepción, the mulatto chocolate-maker. "But there are days," she recalled, "I did not interact with him."[43] Willing to acknowledge having had adulterous sex, Leonor wanted to be sure she was not judged as a concubine. The testimony of Leonor's lover, Andrés de Oliva, a *mestizo,* corroborated her account. He said that he had "entered" but did not inhabit her house, "[though] in that time I had known her carnally."[44] Although another woman, the 24-year-old mulatto Ana, was not reluctant to admit to her previous sexual activities, she declared that "in the time mentioned I have repeatedly known him [Agustín de Loya] carnally but now it has been awhile."[45]

Here then are blacks and mulattos talking about sex, exhibiting their desire beyond the sanctity of the conjugal union. But as Foucault observed, "the central issue" doesn't reside in sex talk. In order to understand how power worked in the ecclesiastical proceedings and the confessional, what matters is "to account for the fact that it [sex] is spoken about, to discover who does the speaking, the positions and viewpoints from which they speak, the institutions which prompt people to speak about it and which store and distribute the things that are said." We must add, however, that the clergy wanted sex to be narrated as a vice, a matter of human frailty, and a form of corporeal debasement. Such an understanding of sex was decidedly Christian, underscoring how much more was at stake for persons who came from a distinct ideological complex than matters of the flesh.[46] The clergy intended for the raids and confessional moments to effect more than a curtailment of "everyday pleasures." In scope and ambition, the clergy's actions were literally configuring Christianity as a religion and restricting cultural expression to Catholic norms.[47]

43. AGN, Bienes Nacionales 442, expediente 44, México, 31 October 1609, "Confesión de Leonor, mulata," in "Proceso del Fiscal del Arzobispado contra Andrés de Oliva, mestizo, zapatero y Leonor, mulata, por amancebados."
44. AGN, Bienes Nacionales 442, expediente 44, México, 31 October 1609, "Confesión de Andrés de Oliva," in "Proceso del Fiscal del Arzobispado contra Andrés de Oliva, mestizo, zapatero y Leonor, mulata, por amancebados."
45. AGN, Bienes Nacionales 442, expediente 41, México, 17 December 1609, "Confesión de Ana, mulata," in "Proceso del Fiscal del Arzobispado contra Agustín de Loya, mulata y Ana, mulata, por amancebados."
46. Sweet, *Recreating Africa,* 50–58.
47. The clergy insinuated Christianity as the sole complex of legitimate beliefs, customs, and

Ecclesiastical raids and trials were instruments of social discipline in which many, if not most, of the proceedings dealt with persons of African descent, and it is surprising that scholars interested in colonial slavery and racial formation have expressed little interest in the minutia of the ecclesiastical courts' regulatory proceedings. Only in relation to marital proceedings have the ecclesiastical courts been the subject of scrutiny. With regard to sexual behavior, the records of the ecclesiastical court remain largely untouched. As transactions that record the enforcement of Christian norms, the proceedings of the ecclesiastical courts underscore that "human sexuality . . . was a source of constant preoccupation for the church."[48] Ecclesiastical raids and the subsequent interrogations were a form of social discipline designed to punish sinners and cow the laity into conformity. But for historians of early modernism, the set of formal procedures (rather than informal mechanisms) serves only to distinguish social discipline from social control. The lack of interest in the institutional proceedings on the part of scholars of slavery and free blacks reflects, in part, the seductive role of violence in the historical imagination. Literary theorist Saidiya Hartman has expressed concern that the trope and image of the brutalized black body has had an anesthetizing effect on contemporary cultural sensibilities and sympathies. In short, we momentarily pause, then genuflect before the traumatized black subject but eventually hurry on and away from the systemic phenomenon that sanctioned such terror.[49]

The narrow focus on the master-slave relationship and the tendency to differentiate between slave society and colonial society in New Spain obscures the existence of a free black population that straddled both domains. New Spain was home to a sizeable free black population whose numbers at the height of the slavery period rivaled those of the slave population. In such a complex social formation, social control had to extend beyond the master-slave divide and the nexus of violence. Even when they attended to social distinctions, historians of New Spain's African past made differentiations only within the world of slaves. In con-

---

practices to replace the preexisting beliefs of Africans and the customs of creoles. According to the Catholic Church, these beliefs and customs represented idolatry. But theologians saw such expressions as much more than a deviation from the one true religion. Indeed, by delineating a domain of Christian orthodoxy, the clergy introduced Indians and Africans to the concept of religion. In a world in which all could be attributed to the ontological, religion served to delimit domain, boundaries, and borders. "It was in the seventeenth century," writes anthropologist Talal Asad, "following the fragmentation of the unity and authority of the Roman church and the consequent wars of religion, which tore European principalities apart, that the early systematic attempts at producing a universal definition of religion were made"; Talal Asad, *Genealogies of Religion* (Baltimore: Johns Hopkins University Press, 1993), 40.

48. Asunción Lavrín, "Sexuality and Marriage in Colonial Mexico: A Church Dilemma," in *Sexuality and Marriage in Colonial Latin America,* ed. Asunción Lavrín (Omaha: University of Nebraska Press, 1989), 49.

49. Hartman, *Scenes of Subjection,* 3–4.

text of the historical neglect that once characterized New Spain's African past, that limited portrayal of the black experience perhaps seemed justified. But this perspective oversimplifies our understanding of a slave society and ignores the free black population. Intellectual compartmentalization bears much blame for this phenomenon. We write—often out of necessity—about discrete entities: a society that is either slave-based or colonial, individuals who are slaves or free blacks, a system of regulation that features social control directed at slaves or social discipline directed at the laity.

But the historical record defies such dichotomization. Society in colonial Mexico was much more complex. By the beginning of the seventeenth century, a substantial mulatto population flourished in Mexico City, and many of these individuals had acquired their freedom. Far from constituting an ephemeral presence in the burgeoning colonial slave society, free mulattos demonstrated a sense of being rooted. Here we simply need to point to individual names. Free blacks had names such as Catalina de Leon, Beatríz de Cardenas, Leonor de la Concepción, Diego Pérez, Ana Gomez, Andrés López, María Maldonado, Melchora Hernández, María de Callexas, Melchor de los Reyes, Melchora de los Reyes, María Vazquez, and María de Guzman. The Africans in the archival record were simply known as Juan, Angelina, Jusepe, and María. Surnames like Angola, Bran, Congo, Mozambique, and Xolofe were gradually attached to the Christian names of the survivors of the Middle Passage. Creolized slaves and recently freed people, such as Ana mulata, were known only by their first name and racial status. Names, especially surnames, illuminate a person's ties to an individual, to a family, and to Christian identity. In some instances, names of individuals also highlight their legal status. As we listen to individuals identify themselves and relate the circumstances that led to their arrest we hear blacks and mulattos talk about how their private lives facilitated sexual encounters.

Sex Talk

The confessions of the accused offer a glimpse of the exterior structure and texture of interracial relationships. We see free women of color acknowledging their complicity in illicit affairs with Spanish men. Although the details the accused offered about their status are limited, what they said reveals the absence of both tangible sexual expressions of patriarchal authority by owners, employers, or patrons and indications of explicit class disparities. The overwhelming presence of artisans and day laborers among the accused points to the absence of patron-client ties in which a powerful Spaniard availed himself of a brown or black woman. Simply put, the ecclesiastical proceedings do not identify any individuals that the clergy deemed worthy of being addressed as Don.

On 5 December 1601, following the corroborating testimony of Jusepe de

Nájera and María de Cepeda, the *provisor* of Mexico's archdiocese ordered the arrest of the black woman María de Guzman and the Spaniard Castro on charges of *amancebamiento*. The next day the 28-year-old María de Guzman offered her confession. María began by stating that she was unaware of the reason for her arrest. But when the *fiscal* asked if it was true that for eight months she "had been in a state of *amancebado* with Castro," María said yes. "In this time," testified María, "he has repeatedly known me carnally but this is not to be understood as being *amancebada* with him."[50]

In 1605, after hearing the testimony of two Spanish women, who lamented how the "said *amancebamiento* is setting a bad example among the persons who know," the ecclesiastical judge ordered the arrest of the mulatto Francisca Ruiz and the Spaniard Juan Blanco. In her confession, 26-year-old Francisca acknowledged that she had known Juan Blanco for two months. She denied the existence of a protracted affair. "I only knew him once carnally," professed Francisca. It is not clear if the couple rehearsed their testimony prior to being arrested, but 26-year-old Juan Francisco Blanco expressed similar sentiments. "What happened," noted Juan Francisco, "the said Francisca . . . came to my house to wash clothes." He then declared, "I knew her once carnally."[51]

In a case from 1601, black slave Catalina Sánchez recalled being scandalized by the affair between Spanish carpenter Juan Martin and free mulatto Melchora de los Reyes as she offered her testimony before ecclesiastical officials. "For seven months," declared Catalina, the couple had been acting "as if they were husband and wife." "The said *amancebamiento* has caused notoriety and scandal in the neighborhood" observed Catalina, "and this is the Truth." The fact that the next witness, Father Diego López del Huerto, was Catalina's owner may explain why Catalina expressed such horror at the presence of an illicit affair. The priest echoed his slave's testimony.[52]

In another case that same year, after lingering in an archdiocese cell for months, Spaniard Francisco Hernández Mellado conceded that he had had a sexual affair with the mulatto Felipa but resisted identifying their interaction as a state of concubinage. "I had carnal access . . . with her," confessed Francisco. Since then, however, he had merely seen her in a chance encounter on the street.[53]

50. AGN, Bienes Nacionales 810, expediente 80, 1601, "Proceso del Fiscal del Arzobispado contra Castro, español, y María de Guzman, negra, por Amancebados."

51. AGN, Bienes Nacionales 416, expediente 7, 1605, "Proceso contra Juan Blanco, español, pescadero, y Francisca, mulata, por Amancebados."

52. AGN, Bienes Nacionales 810, expediente 6, 1601, "Proceso del Fiscal del Arzobispado contra Juan Martín, español, carpintero, y Melchora de los Reyes, mulata, por Amancebados."

53. AGN, Bienes Nacionales 810, expediente 19, 1601, "Proceso del Fiscal del Arzobispado contra Francisco Hernández Mellado, arriero, y de Felipa, mulata, esclava, por Amancebados."

Patriarchal ties also seem absent in the 1601 case involving Bernado de Sande and the mulatto slave Juana, since the Spanish lover was not her owner. Although Bernado denied the allegations of concubinage, he confessed that "I knew her carnally." But he noted that "more or less it has been a year since I last saw her." Bernado offered no explanation why that was the case (if indeed it was).[54] In another case from the same year involving a relationship between a European and a person of African descent, 26-year-old Portuguese Jerónimo Luís affirmed his year-long relationship with the black slave Luísa when questioned. Although she was another man's property, Luísa was, by her consent, Jerónimo's lover.[55] In another instance from 1609, ecclesiastical officials arrested a slave woman and a Spaniard even though nothing suggested that the woman, Leonor, was the object of control and desire. When questioned about her relationship with Jusepe de Perea, Leonor denied even knowing him.[56] In a similar case, María Callexas, a 40-year-old free mulatto widow, was unlikely to be Juan de Pedraza's object of control. She confessed to having known the Spaniard Juan for six years, during which they had cohabited for one year. At the time of her arrest, she said that she had been separated from Juan for a month.[57] In another case, it seems likely that 26-year-old Matias Cabello lacked the means—beyond his status as a Spanish male—to have patriarchal control over the free black Pascuala. While his neighbors charged that the couple had been cohabitating for nearly a year, Matias claimed that nothing had happened. In so doing, he denied having indulged in simple fornication or the more serious offense of concubinage.[58]

Instances implying patriarchal authority do surface in the ecclesiastical proceedings, especially cases involving relationships between Spanish men and women of color. Yet here too the fragmentary evidence is ambiguous. Following formal charges by the *fiscal* Antonio de Castro and corroborating testimony from Francisca de San Juan and a Spaniard identified as Vicente, ecclesiastical officials arrested Spaniard Pascual Rengifo and a mulatto allegedly named Mariana. After letting Pascual linger in jail for six months, the judge and *fiscal* finally attended to Pascual's confession. Pascual denied knowing a woman named Mariana but suggested that a woman named Jerónima might be the right person. "I have had car-

54. AGN, Bienes Nacionales 810, expediente 24, 1601, "Proceso del Fiscal del Arzobispado contra Bernardo de Sande, español, y Juana, mulata, esclava, por Amancebados."
55. AGN, Bienes Nacionales 810, expediente 59, 1601, "Proceso del Fiscal del Arzobispado contra Jerónimo, portugues, mesillero, y Luisa, negra esclava, por Amancebados."
56. AGN, Bienes Nacionales 810, expediente 125, 1609, "Proceso del Fiscal del Arzobispado contra Jusepe de Perea, bordado, y Leonor, mulata, por Amancebados."
57. AGN, Bienes Nacionales 810, expediente 102, [1601], "Proceso de Luís de Quiros, Fiscal del Arzobispado contra Juan de Pedraza, español y María Callexas, mulata, por Amancebados."
58. AGN, Bienes Nacionales 810, expediente 120, [1601], "Proceso del Fiscal del Arzobispado contra Matias Cabello, mesillero y Pascuala, negra soltera, por Amancebados."

nal access and communication with her," Pascual acknowledged. Though Pascual was married, the judge sent him home with the customary warning. But four years later, rumors surfaced that Pascual and Mariana were at it again. Now additional witnesses, aware of the couple's previous arrest for *amancebamiento*, alleged that the concubines had had three children. On 12 August 1606, Pascual stood before the ecclesiastical judge accused of concubinage for the second time. He identified himself as a 38-year-old merchant (*tratante*) married to María Díaz. Pascual acknowledged that he had known the free mulatto Mariana for four years. "In that time," said Pascual, "I have known her carnally [but] a year ago I distanced myself from the said *amancebamiento*." He confessed, however, that he had brought their daughter gifts and had thus seen Mariana since the purported end of their relationship. Aware that his case looked grim, Pascual professed that this Mariana was not the same woman with whom he had previously consorted.[59] It is unclear how the case ended. We can assume on the basis of precedent that the couple simply received a reprimand and a two-peso fine.

The relationship between Spaniard Blas Rodrigues and free mulatto María Maldonado is another potentially patriarchal affair between interracial lovers. After the routine denunciation and corroborating testimony by two Spaniards in this 1601 case, ecclesiastical officials ordered Blas and María's arrest. In his confession—he was the only one to appear—Blas initially denied the *fiscal's* allegations. But then he relented, acknowledging that he had known María for five years. Blas declared that for the first two years they had been lovers but that this was no longer the case. In order to provide for their four-year-old daughter, he did, however, visit María.[60]

A final example of a potentially patriarchal interracial affair involved Beatríz de Cardenas and the aging Spaniard Gaspar de Trejo, who as I noted earlier stated that "as a man" he had known the 35-year-old free mulatto. The case began in a routine way, but the corroborating testimony offered by Carlos de Trejo, whose relationship to Gaspar is not stated in the archival record, suggests that relatives and possibly resources were involved. Indeed, the presence of the 60-year-old Spaniard Alfonso, Gaspar's peer (who, aside from the occasional priest, was the only man of substance called to testify in all of the ecclesiastical proceedings), hints at the possible stakes involved. Hernández testified that the relationship between Gaspar and Beatríz was over a decade old and had produced two children, but he did not explain why he had not come forward earlier to disclose the affair. When she was questioned by the *fiscal*, Beatríz conceded that she had known Gaspar for fifteen

59. AGN, Bienes Nacionales 810, expediente 36, 1601, "Proceso del Fiscal del Arzobispado contra Pascual Rengifo y María Ana, mulata, por Amancebados."

60. AGN, Bienes Nacionales 810, expediente 92, 1601, "Proceso del Fiscal del Arzobispado contra Blas Rodríguez, español, y María Maldonado, mulata, por Amancebados."

years. But while she acknowledged "having repeatedly interacted with him carnally," she insisted that the sexual affair was a matter of the past. Beatriz testified
that she only came to wash Gaspar's clothes since no one else took care of him. She
categorically denied that Gaspar was the father of her children. In this instance we
identify aspects of a patriarchal relationship. Beatríz—the younger mulatto woman and former slave (*libre de cautiverio*)—was attending to the personal needs of
an aging Spaniard. But even here the evidence is far from conclusive. Beatríz came
and went, and she had children that she alleged were fathered by another man. The
assumption that Gaspar wielded patriarchal authority as patrician, employer, and
lover must be counterbalanced with the personal autonomy Beatríz displayed.[61]

Because most of the ecclesiastical cases involved free mulatto women in relationships with Spanish males and not free black men in relationships with Spanish
women, the evidence from the raids suggest that the manumitted and free population in Mexico was largely composed of women. The ecclesiastical sources corrob-
orate historian Frederick Bowser's conclusions from notary records: Gender was
indeed a factor in whether or not a slave was manumitted. By acknowledging this
relationship we engender the story of freedom, as recent writers, including Jennifer
Morgan, have done with regard to slavery.[62] What implications derive from the
fact that black women were the first to be freed? In light of Patterson's emphasis
on "natal alienation" as slavery's "constituent element," what consequences flowed
from a free womb? The social history answer is, of course, free children. If gender
shaped the experiences of slavery and manumission, it had a similar effect on the
experiences of freedom and modernity.

By identifying personal autonomy in the midst of the cataclysmic age we
bring into relief the earliest recorded instances of black freedom. Far from being
a trivial matter, delineating personal autonomy is a critical historical endeavor. In
the wake of the objectification of the Middle Passage and the enslavement process,
personal autonomy—initially in the form of a limited amount of time and space
to form informal yet fleeting social relations—nurtured a divide between master
and slave, thus tempering the effects of social death. The personal autonomy individuals exhibited in the ecclesiastical cases staved off the master's totalizing aim of
defining slaves as objects and a category of labor that was the extension of his/her
will. But the raids also show blacks and mulattos defying the will of the Catholic
Church to cast them into compliant Christians. Finally, the voices in the archive
also reveal that relations between blacks and Spanish elite were not completely
ensnared in patriarchal bonds.

61. AGN, Bienes Nacionales 442, expediente 8, 1609, "Proceso del Fiscal del Arzobispado contra
Gaspar Trejo y Beatríz, mulata, por Amancebados."
62. Frederick P. Bowser, *The African Slave in Colonial Peru, 1524–1650* (Stanford, Calif.: Stanford
University Press, 1974); Morgan, *Laboring Women.*

Historian Kim Butler has argued that the Brazilian and in general the Latin American social order rested on a system of patronage in which both the relationship between patron and client and dependence were central.[63] Blacks in Brazil came to rely on patrons for employment and social mobility, a pattern that historian R. Douglas Cope has brilliantly described among plebeians—including blacks and mulattos—in seventeenth-century New Spain.[64] But sources matter, and perhaps their conclusions reflect the particularities of records that track material life. Ecclesiastical sources, as we shall see, document a different reality: ethnic Africans and mulattos manifested little actual dependency on the Spaniards with whom they shared social intimacy. In short, the various relations between mulattos and Spaniards attest to shared cultural affinities as creoles and plebeians.

The clergy that led the ecclesiastical raids were not just interested in illicit interracial relationships. They also focused their gaze on illicit relations among black and mulatto couples. On 3 January 1601, *fiscal* Luís de Quiros presented formal charges against the free mulattos Melchor de los Reyes and María Vazquez for being *amancebados*. Spaniard Juan Gallegos, from the barrio of Santa María, offered corroborating testimony about the illicit affair. Juan Gallegos testified that the couple had been cohabiting for a year, which raises the question of why did he not come forward earlier. As a Spaniard and evidently a God-fearing Christian, what compelled Juan Gallegos to wait for a year? Did he come forward of his own free will or was he cajoled by the *fiscal*? Answers to these questions are elusive, but the timing of Juan Gallegos's confession invites curiosity. The second witness, Spaniard Juan de la Cruz, affirmed the affair's existence but testified that the pair had been cohabitating for six months. "I have seen them . . . with each other," recalled Juan. "What [is] more . . . other times I saw the said mulatto [María] go to the house of the said mulatto [Melchor]." Juan de la Cruz claimed that the affair had resulted in a child. "María Vazquez told me," he said. Juan de la Cruz's reference to a love child suggested more than fleeting consensual sex. If the story was true, Melchor de los Reyes and María Vazquez had forged, as best as they could,

63. Kim D. Butler, *Freedoms Given, Freedoms Won: Afro-Brazilians in Post-Abolition São Paulo and Salvador* (New Brunswick, N.J.: Rutgers University Press, 1998), 18–23.

64. Butler, *Freedoms Given, Freedoms Won*, 21. Cope notes that in the economy and in relation to work, *castas* relied on patricians; see Cope, *The Limits of Racial Domination*, 86–105, esp. 104. This dynamic is not evident in the archival sources that detail the marriage patterns of Angolans and free blacks or delineate patterns in witness selection. I think this speaks directly to the ways that Africans and their descendants delimited a sphere of intimacy, underscoring a distinction between the social structure and interiority of their lives. This process identifies the silhouette of an interior space that often has been overshadowed by the metaphors of work and power. But the social logic of the moral economy underscores that work and power shaped and in turn are shaped by these interior structures and relationships. The way that capitalism, for instance, is transformed reflects the particular logic of the social landscape that it encounters. As I argue throughout, but in particular in chapter five, this silhouette requires some attention before we can simply categorize the population of African descent as *castas*.

the semblance of a family life. The allegations that they had been cohabiting "for a year" suggest that the relationship resembled a family. In the Church's eyes, the couple's relationship was illicit, but Melchor and María's behavior was a popular practice among the laity. In subjecting the popular to scrutiny, the Church emphasized the difference between the sanctioned and the unsanctioned.[65] Insisting on this difference as the principal lesson of the confessional moment.

Two days after the couple's arrest, Melchor de los Reyes appeared at the hearing and identified himself as a single 25-year-old. In that confessional moment Melchor attested, despite what he and María shared, that he was "single." They had not contracted vows or petitioned for a marriage license. In the Church's eyes, Melchor was single, and in order to signify his understanding of and respect for Catholic orthodoxy Melchor needed to say as much. Here then we see the Catholic disciplinary mechanism at work at its most fundamental level. By delineating the parameters of even the simplest answer—I am single—it forestalled alternatives, even when such alternatives were widely manifest among the laity. In this confessional instance, the church shaped the individual in a manner that was not dissimilar from how social death transformed the African into a slave. Building on Claude Meillassoux's formulation of social death, Patterson identifies "several transitional phases." But the inaugural moment of "social negation" involves the slave being "violently uprooted from his milieu" followed by a process of desocialization and depersonalization. The ecclesiastical raid that resulted in Melchor's arrest resembled being "violently uprooted." He was dramatically removed from his neighborhood and the neighbors whose behavior he emulated. In reminding Melchor of sanctioned norms, the clergy brought into effect a process of desocialization. In other words, Melchor was not to engage in the customs that his neighbors practiced. In coercing Melchor to deny his social existence with María—I am single—the clergy presided over a process of depersonalization. Melchor could not lay claim to his desire and the reality that he had forged a life with María in Christendom but beyond Christian orthodoxy.[66] At the same time, the *fiscal* demanded that he acknowledge his sin. The *fiscal* asked him if he knew the reason for his arrest (*Preguntado si sabe la causa de su prison*?). "They told me," replied Melchor, "that it was for being *amancebado* with a free mulatto named María Vazquez." Next, the *fiscal* wanted to know if Melchor "knew the said María Vazquez and for how long." Melchor responded that for a year he had interacted with María Vazquez. Then the *fiscal* posed the central question: "Have you been

65. Lewis, *Hall of Mirrors*, 5–8.
66. AGN, Bienes Nacionales 810, expediente 6, 5 January 1601, "Confesión de Melchor de los Reyes," in "Proceso del Fiscal del Arzobispado contra Melchor de los Reyes, mulato zapatero y María Vazquez, mulata, por amancebados."

amancebado with the said María Vazquez, mulato, and have slept and eaten with her on a table and in a bed and have you known her carnally?" "Yes," said Melchor, "but we were freed from our love three months ago."[67] The case ended with the customary warning, thus leaving us to ponder the fate of Melchor and María beyond the proceedings.

Just weeks after the free mulattos Jusepe de la Cruz and Melchora Hernández began living together, the *fiscal* was apprised of their illicit affair. On 11 August 1601, he leveled formal charges of *amancebamiento*. After asking two Spaniards, Agustín Martínez and Juan Salazar, to substantiate the accusation, the *fiscal* had the couple arrested. In a city of tens of thousands where thousands of Africans and an even greater number of Indians arrived annually, the *fiscal* had received word of a budding illicit affair that both witnesses alleged was a month old at best. A week later, on 18 August 1601, Jusepe de la Cruz gave his confession. "I am eighteen and single," noted Jusepe. Asked "if he knew the reason for his imprisonment"—a formulaic but leading question that sought to elicit, not coerce, the truth—Jusepe stated that he was uncertain yet assumed that it was related to his arrest along with Melchora, "being that I and the so said were nude." "How long," asked the *fiscal*, "have you known Melchora?" "Fifteen days," replied Jusepe. Ignoring Jusepe's response, the *fiscal* queried, "Is it true that for three months you have been and presently are in a state of *amancebado* with the so said eating, sleeping with her . . . and knowing her carnally?" "It has not happened as such," protested Jusepe. "What did happen is that two weeks ago I approached her [Melchora] with the intention of marrying her . . . but the said *fiscal* caught us sleeping together."[68] Next the *fiscal* turned to 14-year-old Melchora Hernández. "Do you know why you have been arrested?" the *fiscal* asked. "For being in a single room together with the said Jusepe de la Cruz," responded Melchora. When asked how long she had known Jusepe, Melchora replied fifteen days. "And in this time," confessed Melchora, "we have always been together . . . and he has repeatedly known me carnally."[69] In the end, the *provisor* ordered the couple to cease their illicit and licit interactions.

Diego Pérez and Ana Gómez are a final example of a free mulatto couple caught in the snare of the ecclesiastical raids at the beginning of the seventeenth

67. AGN, Bienes Nacionales 810, expediente 6, 1601, "Proceso del Fiscal del Arzobispado contra Melchor de los Reyes, mulato, zapatero, y María Vazquez, mulata, por Amancebados."

68. AGN, Bienes Nacionales 810, expediente 65, 18 August 1601, "Confesión de Jusepe de la Cruz," in "Proceso del Fiscal del Arzobispado contra Jusepe de la Cruz y Melchora, mulatos libres solteros por amancebados"; AGN, Bienes Nacionales 810, expediente 65, 1601, "Proceso contra Julepe de la Cruz, mulato libre, sombrero, y Melchora, mulata libre, por Amancebados."

69. AGN, Bienes Nacionales 810, expediente 65, 18 August 1601, "Confesión de Melchora Hernández," in "Proceso del Fiscal del Arzobispado contra Jusepe de la Cruz y Melchora, mulatos libres solteros por amancebados."

century. After registering his accusation against them in 1609, the *fiscal* called on two witnesses. Both were Spaniards. Since Diego and Ana allegedly lived in the house of an *alguacil,* Alonso Díaz, his absence as witness poses some interesting questions. After all, the constable escorted the *fiscal* on his raids and was invariably summoned by ecclesiastical and Inquisition officials, although another *alguacil* had carried out this arrest. Did Alonso Díaz know about his tenants? Did he care? If not, how did he reconcile his indifference with his status as a royal constable? Diego, an 18-year-old, was the first to testify. As a single man he had known Ana Gomez for a month. "I have repeatedly known her carnally," observed Diego. Ana Gomez denied the charges. "The said Diego Pérez," confessed Ana, "was going to be my son's conformational godfather." As the lover of her son's godfather, Ana would have been engaged in spiritual incest with Diego. Since the case ended abruptly, it remains unclear who was lying. But here we see Ana Gomez actively courting the judge's favor as a Christian and a mother.[70]

In most slave societies, autonomous free blacks embodied a visible threat to the social order, and the ruling elite throughout the Americas restricted their access to liberties. But in Mexico, free coloreds pressed their personal autonomy in the hope of grasping liberty. They lived on their own without the presence of a patrician Spaniard. In the proceedings, witnesses repeatedly used formulaic language that stated that they had seen couples *comer y dormer a una mesa y cama como sí fueran marido y mujer* (eating at a table and sleeping in a bed as if they were husband and wife). Often modifying their declarations with such phrases as "I have seen them," "I have repeatedly seen them," and "I have seen them many times," the witnesses then would add a period of time.[71] This language implied that the offenders—mostly free mulatto women—had the personal autonomy (defined in terms of mobility, space, and time) to sustain what was in the Church's eyes an illicit affair but to them was their own personal business. This autonomy contradicts the scholarly characterization of free black life. These individual black experiences were lived outside the boundaries of analyses that emphasize commodification, labor, and race. Individuals used their autonomy to forge lives and engaged in social practices that reflected their desires. In asking about their transgressions, the *fiscals* were not concerned about confining free mulattos to a labor market or, for that matter, with subordinating them to the caste system. What they defined as transgressions touched only on matters of Christian being. This suggests that in

70. AGN, Bienes Nacionales 442, 14 December 1609, "Proceso del Fiscal del Arzobispado contra Diego, mulato, carnicero, y Ana Gomez, mulata soltera, por Amancebados."

71. AGN, Bienes Nacionales 442, expediente 33, 1609; AGN, Bienes Nacionales 442, expediente 8, 1609; AGN, Bienes Nacionales 810, expediente 65, 1601; AGN, Bienes Nacionales 810, expediente 6, 1601.

the early seventeenth century, free blacks had created areas of private and community life reflective of their desires, not those of colonial authorities.

In regulating personal behavior and private lives, the proceedings reinforced dogma (the formalized teachings of the parish priest), but they also constituted the licit and defined the illicit. Such focused attention on private lives and individual behavior involved more than regulation. It delineated for the accused the existence of the individual, the site of the soul. The teachings and regulations of Christianity spelled out the permissible and configured the individual as the agent responsible for his or her soul. For numerous blacks and mulattos, including Beatríz de Cardenas, Leonor de la Concepción, Diego Pérez, Ana Gomez, Andrés López, María Maldonado, Melchora Hernández, María de Callexas, Melchor de los Reyes, Melchora de los Reyes, María Vazquez, María de Guzman, and Catalina de Leon, this form of the self was relatively new. Even twenty-five years after her baptism, the clergy's teaching of Christian personhood was a novel concept for Catalina de Leon.[72] In all likelihood the illicit offspring of an African mother and a Spaniard (she was not identified as a *hija legitima*) who was born sometime in the 1580s, Catalina was reared in a Christian landscape. If she was fortunate enough to have been reared by her mother, then an African sense of self, which itself was in the process of changing, competed with the identity the clergy extolled. As a Christian in a fragile Christian landscape, Catalina de Leon was still acquiring the rudiments and mysteries of faith. In the ecclesiastical proceedings, Catalina was formally reminded that as an individual she was responsible for her behavior and her soul. In asking "was it true" that for the last six months "you have been and at present are publicly *amancebado* with the so said treating and knowing him carnally as if you where his wife," the *fiscal* clarified both the licit and the illicit and called into relief Christian personhood. As a good Christian, Catalina should aspire to legally marry and engage in carnal intercourse only with her husband. For all the accused, the proceedings were an ominous reminder that they had souls for which they, as individuals, were accountable.

The activities of the ecclesiastical court encourage a reconsideration of the perspective that masters and patricians were the exclusive loci of power in matters related to persons of African descent. In its focus on this creolized population, the Catholic Church sought to discipline both creoles and newly arrived Africans. We see the spectacle of the clergy deploying disciplinary strategies among free blacks and mulattos to keep other members of the laity in check. Ecclesiastical discipline cut across domains that scholars of Mexico conceive as hermetically distinct, re-

72. AGN, Bienes Nacionales 442, 21 March 1609, "Mandamiento de prison contra los culpados," in "Proceso del Fiscal del Arzobispado contra Diego de Salinas, sombrerero y Catalina, mulata, por amancebados."

minding us that New Spain's slave society was not separate from the world of free blacks.[73]

In glimpsing how Church and state claimed the right to discipline free blacks and mulattos, we see the workings of Spanish governance. In the early seventeenth century, a domain of modern state power gained ascendancy over the social landscape. The discipline practices (the Inquisition) of a bureaucracy (the Church) were designed to rationalize Spanish rule and bolster its authority. Masters, slaves, and free persons were caught up in the shifting practices of power expressed through the modality of Catholic modernity. The threat that mobile slaves and free blacks constituted in seventeenth-century New Spain was secondary to the paramount objective of power—Christian orthodoxy. Christianity played the dominant role in controlling slaves and free blacks in the early seventeenth century.

In seventeenth-century New Spain, the absolutist state did not view the physical liberty of dependents—slaves, servants, offspring, and wives—as the paramount threat to the social order. Enforcing Christian orthodoxy was more important to royal officials than controlling the threat to patriarchal authority the movement and mobility of free blacks represented. In this respect, Spanish America varied dramatically from Anglo America, where officials of the colonial state placed their power at the service of patriarchy in controlling the mobility and growth of the free black population. Carole Shammas's conclusion that "patriarchs were supposed to control the movement of their dependents" and that "when they no longer could do so, the system fell apart" does not apply to New Spain.[74] In New Spain, manumission decreased the number of slaves, but the system in which bondage and freedom were embedded survived the growth of the New World's first and largest free black population. As the following case illustrates, the clergy and the inquisitors displayed a keen interest in regulating the private lives of ordinary free blacks so as to uphold the social order.

On 9 November 1609, as the inquisitors presided over matters of faith and state, they were distracted by a commotion in the Inquisition's cells, where an inmate who had been remanded into custody for having fled a textile mill (*obraje*)

---

73. J. Jorge Klor de Alva, "The Postcolonization of the (Latin) American Experience: A Reconsideration of 'Colonialism,' 'Postcolonialism,' and 'Mestizaje,'" in *After Colonialism: Imperial Histories and Postcolonial Displacements*, ed. Gyan Prakash (Princeton, N.J.: Princeton University Press, 1995), 241–275.

74. Shammas has recently revisited the critical importance of bureaucracies as a way to distinguish between Spanish America and Anglo America. She argues that "the rather underdeveloped state of governmental institutions enhanced the authority of the household head. . . . No colony adopted any of the measures popular among the propertied in late seventeenth- and eighteenth-century England to counter the trend of household head individualism. The strict family settlement, marriage settlements and the 1753 Act Against Clandestine Marriages all reminded household heads and would-be household heads of their lineage obligations. The enforcement of these legal arrangements, however, depended on judicial and church bureaucracies that never materialized in colonial America." Shammas, "Anglo-American Household Government in Comparative Perspective," 126.

wanted to offer a self-denunciation.[75] Identified as Francisco de Castañeda, a free mulatto tailor, the inmate requested an audience "in order to confess before our lord." When they heard the petition, the inquisitors ordered that Francisco be escorted to the tribunal later that day to be examined for the sin of bigamy. The subsequent proceedings provide a detailed examination of Francisco de Casteñeda's life, his family genealogy, his exposure to Christianity, and the circumstances under which he became a bigamist. Francisco's self-denunciation and his testimony's revelation of how the Inquisition placed an individual's entire community on trial reveal the workings of modern power in the seventeenth century. In the context of a burgeoning slave society, Francisco de Casteñeda's status and mobility did not threaten the social order; he was able to travel freely and socialize with slaves and servants. But when his behavior did not conform to Christian orthodoxy, he did constitute a threat. And the inquisitors had to contend with that threat.

After spending time in the oppressive confines of an *obraje,* Francisco de Castañeda was ready to talk. As a Christian, Francisco knew he had options that could change his condition. On being exhorted by the inquisitors' ritual rhetoric to divulge his crimes, Francisco began by offering his autobiography. He identified himself as a mulatto and legitimate son of Spaniard Juan de Castañeda and Elena, a free mulatto. He was reared in his parents' household in the barrio of Monserrate in Mexico City, after which he married an Indian native of Orizaba, María de la Cruz. The wedding was a formal affair. The couple received their wedding license from Dr. Salamanca, a priest in the archdiocese. They celebrated their nuptials in the company of Spaniards and *mestizos* in the house of a fruit vendor, Juan Gallegos; Gallegos and his wife served as godparents (*padrinos*). Two months later, the couple was veiled in the parish church of Santa Veracruz. While an individual named Sancho Gonzalez presided, Miguel Ortiz and his wife Isabel de Villalobos, residents of the barrio of Monserrate and possibly acquaintances of Francisco's parents, sponsored the ceremony.

After four years of marriage, Francisco left his wife and moved to the pueblo of Queretaro, where he gained employment as a tailor. Three months later, he contracted a second marriage with the mulatto Gerónima de la Cruz. Francisco repeated the formalities that had united him in matrimony with María. Such formalities, even for persons of African descent, were initiated by identifying family genealogies, and Francisco identified Gerónima as the legitimate daughter of the deceased free black Juan Bran and the deceased Indian Catalina Herrera. He related how a Franciscan friar, Fr. Alemán, married them in a monastery; the free mulatto couple Pasqual de Salazar and María de Serrano served as *padrinos*.

---

75. AGN, Inquisición 470, folios 309–363, "Proceso contra Francisco de Castañeda, mulato libre, sastre, natural de la ciudad de México por casado dos Veces."

Francisco's bliss lasted for a month before his conscience troubled him into confessing his error. But before he could return to Mexico City to confess, he lost a pair of gloves while working in Tezcoco, for which the owner had him arrested and placed in an *obraje,* where he could work to repay the debt. After experiencing repeated abuse, Francisco fled in the company of some Indians, but when the *obraje* owner found him in Mexico he returned to the textile mill "so that he could not come to the Holy Office."

Francisco's confession caught the inquisitors' attention. They wanted to know the names of the ecclesiastical official and the witnesses that presided as he and Gerónima de la Cruz had petitioned for a marriage license in Queretaro. In asking for the names of his witnesses, the inquisitors brought a fragment of Francisco's community under scrutiny. Francisco gave the names but noted that he had hidden the truth from free mulatto mule driver Miguel Hernandez and the *mestizo* Francisco. Next, the inquisitors asked if María de la Cruz was alive and if so, to describe her and name their children. Francisco characterized María as a woman between the ages of eighteen and twenty with a small thin body who had borne him two sons—Juan de Castañeda, named after his father, and Nicolas, who had previously died. The inquisitors asked Francisco what motivated him to marry a second time. "Did you know not to do it?" queried the *fiscal.* Acknowledging that he fancied Gerónima, Francisco declared that "the devil blinded me into doing it" (*que le cego el demonio para hazerlo*), since he knew not to marry a second time. After this confession of desire, Francisco again pleaded for clemency. In order to determine if Francisco was a heretic, not merely a bigamist, the inquisitors questioned him about his conscience. Francisco responded that he felt remorse for having violated the sacrament of marriage for no other reason than having desired Gerónima de la Cruz. He told the inquisitors where to find Gerónima, describing her as a tall young woman "beyond the age of twenty."

After remanding Francisco into custody, the inquisitors dictated a letter addressed to officials in Queretaro's Franciscan monastery that asked for information about Francisco and Gerónima's marriage. Embodied in the inquisitors' request was a bureaucratic confidence that no act, individual, or transaction stood beyond the purview of Church and state. In tone and practice, the Holy Office wielded authority in a decidedly modern manner. The Inquisition conceived of free blacks and slaves as part of the larger population whose private lives needed to be managed "in its depth and its details."[76] While the universal application of canon law positioned slaves and free blacks on the same legal plane as Spaniards—as people

76. Michel Foucault, "Governmentality," in *The Foucault Effect: Studies in Governmentality with Two Lectures by and an Interview with Michel Foucault,* ed. Graham Burchell, Colin Gordon, and Peter Miller (Chicago: University of Chicago Press, 1991), 102.

of reason (*gente de razon*)—everyday practices of power diminished that equality before the law. According to Irene Silverblatt, the Inquisition

> was developing a structure and logic apart from dynastic boundaries; it was formally organized according to principles of rationality; it was imagined as being greater than the sum of its individual officeholders; and it was careful to legitimate its practices through an appeal to public welfare. In sum, the Inquisition was a bureaucracy that typified the evolving institutions of the emerging modern world: it was a state structure in the making.[77]

In the Christian commonwealth, even two obscure free mulattos had personal identities—Francisco de Castañeda and Gerónima de la Cruz—that could be regulated and disciplined.

The inquisitors placed Francisco's familiars on trial when they mined his testimony for evidence of wrongdoing. In their dispatch to Queretaro, the inquisitors identified the individuals who were to be questioned about the bigamist marriage. Among those named as potential witnesses were the free mulatto Gerónima de la Cruz; the married free mulattos Pasqual de Salazar and María de Serrano, who served as *padrinos;* Mariana, the slave of Juan Rodriguez Galan; and Ines, Juan Rodriguez Galan's free mulatto servant. According to the inquisitors' instructions, the Franciscan authorities were to question all of them to find evidence about the marriage of Francisco and Gerónima and to assure themselves that these individuals upheld Christian orthodoxy "in its depths and its details."

A month later the Franciscans had complied with the instructions of the inquisitors. Suddenly Francisco's confession and his story acquired a different twist. Juan Pasqual, a 50-year-old free black (*de color moreno*), testified that he was present at Francisco and Gerónima's wedding. While confirming that Fr. Sebastian Alemena had presided over the ceremony in which Pasqual de Salazar and his wife María de Serrano served as *padrinos,* Juan Pasqual said that Francisco had deceived him and others as to his single status. In Mexico, Juan learned and "saw with my own eyes" that Francisco was already married. He learned of Francisco's deception when Francisco's parents, a Spaniard named Castañeda and his mulatto wife, questioned him about the whereabouts of their son. As proof of his Christian conscience, Juan accompanied Francisco's parents to the Holy Office to offer his confession when he learned of Francisco's true marital status and realized that he

---

77. Irene Silverblatt, *Modern Inquisitions: Peru and the Colonial Origins of the Civilized World* (Durham, N.C.: Duke University Press, 2004), 10–11. Silverblatt's argument has antecedents in the historiography of the emergence of the medieval "persecuting society." This is a critical starting point for understanding how persecution tied in to the centralization of power rather than seeing it as a religious issue. See R. I. Moore, *The Formation of a Persecuting Society: Power and Deviance in Western Europe, 950–1250* (New York: Oxford University Press, 1987); and Christine Caldwell Ames, "Does the Inquisition Belong to Religious History?" *The American Historical Review* (February 2005): 13–16.

had unwittingly aided a bigamist. But this effort was thwarted when they were unable to locate an inquisition official. Soon thereafter, Juan Pasqual left Mexico, leaving Francisco's parents with the burden of confessing.

Mariana de la Concepción's testimony was equally damning for Francisco. The slave of Juan Rodriguez Galan (who was also Gerónima's employer) stated that she had known Francisco for three years. In the course of those years "before he married Gerónima de la Cruz," the couple had been "in a state of *amancebamiento*." After Juan Rodriguez Galan's wife Gerónima de los Angeles repeatedly found the two lovers in a compromised state, she had Francisco arrested in order to force a legitimate union. According to Mariana, Francisco informed Gerónima de los Angeles that he was already married. Adamant that Francisco marry her servant, Gerónima threatened the couple until they finally relented. Wedding proceedings followed. But Gerónima de los Angeles prevented the nuptials from being celebrated in her house and prohibited Mariana and others from attending the festivities.

The free mulatto Melchora de los Reyes, an eighteen-year-old servant of Juan Rodriguez Galan, corroborated Mariana's testimony. Melchora knew that Francisco was involved with her sister, Gerónima de la Cruz. She too confessed that the common-law relationship ended when Gerónima de los Angeles found the couple in a compromising situation. Threatened with arrest, the couple opted for a legal union. Melchora recalled that "because her mistress was angry," she did not allow her to "go to the Church" to attend her sister's wedding. After the festivities, Francisco fled Queretaro.

In offering their testimonies, the wedding attendees and Gerónima de la Cruz's familiars did more than substantiate the existence of a marriage. They provided evidence that Francisco and Gerónima had lived in a common-law arrangement until Gerónima da los Angeles forced the couple to legitimize their union. They knew and to a certain extent condoned the relationship. The tone of their testimony suggests that the witnesses understood themselves to be under scrutiny. Juan Pasqual noted that this was why he attempted to bring the matter to the inquisitors' attention. But ultimately his efforts as a good Christian failed. Mariana and Melchora implied that they were not aware of Francisco's previous marriage, which absolved them from responsibility for bringing evidence of wrongdoing to Inquisition officials. Whether such claims were truthful cannot be determined, but in suggesting as much the two black women presented themselves as good Christians.

Gerónima de la Cruz, Francisco's second wife, also cloaked her testimony in the shroud of ignorance. She confessed that she had lived in a common-law arrangement with Francisco but then was "caught and yelled at" by her mistress and was coerced into a marriage. Claiming to learn about Francisco's previous marriage only after marrying him, Gerónima professed her innocence. In offering these fragments of their lives to the presiding officials, the various individuals underscored their awareness of the stakes involved. In questioning them about their behavior, the inquisitors sought to regulate slaves and free blacks alike as part of the Christian population.

The Franciscan officials in Queretaro appended a copy of the *informacíon matrimonial* to their letter to the inquisitors in Mexico City. The penchant for detail and its preservation enabled them to locate positive proof that Francisco and Gerónima had contracted a marriage. Through the *informacíon*, we learn that Francisco had presented two witnesses, the free black Francisco Hernandez and the Indian Francisco Sanchez, to attest to his single status. Both men confessed that they had known Francisco in Mexico and offered testimony on behalf of Gerónima, though they did not indicate how long they had known her. A third witness, Francisco de Sosa, who was over thirty years old, acknowledged that he had known Francisco for four months but declared that had known Gerónima de la Cruz "since she was a girl." Evidently the Franciscans had doubts about the testimony of the two Franciscos and demanded that additional information be brought forth to verify Francisco de Castañeda's truth claims. Francisco promptly complied and offered witnesses with whom he shared longer and more intimate ties. On the basis of a five-year friendship with Francisco and his familiarity with Francisco's parents, the mulatto Diego Perez vowed that the groom was free from any marital impediments. The *mestizo* Francisco Hernandez noted that his relationship with Francisco could be dated back to when "he [Francisco de Casteñeda] had the use of reason." Like Diego Perez, Francisco Hernández claimed to know Juan Casteñeda and his wife Elena de Torre. In a universe that numbered souls in the millions, Inquisition officials could be confident that their ecclesiastical subordinates adhered to protocol by recording minute details involving the lives of free blacks. In this respect, the private life of free blacks—especially behavior touching on matters of the soul and Christian orthodoxy—was not allowed to extend completely beyond the purview of the nascent state.

With the cessation of the Queretaro investigation, the proceedings shifted back to Mexico. On 12 December 1609, the Inquisition's *fiscal* Pedro de Fonesca asked that Francisco be officially charged with bigamy. Two days later the Holy Office initiated formal proceedings against him. After four days of testimony from witnesses who were present at Francisco and María de los Angeles's wedding, the inquisitors examined the marriage register from the parish of Santa Veracruz. Ascertaining that the wedding had taken place on 11 April 1604, the inquisitors turned their attention to Francisco de Casteñeda.

In the course of the two *audiencias*, a brief trial, and judicial sentencing, they repeatedly questioned Francisco about his family genealogy, the course of his life, and his two marriages. They wanted to assure themselves that Francisco was not a hardened heretic. They also wanted to discern the degree to which Francisco was familiar with Christianity. In the process, the inquisitors brought into relief the formalities that defined a good Christian—formalities that applied to all *gente de razon,* including free blacks. In a series of leading questions, the *fiscal* asked Francisco to state if he had been baptized and confirmed. Did he attend mass, confess, and participate in the Eucharist at the times the Church ordered? Francisco answered in the affirmative, noting that he had most recently confessed prior to his arrest in Texcoco's convent of San Francisco. When ordered to demonstrate his instruction as a Christian, Francisco signed and crossed himself while reciting the Paternoster, the Ave Maríe, the Creed, the Salve Regina, and the Ten Commandments. At the conclusion of this Christian recital, an inquisitor recorded that Francisco had "said them well in Latin" (*en romance bien dichos*). Despite this performance or perhaps since Francisco knew better, the inquisitors unanimously found him guilty of bigamy. In an *auto de fe* celebrated in March 1610—four months after his initial confession—Francisco, dressed in a *sanbenito* (penitential garment) and the insignia of a bigamist with a noose around his neck while carrying a candle, experienced ritual humiliation as he and the other penitents were paraded through Mexico's streets. After receiving 100 lashes, the young free black who had confessed that desire had made him sin was exiled from family and friends for a period of four years. For the inquisitors, the affair culminated in the cathedral on 14 March 1610, when officials read the sentences out loud before the viceroy and the assembled mass, which included Francisco's relatives.

*   *   *

Overlapping and entangled strategies of discipline challenge the perspective that insists that dominance shifted from slaveholders to the imperial/colonial/national state in the transition from slavery to freedom. New Spain's masters competed with the church's disciplinary authorities to bend the will of Africans. Though in competition, these distinctive sites of power complemented each other in the violent remaking of Africans into Western objects—black Christians. The simultaneity that informed the workings of these distinctive sites of power constituted a disciplinary regime. As historian Diane Paton observed in the context of colonial Jamaica, "Conventional periodization tends to reinforce an assumption of a complete break between slavery and 'freedom.'" Skeptical of this divide and its denial of articulating disciplinary practices, Paton contends that "the history of punishment and the history of the transition from slavery to free labor are ripe for consideration alongside each other because of the conceptual connections and contradictions among slavery and different forms of punishment."[78] From the

78. Diana Paton, *No Bond but the Law: Punishment, Race, and Gender in Jamaican State Formation, 1780–1870* (Durham, N.C.: Duke University Press, 2004), 4–5.

conventional perspective—which Paton criticizes—the tendency has been to see distinct expressions of power (read pre-modern and modern) as being sequential rather than coterminous.[79] But in Spanish America, practices associated with the discipline of free persons also applied to slaves. And the reverse was true as well. In focusing on the proceedings of the ecclesiastical courts we see a demonstration of how Catholicism, as a form of modern power, implicated both slave and free.

The story before us involves far more than the workings of Catholic modernity. Through the regulation of the laity the clergy gathered evidence about private lives. As blacks and mulattos revealed their offenses to the clergy and inquisitors they offered glimpses of the lives and relationships they had forged. Of course, these details emerged in the context of a trail. But the accused literally tell us that their lives—their private lives—operated both within and beyond the confines of the labor market. By means of their private lives—in the first instances claims to personhood and then the ability to come and go as they pleased—blacks and mulattos established specific relationship that defined their communities. As Africans, blacks, and mulattos claimed personhood and private lives, they brought personal liberty into relief, a liberty in which African and their descendants could insist on their Christian identities as family members and kinfolk.

79. Scholars in some instances have documented what the enslaved perceived as the divide. Patterson offers the following quote: "Isaiah Butler, another South Carolina ex-slave, observed: ''Dey didn't have a jail in dem times. Dey's whip 'em, and dey's sell 'em. Every slave know what "I'll put you in my pocket, Sir" mean'" (in Patterson, *Slavery and Social Death*, 6).

TWO

Genealogies of a Past

German political philosopher Karl Marx eloquently questioned the notion of historical transcendence by asking "What is a Negro slave?" His answer: "A man of the black race. . . . He only becomes a slave in certain relations."[1] Slaves (and consequently slavery) continually had to be made. Africans in the seventeenth century were made into slaves through specific relations of domination that marked them as distinct both from sixteenth-century arrivals and from others who experienced slavery in seventeenth-century New Spain. This chapter describes that historical process.

In 1646, New Spain's 35,089 enslaved Africans constituted the largest concentration of Africans in the urban New World. The African population in New Spain also represented the second largest assemblage of Africans in the Americas.[2] As is evident in table 2.1, together with New Spain's 116,529 blacks and mulattos, slave and free, the African population formed the largest black society in the Americas.

Despite colonial Mexico's rich historiography of ethnicity, a curious omission prevails. Though scholars acknowledge the size of the African population, its cultural significance remains largely unexamined. In light of the numerical ascendancy of Africans over Spaniards throughout the colonial period, this omission

---

1. Karl Marx, *Wage Labour and Capital* (New York: International Publishers, 1937), 29.
2. On the basis of the Harvard database *The Trans-Atlantic Slave Trade: A Database on CD-ROM* (ed. David Eltis, Stephen D. Behrendt, David Richardson, and Herbert Klein [New York: Cambridge University Press, 1999]), Africanist Joseph Miller states that there "were 15 successful crossings [to the Americas] from Central Africa in the 1590s, 30 in the 1600s, 47 in the 1610s, 27 in the 1620s, 21 in the 1630s and none in the 1640s." During this period, Spanish American cities competed with Brazil as the principal recipients of enslaved Africans. "Central Africans," Miller writes, "thus dominated the initial slave populations of the Americas at the beginning of the seventeenth century, with approximately equal numbers in Spanish cities and on sugar plantations in Brazil." Joseph C. Miller, "Central Africa during the Era of the Slave Trade, c. 1490s–1850s," in *Central Africans and the Cultural Transformations in the American Diaspora,* ed. Linda M. Heywood (New York: Cambridge University Press, 2002), 26–27.

TABLE 2.1. POPULATION OF NEW SPAIN BY REGION AND ETHNIC GROUP, 1646

Region[1]	Europeans	Africans	Indians	Euro-Mestizo[2]	Afro-Mestizo[3]	Indo-Mestizo[4]
Mexico	8,000	19,441	600,000	94,544	43,373	43,190
Tlaxcala	2,700	5,534	250,000	17,404	17,381	16,841
Oaxaca	600	898	150,000	3,952	4,712	4,005
Michoacán	250	3,295	35,858	24,396	20,185	21,067
Nueva Galicia	1,450	5,180	41,378	19,456	13,778	13,854
Yucatán	750	497	150,053	7,676	15,770	8,603
Chiapas	80	244	42,318	1,140	1,330	1,482
Totals	13,830	35,089	1,269,607	168,568	116,529	109,042

Source: Gonzalo Aguirre Beltrán, *La población negra de México,* 2nd ed. (México: Fondo de Cultura Económica, 1972), 219.

1. Archdiocesan boundaries defined the regions employed in this census.
2. Denotes racially mixed persons who, for reasons of residency and public perception, were classified as Euro-Mestizos. Such individuals included, for example, the legitimate son or daughter of a Spanish-Indian union (a *mestizo/a*). Castizos and to a lesser extent light-complexioned moriscos were also defined as Euro-Mestizos.
3. Afro-Mestizos were usually racially mixed persons with either one or both parents of African descent. They and/or one of their parents were also partially of Spanish descent. The names most commonly used for such individuals were *mulato* or *pardo.*
4. These were invariably mestizos or the offspring African-Indian unions who lived among indigenous peoples. Their cultural orientation and phenotype often resembled that of Indians.

seems glaring. But when we acknowledge that during the same period slaves and free blacks constituted the majorities of the principle urban centers—the sites of Spanish power—the absence of scholarly attention becomes rather ominous.

Basic social and cultural questions still need to be framed in relation to the African population. We know so little about the domestic arrangements of persons of African descent that even our knowledge about which questions we need to ask concerning gender, sexual, and family conventions among Africans remains provisional. Did a family structure exist among enslaved Africans?[3] If so, what was its nature and on what social logic did it rest? How did the family structure

3. In the study of Afro-Latin America, the family is a fundamental and remarkably undertheorized concern. The cognitive orientation that shapes research priorities can best be expressed by the intellectual framework that informs family studies. Anthropologist Jack Goody has noted that "for the last hundred and fifty years the study of the European family and marriage has been dominated by the growing preoccupation of scholars about their links with the great events that took place in the West at the outset of the modern period. What was the relationship of the family with the Reformation outside and inside the Catholic Church, with the growth of capitalism and the coming of industrial society?" Goody observes that this "question has world-wide implications. For the problem of the 'rise of the West', which gripped the intellectual imagination of Marx, Weber, and countless others, is closely linked with 'the uniqueness of the West.'" This formulation engaged our attention in chapter 1, but there and throughout I am intent on discerning the role that the family and kinship played in the lives of Africans and their New World descendants. This viewpoint has not been a pressing concern for family studies in colonial Latin America. Jack Goody, *The Development of the Family and Marriage in Europe* (New York: Cambridge University Press, 1983), 1.

of Africans change over time? What social consequences, if any, flowed from the changing family structure? What were the cultural implications, if any, of these structural changes? Did the existence of the family and its structural changes enable family members to have access to freedom? Asked differently, what is the relationship between an emergent private life, individualism, and freedom?

Building on the argument that among blacks, private lives were channeled through Christian discipline, this chapter examines how Africans used Christian matrimony to create ethnic ties. Another way of interpreting this process is to view African appropriation of Christian matrimony as part of the inaugural moment in the formation of private lives. In fact, what scholars define as ethnicity in seventeenth-century New Spain should also be interpreted as a process of individualization, a process from which Africans emerged with private lives. The claims Africans staked as husbands and wives in the sixteenth century would foster ethnic collectivities in the first half of the seventeenth century. In suggesting as much I am claiming that enslaved Africans in Spanish America were some of the first individuals in early modern Christendom to construct private lives largely unencumbered by primordial traditions.

Because the sixteenth-century slave trade that brought thousands of West Africans to New Spain resulted in both the presence of African survivors and the emergence of a creole population, a distinct understanding of African cultural formation seems necessary for the seventeenth century. Much of this chapter focuses on persons who were identified and who self-identified as Angolans. Many of these individuals landed as slaves in New Spain between 1595 and 1622 and found their way to Mexico City, where they joined West Africans, especially *negros criollos* (black creoles), both slave and free, along with Spaniards and Indians. African cultural formation in New Spain in the first half of the seventeenth century was not a novel phenomenon; its history dates back to the conquest, if not before. Instead of insisting on a cultural continuity whereby West-Central Africans in New Spain simply were swept up in the cultural vortex created by West Africans, the evidence suggests that constant innovation characterized the African pattern, resulting in a plurality of New World ethnicities—the fashioning of multiple African identities.[4] In depicting this cultural process, scholars have often privileged the notion of radical disjuncture, but now we understand that a much more subtle dynamic was at work. While the Spaniards' use of the term Angolan to describe all Africans underscores a linguistic and therefore cultural break with the West African past

4. Miller, "Central Africa during the Era of the Slave Trade, c. 1490s–1850s," 22; Paul E. Lovejoy, "Identifying Enslaved Africans in the African Diaspora," in *Identity in the Shadow of Slavery,* ed. Paul E. Lovejoy (New York: Continuum, 2000), 3.

5. My work builds on the work of art historian David Brown, who focuses on "changing forms over time" instead of "thickly delineated historical and sociopolitical contexts." This shift in focus enables him to "situate changing forms" in ways that step outside "airtight frameworks of local and global sociohistorical explanation"; see Brown, *Santería Enthroned,* 8. I am convinced that a local dynamic

that was signified by the use of such terms as Bran, Biafara, and Gelofo, these ethnic terms were channeled through a Christian cultural dynamic that provided continuity. The numerical preponderance of Angolans and creoles in the first half of the seventeenth century served to distinguish the cultural dynamic of that century from New Spain's sixteenth-century African past. As products of distinct African cultural traditions and practices, most creoles and Angolans configured each other as strangers. In New Spain's complex social landscape, the shared experience of race and slavery was not enough to forge a collective African, slave, or black consciousness. By embracing Christian customs, however, these discrete "black" populations steadily began to resemble each other. In time—through the course of the first half of the seventeenth century—this resemblance moved beyond form and ultimately permeated the cultural logic of daily existence. In urban New Spain, Christianity rather than race or slavery provided the structural contours of blackness. Christianity also offered the enduring structural presence that tenuously linked the sixteenth to the seventeenth century. For these reasons, the genealogies of blackness were largely rooted in Christianity.

A brief note on method may be useful here. In this and the subsequent chapter, I draw on a careful examination of thousands of marriage petitions (*informaciones matrimoniales*) for the period 1584–1650 in which Africans and creoles were present as bride, grooms, and wedding sponsors. I have configured some of this data into tables that are dispersed through the following two chapters. But in an effort to illuminate the significance of the data, I have framed significant parts of the next two chapters around the personalities of two wedding parties—one for the Angolan bride and groom Angelina and Juan and the other for creoles Nicholas de la Cruz and Clara—in 1633 and 1634. Far from being exceptional, the wedding parties and especially the bride and groom (*novios*) underscore the simultaneity of cultural and social formation among persons of African descent. In both cases, Christian conjugality mediated the sociocultural process but with distinct valence for each wedding party. For Angelina and Juan, the marriage affirmed their New World ethnicity as Angolans while the proceedings enabled Nicholas and Clara to embrace their creole identities. But rather than search for differences to distinguish the ethnic couple and the creole couple (a standard line of inquiry among scholars), we benefit by viewing these fragments of a wedding and a wedding party as social forms that embodied the cultural symbiosis that characterized the first half of the seventeenth century.[5] This approach demands more than an examination of

---

shaped by the specific expression of Christianity in New Spain is the predominant "form," if you will, in the landscape of colonial Mexico and the Afro-Mexicans who lived there. Even the disciplinary mechanisms that produced the colonial archive largely reflect a local dynamic (specific inquisitors) as opposed to some larger remote process. What this then means is that I am keen on representing black cultural forms through what art historians might identify as a formalist method. Cultural logic and cultural forms are profoundly historical, specific to place and time.

the ways the concept "Angolan" brought the *criollo* presence and experience into relief. At its core, my depiction of the cultural dynamic necessitates an exploration of time and being in the period under discussion. Posed as a question, were Juan and Angelina engaging in the same cultural practices as the Nicolas and Clara? By situating this question in a specific period—the 1630s—this and the next chapter locate the complex process of cultural formation in which Angolans defined themselves in the context of an urban society that coexisted with a creole population composed largely of free blacks and mulattos. These two chapters serve to modify our perspective on African and black cultural formation in the Americas. Linear progress did not characterize the transition from ethnic Africans to successive generations of creoles. Cultural articulation was specific but also emerged in a cultural crucible shaped by Christianity and Spanish cultural forms (language, private property, the law, and customs).

In the Catholic Crucible

Catholicism's long and complex relationship with Africans and their New World descendants—slaves—is one of history's best-guarded secrets. By the time of the Protestant Reformation, Catholicism had experienced a century of interaction with Africans, both in Guinea and in the steadily unfolding Atlantic world—a world that included Europe, the Atlantic islands, and the Americas. While much of Catholicism's relationship with Africa and Africans was mediated through the slave trade, contemporary and modern observers have often overlooked the extent of the Church's involvement with New World slavery during its formative period and subsequently as the single largest owner of slaves in the Americas. To this day, black Catholics outnumber black Protestants or adherents of any other New World African religion. Despite the preponderance of black Catholics, black religiosity in the Americas is still largely associated with the Christianity of Protestant denominations or sects. But the history of the early Americas illustrates how African Christianity was channeled through Catholicism.

On 11 July 1633, Angolans Angelina and Jusepe entered Mexico City's cathedral intent on winning sanction for the marriage they desired. Upon receiving their request, the vicar, Fray Luís de Cifuentes, asked the couple to provide evidence of their unmarried status. At that moment, Angolans Juan and María de la Cruz, who had accompanied Angelina and Jusepe on their mission, stepped forward to testify that neither was married and that the two were not closely related. A day later, after weighing the evidence, Luís de Cifuentes granted the couple their wish. Unless someone came forward with incriminating evidence in the next twenty-one days (the time period when the banns would be read three times), Angelina and Jusepe would marry. Since no one challenged the match, the couple wed in August 1633.[6]

Angelina and Jusepe were not unusual. Although they believed in a poly-theistic pantheon, these beliefs existed in a Christian cultural context, and many Angolans like them embraced the sacrament of a Christian marriage. Though some hesitated to do so under normal circumstances, even the culturally recalci-trant often renounced their common-law arrangements, what the Church referred to as concubinage, on the threshold of death.[7] Many Africans felt led by moral imperatives to petition for absolution of the mortal sin of living in a common-law arrangement. Even individuals who refused to abide by Christian values in other aspects of their lives ascribed symbolic importance to a church-sanctioned union. Fear of eternal hell, perhaps an index of an individual's degree of creolization, often prompted those living in a state of *amancebamiento* to marry, revealing the degree to which Christianity had permeated their consciousness.[8]

Seven decades after the conquest, New Spain's clergy routinely received mar-riage petitions from Africans. The frequency of these petitions increased after the viceroyalty's first inquisitor general, Pedro de Moya y Contreras, became arch-bishop and introduced ecclesiastical reforms in accordance with the Council of Trent (1545–1563). In 1569, Moya y Contreras arrived in Mexico City intent on inaugurating the era of Catholic renewal in New Spain. Moya y Contreras and the Inquisition asserted both royal authority and clerical reforms designed to bol-ster the ecclesiastical structure through which the Crown asserted its dominion over the behavior and therefore the souls of the faithful. Thus, the tribunal di-rected its proceedings against Protestant heretics, *conversos* suspected of still being Jews, and the amorphous *republica de los españoles,* a group that included errant Spaniards, *mestizos,* and the variously defined descendants of Africans. After Moya y Contreras installed the tribunal and presided over a series of spectacular *autos de fe,* he was appointed archbishop of Mexico, a position that enabled him to impose reforms on the clergy, the social group explicitly concerned with the spiritual life of the faithful. These reforms led to greater discipline and regulation.

After New Spain held the Third Provincial Council (1585), which affirmed the Tridentine reforms and set ecclesiastical policy for the colony's diverse inhabit-ants, marriage petitions appeared with increasing regularity. From the ecclesiasti-cal perspective, a marriage petition symbolized order (*policía*) in the Christian commonwealth (*república Cristiana*), an order that organically tied individuals through conjugality to the temporal and sacred sovereigns. Marriage linked the

6. Archivo General de la Nación (Mexico City, Mexico), Matrimonios, Primera Seria, (hereafter AGN, Matri.), tomo 47, expediente 8, folios 17–18.
7. The Catholic Church defined *amancebamiento* as the state of concubinage. Additional exam-ples of this practice are located in AGN, Matri., tomo 81, expediente 35, folios 102–103; AGN, Matri., tomo 29, expediente 95, folios 233–234; AGN, Matri., tomo 113, expediente 69, folio 176; AGN, Matri., tomo 7, expediente 85, folio 274; AGN, Matri., tomo 126, expediente 18, folio 54.
8. Carlos M. N. Eire, *From Madrid to Purgatory: The Art and Craft of Dying in Sixteenth-Century Spain* (New York: Cambridge University Press, 1995).

realm of Spain's sovereign with those of the wedding party, thereby ensuring both social order and legitimacy. Marriage petitions and the rituals surrounding them became standard features of social life in seventeenth-century urban New Spain.

As a customary practice, Christian matrimony highlights the prominence of Catholic institutions and practices in the lives of Africans and their creolized descendants. Marriage and its ritualized proceedings also signify how patrimonial authority gained currency among persons of African descent. By embracing the institution of marriage, Africans legitimized their desire to forge ethnic and other affinity ties. Although Christian matrimony instilled identities that conformed with Catholic sovereignty, in most instances neither masters nor the clergy played a visible role in this cultural appropriation of Catholicism. For strategic reasons, Africans and their descendants forged their own paths.[9]

Through its regulation of marriage, the Catholic Church recorded the desires of a diverse ethnic community of persons of African descent. Through these recorded instances of desire, we glimpse the emergence of a culture.[10] I view the choices persons of African descent made regarding spouses and sponsors as an expression of cultural desire. While legally sanctioned marriages were by definition Christian, cultural imperatives that prompted Africans and their descendants to marry did not always reflect the workings of a Christian conscience. Persons of African descent married for various reasons, both in and out of the Catholic Church. The process of spouse and sponsor selection, however, reveals a flourishing community life and a culture in formation. Our task is to discern the cultural logic of this process.[11]

9. Richard Price, *First-Time: The Historical Vision of an Afro-American People* (Baltimore: Johns Hopkins University Press, 1983); Price, *Alabi's World*; Sylvia R. Frey and Betty Wood, *Come Shouting to Zion: African American Protestantism in the American South and British Caribbean to 1830* (Chapel Hill: University of North Carolina Press, 1998); Laura de Mello e Souza, *The Devil and the Land of the Holy Cross: Witchcraft, Slavery, and Popular Religion in Colonial Brazil,* trans. Diane Crosklaus Whitty (Austin: University of Texas Press, 2003); Jon Sensbach, *Rebecca's Revival: Creating Black Christianity in the Atlantic World* (Cambridge, Mass.: Harvard University Press, 2006)

10. The point here is that ritual declarations and testimonies are granted valence in a Christian society by the act of being recorded. Recorded experiences thus compete with other manifestations of history and memory. A degree of tension (if not conflict) informs the coexistence of competing modalities that shape the self and the collective. While other modalities may flourish beyond regulatory proceedings, recorded instances steadily gain authority through legitimacy in a legalistic culture such as the culture of Spanish and Christian colonialism.

11. In the past, scholars have been quick to read meanings into marriage registers. Marriages between variously defined persons present proof that individuals conformed or resisted the norms of an ideological informed social structure. But R. Douglas Cope cautions against a facile reading of marriage registers, especially for interracial unions: "We must not be too eager to fit plebeian behavior into systems of meaning devised by the elite. A mulatto marries a *mestiza*. Who can say what combination of affection, sexual desire, family considerations, and economic calculations went into this decision? We cannot know, from that act itself, whether one partner exulted in an opportunity or the other agonized over marrying 'down'"; Cope, *The Limits of Racial Domination*, 82–83. However, an *informacíon matrimonial* offers slightly more biographical details about individuals than a marriage register, thus enabling a more contextualized conjecture about its meaning.

Rules, prescriptions, and taboos shaped patterns of marriage, kinship, and descent. Communities and their members abide by prescriptive norms to avoid violating existing taboos or engaging in defiling acts of pollution. For anthropologists, such behavior has long underscored the cultural as opposed to the natural dimension of kinship practices. Social practices are cultural cues that individuals internalize in the course of being socialized as part of a particular community. But from where do these practices and the norms that sustain them derive? How are we to understand the emergence of a new set of practices and norms among individuals who in the not-so-distant past were cultural outsiders, people whose various ancestors and kin adhered to different practices and norms? Why and when did these practices take hold? What purpose did they initially serve? Answers to these questions bring into relief the cultural logic that prompted Christian notions of family relations (husband, wife, offspring [*hijo/a legtimato/a, hijo/a natural*], etc.). They help explain how individuals such as Jusepe and Angelina used a Christian marriage to effect both a private life and ethnic ties and they help us understand the profound consequences of that choice—the internalization of Christian norms.

African Kinship Structures

When Angelina and Jusepe petitioned to have their union legitimized, they were departing from the practices of their Angolan ancestors. For West-Central Africans, monogamy, the Christian conjugal unit, the role of free will in the process of spouse selection, and normative assumptions about gender and domestic relations required cultural modifications that threatened an always-already-fragile social organization and values. Christianity and its family structure challenged West-Central Africans because their cultural identities, like those of others, were the products of contextualized family and kinship systems.

Lineage was the foundation upon which seventeenth-century West-Central African cultures rested. Though regional circumstances produced local variations, lineage was omnipresent throughout West-Central Africa, extending as far east as present-day Zambia. A shared kinship ideology accompanied this structural uniformity. The lineage structure was hierarchical and multi-tiered. At bottom, the *futa,* the conjugal unit, united males and females for procreation and social reproduction. The *futa* also provided its members with a collective identity based on descent. It defined status, rights, and customary obligations. Above all, however, the *futa* was a productive unit that controlled the labor of its members and provided them with access to land. The household, or *vumu,* consisted of a collection of lineages "whose function is to own land and allocate tracts to lineages."[12] The

12. Wyatt MacGaffey, "Lineage Structure, Marriage and the Family amongst the Central Bantu," *Journal of African History* 24, no. 2 (March 1983), 175.

household adjudicated differences between lineages over land and labor. Although the *futa* exercised rights over the labor of its members, it was the household that actually "own[ed] the persons of its members, slave and free."[13]

The *kanda,* or clan section, occupied the highest tier in the West-Central African lineage structure, uniting related households. Among its many functions, the *kanda* regulated cultural practices and behavior, shaping spouse selection and the kinship networks of *kanda* members. As an exogamous social institution, the *kanda* obligated its members to marry individuals of another clan section in order to avoid incest taboos. Since *kandas* operated on the basis of virilocality (a practice whereby wives resided with their husbands), the marriage of a male member represented an economic acquisition and served to create reciprocity between two *kandas.* Females and males were not united for emotional reasons. In the West-Central African "ethno-political economy" in which wealth was associated with labor, marriage was an economic relationship between two *kandas.* An individual who had numerous wives and dependents acquired an elevated status because he controlled an army of laborers. In addition, he could rely on an elaborate network of relationships when the need arose. In the virilocal context, the marriage of a female constituted a loss for her *kanda,* which demanded compensation in bride-wealth. Moreover, matrilineal descent patterns ensured that the offspring of any union belonged and were culturally obligated to their maternal kin, from whom children reckoned descent and acquired access to land.

This lineage structure and its cultural practices were essential to the West-Central Africans transported to the Americas. Conceivably, the *kanda* ideology shaped the initial kinship practices and beliefs among West-Central Africans who landed in the New World. But as these Africans confronted new situations, they increasingly employed Christian kinship ideology to maintain contact with the past and define the present.

Confronting Christianity

In the New World, slavery and Christianity provided an ideological arena in which transplanted African social institutions acquired different functions. Although the families of former residents of West-Central Africa and Western Europe had common features, the form developed distinct imperatives in different cultures. The Western European family featured an atomized conjugal unit, Christian kinship and descent patterns, and a nascent individualism that were all alien notions to seventeenth-century West-Central Africans.

Christianity produced changes in the social structure and kinship ideology of West-Central Africans through conversion and cultural suppression. These chang-

13. Ibid.

es precipitated changes in cultural practices and identities.[14] In fact, before contracting a Christian marriage, West-Central Africans assumed new gender roles that roughly conformed with the requirements of Christianity. Since gender reflected reigning norms and the social conventions through which sexually defined beings could enable desire, the act of becoming a Christian shaped how Africans experienced themselves as men and women. Gender, far from being self-evident, was constantly subject to change for African arrivals. European constructions of gender norms informed the ways converted Africans who embraced Christian matrimony experienced their lives as slaves and subjects.

Despite the cultural loss that conversion to Christianity entailed, thousands of West-Central Africans, like Angelina and Jusepe, sought marriage in the Catholic Church. What were the cosmological and personal imperatives that led Angolans to embrace the Christian conjugal unit? What was their understanding of Christianity, the Christian family and kinship structure, and marriage? More important, how did seventeenth-century Angolans and other Africans adjust to the potential cultural conflict between their African and Christian identities as they forged, maintained, and sanctioned their ethnic cohesiveness through Christianity? Definitive answers will always be elusive, but it is clear that the Christian family was instrumental in the lives of people like Angelina and Jusepe. The prevalent and recurrent behavior patterns of such individuals and their neighbors demonstrate that they used the European Christian model of family life to construct their particular New World communities.

The Christian worldview that informed prevalent behavioral patterns is of interest, but so are the ethnic and racial identities that informed spouse selection, kinship networks, and friendships. As we shall see, identities and social networks were mutually constitutive. The union of Angelina and Jusepe epitomized their Christian consciousness. Similarly, the marital alliances of thousands of Africans and those of their descendants illustrate how New World identities and private lives assumed tangible expressions around well-defined but not immutable boundaries. One guiding question maintained and reproduced such boundaries: Do *we* intermarry with *them*?

In recent years, studies of the African past and the New World experiences of blacks have explicitly focused on the self. In a decisive shift from rooting the sub-

14. Richard Price has captured this phenomenon among the Saramakas of Suriname. Aware that literacy would allow them greater understanding of and access to the "white world," the Saramakas sought to have some of their children educated by the Moravian missionaries. According to Price, "The toll exacted over the centuries for this privilege remained constant: intense pressure to renounce 'heathen' ways and break off relations with non-Christian family and kinfolk. Saramakas then as now were caught in this terrible bind, knowing that literacy was a password to an understanding of the outside world and the key to being able to manipulate it, but also knowing that its acquisition entailed what was, for them, a truly Faustian bargain, the willingness to sell their souls"; Price, *Alabi's World,* 67–68.

jectivities of slaves in materialist categories derived from labor or racial subordination, scholars presently stake claims around the issues of ethnic provenance, place of birth, Africanisms, and creolization.[15] These scholars underscore the centrality that cultural heritage played in defining the ethnic identities and experiences of the enslaved. The focus on cultural heritage in current scholarship returns us to one of the foundational concerns of Afro-American studies: What cultural logic informs the New World black experience? "The African impact in the diaspora went far beyond culturally diluted survivals," insists historian James H. Sweet, who implies that African cultural traditions were more important to newly arrived Africans than the colonial culture they encountered. Sweet is convinced that "Africa arrived in the various destinations of the colonial world in all of its social and cultural richness, informing the institutions that Africans created and providing them with a prism through which to interpret and understand their condition as slaves and as freed people."[16] Sweet and others believe that African social and cultural traditions were remarkably immune to the onslaught of the slave trade and New World slavery. "Indeed," writes Sweet, "the tenacity of certain core beliefs can be measured more effectively across time and space."

As a cultural theorist, Sweet's emphasis borders on black structuralism. Yet rather than simply dismiss such cultural characterizations as essentialist, we must acknowledge the widely shared nature of his views, which also constitute a political response to a long and deeply held view that Africans and their New World descendants are a people without history. Today such views are less prevalent, but in its place another dilemma has arisen: Which African past survived and what are its limits for writing about the formation of black cultures? "While scholars who study slavery in the Americas sometimes recognize the African background as 'important,'" observed Africanist Paul Lovejoy "they usually do not examine the specific historical contexts from which the enslaved came. They nod in the direction of Africa, but they do not adopt a perspective from Africa. It is as if individuals stopped being 'Africans' once they were on board 'European' ships."[17] To cite but one example, we can examine historian Alida Metcalf's study of the family in

15. Richard Price, *Travels with Tooy: History, Memory, and the African American Imagination* (Chicago: University of Chicago Press, 2008), 207–308; David Scott, "This Event, That Memory: Notes on the Anthropology of African Diasporas in the New World," *Diaspora: A Journal of Transnational Studies* 1, no. 3 (1991): 281–284; Lovejoy, "Identifying Enslaved Africans in the African Diaspora," 1–29; Palmié, *Wizards & Scientists*; Gomez, *Exchanging Our Country Marks*; Sweet, *Recreating Africa*; Joseph C. Miller, *Way of Death: Merchant Capitalism and the Angolan Slave Trade, 1730–1830* (Madison: University of Wisconsin Press, 1988); Joseph C. Miller, "Central Africa During the Era of the Slave Trade, c. 1490s–1850s"; Brown, *Santería Enthroned.*
16. Sweet, *Recreating Africa*, 2.
17. Lovejoy, "Identifying Enslaved Africans in the African Diaspora," 12–13.

early Brazil, a pioneering work that theorized the black family in ways that is still an exemplar. Metcalf explained her objective as follows: "The inheritance of cultural attitudes and economic resources from generation to generation among the people of this community Santana de Parnaíba [the majority of whom were slaves and small farmers], from the time when the Portuguese first landed on the coast of Brazil in 1500 to the birth of the Brazilian nation in 1822, is the subject of this book."[18] Metcalf is concerned with family strategies, the same cultural dynamic I seek to delineate. For Metcalf, "family strategies became a cultural inheritance that shaped the community and the development of the western frontier." But Metcalf depicted Africans as a people without history, thereby reproducing the interpretive gesture that prompted Sweet's and Lovejoy's critique—a critique we share even though we disagree about how one might actually tackle the job of representing the African past. Despite an interest in "cultural attitudes" among scholars who study people that included a substantial number of slaves, Metcalf proceeded as if all of her subjects were and had always been Western. At issue is a presumed universality in which the uniform Western subject motivated by economic rationality stands in for all else. But when and under what circumstances did this cultural logic come to characterize the New World African experience?

Variations on the African Past

In 1633, Juan testified before the ecclesiastical authorities that he and Angelina had "come together to this kingdom." Juan also noted that "for six years I have communicated" with Angelina in Mexico City. If by 1633 they had lived in New Spain for six years, they probably arrived in 1627 on the *Nuestra Señora de la Piedad,* the only registered slave ship for that year, which arrived with 152 West-Central Africans.[19] After disembarking in Veracruz, the survivors were inspected by royal officials and rested briefly in a new environment characterized by oppressive humidity and a constant plague of mosquitoes. After several days, the Africans faced hordes of interested buyers who violated and humiliated them with touches and penetrating stares. Angelina and Juan and their remaining shipmates next had to endure the arduous journey from Veracruz to the viceregal capital.

18. Alida Metcalf, *Family and Frontier in Colonial Brazil: Santana de Parnaíba, 1520–1822* (Berkeley: University of California Press, 1992), 1.

19. Juan is quoted as saying in 1633 that "for six years I have communicated" with Angelina in Mexico City. Matrimonios, tomo 47, expediente 8, folios 17–18, AGN. Enriqueta Vila Vilar has compiled a list of registered slave ships for the sixteenth and seventeenth centuries. Her research indicates that the *Nuestra Señora de la Piedad* was the only registered slave ship that entered the Veracruz port in 1627; see *Hispanóamerica y el comercio de Esclavos* (Sevilla: Escuela de Estudios Hispano-Americanos de Sevilla, 1977), appendix.

When Angelina and Juan had completed the steep and difficult climb from the tropics of Veracruz to Mexico City's temperate climate, their new lives as Mexican slaves began.

Separation, death, deprivation, and humiliation marked the contours of the forced migration from Angola to New Spain. Merchants' ledgers record mortality rates and profits but are silent about the cultural, psychological, and spiritual tolls the Middle Passage extracted. As they recovered from the physical horrors of their transatlantic voyage, African survivors had to make tremendous cultural adjustments, the most profound of which transpired in the cosmological realm. The experiences of Angelina, Jusepe, María, and Juan suggest that they had undergone this process and had embraced certain changes. They were Africans for whom ethnicity that was formerly expressed in lineages now found expression in spouse selection and friendship ties. Angelina, Jusepe, María, and Juan were aware of ethnicity as a component of their identities, but they understood and possibly accepted the tenants of Christianity, thus indicating the coexistence of (at least) dual and potentially conflicting identities.

Among scholars of Mexican history, the lack of interest in the African past from which people like Angelina and Jusepe, María, and Juan had been uprooted raises conceptual difficulties for those who study cultural formation. Mexican historians' narratives of the colonial period tend to depict Africans as culturally bereft people. This intellectual practice stands in marked contrast to the ways they engage the Native American past.[20] Even for a population whose members confronted colonialism as individuals, the past played some role in the colonial encounter. Yet the claim that Africans entered the Americas as individuals divorced from their collective traditions serves to excuse historians' lack of engagement with the African past and denies the fact that individualism was a process.[21] Armed with an understanding of the African past, we can see that the analytical framework of individualism conceals the ways that seventeenth-century arrivals from West-Central Africa emerged as Angolans and then formulated communities based on ethnic ties through the vehicle of Christian matrimony.

For Western-trained historians, understanding the transition from African to Western cosmologies that Angolans underwent poses several methodological and interpretive problems. How do we demonstrate that Central African cosmologies matter when Western rules of evidence configure the historical archive in decid-

20. To this day, the study of African cultural formation in New Spain and in early Latin America lacks such brilliantly conceived studies of Spanish-Indian interaction as Rebecca Horn's *Postconquest Coyoacan: Nahua-Spanish Relations in Central Mexico, 1519–1650* (Stanford, Calif.: Stanford University Press, 1997), a study that theorizes through space and time and specific political and economic practices

21. Claudio Lomnitz-Adler, *Exits from the Labyrinth: Culture and Ideology in the Mexican National Space* (Berkeley: University of California Press, 1992), 268–274.

edly narrow ways? Also, how can historians avoid charges of mythical or structural interpretations of the African cultural past? Despite these conceptual dilemmas, our understanding of New Spain is not complete until we engage with these issues. Slaves such as Angelina and Jusepe had an African past that helped shape their identities in New Spain.

From childhood, West-Central Africans had been acquainted with Mpemba, "the land of the death" that was located in the west across a large body of water in which deceased spirits with white skins ruled. Local elders passed a prophecy from generation to generation: "A man's soul does not dwell in the grave after his death but leaves it to become a ghost [n'kuyu] in the land of the dead, which is called ku mpemba a fula. In the land of the dead there are villages, waters, and hills, as there are here [vava nsi]. He must first cross the water, climb the hill, and descend to arrive in the country [mu si] of Mpemba a Fula. . . . When he arrives, they paint him with tukula-red so that his body becomes parti-colored [mfumfukutu]. They are healthier than we. They go to the Europeans to travel and to buy things. They work and have plenty to eat."[22]

For the approximately 75,000 West-Central Africans who arrived in Mexico from 1595 to 1640, the prophecy surrounding Mpemba appeared to have been fulfilled. Although the prophecy stated that only the souls of the dead made the voyage, perhaps the enslaved saw themselves as having experienced a spiritual death. In fact, the widely shared BaKongo cosmology identified two juxtaposed worlds, "this world" and the "land of the dead." Death defined the space beyond what was known—life outside of the village and separation from one's lineage.

As the ship that carried Angelina and Juan tossed on the waves of the Atlantic, the Mpemba mythology must have assumed the air of frightening reality. Those unaware of the BaKongo prophecy had different legacies through which they saw Europeans, interpreted the significance of the Middle Passage, and understood their arrival in the Americas. Even after sustained European and African contact along the Bight of Biafra, Olaudah Equiano, an Ibo, interpreted his fate among Europeans in supernatural terms: "I was now persuaded that I had gotten into a world of bad spirits and that they were going to kill me. Their complexions too differing so much from ours, their long hair and the language they spoke (which was very different from any I had ever heard) united to confirm me in this belief."[23] Even if we question the veracity of Equiano's account—which a number of scholars

22. Wyatt MacGaffey, *Religion and Society in Central Africa: The BaKongo of Lower Zaire* (Chicago: University of Chicago Press, 1986), 45–46; also see Wyatt MacGaffey, "Cultural Roots of Kongo Prophetism," *History of Religions* 17, no. 1 (1977): 177–193; Wyatt MacGaffey, "Kongo and the King of the Americans," *Journal of Modern African Studies* 6 (August 1968): 171–81.

23. Olaudah Equiano, *Equiano's Travels: His Autobiography, The Interesting Narrative of the Life of Olaudah Equiano or Gustavus Vassa the African,* ed. Paul Edwards (London: Heinemann Educational Books, 1967), 25.

have done—it is still critical to acknowledge that Africans brought their own beliefs into the encounter with Europeans. West Africans and West-Central Africans filtered their experiences through myths, beliefs, or prophecies that predated the arrival of the Europeans. For West-Central Africans, the Portuguese phenotypes, the voyage across the Atlantic, and the Spanish presence in New Spain probably heightened the levels of anxiety about the Mpemba prophecy.

For enslaved West-Central Africans, the relevance of the Mpemba prophecy did not end with the Middle Passage. The elders had predicted that a man "must first cross the water, climb the hill and descend to arrive in the country of *Mpemba a Fula*."[24] This route described the voyage from Angola to Mexico City. After disembarking at Veracruz, the enslaved Africans had to climb the mountainous road to Mexico City, and after they reached the valley of Mexico, they descended into the city. The coincidence between the topography in the Mpemba prophecy and the journey from Angola to Mexico City surely reinforced the conviction of many West-Central Africans that they had arrived in the "land of the dead." Even the most dubious must have felt that their cosmology was reaffirmed after seeing swarthy Spaniards dominating and exploiting the reddish-brown indigenous peoples, a fulfillment of another part of the prophecy.

The perception that they had arrived in Mpemba had profound cultural implications for West-Central Africans. They not only had to reaffirm ancestral beliefs but also had to be predisposed to simultaneously embrace the beliefs of the white people (*bamindele*). Although the Mpemba prophecy helped rationalize the Middle Passage and later experiences, those who believed it must have grown increasingly suspicious of its truth over time. Contact between new and earlier African arrivals and social intercourse with black creoles likely undermined the explanatory power of the Mpemba prophecy. Some Africans probably began to blame witchcraft and sorcery, the failure of individuals or groups to propitiate the ancestors or deities, or the omnipotence of the Christian god. Some Africans became increasingly predisposed to a process of ritual remediation through which they sought to improve their lives in Mpemba and their status with African deities. When this failed, some Africans began to view the Christian god with awe and became willing to embrace aspects of Christianity. Yet Africans did not abandon their ancient cosmos or become exclusively Christian. Selected African beliefs coexisted alongside aspects of Christianity. Only as the memory of the African deities faded did Christianity come to dominate the black cosmos. Even then, ancestral beliefs and practices continued to influence the lives of Africans and their descendants.[25]

24. MacGaffey, *Religion and Society in Central Africa,* 46.
25. Gomez, *Exchanging Our Country Marks;* Morgan, *Slave Counterpoint;* Sweet, *Recreating Africa.*

Although intangible manifestations of culture persisted, African social institutions often were transformed to the point where they resembled those of other sociocultural groups in New Spain. Practical considerations reinforced by the peculiarities of the slave trade and slavery, a new sociocultural environment, and the ideological and structural dimensions of Christian social control affected Africans' cultural practices in innumerable ways. In a colonial context, cosmological and practical considerations provided a strong impetus for change.[26] Despite such cultural pressures, the creolization of the African population and its cultural practices that began in the sixteenth and seventeenth centuries was never complete.

Although the Mpemba myth prophesied that the inhabitants of the "land of the dead" would be distinguished by their white and red phenotypes, the preponderance of blacks in Central Mexico must have startled the West-Central Africans who arrived during the first half of the seventeenth century. Was it not prophesied that blacks would be transformed into whites? How did the new arrivals interpret the black presence that included kin, former friends, and various peoples who defined themselves as Bran, Wolof, and Biafra? The black presence surely fostered doubts about the prophecy and about whether New Spain was indeed the "land of the dead." These doubts probably gained strength as the new arrivals interacted with "the dead," who after a time resembled spirits, ghosts, or ancestors less and less. This realization awoke many people to the reality of New World slavery. One must ponder the feelings of individuals such as Angelina and Juan when they learned that Mpemba was in actuality Mputo, the "land of the whites."

For readers dubious about cosmological renderings of the Central African past, one might offer a more familiar narrative. Here the emphasis is on discerning where seventeenth-century Africans originated. The rules of evidence privilege the numbers derived from merchant ledgers and thus impose early modern European notions of polity, ethnos, and cultural proclivities recorded there.[27] Even

---

26. Alfred Métraux, *Voodoo in Haiti,* trans. Hugo Charteris (New York: Schocken Books, 1972); Price, *Alabi's World*; Gomez, *Exchanging Our Country Marks*; Palmie, *Wizards & Scientists*; Brown, *Santería Enthroned*; Jean Comaroff, *Body of Power, Spirit of Resistance: The Culture and History of a South African People* (Chicago: University of Chicago Press, 1985); Enid Schildkrout and Curtis A. Keim, *African Reflections: Art from Northeastern Zaire* (Seattle: University of Washington Press, 1990).

27. In offering this vantage point as a possibility, I nonetheless concur with anthropologist Stephan Palmié's critique of the empiricist fantasy that informs the method of slavery scholars and Africanists who insist on a relationship between the slave trade and cultural specificity. Palmié wrote, "In recent decades, a burgeoning historiography of slavery has provided us with a truly stunning wealth of aggregate data on how human beings . . . lived and died in New World cane fields and slave barracks. . . . Regardless of whatever mixture of zeal, caution, and care went into the compilation and analysis of the sources from which such data were synthesized, regardless, also, of how important some of these findings may prove in correcting previous conceptions of New World slavery, there is an ultimately quite frightening sense of irrelevancy in all this." Palmié argues that the very sources on which our representations hinge—precisely because they were conceived in objectification that sanctioned terror—can never capture the horror associated with New World slavery. Palmié, *Wizards & Scientists,* 8.

this empirically driven context requires cultural speculation, as the student of colonial Mexico must link Western configurations of African history with specific
peoples as they emerged as slaves. Both options are fundamentally limited in what
they can convey, but the images that we generate as a result of the available sources
may offer the greatest restrictions. As anthropologist Stephen Palmié observed in
his brilliant study on nineteenth-century Cuba, the problem "is that the person he
the slave Tomas] may once have been remains beyond historiographic recovery
because the nature of the evidence we deem admissible simply erases his historical being and subjectivity."[28] Thousands of West-Central Africans were uprooted
by the consolidation of the Kongo kingdom in the late fifteenth century, the rise
of the Mbundu kingdom, the Jaga invasions of the Kongo kingdom in the sixteenth century, the gradual disintegration of the Kongo kingdom, and the various
Angolan wars that erupted in the seventeenth century.[29] Military conflicts and ex-
changes of dependents created the initial slaving frontiers, and the people sold to
the Portuguese slave traders who operated in West-Central Africa tended to come
from certain ethnic groups. This was especially evident in New Spain between 1595
and 1640, when most enslaved Africans came from the region west of the Kwango
River, south of the Zaire River, and north of the port of Benguela. Conceivably, at
a given moment, a particular slave frontier provided the bulk of Africans. Those
who defined themselves as being from "the land of Angola" used this label to refer
to linguistic and cultural similarities they shared with specific ethnic groups. This
coincided with the Iberian tendency to homogenize Africans on the basis of their
port of embarkation. In other words, Africans may have identified themselves to
Spaniards by geographical origins and simultaneously distinguished among themselves on the basis of linguistic and cultural differences. During the slave trade,
"Angola" included the ports of embarkation along the Luandan coast, including
Luanda, Lobito, and Benguela. While Europeans simply defined the enslaved from
the region as those from the "land of Angola" or the "land of the Congo," Africans
did not forget primary identities that the Mbundu, Ovimbundu, Imbangala,
Pende, Sonyo, Kongo, Soso, Zombo, and Tyo (Teko) peoples carried with them to
the Americas.

In the initial years of the slave trade, many West-Central Africans who were
sold to Europeans were dependents of elite people, including male slaves, impover-

<hr>

28. Palmié, *Wizards & Scientists*, 8–9.
29. Useful studies that document the political evolution of West-Central Africa include David
Birmingham, *Trade and Conflict in Angola: The Mbundu and Their Neighbours under the Influence of
the Portuguese, 1483–1790* (Oxford: Clarendon, 1966); Anne Hilton, *The Kingdom of Kongo* (Oxford:
Clarendon, 1985); Joseph C. Miller, *Kings and Kinsmen: Early Mbundu States in Angola* (Oxford:
Clarendon, 1976); Miller, *Way of Death*; Thomas Q. Reefe, *The Rainbow and the Kings: A History of the
Luba Empire to 1891* (Berkeley: University of California Press, 1981); John K. Thornton, *The Kingdom
of Kongo: Civil War and Transition, 1641–1718* (Madison: University of Wisconsin Press, 1983); Jan
Vansina, *Kingdoms of the Savanna* (Madison: University of Wisconsin Press, 1966); and Jan Vansina,
The Children of Woot: A History of the Kuba Peoples (Madison: University of Wisconsin Press, 1978).

ished cultivators, and individuals uprooted by war, drought, famine, and/or debt.[30] Exchange of dependents took place within a reciprocal trading network controlled by elites that extended from the interior to the coast; the enslaved ultimately found themselves in Portuguese hands as payment for European goods. Although it is impossible to establish the number or percentage of dependents thus transferred into European hands, their presence was substantial.

Slaves and dependents probably did not seek to re-create the ideological basis on which their status in Africa had rested. Those who were most likely to be enslaved in the New World of the seventeenth century had been socially degraded beings in Angola and they had no reason to embrace the more lowly aspects of their Old World status. Cross-cultural examples have demonstrated a propensity among the marginalized to discard stifling, oppressive practices when new opportunities arise. This is true even when discarding oppressive practices involves changing one's cultural identity. Perhaps the victims of the transatlantic slave trade chose this course by re-creating an African past devoid of the ideology and practice that had legitimized their subordination. If this process did take place, a new cultural synthesis had to emerge.[31]

Of course, the principal victims of the transatlantic slave trade—the youth and the marginalized—carried a particular but often imperfect understanding of the worlds they had left behind. They filtered their cultural understanding through the prisms of gender, age, status, and lineage. Despite the fact that males and females, subordinates and elites, youth and their elders were socially and culturally interdependent, no one was likely to reproduce the corpus of African beliefs, symbols, and cultural and situational meanings in its entirety. Victims of the transatlantic slave trade carried a cultural perspective that largely mirrored their gender, age, and status. Such individuals were differently suited than were free Africans to reconstruct cultural forms and practices. In the final analysis, what mattered to enslaved Africans in the Americas was not the authenticity of certain cultural forms or practices but their efficacy in making daily life bearable. Above all else, the forms and practices that Africans introduced and created had to be functional. Indeed, as victims of the slave trade encountered alien peoples, grappled with unpredictable realities, and met an array of new cultural forms, they had to scrutinize existing ontologies and cosmologies—what one observer has termed "the functional revaluation of the categories."[32] In this process, Africans discarded, retained,

---

30. *Dependents* refers to individuals who were beholden to elites or their patrons. For example, junior kin, women, children, and slaves were dependent on the lineage head, who in turn was a cultivator, soldier, or vassal in a state of dependency with regard to an elite patron. See Miller, *Way of Death*, 40–104.

31. This insight flows from Victor Turner, *The Ritual Process: Structure and Anti-Structure* (Ithaca, N.Y.: Cornell University Press, 1969); and Claire C. Robertson, *Sharing the Same Bowl: A Socioeconomic History of Women and Class in Accra, Ghana* (Bloomington: Indiana University Press, 1984).

32. Marshall Sahlins, *Islands of History* (Chicago: University of Chicago Press, 1985), ix.

and modified some old forms and borrowed selectively from others, thus effecting a cultural transformation.

Rethinking Social Death

Over the past twenty years, social death has been the dominant organizing metaphor through which scholars of slavery and therefore black life represented the slaves' cultural experience. As a metaphor, social death centers power as the defining category that informed slave life and culture. The representative slave emerges as the ultimate nonperson constrained from asserting an independent existence. As chattel, the slave allegedly did not constitute a being beyond the master's confining grasp. This analysis argues that perhaps only the master possessed the authority and will to imagine an autonomous slave existence. Even as a person, the slave did not have sufficient authority to insist that her/his humanity be acknowledged. In a slave society and a society with slaves, social death aptly characterized an important (if not the defining) component of the slave and thus black experience. But in relationship to colonial Mexico, where the slave acquired a juridical identity as a vassal and a person with a soul, this formulation needs to be questioned. When did social death exist in the life of a slave? Were Angelina and Jusepe socially dead? The complex configurations of gender and ethnicity that shaped the desire to contract marriage and the resulting kinship ties that subsequently emerged challenge the ideological construction of social death. As the narrative of the slave experience, social death assumes a uniform African, slave, and ultimately black subject rooted in a static New World history whose identity originated in being property and was confined to slavery. It absorbs and renders exceptional evidence that underscores the variegated nature of experience and consciousness. Thus the normative assumptions about the experiences of peoples of African descent project the "black" cultural experience as timeless and universal.[33]

But in the first half of the seventeenth century, ethnic networks reigned ascendant among New Spain's African population, as tables 2.2, 2.3, and 2.4 show. Within the dual contours of Christianity and slavery, an ethnic interiority emerged. Through Christian marriages, Africans inaugurated and sustained the process of ethnogenesis, the creation of social networks inside the structures of domination. African ethnicity was invoked through the requirements of Christian marriage rituals; we could say that African ethnicity was channeled through Christianity. By means of participating in Christian rituals, some slaves became ethnics, a process that calls into question the legitimacy of the ideological construction of social death as applied to colonial Mexico.

33. For an elaboration of black structuralism, see the preface to this volume.

TABLE 2.2.

LENGTH OF TIME WITNESSES OF ANGOLAN COUPLES HAD KNOWN THE BRIDE OR GROOM, 1595–1650

Amount of Time	Number	Percent
One year or less	3	0.2
2–3 years	22	1.8
4–5 years	128	10.7
6–7 years	444	37.1
8–9 years	349	29.2
10–11 years	138	11.5
12–13 years	67	5.6
14–15 years	14	1.2
16–17 years	7	0.6
18–19 years	2	0.2
20–21 years	17	1.4
"Many years"	5	0.4
Totals	1,196	99.9

Source: Matrimonios Primera and Tercera Seria, AGN.

Table 2.2 illustrates that over one-third (37.1 percent) of Angolan marital sponsors had known the bride and/or the groom for six or seven years. Indeed, over 83 percent of Angolans who testified on a couple's behalf had known the bride and/or the groom for between six and thirteen years. Such ties underscore the existence of a critical mass of Angolan survivors who renewed enduring and forged new ethnic ties. Juan and Angelina had maintained contact after being separated in Mexico City, which is not surprising since they had known each other since childhood.[34] Having endured the process of enslavement and the horrors of the Middle Passage together, Juan and Angelina probably came to depend substantially on one another as they confronted an alien environment, encountered foreign peoples, and wit-

34. In his testimony, Juan stated: "Since I can remember I have known Angelina . . . for she is my sister and we have come to this kingdom together." AGN, Matri., tomo 49, expediente 8, folios 17–18. It is possible that Juan employed the term "*hermana*" as he would have in West-Central Africa. According to Anne Hilton, "Throughout their known history the Kongo normally reckoned descent for the purposes of land-holding in terms of their relationships with *kanda*, not with individuals. Thus the term 'brother' was applied to all members of ego's *kanda* who could also be called collectively 'mother,' 'father' referred to all members of ego's father clan and 'child' referred to all member of ego's child's clan. A free man could normally depend upon four 'chiefs' to interest themselves in his affairs. These were the lineage heads of his mother's (i.e., his *kanda*), his father's and his paternal and maternal grandfather's *kanda* or *kanda* segment." Hilton, "Family and Kinship Among the Kongo South of the Zaire River from the Sixteenth to the Nineteenth Centuries," *Journal of African History* 24, no. 24 (1983): 190. Igor Kopytoff and Suzanne Miers have cautioned scholars that "the metaphorical use of kin terms may be deceptive and should not, above all, be taken at their Western face value." Kopytoff and Miers, *Slavery in Africa: Historical and Anthropological Perspectives* (Madison: University of Wisconsin Press, 1977), 25.

nessed strange customs. As they sought to impose meaning on their experience, the two also relied on the presence of other Angolans, including Jusepe and María de la Cruz, with whom they shared linguistic and cultural similarities. Although the circumstances surrounding their courtship are unknown, Jusepe and Angelina apparently had opportunities to see one another regularly. The marriage witnesses, Juan and María de la Cruz, stated that Jusepe and Angelina "ordinarily interacted in this city," suggesting that they had some freedom of movement. Such mobility was related to a person's occupation and the errands at hand. Angelina and her brother Juan, for example, belonged respectively to a shop-owner and merchant, both of whom conducted business in the *plaza*. During their working hours, they had opportunities to interact with family and friends. Although they were dispersed throughout elite households, enslaved Angolans nonetheless forged vibrant and enduring ties with persons similarly defined.

Strategic Conjugality

In seventeenth-century Mexico City, most slaves were employed largely as domestics and artisans and most Angolans lived with a small multiracial nucleus of household staff. Among the 330 identified Angolan married couples who were married in Mexico City's wealthiest parishes in the first half of the seventeenth century, only 100 had the same master. The couple Manuel and María, who were both owned by Juan Bautista de Avilar, were among this group.[35] Couples such as Manuel and Gracía or Domingo and Inés were rather fortunate since they lived on the same street, albeit in different households.[36] Cristóbal and Luisa also had different masters yet lived in the same neighborhood.[37] But the significance of spatial proximity was shaped by the whims of masters and the resourcefulness of slaves. In this context, exogamy—partnering with a differently identified individual in the same household—was a viable option. But many Angolans chose to forge marriage ties with other Angolans who lived on different streets, in distant barrios, and even in faraway towns. Despite the hardships that continuing such contacts entailed and in spite of the fact that most Angolans interacted daily with members of other ethnic and racial groups, they established their most intimate associations with persons similarly defined. As table 2.3 shows, 72 percent of enslaved Angolans selected Angolans as spouses. Though we cannot be certain of the true meaning of "Angolan," the table underscores the value that Angolans accorded to their New World ethnicity.

35. AGN, Matri., tomo 10, expediente 69, folio 166; AGN, Matri., tomo 5, expediente 43, folio 151; AGN, Matri., tomo 5, expediente 101, folio 278.

36. AGN, Matri., tomo 63, expediente 68, folios 17–18; AGN, Matri., tomo 10, expediente 153, folio 355.

37. AGN, Matri., tomo 29, expediente 96.

TABLE 2.3.
SPOUSE SELECTION PATTERNS OF ENSLAVED ANGOLANS IN MEXICO CITY, 1595–1650[1]

Ethnicity and Status of Spouse:[2]	Number	Percent
Enslaved Angolan	330	72.0
Enslaved Creole	37	8.1
Enslaved Bakongo	28	6.1
Enslaved Person from Terra Nova	14	3.0
Indian	9	1.9
Enslaved Person from Mozambique	7	1.5
Enslaved Bran	5	1.0
Person from São Tomé	5	1.0
Chino	5	1.0
Mestizo	4	0.9
Anchico	2	0.4
Carabalí	2	0.4
Mandinga	2	0.4
Biafra	2	0.4
Person from Cabo Verde	1	0.2
Enslaved Mulatto	1	0.2
Unknown	4	0.9
Total	458	99.4

Source: Matrimonios Primera and Tercera Seria, AGN.

1. The marriage records on which this table is based were drawn from the *sagrario* and the cathedral in Mexico City and the parishes of Santa Veracruz and Salto del Agua. Consequently, the sample is confined to the principal parishes of Mexico City where the wealthiest Spaniards and their servants lived.

2. Unless otherwise indicated, persons are assumed to be free.

The spouses Angolans selected affirmed their perception that they were distinctive people. Despite the restrictions slavery imposed, persons of African descent used their juridical rights as Christians and their mobility to stake claims on their identities as Angolans. By establishing the foundations of their lives in the act of marriage, Angolans ensured that their ethnic identities and the Angolan community were mutually reinforcing, and they reproduced those identities through ties of consanguinity and affinity. In the dynamic process of redefining themselves in the New World, Africans utilized their Christian personae to forge identities beyond their juridical status as slaves. By asserting their ethnic identities, Angolans simultaneously exhibited social selves beyond the categories of labor and property.

Angolan marriage practices were not, however, classical expressions of endogamy. The peculiarities of the transatlantic slave trade prevented Angolans from reproducing preexisting marriage and kinship patterns. Moreover, Angolans and their descendants were denied the institutional power that was crucial to enforcing and transmitting African cultural norms. Angolans relied on family and community pressure, social conformity, and socially constructed personal preference to create solace with individuals of similar heritage. This behavior was not peculiar to Angolans. In the absence of institutionally enforced laws, collective sensibilities and an informal code of conduct played a large role in establishing community norms and shaping personal choices. The decision of an Angolan to select another Angolan as a mate reflected individual choice conditioned by the prevailing ethnic sensibility.

Ethnic sentiment, however, did not insulate Africans from the burdens of slavery and the weight of a Christian colonialism intent on regulating their souls. Cohesiveness and ethnic boundaries protected the enslaved but were simultaneously porous and malleable. The multiple identities manifest among persons of African descent reflected the dynamic relationship between slavery and Christianity. As table 2.3 illustrates, New Spain was home to various peoples from Africa, including Angolans, BaKongos, Bran, Carabalí, and Mandingos. Though 72 percent of Angolan marriages involved other Angolans, 28 percent of the Angolans selected spouses with different identities. In addition, 91 percent of Angolan marriages involves a spouse who was also enslaved. Here then we see how slavery and Christianity intersected in the lives of seventeenth-century Africans. But racial slavery and racial oppression did more than fuse the identities and experiences of peoples of African descent. Since Africans of various origins viewed the world through related but different prisms, they ascribed different values to and had varied understandings of endogamy, the rigidity of boundaries, and social relations. This pattern was similarly manifest among the diverse population of creoles.

Arguably, no collective African identity existed in New Spain. Only through their contact with the non-African "Other" did Africans manifest a tenuous collective consciousness. In some instances, they internalized an imposed Africanity, but one cannot document this as generally true for Africans in New Spain or throughout the hemisphere. Uprooted and atomized as they confronted circumstances over which they had no control, the various cofflemates and shipmates, drawn from diverse ethnic groups, forged a tenuous collective consciousness. According to Africanist Joseph Miller,

> For the enslaved . . . notions of belonging must have faded as their pasts receded behind the hills and valleys behind them and as the suffering of the slave trails and markets through which they passed overwhelmed the condemned. New identities, in terms that their new masters understood better, more relevant to the slaves' present and future lives, were simultaneously forming to bind people according to the markets where slavers assembled them in coffles, when they boarded ships, and the individual ships that carried them to the New World.[38]

38. Miller, *Way of Death,* 23.

Table 2.4. Spouse Selection Patterns of Africans by Ethnicity in Mexico City, 1584–1640[1,2]

Ethnicity of Spouse	BaKongo	From Terra Nova	Bran	From Biafra	From Mozambique	From São Tomé	Bañol	Gelofe	Biojo	Mandinga
Anchico	1	0	0	0	0	0	0	0	0	0
Angolan	28	14	5	2	7	5	0	0	0	0
BaKongo	14	1	2	1	1	2	0	0	0	0
Bañol	0	0	0	0	0	0	2	0	0	0
From Banguela	0	1	0	0	0	0	0	0	0	0
Black	3	1	2	1	3	0	0	0	0	1
From Biafra	0	1	1	2	0	1	0	0	0	0
Bran	0	1	8	0	1	0	0	0	0	0
Chino/a	0	0	1	1	0	0	0	0	0	0
Gelofe	0	0	0	0	0	0	0	1	0	0
Indian	2	0	1	0	1	0	1	0	1	0
Lucumi	0	0	0	0	0	1	0	0	0	0
Mestizo/a	2	0	0	0	0	0	0	1	0	0
From Mozambique	0	0	1	0	1	0	0	0	0	0
From Terra Nova	2	13	1	0	2	0	0	0	0	0
Xoxa	0	1	0	0	1	0	0	0	0	0
Zape	0	0	0	0	1	0	0	0	0	0
Unknown	0	0	4	1	0	0	0	0	0	0
Total	**52**	**33**	**26**	**8**	**7**	**9**	**3**	**2**	**1**	**1**

Source: Matrimonios Primera and Tercera Seria, AGN.

1. Although Angolan spouses are included in this table, the list of individuals from which this table was constructed excludes ethnic Angolans as the individuals who chose spouses. See table 2.3 for the spouse selection patterns of ethnic Angolans.

2. The marriage records on which this table is based are drawn from the *sagrario* and the cathedral in Mexico City and the parishes of Santa Veracruz and Salto del Agua. Consequently, the sample is confined to the principal parishes of Mexico City where the wealthiest Spaniards and their servants lived.

Shared experiences alone could not forge an enduring collective identity. Some enslaved Africans subsumed their internal differences in the crucible of racial slavery, while others transported preexisting ethnic rivalries to the Americas.[39] And yet the seventeenth-century slaving frontier made new collective identities more likely by shifting the geographical concentration of the victims of the slavers, which in turn enabled a linguistic and cultural convergence under which a fleeting ethnic sensibility flourished.[40] Identities shaped in Angola were renegotiated in New Spain.

The cultural dynamism of the slaving frontier, the slave trade, and planter preference undermines the once prevalent yet facile assumption that racial oppression alone made a single collective African consciousness possible.[41] In their mundane daily lives and most intimate choices, Africans made distinctions on

39. The exchange between Monica Schuler and Richard Price in "Afro-American Slave Culture" suggests that the identities of enslaved Africans manifested themselves, on the one hand, in ethnic consciousness and, on the other, in pan-ethnicity. Identity was invariably linked to the slave trade and a society's ethnic composition. The preponderance of a given ethnolinguistic group, as in the case of Jamaica, often resulted in stratification along ethnic lines. Slave societies such as Suriname and British North America that received a wider range of enslaved Africans than did Jamaica tended to experience pan-ethnic consciousness very early on. As the Suriname case makes clear, pan-ethnic alliances were often intersected by a collective consciousness based on legal status (maroon versus enslaved), the estate to which individuals belonged, and New World lineage ties. See Price, "Commentary Two," *Historical Reflections* 5 (Summer 1979): 141–149; and Price, *Alabi's World.* In seventeenth-century New Spain, both phenomena—narrowly defined ethnicity and pan-ethnicity—co-existed among persons of African origins.

40. Miller has defined the "slaving frontier" as the "moving frontier zone of slaving violence." Its geographical contours

took shape with the first border raids of the newly centralized Kongo kingdom shortly after 1500 and continued in the shudders that ran through that state in the late sixteenth century. . . . Kongo violence fed the initial Portuguese purchases of slaves in west central Africa. The sixteenth-century growth of the Mbundu kingdom of the Ngola a Kiluanje and a similar collapse of its conquered domains into partisan struggles in the 1620s, though complicated by the interference of Portuguese armies in the internal politics of the African state in the "Angolan Wars" of the seventeenth century, advanced the slaving frontier south from the Kongo beyond the Kwanza. It also set Luanda-based slaving on the war footing it featured for the first half of the seventeenth century.

Miller, *Way of Death,* 141, 140–169, and passim. David Birmingham's *Trade and Conflict in Angola* also provides a geographical sketch of the "slaving frontier."

41. In a pathbreaking book, Sidney W. Mintz and Richard Price suggest that Afro-Americanists have viewed the early interaction between Europeans and Africans too narrowly as a one-dimensional encounter between two distinct cultures. Mintz and Price criticize this encounter model on the basis that it grossly oversimplifies the African and European experiences. See Mintz and Price, *An Anthropological Approach to the Afro-American Past,* 4. Despite Mintz and Price's caution, scholars continue to homogenize the experiences of Africans and their diverse cultural heritage. Some scholars, in fact, have made conclusions about West and West-Central Africans based on the cultural practices and experiences of East Africans. In her discussion of time among black Virginians, Mechal Sobel, for example, relied on ethnographic accounts of the Nuer, an East African ethnic group. Most, if not all, black Virginians were descendants of West and West-Central Africans. Michel Sobel, *The World They Made Together: Black and White Values in Eighteenth-Century Virginia* (Princeton, N.J.: Princeton University Press, 1987), 26–29.

the basis of ethnicity and affinity ties with specific individuals. In fact, we must question scholarly assertions that New World Africans established communities in which ethnicity did not prevail.[42] Such assertions wrongly attribute cultural homogeneity, cultural stasis, and mythical racial and slave consciousness to Africans. During moments of crisis—usually slave rebellions and collective flight—ethnic identities were subordinated to an overarching African, black, or slave consciousness. Such episodes were unusual, brief, and rarely if ever manifested among the total slave population. Indeed, such expressions resembled ethnic alliances more than the subordination of ethnicity. After the need for cooperation had waned, in fact, ethnic distinctions resurfaced, including rivalries.[43]

42. This is especially true for works produced in the 1980s on Africans in what today constitutes the United States. Sterling Stuckey, for example, has stated that "what we know of slave culture in the South, and of that of blacks in the North during and following slavery, indicates that black culture was national in scope, the principal forms of cultural expression being essentially the same. This is attributable mainly to the similarity of the African regions from which blacks were taken and enslaved in North America and to the patterns of culture shared more generally in Central and West Africa." Stuckey, *Slave Culture*, 82. For a similar argument, see Margaret Washington Creel, *"A Peculiar People": Slave Religion and Community-Culture among the Gullahs* (New York: New York University Press, 1988).

43. Much remains to be discovered about ethnicity among enslaved Africans. See, for instance, David Barry Gaspar, *Bondmen & Rebels: A Study of Master-Slave Relations in Antigua, with Implications for Colonial British America* (Baltimore: Johns Hopkins University Press, 1985); Mary C. Karasch, *Slave Life in Rio de Janeiro, 1808–1850* (Princeton, N.J.: Princeton University Press, 1987), 3–28, 254–301; Mieko Nishida, "Ethnicity and Manumission in Urban Slavery: Salvador, Brazil, 1808–1888," paper presented at the Carolinas Colonial Latin America Seminar, Durham, North Carolina, April 1991; Joao José Reis, "Slave Rebellion in Brazil: The African Muslim Uprising in Bahia, 1835" (Ph.D. diss., University of Minnesota, 1982); Joao José Reis, *Slave Rebellion in Brazil: The Muslim Uprising of 1835 in Bahia*, trans. Arthur Brakel (Baltimore: Johns Hopkins University Press, 1993); and Monica Schuler, "Akan Slave Rebellions in the British Caribbean," *Savacou* 1 (June 1970): 8–31. These works transcend the traditional African-creole dichotomy and are quite suggestive with regard to ethnicity.

More recent inquiries have revealed the usefulness of ethnicity as a category of analysis in New World slave societies. Nevertheless, ethnicity needs to be deconstructed along lines of gender, age, and status, since these may have constituted the primary nexus in which enslaved Africans most frequently operated. See the following selections in *Identity in the Shadow of Slavery*, ed. Paul E. Lovejoy (New York: Continuum, 2000): Lovejoy, "Identifying Enslaved Africans in the African Diaspora," 1–29; Jane Landers, "*Cimarrón* Ethnicity and Cultural Adaptation in the Spanish Domains of the Circum-Caribbean, 1503–1763," 30–54; Douglas B. Chambers, "Tracing Igbo into the African Diaspora," 55–71; and Sandra E. Greene, "Cultural Zones in the Era of the Slave Trade: Exploring the Yoruba Connection with the Anlo-Ewe," 86–101. See also these selections in *Central Africans and the Cultural Transformations in the American Diaspora*, ed. Linda M. Heywood (New York: Cambridge University Press, 2002): Linda M. Heywood, "Introduction," 1–18; Joseph C. Miller, "Central Africa during the Era of the Slave Trade, c. 1490s–1850s," 21–69; Mary C. Karasch, "Central Africans in Central Brazil, 1780–1835," 117–151; Elizabeth W. Kiddy, "Who Is the King of the Congo? A New Look at African and Afro-Brazilian Kings in Brazil," 153–182; Robert W. Slenes, "The Great Porpoise-Skull Strike: Central African Water Spirits and Slave Identity in Early-Nineteenth-Century Rio de Janeiro," 183–208; Wyatt MacGaffey, "Twins, Simbi Spirits, Lwas in Kongo and Haiti," 211–226; Jane Landers, "The Central African Presence in Spanish Maroon Communities," 227–241; and Hein Vanhee, "Central African Popular Christianity and the Making of Haitian Vodu Religion," 243–264. Other useful explorations include Sweat, *Recreating Africa*; and João José Reis, *Death Is a Festival: Funeral Rites and Rebellion in Nineteenth-Century Brazil*, trans. H. Sabrina Gledhill (Chapel Hill: University of North Carolina Press, 2003).

The importance of ethnicity lies primarily in the function it performed among Africans in sixteenth- and seventeenth-century New Spain. The functional boundary depended less on authentic differences than on perceived and imposed linguistic and cultural similarities. One scholar has stated, "The ethnic boundary canalizes social life—it entails a frequently quite complex organization of behavior and social relations. The identification of another person as a fellow member of an ethnic group implies a sharing of criteria for evaluation and judgment. . . . On the other hand, a dichotomization of others as strangers, as members of another group implies a recognition of limitations on shared understandings, differences in criteria for judgment of value and performance, and a restriction of interaction to sectors of assumed common understanding and mutual interest."[44] Even an impressionistic examination of seventeenth-century African marriages, like that of Angelina and Jusepe, magnifies the existence of such boundaries.

In general, African patterns of spouse selection in the New World were neither random nor indiscriminate. Africans differentiated themselves through perceived ethnic criteria. The evolution from an ethnic African to black creole population, as we shall see, did not involve a pan-African transitional period. In part, the absence of an African identity was the result of the primacy of ethnicity—real and imposed. The ethnic cohesion of Africans could not be transferred intact to subsequent generations. When the slave trade to New Spain declined after 1640, ties of African ethnicity also waned. As creoles, Afro-Mexicans could not reproduce the ethnicity of their parents. Only the African-born could accomplish that task. The mass of incoming West Africans were the harbingers of African ethnicity in sixteenth-century New Spain. When West-Central Africans, Angolans in particular, came to outnumber West Africans in the first half of the seventeenth century, they emerged as the principal architects of African ethnicity by means of spouse selection and the construction of an elaborate network of relationships. Ironically, they legitimized their ethnicity through Christian matrimony.

At that very historical moment and in the same site, a distinct group of blacks and mulattos exhibited a parallel cultural process. They too built social networks that hallowed additional space within the contours of Spanish domination. Here again, Christian conjugality served as the vehicle whereby persons of African descent forged social networks and mediated cultural similarities. But in this case, blacks and mulattos—who by definition constituted creoles—forged a distinctive interiority. Black creoles were not, however, divorced from the African past. Even though Africans and creoles did not re-create an African cultural environment, African parents and ancestors molded their ethnic heritage to fit New World

44. Fredrik Barth, "Introduction," in *Ethnic Groups and Boundaries: The Social Organization of Culture Difference,* ed. Fredrik Barth (Boston: Little, Brown & Co., 1969), 15.

circumstances. On the whole, Africans and their descendants maintained their relatively autonomous identities and cultural boundaries. During the course of the seventeenth century, Africans and creoles initiated the structuring of boundaries through spouse selection. Coexisting and overlapping boundaries reflected the multiple identities and consciousnesses manifested by the black population. But the process was never static. Even the most enduring boundaries continually changed.[45]

45. The phrase "primary associations" is a slight semantic modification of Milton M. Gordon's "primary relationships" and refers to the most intimate ties of friendship and kinship. Gordon defined "primary relationships" as those that are "personal, intimate, emotionally affective, and which bring into play the whole personality, as contrasted with *secondary relationships*, which are impersonal, formal, and segmentalized, and tend not to come very close to the core of personality." Milton M. Gordon, *Assimilation in American Life: The Role of Race, Religion, and National Origins* (New York: Oxford University Press, 1964), 32.

THREE

Creoles

The origin of the creole lies in African social reproduction in the New World.[1] African women of sixteenth-century New Spain bore children despite the hardships of the Atlantic passage, the new disease environment, and the misfortunes of slavery. Their surviving offspring and the offspring of African men and Spanish and Indian women created the nucleus of the creole population. As a Spanish construct, the authorities mobilized the term *criollo* with the intent of defining and thereby regulating this population. But the real significance of the term "creole" derived from its relational meaning—"not African." Creoles were persons of African descent born in the Indies. This was one of a number of terms Spaniards used to differentiate the non-Spanish population. (They identified arrivals from Guinea who did not speak Spanish or Portuguese as *bozales*. Africans that spoke a romance language or manifested Christian customs acquired the elevated label of *ladino*.) Beyond its foundational meaning of a person born of Africans living in the New World, the term "creole" also came to refer to particular regions of the Indies.

Because of the absence of quantitative demographic data, births and birth rates among Africans have invited scant attention in Spanish America. We know that in the first half of the sixteenth century, the number of African arrivals overshadowed the number of births among creoles. But the qualitative data suggests that by the end of the sixteenth century, West Africans had produced a creole population whose numbers rivaled that of their parent population.[2] By the seventeenth century, the creole population was growing rapidly, although it was not yet self-sustaining. In 1646, New Spain's 116,529 creoles easily outnumbered the

---

1. Morgan, *Reproduction and Gender in New World Slavery*.
2. Bennett, *Africans in Colonial Mexico*, 19–20, 22, 27.

35,089 Africans, although we don't know how many slaves and freepersons made up the membership of either population.[3] The emergence of this creole population is an unexamined enigma.

Rather than address here what happened to Mexico's black population—a standard strategy of scholars—we would greatly benefit from efforts to narrate the creole experience. The following questions could serve as our signposts. In what ways was the creole experience in the first half of the seventeenth century similar to that of the African population that simultaneously lived in New Spain? How were creole experiences distinguished from those of Africans? By bringing these seemingly simple questions to our reading of the records in the ecclesiastical archive we outline a history of creoles that transcends the conventional narrative arc from slavery to freedom. What we find is a truly dense creole social life. As we shall see, creoles fortified existing forms of personal autonomy, thereby adding layers to the nascent black interiority of seventeenth-century New Spain.

As slaves and free people, creoles appeared frequently in the ecclesiastical records. In the records of social transactions—baptism, marriage petitions, and *amancebamiento* proceedings—they often demonstrated an autonomous social existence in the spouses and sponsors they selected. There is a distinct pattern to the spouses creoles chose as desirable and the witnesses they felt were trustworthy. These choices can be interpreted as components of identity formation. As a New World social type, creoles did not emerge with a self-conscious identity; they had to forge a new identity for a new people. Over the course of the seventeenth century, creoles created and reinforced their identities in the context of the Christian marriage market. In the first half of the seventeenth century, when the slave trade was a presence that loomed over every aspect of daily life, creoles chose sponsors largely based on ethnicity; those of Angolan descent choose others who shared that lineage. But kinship and affinity also weighed heavily when they elected who would be their witnesses in their rites of passage.

As creoles registered their presence in and through administrative structures that were designed to regulate and govern them, they underscored the ways that Christian-inflected language and cultural practices shaped their lives. Creole cultural practices—from ways of reckoning time, space, and the self to ways to resolve disputes—drew heavily on Christianity. The descendants of Africans embraced Christian marriage for a variety of reasons. This chapter documents the ways that creoles expressed a modicum of agency in their engagement with Catholicism. By mediating their social practices through Christian tropes, creoles brought into relief the discursive boundaries of seventeenth-century self-fashioning, all the while highlighting forms of identification that colonizers rarely acknowledged. Creoles

3. Aguirre Beltrán, *La población negra de México.*

built on practices in evidence among the ethnic African population. Such practices were also widely deployed among Indians (Indios), Spaniards (Españoles), and the variously defined mixed-race populations. But in all instances the social practices of creoles, Indians, or Spaniards became the traditions associated with an allegedly authentic group. Seventeenth-century creoles, who were less than a generation removed from the invented African ethnicity of their parents, were still assimilating Christian cultural practices. Yet in using Christian practices, creoles constructed private lives as men and women, husbands and wives, offspring and kinfolk. Ironically, in embracing Christian practices, creoles created greater social autonomy from Spaniards.

*   *   *

Nicolás de la Cruz, also identified as Nicolás de los Reyes, was in trouble. In 1634, as the free mulatto and native of Mexico City confronted bigamy charges in the viceregal capital, he stood before the tribunal of the Holy Office of the Inquisition to answer questions about his relationship with two slave women, Mariana de San Miguel and Clara Hipolito. These were serious allegations. If the inquisitors found Nicolás guilty, his punishment would include a long period of exile from friends and family. As was customary, the inquisitors canvassed widely among the associates of the accused—family, friends, and workmates—both to assure a judicious decision and to reinforce the perception of their omnipotence. Over the course of a year, the tribunal gathered evidence from Nicolás's acquaintances, many of whom had been present at both wedding festivities.[4]

In both of his marriages, Nicolás underscored the importance of residential and occupational ties in the selection of spouses and sponsors. He met Clara Hipolito, his first wife, when they both lived and worked in the Mexico City parish of Santa Veracruz. As Doña Juana Velazquez's black creole slave, Clara had enough time and freedom of movement to interact with her suitor. Antonio de la Cruz, a *ladino* from Mozambique, testified that Clara was free to spend nights with Nicolás in the house of his employer but "in the mornings went to her mistress's home . . . in the neighborhood of las Mercedes." When they petitioned for their *información matrimonial*, Nicolás and Clara had known each other for at least eight years. After receiving their marriage license, the couple celebrated their nuptials. During the ceremony a different set of sponsors presided than the ones the couple had called on for their marriage petition. The presence of Francisco, a Xolofe, and his wife Maria, who was from Mozambique, illustrate how ethnicity overlapped with occupational and residential ties when sponsors were chosen.

<hr>

4. AGN, Inquisición 381, expediente 8, 1634–1635, "Proceso de Nicolás de la Cruz, mulato libre, natural de la Ciudad de Mexico City, y por otro nombre Nicolas de los Reyes."

Clara's community centered on ethnicity; many of the assembled wedding guests, including her mother, María Macua, Manuel, and María, identified Mozambique as their place of origin.

But the marriage ended abruptly. When Clara's mistress moved to Querétaro, Clara left her husband. Although some individuals defended their marital rights tenaciously, Clara and Nicolás did not. "We parted," confessed Clara, "after he quarreled with me about a short skirt."[5] Clara's departure merely finalized an emotional separation that already existed.

When he married a second time, Nicolás again drew on occupational and residential proximity when he chose his spouse and his sponsors. As an employee of Pedro de Sierra, an *obraje* owner, Nicolás came to know Mariana de San Miguel, a creole slave. When they selected their marriage witnesses, Nicolás and Mariana chose inhabitants of the *obraje*, which in the seventeenth century was an enclosed workhouse staffed by an assortment of slaves and servants. Juan de la Cruz, the black slave of Pedro Sierra, had known Nicolás ten years, six in Mexico City and the rest in the *obraje*. Free mulatto Manuel de la Cruz had known Nicolás twenty years "more or less," eleven in Mexico City and the remaining years in the *obraje*. Mariana presented Pedro Losano, a mulatto slave, and Juan Alonso, a *chino* (a person from the East Indies), as witnesses. Both witnesses were enslaved to Pedro Sierra and testified that they had known Mariana for the entire five years they had been in the *obraje*. At the nuptials, Juan and his wife, Catalina, two slaves "from the land of Anchico" who belonged to Pedro Sierra, presided as *padrinos*. Two years after the nuptials were celebrated, rumors circulated in the *obraje* that a black women in the Coyoacan market (*tianguez*) was searching for Nicolás, saying "she was the mother of his first wife." "Everyone in the obraje," noted Mariana, "knew for sure that the said Nicolás de los Reyes or de Pisa was married with the said black woman before he married me."[6]

What compelled Nicolás to marry for a second time? Although periodic ecclesiastical raids, as we saw in chapter 1, resulted in fines and elicited acts of contrition from individuals caught in common-law arrangements, the clergy grudgingly tolerated concubinage. The Church manifested its tolerance in the distinct ways it punished offenders. Although the ecclesiastical courts prosecuted those accused of *amancebamiento*, it handed bigamists over to the Inquisition. Matrimony was a sacrament, and those who embraced Christian conjugality had to conform to monogamy. Individuals who chose Christian matrimony and then violated its sanctity risked severe punishment. For these reasons, Nicolás's decision seems even more mysterious.

5. AGN, Inquisicíon, Tomo 381, expediente 8, 1634–1635.

6. AGN, Inquisición 381, expediente 8, 1634–1635, "Proceso de Nicolás de la Cruz, mulato libre, natural de la Ciudad de Mexico City, y por otro nombre Nicolas de los Reyes."

Yet his decision to marry within the Catholic Church conformed to the patterns of his community. Africans and creoles embraced Christian marriages with growing regularity over the seventeenth century. Christian matrimony was an important reality. Though we can only speculate about motives for converting to Christianity and contracting a Christian marriage, thousands of Africans and an even greater number of creoles availed themselves of the sacrament of matrimony, perhaps prompted by a combination of ontological fear, strategic calculations, and faith. By the middle of the seventeenth century, Christian marriage had become the norm for creole slaves and free blacks. In electing to marry, creoles acquired rights as well as obligations. For creoles, as we shall see, such rights extended beyond the conjugal couple. Children acquired the publicly acknowledged status of legitimate child (*hijo legitimo,* the child born to legally wed parents, as opposed to the *hijo natural,* a child born out of wedlock).[7] Daughters were publicly acclaimed as maidens (*doncellas*), a status that reflected and bestowed family honor. These and other terms allude to a variegated social experience that was inextricably bound up with the private life of black folk, a life the conventional narrative of slavery and freedom shrouds.

As a form of cultural appropriation, creoles' requests for Christian matrimony brings into focus the absence of urban paternalism in binding creoles—slave and free—to the Church and thereby to the Catholic sovereign in Spain. Even in the semi-closed world of Pedro Sierra's *obraje,* creoles staved off uninvited masterly intrusions in their social existence. Nicolás de la Cruz was incarcerated nearly a decade for an undetermined reason in Sierra's *obraje* just south of Mexico City, but even in jail he managed to sustain ties with individuals he had known earlier in Mexico—free mulatto Manuel de la Cruz and Pedro Sierra's black slave Juan de la Cruz—and forge new connections with others confined to the textile mill. When the black creole (*negra criolla*) Mariana de San Miguel married Nicolás, she did not ask her master, Pedro Sierra, to preside as *padrino.* And Sierra did not attend the nuptials, at which five of his slaves were present. Mariana and Nicolás selected their witnesses and matrimonial *padrinos* from Pedro Sierra's labor force, but they restricted the master's physical presence in their social existence. The choice about who would be part of their social world was theirs.

In the less confining orbit of Mexico City, creoles were even more resolute in excluding patricians from symbolic roles as witnesses and sponsors. Clara and Nicolás drew on long-standing ties when they selected witnesses for their wedding. *Mestizo* tailor Juan Vazquez had known both for twelve years, while Antón de Santillana, an enslaved Angolan, had known Nicolás "since birth and thereafter

---

7. Daisy Rípodas Ardanaz, *El matrimonio en Indias: Realidad social y regulación jurídica* (Buenos Aires: Fundación para la Educación, la Ciencia y la Cultura, 1977); Twinam, *Public Lives, Private Secrets,* 26–27.

saw him grow." Nicolás and Clara selected sponsors from among their social intimates. A similarly intimate assortment of individuals surrounded the couple at their nuptials. The guests included the *padrinos* Francisco Xolofe (Wolofo) and his wife María Mozambique, the *indio ladino* Juan, an unnamed black man, Manuel Mozambique, and Clara's mother, María Macua. During the first half of the seventeenth century, urbanized creoles built an independent social world within the city that was principal site of Spanish power.

Cities were the polis from which Spanish authority radiated out to the rural landscape. Patricians were one of several loci of power intent on controlling persons they saw as dependents. Cities were also the sites of repeated conflicts between Church and state, patricians and plebeians. In the urban crucible, jurisdictional conflicts—which are often framed as the conflict between canon, civil, and criminal law—came to the fore and patriarchs confronted endless challenges from dependents over existing obligations and the bundle of rights that extended from Church and state. While demanding masters often limited their slaves' engagement with Catholicism on grounds that Christianity competed with the slaves' status as commodities, the patrician's sense of honor and Christian benevolence made it possible for many plebeians to fulfill their Christian obligations. Rather than focus on why patricians allowed practices that undermined their authority, we should ask how creoles initiated an autonomous Catholic existence. An examination of marriage petitions illustrates how creoles utilized Christianity in order to create a black interior life.

Mexico's creoles forged dense networks of relationships in the first half of the seventeenth century. Family formation—expressed in and through the language of Christianity—offers a glimpse of these networks. In their face-to-face world, creoles, like Africans, valued long-term relationships. For creoles, however, familiarity competed with kinship ties in the seventeenth century. As early as the first half of the seventeenth century, creoles displayed sentimental ties to a particular place that through the memory of kin had acquired meaning. But they also maintained actual family connections. They were not rootless and without kin and intent on social mobility, as they appeared to be in the minds of an anxious Spanish elite and (all too often) in the historical record. Their social world was much more complex. Indeed, the relative frequency with which seventeenth-century creoles called on blood and symbolic kin calls into question the extent to which social death defined the cultural world of creoles.

"Many Years"

Urban life enabled relatively stable relationships to flourish among Africans and creoles. Urban spaces—streets, plazas, and the homes of the elite—compensated for the atomized nature of urban slave-ownership. Servants often had consider-

TABLE 3.1.
LENGTH OF TIME WITNESSES OF MULATTO COUPLES HAD KNOWN THE BRIDE AND/OR
GROOM, 1591–1650

Amount of Time	Number	Percent
Less than one year	0	0.0
1–2 years	8	2.3
2–3 years	17	4.9
5–6 years	75	21.9
7–8 years	46	13.5
9–10 years	54	15.8
11–12 years	32	9.4
13–14 years	15	4.4
15–16 years	16	4.7
17–18 years	5	1.5
19–20 years	8	2.3
Over 21 years	4	1.2
Notions of forever[1]	55	16.1
Unknown	6	1.7
Total	341	99.7

Source: Matrimonios Primera and Tercera Seria, AGN.

1. Includes "since he could remember" (*desde sabe recorder*), "since he had the judgment of reason" (*desde tiene jurado de razón*), "since he was a child" (*desde que era nino*), "since he was born" (*desde que era criatura*), "since forever" (*desde siempre*), "many years" (*muchos años*), "since they brought her [from Guinea]" (*desde que la tajeron [de Guinea]*).

able mobility. Between house and street, Mexico's African and creole populations gained the social networking advantages typically associated with plantations. The large number of people living in cities more than compensated for the disparity in the number of slaves and servants attached to urban rather than rural patriarchs. While the threat of sale, inheritance patterns, or a patron's shifting fortunes always lurked in the background, most buyers, heirs, and creditors also lived in Mexico City. In the city, the stability of families and friendships—defined narrowly around the ability to interact—did not depend on a single patron. The testimony in the marriage petitions about the length of time witnesses had been acquainted with the bride or groom underscores the stability of relationships (see table 3.1). In the testimony of witnesses for the period 1591–1644, over 92 percent of the individuals had known each other five or more years. Sixty percent of the witnesses had known the bride and/or groom for between five and twelve years. Fourteen percent of matrimonial sponsors had known the bride and/or groom for thirteen years or more; this figures increases to 31 percent when the nonquantitative notion of "forever" is included. Creole stability emerged in New Spain's principal

urban center and the core of its slave society, Mexico City. For a population whose origins lay in natal alienation, years mattered.

In 1598, a wedding party entered the *sagrario,* the administrative center of the cathedral, intent on securing a marriage license for the prospective bride and groom, Miguel de Xaso and Magdalena. Lázaro, a 27-year-old free mulatto, had known the free mulatto Miguel for four years. Similarly, an unnamed 25-year-old Angolan slave vouched that the free mulatto Magdalena, whom he had known for five years, was unencumbered with impediments to marriage. Under oath, two unnamed enslaved black women (*negras*) declared that they had interacted with Miguel and Magdalena for twelve and ten years, perhaps as residents of the same barrio in which ties of work, family, and leisure mitigated differences between the enslaved and the free. As they sought to contract a marriage with each other, the free mulattos Magdalena and Miguel relied on long-standing ties with an African and with creole slaves.[8]

In 1610, a widow and a widower also drew on long-standing ties when they selected their marital witnesses. Juan Baptista, a free mulatto, relied on the 30-year-old *mestizo* Sebastian Hernandez and the Spaniard Diego Pérez. Sebastían, who had known Juan for eighteen years, revealed that Juan's wife had died a year earlier. Diego, who had interacted with Juan for seventeen years, said the same thing. Leonor, the prospective bride and also a widower, presented two witnesses. Both claimed that her husband Pedro Martín, a *mestizo,* had died eight years earlier. Juana Luísa, a 35-year-old mulatto, based this claim on twelve years of intimacy with Leonor. Diego Díaz, a 31-year-old, had learned this information during his 16-year relationship with Leonor. Preexisting ties that linked the respective witnesses to previous marriages—distinct symbolic communities—now united the survivors in holy matrimony. Juan and Leonor's second wedding extended specific community boundaries. The ritualized proceedings brought individuals defined as mulattos, Spaniards, Indian, and *mestizo* together.[9]

Another widow from 1610 records demonstrated the deep ties that united creoles. Eight months after María de la Encarnación's husband died, the 20-year-old free mulatto stood before the ecclesiastical authorities with a prospective groom, Luís, a black creole slave, to petition for a marriage license. One of her witnesses, Juan de Carate, a 20-year-old mulatto slave, acknowledged that her husband, Antonío de la Cruz, had died eight months earlier. He based this information on having interacted with María for six years. Cristóbal de Santa Ana, a 22-year-old free black creole "who lives in the house of a merchant," had known the bride for eight years. Juan, a creole slave, testified that he had been acquainted with Luis

8. AGN, Matrimonios 61, expediente 68, folios 268–70, 1598.

9. AGN, Matrimonios 61, expediente 26, folio 137, 1610. An identical example appears in AGN, Matrimonios 75, expediente 112, folio 380, 1620.

for six years. Domingo López, a 40-year-old Spaniard, had known the prospective groom for twelve years. Domingo underscored the intergenerational nature of their relationship, noting that he had known Luís "since he was a little boy."[10]

A final example of enduring ties among creoles involving a widow and a widower comes from 1629. In that year, the mulatto slave Sebastián Meléndez and the free mulatto Magdalena Sanchez petitioned for a marriage license. Gerónimo, a 50-year-old free mulatto, had known Magdalena for eight years. Francisca Camilla, a 23-year-old free mulatto, had interacted with Magdalena for the same amount of time. Ana María, a 25-year-old *mestiza* who was married to a Spaniard, testified to an intimacy of "many years" with Sebastián Meléndez and said that that his wife had died two months earlier. Catálina de Espinoza, a 50-year-old Bran slave, had forged a relationship with Sebastián for an undetermined amount of time but declared that since his wife had died two months earlier he was unencumbered.[11]

Evidence that creole slaves had known each other for long periods surfaces frequently in the testimony. In 1629, the mulatto slave Juan López and the 27-year-old *mestiza* Ursula de San Nicolás entered the *sagrario* to request a marriage license. The couple presented four witnesses. Diego de San Nicolás, a 40-year-old creole slave, said that he had a 30-year relationship with Juan. De Castellano, a 20-year-old mulatto slave, had interacted with Juan for an undetermined number of years. Sebastián Hernández, a 45-year-old creole slave, had known the prospective bride for five years. The 50-year-old free black Alonso de Avíles had known her for eight years.[12] In 1631, we find another example of the enduring ties that united a wedding party. Juan Roman, a mulatto slave owned by Juan Pérez the butcher, wanted to marry the black creole slave Apolonía. Though both had different masters, Juan and Apolonía insisted on a conjugal union. Cristobal de Agusto, a 40-year-old slave, had been familiar with Juan for twelve years. Mateo de la Cruz, a 23-year-old *mestizo,* had known Juan for twelve years. In testifying on behalf of Apolonía, Francisca de la Cruz, an 18-year-old free mulatto, said that he had known her for ten years. Leonor, a 40-year-old *mestiza,* had interacted with Apolonía since the time Apolonía was eight.[13] From Juan and Apolonía's perspective, the relationships that they had sustained with their matrimonial sponsors enabled them to envision a relatively stable marriage even though they were enslaved. As the wedding party, the bride, the groom, and the witnesses formed a social network despite their differences in status while ethnicity would enable the slaves Juan and Apolonía to enjoy their conjugality.

A final illustration of long-standing ties among creoles involves two free mu-

---

10. AGN, Matrimonios 64, expediente 79, folios 245–250, 1628.
11. AGN, Matrimonios 113, expediente 12, folio 35, 1629.
12. AGN, Matrimonios 10, expediente 58, folio 131, 1629.
13. AGN, Matrimonios 7, expediente 50, folio 191, 1631.

lattos, Juan de Santiago and Ana de Fonesca. In 1644, the prospective couple stood before the ecclesiastical authorities seeking a marriage license. Ana presented Lorenzo, a free mulatto, as witness; he declared that he had known her for six years. Cristobal said the same of his relationship with Juan. An unnamed *mestizo* said that he had been friends with Juan for twenty years. In that time, he saw Juan's wife, also named Ana, die. He observed that she was "buried in the Chapel of the Morenos in the Convent of Santo Domino."[14]

Thirty-year relationships may have been an exception, but decade-old ties seem quite common for creoles, free and slave alike. This longitude attests to growing stability among Mexico's creole population. In the marriage petitions, we see evidence that individuals imbued these relationships with sentimental value. Ecclesiastical authorities were not interested in sentiment. For them, all that counted was the number of years the witnesses had known each other. But the prospective couples and their matrimonial witnesses translated years into distinct notions of familiarity.

Birth and Blood Ties

In 1612, as free mulatto Lázaro de la Espinosa and mulatto slave Francisca de los Reyes petitioned ecclesiastical authorities for a marriage license, an anxiety rooted in status informed the ritual proceedings. Lazaro's mother opposed her son's decision to marry Francisca on the grounds that she was a slave. Francisco de San García, a 25-year-old Spaniard, had known the couple for seven years and testified that "they had been and still are in a state of concubinage." Francisco blamed Lazaro's mother for the couple's sinful life. "She did not want her son to marry Francisca de los Reyes," observed Francisco, "since she was a slave." "She [Lázaro's mother]," Francisco concluded "tried to impede the marriage." Juan, a 22-year-old Spaniard, was less forthcoming, declaring simply that he had known the couple five years. As Lázaro and Francisca voiced their request to be married, the presence of Lázaro's mother brought differences to the fore. She opposed her son's marriage to a creolized mulatto. Even though Francisca's surname indicates that she was a person with defined genealogical ties, she was a slave. For years Lázaro had accommodated his mother's concern and lived in a state of *amancebamiento* with Francisca. But now the couple wanted a church-sanctioned marriage.[15]

In a slave society, kinship was not a given. Even creoles, both free and enslaved, could not assume that both or even one parent would be present in their lives. Natal alienation—the absence of ascending and descending lineage—is a critical

14. AGN, Matrimonios 19, expediente 74, folios 187–188, 1644.
15. AGN, Matrimonios 65, expediente 16, folios 72–73, 1612.

feature of the slave experience in Spanish America. Although neither Lázaro nor his mother was a slave, according to the records, his mother was the offspring of a slave. As a free woman, she staked claims in the well-being of her son. Such claims, rooted in Christianity and freedom, stands in contrast to what Orlando Patterson calls a genealogical isolate, an individual with no claims or obligations to ancestors.[16] As a free person, Lázaro's mother expressed rights regarding her son. He was legitimately hers—her offspring. Yet, as this case illustrates, a maternal presence was not synonymous with family harmony.

A less cantankerous mother appeared in the marriage petition involving the free mulattos Marcos Hernández and María de los Angeles. In 1628, Mexico City native Marcos Hernández petitioned to marry María de los Angeles, a native of Toluca. Marcos chose 25-year-old Pedro Hernández, the son of a Spaniard and a mestizo (a *castizo*), to vouch for the fact that he was single and did not have any kinship ties to his prospective bride, María. Pedro rooted his claims in a twelve-year relationship with Marcos. An unnamed 22-year-old mulatto native of San Mateo de Atengo who lived on the haciendas of the Count of Calimaya said he had known María "since he could remember." María Magdalena, a 40-year-old free black woman, simply noted that she was Marcos's mother and had known the bride for six years.[17]

A final example of a creole drawing on parental testimony in the course of seeking a marriage license involved regional migration and long-standing familiarity between a groom, his matrimonial sponsors, and the parents of the prospective bride. In 1633, Spanish carpenter Juan Nicólas Castillo sought to contract marriage with the free mulatto Teresa de Vilchéz. Francisco de Vera, a 33-year-old mulatto, said that he had known Juan for twelve years. Francisco had known Juan in Puebla and had maintained contact with him after they both moved to Mexico City. Francisco had also interacted with Teresa for the six years he had lived in her father's household, and it is likely that Juan had come to know his future bride through his friend. Following Francisco's testimony, a 35-year-old free black woman named Agustína spoke up. Identifying herself as Francisco's wife, Agustína said that she had known Juan since he was a boy of fourteen living in Puebla de los Angeles. Next, the ecclesiastical authorities heard from Juan de Vilchéz, a 30-year-old mulatto who asserted his paternal claim over Teresa. "She is my daughter," he declared. A second parent was present as well. The scribe noted that María de Vilchéz, a 30-year-old free mulatto, was "Teresa's legitimate mother." For creoles,

---

16. "Not only was the slave denied all claims on, and obligations to, his parents and living blood relations but, by extension," observed Patterson "all such claims and obligations on his more remote ancestors and on his descendants. He was truly a genealogical isolate." Patterson, *Slavery and Social Death*, 5.

17. AGN, Matrimonios 28, expediente 127, folios 343–344, 1628.

the presence of both parents was rare but occurred with increasing frequency in the first half of the seventeenth century. The appearance of parents as matrimonial sponsors highlights the importance that Juan de Vilchéz, María de Vichéz, and Teresa de Vilchéz placed on family ties as the identifiable core of their community. From the testimonials, we also learn that long-standing acquaintances from a distant city had maintained contact after relocating to the viceregal capital. It was through this nexus that Juan Nicolás Castillo and Teresa de Vilchéz found each other.[18]

Most creoles in the first half of the seventeenth century could not call on parents to testify on their behalf as they petitioned for marriage. High mortality rates, illicit relations, and slave sales prevented many creoles from relying on their parents as matrimonial sponsors. When parents and children were sold, creole parents and children could not rely on the clergy to intervene, as their parents had. On the basis of canon law, the church limited its protection to husbands and wives, but not ties between parents and children.

In the examples from the archive, freepersons, not slaves, had the privilege of being present in their children's lives. Parents of Spaniards, *mestizos,* and Indians appeared with greater regularity as matrimonial sponsors in creole marriage petitions. For example, in 1628, the mulatto slave and native of Mexico (*criollo de Mexico*) Tomás de Torre stood with the newly widowed Ana María before the ecclesiastical authorities. Seventeen days after her husband, a black man named Mateo, had died, Ana María, a mestiza, decided to marry Tomás. But Ana María did not act in haste. She had known Tomás since their childhood. Ana María's mother, Violente de los Reyes, who identified herself as a *china,* noted that Tomás had been familiar to her "since he was a child." Diego Ximenez, a mulatto slave and native of Mexico (*natural de Mexico*), also emphasized the long-standing familiarity that united the prospective couple and the wedding party. Diego recalled knowing Tomás "since they were children" together and Ana María from the time she was two. For church officials, this was credible testimony. The presiding priest concluded the formalities by questioning Ana María's desire to marry a slave. But in the universe of a slave society in which thousands of *bozales* (Angolans) were introduced to each other every year, Tomás's status as a native mulatto with deep ties to the bride and her family overshadowed concerns about status. Within limits, familiarity tempered status.[19]

Lifelong familiarity also played a role in the marriage petition of Juan Agustín and Francisca Beatríz. In 1629, the free mulatto escorted his prospective Indian bride into the *sagrario* to request a wedding license. Two accompanying witnesses

---

18. AGN, Matrimonios 5, expediente 123, folio 332, 1633.
19. AGN, Matrimonios 28, expediente 25, folios 66–67, 1628.

testified that the couple lacked impediments. Melchor Benardino, a 60-year-old Indian, testified that he had known Juan "since he was a very little boy." Melchor also stated that Francisca was his daughter and that she had been a widow for six years. María Jerónima, a 50-year-old Indian, said that she was Francisca's mother and the wife of Melchor. Juan had been familiar to her too "since he was a young boy." Francisca and Juan had known each other since childhood. Now years after Francisca's husband had perished, a former childhood friend had become an acceptable spouse.[20]

Parental testimony carried weight with the ecclesiastical authorities. Who better than a parent would know if their child had consanguineous impediments to a prospective marriage? For the child, a parent's willingness to serve as a matrimonial sponsor was quite meaningful. For one thing, the presence of a parent signified approval of the union. The presence of parents as matrimonial sponsors delineated the importance that sponsor selection played in community formation and suggests that community ties were increasingly reinforced with family members.

For creole offspring and descendants of slaves, the process of defining a community could not be restricted to parents. In lieu of parents, some individuals called on other relatives to serve as their matrimonial sponsors. Kin ties highlight the growing complexity of creole kinship patterns in the seventeenth century. In 1628, *castizo* Francisco Santos and free mulatto Francisca de Mesa requested a marriage license. Although the bride Francisca was a native of Toluca, she shared two witnesses with Francisco, 50-year-old mulatto Juana de Morales and 25-year-old *mestizo* Andres Martínez. Both had known the couple as children. In marrying, the couple probably formalized a relationship that dated back to their youth in a nearby town. Next came Elena Gonzalez, a 40-year-old mulatto. As a relative, she spoke with authority about Francisco's unencumbered state. In her declaration that she had known Francisco "since he was born being that he was her nephew," Tia Elena provided a fragmentary but invaluable glimpse of the expansive familial ties among creoles in the first half of the seventeenth century.[21]

"Since Birth": Metaphors of Forever

In 1621, the matrimonial sponsors in creole wedding parties underscored the symbolic role that witnesses occupied as the cornerstone of the social network of the bride or the groom. Language that implied that a sponsor had known one or the other or both from their birth attests to the longevity of creole connections in the

20. AGN, Matrimonios 10, expediente 154, folio 352, 1629.
21. AGN, Matrimonios 28, expediente 136, folios 359–360, 1628.

fragmented and truncated universe of a colonial slave society. Over the course of the seventeenth century, these connections slowly transcended the natal alienation that characterized the process of enslavement and even typified the slave experience. Utterances such as "since she was born," "since they were children," "since he was a boy," "since she had the judgment of reason," "since he could remember," or simply "forever" illustrated a familiarity that transcended declarations of a fixed number of years. Creolized slaves and free persons voiced this language of sentiment in many cases. Of course, slave and free were addressing the priest and his scribe, but they were simultaneously bearing witness, testifying, literally professing to each other at that moment. The language spoke of a deeper form of knowing than the knowledge of passing acquaintances.

Such language carried great weight in the ritual proceedings. But it also emphasizes that sponsor selection was a deliberate practice that involved the dense ties and networks that creoles were forging in the first half of the seventeenth century. In these declarations, we find the essence of creole communities. As the free mulatto couple Jusephe de Rojas and Isabel de Cervantes petitioned for the sacrament of matrimony, two *mestizos* in their early twenties testified on the bride's behalf. Both men noted that they had known Isabel since they could remember, Juan offering the slightly different language "since she had the judgment of reason." This language bore witness to the deep ties connecting Lorenzo, Juan, and Isabel de Cervantes—they had known each other forever. The groom marshaled individuals whose ties were not as long, perhaps because Jusephe was not a lifelong resident of Mexico City. The 20-year-old mulatto slave Francisco Hernández testified that he had known Jusephe, whom he identified as Juan, for four years. The free mulatto tailor Juan Francisco had been acquainted with the groom for six years.[22]

A similar pattern was evident in the case of María de la Cruz and Domingo de las Nieves. María, a ladina Indian, and Domingo, a free mulatto, sought a marriage license in 1629. María was a native of Jalapa who had lived in Mexico City for three years but had maintained ties with acquaintances from her hometown. Blas de Alvarez, a 23-year-old black creole slave, said that he had known María in Mexico for the last three years and before that in Jalapa for two years. Lucas, a sixteen-year-old *mestizo,* had known María since he was eight years old when they both lived in Jalapa. Domingo's witnesses offered comparable ties. Francisco Vazquez, a 44-year-old free mulatto, had been acquainted with Domingo since birth. The

22. AGN, Matrimonios 85, expediente 15, folios 27–28, 1621. How did this imbalance play out after the marriage? In theory, as Jusephe's wife, Isabel would have to be guided by the patriarchal practices that her husband imposed. Would he welcome Isabel's strong ties to friends and place as an extension of his own world and social networks? If not, how would the tension be resolved? Answers to such questions are elusive in most *informaciones matrimoniales* from this period. But as we will see in chapter 5, the *informaciones matrimoniales* from a later period, along with Inquisition and ecclesiastical records, offer some answers to these questions.

25-year-old Diego de la Cruz testified that his relationship with Domingo dated back to the time when Domingo first "had the use of reason."[23]

In 1628, the mulattos Jeronimo Ventura and Francisca de la Cruz requested a marriage license. After the routine and ritualized formalities, the priest pointedly asked Francisca if she consented to marrying a slave. In underscoring Jeronimo's slave status at that moment—a ritual within a ritual—the priest was assuring himself and the bride that she had decided to enter matrimony with a bondsman of her own free will. Francisca, the priest's question pointed out, was choosing to marry an encumbered man. For Francisca and members of the wedding party, Jeronimo's status was not an issue. Diego de Avalos, a mulatto slave, vouched that he had known Francisca "since she was an infant" while another Jeronimo testified that he had known her for fifteen years. On the basis of these longtime relationships, the two men sought to verify that the couple had no impediments to their marriage. Juan Lorenzo de Noguesa, a 44-year-old self-identified Bañol slave, voiced similar sentiments. He had known Jeronimo for twelve years. The final witness, a free black woman named Ana María who was married to the free mulatto Juan Fraile, also said that she had known Francisca since birth. Status played no discernible role in the composition of this wedding party. As longtime acquaintances both free and slave, an African and mulattos had forged bonds with each other. In asking Francisca if she willingly wanted to marry a slave, the priest momentarily reified Jeronimo's status as a slave. But this issue was the Church's concern, not Francisca's. In marrying Jerónimo, Francisca embraced an individual with whom she had long-standing ties who happened to be a slave.[24]

A similar scenario was manifest in the marriage between María Hernández and her groom, Juan. In 1628, Juan, a widower who was identified as a *mestizo* and the son of a mulatto, and his prospective bride, mulatto slave María, presented witnesses with whom they shared lifelong ties. Blas de la Cruz, a 26-year-old mulatto slave, had known María "since birth" and Juan for twelve years. An unnamed 30-year-old black slave, a "ladino in the Castilian language," had known María "since a child" and Juan for four years. María de la Cruz, an indigenous woman, had interacted with Juan for "many years." In supporting their claims of familiarity, all of the witnesses testified that Juan had been a widower for the past four months. As the vicar weighed the evidence, he asked Juan if it was his desire to marry a slave. In posing the question, the priest reminded Juan and all those present that Spaniards customarily did not join in holy matrimony with individuals of degraded status, which for elites in New Spain meant descendants of Africans and slaves.[25]

---

23. AGN, Matrimonios 10, expediente 211, folio 492, 1629.
24. AGN, Matrimonios 28, expediente 55, folios 144–145, 1628.
25. AGN, Matrimonios 28, expediente 134, folios 354–355, 1628.

Clerics also reminded Indians that equal status and racial endogamy were the norm. In questioning marital choices that violated these norms, the clergy brought a Spanish-imposed divide into relief. But they deferred to the Christian ideal of free will, albeit grudgingly. In 1631, when 22-year-old Magdalena de la Cruz, an Indian, and Diego, a mulatto slave, petitioned for a marriage license, they presented four witnesses. Juan de Soto, a 25-year-old *mestizo,* had known Magdalena since birth and since that time had watched her grow up. María de los Reyes, a 33-year-old free mulatto, offered the same testimony. An unnamed 25-year-old free black creole had known the groom for five years. Lorenzo Herrera, a 23-year-old Spaniard, had known Diego for a year longer. After hearing the testimony, the vicar asked Magdalena—through Indian interpreter Diego de Mendoza—if she had decided to marry a slave of her own free will.[26]

A similar thing occurred on November 22, 1633, when Pedro Camaria, a mulatto slave, and María Magdalena, a 40-year-old Indian, wanted to marry. After the priest posed the question about Pedro's slave status and asked María if she was willingly entering the marriage, he turned to the witnesses. Andrés de la Cruz, a black slave owned by the same master as Pedro, stated he had known the prospective groom "since he had the use of reason." Andrés noted that Pedro had been married to *mestiza* Beatríz de Guzman, who had died on November 17th of 1633, "the day of San Gregorio," and said that María's husband had perished "ten or eleven years ago." Thirty-four-year-old Diego Francisco de Villalobos, a free mulatto, had known María for twenty years, and he corroborated that her husband had died eleven years earlier. Diego's relationship with Pedro was of equal length; he too noted that Pedro's first wife Beatríz had died five days earlier. Less than a week after his wife's death Pedro was prepared to reenter matrimony, but not with a stranger. He and María had known each other for at least twenty years.[27]

In a final example involving the question of free will and a union between a person of Indian ancestry and a mulatto, we glean why clerics carefully questioned individuals who brought petitions involving differences in legal and racial status. In 1628, a year and a half after his first wife, the Indian Angelina, had died, mulatto slave Sebastian de Mora sought another marriage. This time he wanted to marry *mestiza* Luísa de los Santos. In marrying a second time, Sebastian was not starting a brand-new life; instead, he was expanding the social network that he and Angelina had built. María de Escobar, a 50-year-old *castiza,* declared that she had known Sebastían for seven years, well before his wife died, but that her ties with Luísa were more enduring. She had known the *mestiza* "since she was a child." Next, Sebastían Nuñez, a 30-year-old *indio* ladino "dressed like a Spaniard," testified that he had interacted with Sebastian for twenty years and that he had been

26. AGN, Matrimonios 5, expediente 34, folio 130, 1631.
27. AGN, Matrimonios 5, expediente 44, folio 153, 1633.

present when Angelina was buried. Catalína, a 50-year-old Spaniard, said that she had known Luisa for seven years. Before granting the couple a license, the vicar, as was routine, asked Luisa if she wanted to marry a slave. In this instance the wedding party included individuals who were well acquainted with both bride and groom. The slave Sebastían maintained the ties that flourished during his initial marriage as he contracted his second marriage.[28]

It does not appear that relationships among creoles in the early seventeenth century were formed on the basis of rigid formulations of legal status. Among creoles, the growing number of free persons steadily interacted with slaves. As we saw in the case of Lázaro's mother, however, status-conscious parents sometimes voiced objections to the desire of their free offspring to marry slaves. But before the second half of the seventeenth century, creole relatives rarely opposed spouse selection. In any case, couples carefully selected their witnesses to avoid a fiasco during the proceedings. Wedding parties reflected the relationships that sustained individuals in the course of daily life. The marriage between Pedro de la Cruz, a black creole slave, and Luísa de la Cruz did not invite much scrutiny beyond the vicar's routine question about whether Luísa, a free mulatto, consented to having a slave husband. For the wedding party, this union did not seem out of the ordinary. Pascual de Torres, a 40-year-old free mulatto butcher, said he had interacted with Pedro for six years. Pascual de Aguijo, a 20-year-old free mulatto servant, had done so for eight years. Juana de la Cruz, a 30-year-old free mulatto servant, had known Luísa for six years. Juan de Ribera had known her "since she was born." Luísa, a 35-year-old *mestizo*, did not hesitate to be identified with slaves and mulattos.[29]

Slave status was a familiar condition for creoles in the first half of the seventeenth century. Yet that status did not prevent enslaved creoles from forming long-term friendships that sustained them. In 1629, a community of slaves belonging to different masters entered the *sagrario* to persuade the ecclesiastical authorities to grant Juan Francisco and Leonor a marriage license. In their desire to wed, Juan, a mulatto slave of Don Diego López de Carate, and Leonor, a black creole slave owned by Francisco Nuñez, seemed stoic about the fact that slavery would structure their conjugal lives. The testimony of the two witnesses underscores the deep ties of this community of slaves. The 36-year-old black creole slave Diego de Avalos had known Juan for six years and Leonor since birth. Anton, a 46-year-old mulatto slave, had known Leonor for six years and Juan since birth. Both bride and groom had lifelong friends by their side as they married.[30]

In another instance from 1629, the 26-year-old free mulatto Francisco Pérez

28. AGN, Matrimonios ?, expediente 95, folios 253–254, 1628.
29. AGN, Matrimonios 28, expediente 136, folios 364–365, 1628.
30. AGN, Matrimonios 88 expediente 299, 1629.

and creole slave Clara de Queros petitioned for a marriage license. The bride and the groom presented the same witnesses. Diego, a 38-year-old creole slave, had been familiar with Francisco "from the time he reached the age of reason" and had known Clara for an undetermined amount of time. The 25-year-old free mulatto Juan de Carmona had known the prospective groom for fifteen years and the bride for eight years.[31] Similarly, in 1631, the 22-year-old free mulatto Agustína de San Miguel sought a license to marry the mulatto slave of Baltasar de la Cruz. The 25-year-old Spaniard Cristóbal de Cordoba had known Agustína "since she was a baby." Gerónimo de Cordoba, a 38-year-old creole slave, had also known Baltasar since birth. Francisco de Chavez, the 25-year-old slave of Mexico's archbishop, testified that he had been familiar with Baltasar for ten years. Eighteen-year-old Spaniard Diego de Medina had known Agustina since he was twelve and she was sixteen.[32]

* * *

Framing Stories from the Archives as Culture

The stories people fabricated and circulated in the oral and aural universe of New Spain not only conveyed experiences but also imposed a structure on daily life in the seventeenth century. While ecclesiastical and inquisitorial proceedings thrived on rumors, rumors also expressed the social worlds of Africans and their creole descendants.[33] When individuals were called by the inquisitors to comment on the behavior or beliefs of an accused friend or acquaintance, they offered more than evidence of Christian wrongdoing. Their words illuminated the social practices and customs of their communities. Ecclesiastical and inquisitorial proceedings contain countless testimonials about relationships and social networks.[34] This evidence—whereby persons of African descent manifested their identities as social beings in their own words and deeds—raises the question of why the limited body

---

31. AGN, Matrimonios 10, expediente 70, folio 168, 1629.
32. AGN, Matrimonios 7, expediente 47, folio 184, 1631.
33. In light of the abundant source material in the Mexican archives on persons of African descent—including biographies, tales, rumors, stories, and even competing versions of incidents—the absence of studies akin to the seminal work of scholars of Afro-America and Africa appears rather stunning. See Rosalind Shaw, *Memories of the Slave Trade: Ritual and the Historical Imagination in Sierra Leone* (Chicago: University of Chicago Press, 2002); Luise White, *Speaking with Vampires: Rumors and History in Colonial Africa* (Berkeley: University of California Press, 2000); and Price, *First-Time*.
34. Richard Boyer, *Lives of the Bigamists: Marriage, Family, and Community in Colonial Mexico* (Albuquerque: University of New Mexico Press, 1995); Twinam, *Public Lives, Private Secrets*.

of cultural analysis has been restricted to a gloss of African ethnicity and the initial generations of creoles.

Previous studies of New World cultural formation have focused almost exclusively on how Africans became slaves and how the enslaved initially created creole cultures.[35] Such studies rightfully privileged the structural constraints that slavery imposed on the formation of African culture in New Spain and the workings of the social order in defining the status of persons of African descent.[36] This structural perspective—framed sequentially around the slave trade, labor, and social mobility—has brought increasing specificity to the African past in the Americas. Yet by emphasizing the social dimensions in which the African presence was mired, the studies of slavery in New Spain also privileged a racial narrative that defined slavery and freedom in the narrowest terms. The narrative until now has privileged the mechanisms whereby the slave trade transformed cultural beings (Africans) into social entities—property and workers. Mexicanists are aware that Africans were transformed into slaves, but they acknowledge only in passing that a social and cultural dynamic was involved as well. As a result, the enslaved figure in the narrative of slavery and freedom merely as objects—those who were defined by their domination and labor. By framing the story in this manner, scholars have moved effortlessly from describing the social oppression of the enslaved to using the lens of race relations to examine the role of blacks in the formation of society in New Spain.[37]

The scholarly neglect of generational cultural dynamics raises several related questions. Can we really reduce the transformation of Africans into slaves to a social process? If not, what cultural practices accompanied the social process? And finally, can the cultural dynamic of the initial generation of creoles be meaningful for successive generations? We need to give actual cultural practices a privileged place in our analysis of persons of African descent. But a cultural framework demands historical specificity. We need to understand that most basic element of

35. Herskovits, *The Myth of the Negro Past*; Melville J. Herskovits, *The New World Negro: Selected Papers in Afroamerican Studies* (Bloomington: Indiana University Press, 1966); Roger Bastide, *African Civilisations in the New World,* trans. Peter Green (New York: Harper & Row, 1971); Mintz and Price, *The Birth of African-American Culture*; John Thornton, *Africa and Africans in the Atlantic World, 1400–1680* (Cambridge: Cambridge University Press, 1992); Richard D. E. Burton, *Afro-Creole: Power, Opposition, and Play in the Caribbean* (Ithaca, N.Y.: Cornell University Press, 1997).

36. Palmer, *Slaves of the White God*; Carroll, *Blacks in Colonial Veracruz*; Cope, *The Limits of Racial Domination.*

37. Cope, *The Limits of Racial Domination*; Lewis, *Hall of Mirrors*; Claudio Lomnitz, *Deep Mexico, Silent Mexico: Anthropology of Nationalism* (Minneapolis: University of Minnesota Press, 2001); María Elena Martínez, "The Black Blood of New Spain: Limpieza de Sangre, Racial Violence, and Gendered Power in Early Colonial Mexico," *William and Mary Quarterly*, 3rd. ser., 61, no. 3 (July 2004): 479–520.

historical inquiry—change over time. With regard to the seventeenth century—which was framed by liberty as much as it was by the slave experience—I insist that freedom, defined by a modicum of control over the self and body, was a multilayered cultural process as well as a social and juridical process. In this chapter, I bring into relief an unexplored facet of creolization.

Criollo (creole) was a key term in the New World lexicon. In the Indies prior to the 1560s, Spaniards applied the term exclusively to blacks and mulattos as a way to distinguish them from Africans labeled *bozales* or *ladinos*. While "*criollo de,*" like "*natural de,*" signified place of birth, a key aspect of the term was its reference to customs—the normative practices associated with a given polity. From birth, *criollos* were familiar with the Christian commonwealth and its customs. For early modern Spaniards, the term *criollo* referred to a way of life that included beliefs, customs, tastes, and proclivities. Though Spaniards initially used the term to refer to place of birth, in time "*criollo*" became synonymous with contemporary definitions of culture.

For Afro-Americanists, the nature, scope, and social logic of creole cultural formation constitute a central theoretical concern.[38] At the most basic level, scholarly efforts to understand the reconstituted African presence in the Americas necessitate an engagement with the theories of creole culture or a critique thereof.[39]

Central to the study of the reconstituted African past is the social logic that guided the survivors of the Middle Passage as they established social and cultural practices in the New World.[40] Scholars have offered various cultural interpretations for lived experienced in the aftermath of the Middle Passage that are premised on the various contact situations that flourished throughout the course of the Atlantic slave trade. Though contemporary scholarship has forged a consensus around the idea that slaves manifested social practices and cultural institutions that reflected their consciousness as social beings, a long-standing debate turns on the issue of cognitive cultural orientation.[41] In other words, to what degree did the enslaved, composed of individuals divorced from their original cultural moorings, construct a fundamentally original cultural synthesis? To what degree did they create a cultural complex on the basis of a shared African logic? Grossly simplified, the question revolves around the extent to which the lives and practices of the enslaved refracted a creole or an African cultural logic. The arguments in this debate have become increasingly layered as scholars have enlisted vast bodies of new his-

38. Palmié, *Wizards & Scientists*.
39. Paul E. Lovejoy, "Identifying Enslaved Africans in the African Diaspora," in *Identity in the Shadow of Slavery*, ed. Paul E. Lovejoy (New York: Continuum, 2000), 1–29.
40. Frazier, *The Negro Family in the United States*; Herskovits, *The Myth of the Negro Past*.
41. Stuckey, *Slave Culture*; Gomez, *Exchanging Our Country Marks*.

torical knowledge, refined their methods in relationship to an expanded definition of the colonial archive, and brought historical scrutiny to long-neglected regions and eras.[42] As a result, for some regions and eras scholars have radically revised, if not transformed, our understanding of slave life and culture. Ironically, this has not been the case for much of colonial Spanish America. The earliest sites of the African presence, though they are the locus of the largest body of extant sources, have received the least amount of scholarly attention.

Another problem related to the dearth of scholarship on the African past in colonial Spanish America concerns the intersection of time and culture. What we know about the cultures of the enslaved has been derived from a narrow yet geographically similar cultural place and time—plantation America. Since the cultural logic of plantation America witnessed the thorough commodification of social existence, especially slave life, our understanding of the African cultural past—which has principally been created from the period of the eighteenth century and beyond—has been derived from unquestionably modern societies.[43] Is it not conceivable that a distinct process of culture formation prevailed in societies that operated with an early modern social logic? Addressing this question demands an exploration of creole cultural formation over the course of the mid-colonial period of New Spain.

Creolization as Process

Seventeenth-century creolization warrants far more scholarly attention than it has received. West-Central Africans and their descendants entered a social landscape that was already forming. Although it is tempting to assume that cultural continuity prevailed, that West-Central Africans were swept up in the cultural vortex West Africans had already inaugurated, the evidence suggests otherwise. The archival record suggests that innovation characterized the identities seventeenth-century Angolans fashioned.[44] Instead of characterizing this process as a radical disjuncture, scholars may benefit from a more subtle reading of the cultural dynamic.

For example, the term "Angolan" is prevalent in the historical record in the seventeenth century, although that past was often signified in the archival record with the terms "Bran," "Biafara," and "Gelofo." This suggests an individual who had experienced a cultural break with the West African past. This was a change: Bran was the African identity that was prevalent in sixteenth-century records in New

42. James Sidbury, *Ploughshares into Swords: Race, Rebellion, and Identity in Gabriel's Virginia, 1730–1810* (New York: Cambridge University Press, 1997).

43. Sidney W. Mintz, *Caribbean Transformation* (New York: Columbia University Press, 1974).

44. Bennett, *Africans in Colonial Mexico.*

TABLE 3.2.

SPOUSE SELECTION PATTERNS AMONG PERSONS IDENTIFIED AS BLACK IN MEXICO CITY, 1584–1650[1]

Ethnicity of Spouse[2]	Number	Percent
Black	223	64.3
Ethnic African[3]	54	15.6
Mulatto/a	26	7.5
Indian	22	6.3
Mestizo/a	13	3.7
Chino	3	0.9
Spaniard	3	0.9
Castizo/a	1	0.2
Morisco/a	1	0.2
Unknown	1	0.2
Total	347	99.8

Source: Matrimonios Primera and Tercera Seria, AGN.

1. The marriage records on which this table is based are drawn from the *sagrario* and the cathedral in Mexico City and the parishes of Santa Veracruz and Salto del Agua. Consequently, the sample is confined to the principal parishes of Mexico City where the wealthiest Spaniards and their servants lived.

2. Blacks are persons who were identified and defined themselves as Negros.

3. The majority of ethnic Africans were Angolans; others included the BaKongo, Mandinga, Bran, Biafra, and persons from Terra Nova and Mozambique.

TABLE 3.3. SPOUSE SELECTION PATTERNS OF MULATTOS IN MEXICO CITY, 1591–1650[1]

Ethnicity/Race of Spouse	Number	Percent
Mulatto/a	99	36.4
Mestizo/a	67	24.6
Black	26	9.6
Spaniard	23	8.5
Indian	22	8.1
Ethnic African	9	3.3
Castizo/a	9	3.3
Chino/a	2	0.7
Unknown	15	5.5
Total	272	100.0

Source: Matrimonios Primera and Tercera Seria, AGN.

1. The marriage records on which this table is based are drawn from the *sagrario* and the cathedral in Mexico City and the parishes of Santa Veracruz and Salto del Agua. Consequently, the sample is confined to the principal parishes of Mexico City where the wealthiest Spaniards and their servants lived.

Spain. In other words, the identity "Angolan" was a break with another African identity present in an earlier period in New Spain, "Bran." This shift in ethnic composition is attributable to the geography of slavery.

When the slave trade ended, distinct communities of creoles were present in New Spain that were largely composed of the offspring of sixteenth-century West Africans and the offspring of seventeenth-century Angolans. The marriage patterns for black creoles and mulattos, which are reflected in tables 3.2 and 3.3, underscore the plurality of identities among blacks and mulattos. Although blacks and mulattos exhibited a greater propensity than Angolans to marry persons of different racial classifications, the majority nonetheless elected persons of African descent as spouses. Among blacks, 87 percent selected a spouse of African descent, though only just over 64 percent selected spouses from their own ethnic group. Nearly 50 percent of the mulattos in the sample married persons of African descent, though only 36 percent of such marriages were with other mulattos. These patterns underscore a propensity among people of African descent to forge specific black unions.

Differences born of discrete African pasts and the timing of the arrival of African relatives from Guinea resulted in distinct expressions of creole identities. Creoles with an African parent or parents had different cultural orientations from individuals whose African relatives had arrived one or two generations earlier. We cannot think of creoles as a homogenous group, and we cannot think of the process of creolization as uniform. To view all creoles as the same ignores the complexity that characterized cultural formation in the middle and late colonial period. We know that for the survivors of the slave trade, ethnic differences precluded the formation of an African or slave consciousness. The same is true for creoles. A new black identity had to be forged from different ethnic practices. But in New Spain this process never resulted in a singular black identity.

For the growing population of black creoles in the seventeenth century, "Africa," if it was remembered at all, took on meaning in relationship to a specific parent. Creoles' understanding of Africa was largely derived from the presence of recent survivors of the Middle Passage, those who were part of the second slave trade, which reached its height in 1622.

How did creoles form bonds with Angolans in the first half of the seventeenth century? Most creoles were the descendants of West Africans, while Angolans were the most recent arrivals from the "land of Guinea." We would expect that as products of distinct African cultural traditions and practices, most creoles and Angolans would have perceived each other as strangers. And we would expect that the great complexity of the social landscape of New Spain would have made it difficult for these two groups to create a collective consciousness, even though they shared the experience of race and slavery. But both groups embraced

Christian customs, and it was through this shared experience that they began to have a common identity. During the first half of the seventeenth century, this shared experience permeated the cultural logic of daily existence. In urban New Spain, Christianity, not race or slavery, provided the structural contours that made a common black cultural identity possible. It was the enduring structural presence that linked sixteenth-century black identity to seventeenth-century black identity. Christianity engaged and structured African ethnicity in a way that bestowed a form of continuity—in the guise of Angolan ethnicity, for instance—but ultimately resulted in cultural disjuncture.[45]

The bigamy proceedings against Juan Francisco de Robledo, a 48-year-old free black, highlights how Christian ways of knowing gradually replaced African ethnicity.[46] Brought to trail in 1593, at the beginning of New Spain's second slave trade, the words of this offspring of a West African mother did not reveal the slightest trace of how the African past competed with Christianity in his life. Professing a Christian conscience, Juan Francisco acknowledged that he had not attended church regularly. But the lessons of his youth were intact. He easily recited the Paternoster, the Credo, the Ave Maria, the Ten Commandments, and the standard confession. The inquisitor noted that he "said all of them well." Aside from categorizing his mother, Andrea, as an African from *tierra nueva,* Juan did not offer evidence of (nor was he asked about) his African past. This neglect was deliberate.[47] In effect, the inquisitor signaled that what mattered was his consciousness as a Christian. Through repetition and periodic command performances, his creole consciousness, which had been created in relationship to Christianity, gained ascendance over the specific African legacy he inherited from his mother, Andrea, and his exposure to the reconstituted African norms during his interactions with Africans and black creoles. As a creole born in 1545, Juan Francisco exhibited the creole practices that flourished in the second half of the sixteenth century: He bore a Spanish name, had a solid command of Christian dogma, and was a practicing Christian, illustrating that there was no singular creole identity in the New

45. Knowing is structured by specific proceedings. From the beginning memory embodied tensions as it sought to reconcile competing systems of meaning. Eventually Christian structuring gained ascendance in the pantheon of remembering. Still, Christianity was not the only system of meaning. Christian versions, in a word, did constitute the sum total of existing memories, histories, and forms of selfhood.

46. AGN, Inquisición, tomo 185, expediente 3, 1593.

47. According to Soviet literary scholar Krystyna Pomorska, "The 'authoritarian word' does not allow any other type of speech to approach and interfere with it. Devoid of any zones of cooperation with other types of words, the 'authoritarian word' thus excludes dialogue. Similarly, any official culture that considers itself the only respectable model dismisses all other cultural strata as invalid and harmful." Pomorska "Foreword," in Mikhail Bakhtin, *Rabelais and His World,* trans. Hélène Iswolsky (Bloomington: Indiana University Press, 1984), x.

Spain of the sixteenth century that we can think of as a baseline.[48] In the course of that century, the distinct bodies of West African *bozales* and *ladinos* remade the African past in a way that was far from generic. The same was true for the seventeenth century.

As mothers, fathers, sisters, brothers, aunts, uncles, godparents, and friends, Africans generated anecdotal yet meaningful reconstructions of the African past. Here we only need recall the testimony surrounding Clara Hipólita, Nicolás de la Cruz's first wife. In the Inquisition proceedings, Clara and the other witnesses, including the accused Nicolás, offered a glimpse of her early life. Early in her childhood, Clara the slave was separated from her enslaved mother, María de la Cruz (alias María Macua). Despite this separation and their slave status, mother and daughter maintained regular contact, thus giving María some authority over her daughter's life. Nicolás de la Cruz acknowledged this influence by initially approaching María, not Clara, with his marriage proposal. Persuaded by Nicolás's appeal, María "spoke to her daughter so that she would marry him." Clara agreed and the couple initiated marital proceedings.[49]

The ethnic origins of the wedding guests and attendants indicate that Clara had been reared among Mozambicans. The godmother (*madrina*) was Mozambican. Symbolically, this was very revealing. Godparents (*padrinos*) were essential to Catholic weddings since they played an active role in the ceremony and sponsored the post-nuptial festivities. *Padrinos* were often selected on the basis of their material circumstances and influence over the bride.[50] Invariably, trusted relatives, highly respected community elders, or the *patrón* and his wife occupied this position. Clara selected María, a slave from Mozambique, and Francisco, her Wolofo spouse—her maternal aunt and uncle by marriage. The two Marías—Clara's moth-

48. "Baseline" refers to a specific cultural form against which previous or successive cultural expressions are assessed. Sidney W. Mintz and Richard Price invoked the term in relationship to their preliminary discussion of Melville Herskovits's ground-breaking contribution to the field of Afro-American studies. See Mintz and Price, *The Birth of African-American Culture.*

49. Clara was more emphatic in her testimony, suggesting that the marriage occurred "by order and with the consent of her mother." This interpretation was independently confirmed by Antonio, a slave who worked with María. The limits of Clara and Nicolás's personal autonomy were made clear once they agreed to be married. After the couple finalized matters, they petitioned Clara's owners for their permission. The owners consented under the condition that the wedding be held in the parish church of Santa Veracruz. AGN, Inquisicíon, tomo 381, expediente 8, 1634–1635.

50. Over a lifetime a person could acquire several sets of *padrinos,* including one for their baptism, one for confirmation, and one for First Communion. *Padrinos* performed important ritual and material services at these events. John M. Ingham, *Mary, Michael, and Lucifer: Folk Catholicism in Central Mexico* (Austin: University of Texas Press, 1966), 82–90. For a description of godparent practices among enslaved Africans, see Stephen Gudeman and Stuart B. Schwartz, "Cleansing Original Sin: Godparenthood and the Baptism of Slaves in Eighteenth-Century Bahia," in *Kinship Ideology and Practice in Latin America,* ed. Raymond T. Smith (Chapel Hill: University of North Carolina Press, 1984), 36–58; and Donald Ramos, "Community, Control and Acculturation: A Case Study of Slavery in Eighteenth-Century Brazil," *The Americas* 42, no. 4 (April 1986): 442–443.

er and her maternal aunt—were sisters who had survived the horrors of the slave trade and were fortunate enough to be reunited in Mexico City. Although they had initially been separated by sale, at the time of Clara's wedding both sisters worked for Juan Gómez de Trasmontes.[51] Antonio de la Cruz, who also worked for Juan Gómez, was another person identified as a Mozambican among the African wedding guests. Collectively, they constituted the identifiable core of Clara's family and ethnic network.[52]

The two Marías, Francisco, and Antonio influenced Clara's childhood and worldview in important ways. From them and other members of their community, Clara learned about a particularized Africa and was introduced to Mozambican cultural practices and beliefs. Their casual everyday social interaction, their gossip and exchange of information, their strengths and foibles, and their daily routine consistently shaped Clara's consciousness. Yet she did not inherit their ethnic identity. For María, Antonio, Francisco, and María de la Cruz, ethnicity was at the core of their beings, the essence of their collective identity. But for Clara, ethnicity was just one of many cultural forces in her life. Like Nicolás, she was a creole whose creole self was shaped by the ethnic group she was born into.

The variety of creole cultures present in seventeenth-century New Spain were manifest in daily patterns of interaction. In their behavior, creoles countered the homogenizing process—expressed by masters and scholars alike—by forging specific ties. Such ties bring into relief concrete manifestations of creole culture that can enrich our analysis of cultural formation and the nature of existing social relations. In the seventeenth century, the creole population forged an image of Africa that was shaped by the massive arrival of Angolans. The resulting creole culture was built around social networks that were informed and shaped by the past of West-Central Africans.

If creolization should have any valence it seems critical that the concept not be confined to an outdated definition of culture that includes physical environment, diet, language, beliefs, kinship practices, and community structures devoid of a politics and a political tradition. At the same time, I am convinced of the need to

---

51. AGN, Inquisición, tomo 381, expediente 8, 1634–1635.

52. Antón de Santillana, an Angolan slave, was also present at the wedding. Although Antón testified on behalf of both Clara and Nicolás, he had known Nicolás longer. Antón stated that "I have known Nicolás de la Cruz . . . since he was born and watched him grow." Nicolás's father may have been Angolan; he identified his mother as a mulatto and his father as a "negro." According to Aguirre Beltrán, the number of Mozambicans in New Spain was insignificant. In a limited sixteenth- and seventeenth-century data base that included 624 ethnic Africans, he found only nine from Mozambique. Gonzalo Aguirre Beltrán, *La población negra de México: Estudio ethnohistorico* (Mexico: Fondo de Cultura Económica, 1946), 240–241. The existence of this network suggests that the number of people who defined themselves and were defined as Mozambicans may have been greater than previously believed. Other Mozambican networks can be located in AGN, Matrimonios 10, expediente 134, 1629; AGN, Matrimonios 10, expediente 173, 1629; and AGN, Matrimonios 71, expediente 13, 1607.

limit the use of creolization as an analytical concept to the encounter process and at most to several generations thereafter. To do otherwise threatens the concept's viability and presupposes the faulty logic that the descendants of Africans were resident aliens whose cultural processes were defined by routes but not by roots. As I hope the previous pages have illustrated, successive generations of Africans and their descendants manifested vibrant and generative roots in colonial Mexico.

For creoles, lifelong relationships often shaped the decision about who to marry and who to call on as a sponsor to a marriage petition. This was a distinct difference from the life experiences of the community of African arrivals. Africans rarely had the opportunity to select individuals whom they had known since birth as a spouse or a sponsor. These creole patterns, which initially emerged in the first half of the seventeenth century, illustrate the relative stability of an urban slave society. Even though creoles lived in a society characterized by death and frequent sales, they nonetheless managed to create a core community of friendship and kin that was intergenerational and interracial and included individuals of varying status. In addition, men and women enjoyed long-term friendships that dated back to childhood. Many other friendships were measured in terms of years, even decades. Such relationships highlight the growing density of friendship and family clusters in the early seventeenth century. The archival record also demonstrates that at a very young age, people created friendships across the dividing lines Spaniard elites wished to create and sustained them into adulthood. The values of the growing creole community, not the norms colonizers tried to impose, determined who creoles chose as lifelong friends.

Spouse selection leading to family formation emerged as the principal means through which peoples of African descent manifested real and symbolic differences—as ethnics and black creoles. In the wake of West Africans and concurrent to the path forged by West-Central Africans, creoles embraced Christian matrimony as a means to legitimize their social existence as men, women, and new people. Through the marriage contract, couples legitimized their claims as husband and wife, as parents, and ultimately as kin. For chattel such claims were by no means trivial.

Matrimonial sponsors occupied a crucial role in this cultural process. Far from fleeting, the connections between sponsors and the wedding couple rested on years of interactions within the boundaries created by work and subsistence. Years of accumulated experiences and memories that moved on a continuum from pleasure to pain informed the testimony, yet there was not much room for the narration of these rich experiences in the stylized ecclesiastical setting. In the proceedings, the clergy demanded testimonies that spoke directly to the matter of impediments. Testimonies needed to be disciplined and confined to the length of time a witness had known the person on whose behalf they spoke. To the clergy, everything else was the prattle of slaves and mulattos, the cacophony of the urban rabble. The matrimonial sponsors conformed to the demands of the church, scripting their testimony accordingly. But the melody of daily life hummed underneath each declaration.

Even as Christian matrimony acquired valence among creoles, allowing them to legitimately channel personal desire, the social existence of blacks was not defined by the boundaries orthodox Christianity sought to establish. In the urban and rural areas to which we turn next, the choices of creoles constantly skirted the boundaries of the licit and the illicit. As creoles created their private lives, sin played a quite prominent role.

FOUR

Provincial Black Life

After establishing villages and cities throughout New Spain, the victorious Spaniards allotted themselves *encomiendas,* royal grants whereby a Spaniard assumed the title *encomendero* of a specific area and with it acquired command—but not ownership—over the resident Indian population. The *encomenderos* collected tribute from the subjugated Indians, who were the earliest source of wealth for the Spaniards in the form of labor and tribute in kind. But the Indian population's demographic collapse over the course of the sixteenth century and the Spanish Crown's efforts to remedy this decline led to the introduction of new mechanisms for extracting Indian tribute, most notably the *repartimiento,* a rotating system of forced labor. It required Indians from a designated village to offer their labor for a finite period of time to a named Spanish recipient. As the Spaniards used the *encomienda* and then the *repartimiento* to extract tribute from Indians, they devised strategies for systematically tapping New Spain's resources. The plantation was the device colonial authorities used, and soon after Cortés granted his followers the first *encomiendas,* the plantation economy in which the African population would figure so prominently began to develop.

In 1590, the Marqués de Villamanrique, New Spain's departing viceroy, drafted a memorable passage about the rural black presence for his successor, Luis de Velasco. He wrote:

> In this land there are great numbers of dangerous and pernicious free Africans and mulattos, as your lordship knows. They are only capable of living as vagabonds, robbing and causing violence. Although they owe tribute to his Majesty, the majority avoids it by not registering as I commanded for all on the pain of death. I sent an order to the *alcaldes mayores* and *corregidores* to register the free Africans and mulattos in their districts. They will also be punished if they absent themselves from the districts where they are registered. This order serves

two purposes. First, his Majesty collects the tribute that must be paid to him. The other intent, more central to the security and well-being of the country, is to command them to gather together for registration and to apportion each one among all the mines, so they can serve there with miners, who will pay them. Others will be apportioned into labor gangs subject to an *alcalde mayor* and not permitted to leave their assigned district or contract without a registered license. This will protect the country from these vagabonds at large and their violence and robberies. The miners will benefit greatly from having these servants to relieve most of the Indians from service. The Africans and mulattos themselves also benefit by earning a steady wage making them more dependable. Their sons will be raised in this life, will enjoy and continue it. I did not have time to carry out this plan. In the government records, your Lordship will find the order, which you can carry out as you see fit.[1]

Villamanrique alerts us to the existence of blacks—both slave and free—in the countryside. The viceroy expressed what historian Nicole von Germeten calls "the long-enduring myth of the violent African vagabond."[2] Von Germeten correctly locates Villamanrique's anxieties in his fear that blacks without masters would constitute a threat to the social order. I am interested in exploring the cultural geography the viceroy's words bring into relief. This chapter explores the presence of slave and free blacks in the countryside, where a different colonial reality existed than in cities. It is clear that some rural individuals were thoroughly mobile and easily traversed the countryside. And as New Spain entered the mature colonial period at the beginning of the seventeenth century, the countryside increasingly featured dense and socially cohesive communities of blacks with which the alleged "itinerants" formed enduring social ties.[3]

In shifting our perspective from Mexico City to Morelos, we bring one of the earliest rural black presences in the Americas into relief. Inquisition sources provide a rare glimpse of rural black life—a life in which family tales and tales about families and friends were central.

Villamanrique's concern about the *vago* (vagabond) exhibited the familiar colonial hysteria about "Africans and mulattos" who supposedly roved the countryside intent on committing crimes.[4] Individuals who were "only capable of living"

1. France V. Scholes and Eleanor B. Adams, *Advertimientos generales que los virreyes dejaron a sus sucesores para el gobierno de Nueva España, 1590–1604* (Mexico City: Porrúa, 1956), 100, cited in von Germeten, *Black Blood Brothers*, 76; see also Palmer, *Slaves of the White God*, 182.

2. Von Germeten, *Black Blood Brothers*, 76.

3. Andrews, *Afro-Latin America*, 17; Helg, *Liberty & Equality in Caribbean Colombia*, 18–79; Metcalf, *Family and Frontier in Colonial Brazil*.

4. Palmer, *Slaves of the White God*, 131; Bowser, *The African Slave in Colonial Peru*, 148, 154, 157–158.

beyond the grasp of Spanish administrative control and whose actions were not dictated by market forces and labor discipline heightened the viceroy's anxieties. For Villamanrique, the autonomy of "free Africans and mulattos" was criminal. With his words, the viceroy acknowledged a social breach. The liberty of "free Africans and mulattos"—their ability to limit Spanish control over their lives—defined them as "pernicious." Intent on remedying this breach, Villamanrique sent an order that confined blacks in the countryside to Spanish settlements, thereby assuring that authorities could monitor their presence, compel them to work, and collect their tribute.

Villamanrique's recommendations to secure "the country" relied on a political-economic approach: collecting tribute and extracting labor. Since the Catholic Church maintained a presence in rural areas that were not endowed with mineral wealth or settled with commercial estates, the lack of reference to the clergy as allies in the project of social control is interesting. In view of New Spain's Catholic renewal, which Villamanrique's predecessor Don Pedro Moya de Contreras had carefully orchestrated in his capacity as inquisitor general (1571–1573), archbishop of Mexico (1573–1591), and then briefly as viceroy (1584–1585), this silence seems curious. Villamanrique's perspective and the solution he proposed suggest that the only entities in the countryside were mines and commercial estates, isolated *alcaldes* or *corregidors* that contained Indians and free blacks—"Africans and mulattos"—who in Spanish eyes resembled *cimarrones*, feral cattle.[5]

During the first half of the seventeenth century, a number of demographic events unfolded. The second slave trade (1595–1640) began, the Angolanization of the African population commenced, the creole and mulatto populations began to dominate among the black population, and the number of free coloreds rose precipitously. These were key events in the overlapping histories of empire and slavery, colonial life and black cultural formation, and they unfolded in both urban centers and the countryside. Although urban areas, where Spanish institutions were concentrated, yielded an abundance of sources about a specific locale over time, this is not the case for rural areas.

This chapter, which draws on inquisition proceedings against bigamists, builds on historian Richard Boyer's pioneering work in *Lives of the Bigamists*, which illustrated how a wide array of sources could highlight intimate details of time, place, and social process.[6] The level of descriptive details the bigamy proceedings contain helps counteract the paucity of source material. A typical bigamy proceeding included a denunciation (*denuncia*), accounts from witnesses (*informaciones* and *ratificaciones*), details of institutional transactions (*informaciones matrimoniales*,

5. Richard Price, *Maroon Societies: Rebel Slave Communities in the Americas* (Baltimore: Johns Hopkins University Press, 1979).

6. Boyer, *Lives of the Bigamists*.

dilegencias), and successive interrogations (*audiencias*). Inquisition records provide descriptions of where people lived and how they made a living, what their juridical status was, and some details about their domestic lives. Above all else, these sources underscore the depth of social connections among blacks and other groups in the countryside. Such connections, in fact, fueled Inquisition proceedings, highlighting the purposeful and invasive nature of moral regulation. The record the Inquisition proceedings left enable us to revise the idea that the lack of order that the alarmed Marqués de Villamanrique described prevailed in the countryside.

In alerting Luís de Velasco to the "dangerous and pernicious" presence of Africans, blacks, and mulattos, Viceroy Villamanrique highlighted the physical autonomy exhibited by some blacks in the countryside. It is important to include rural blacks in any study of the colonial period in Mexico. As historian Patrick Carroll recently noted, "Mexico's population was overwhelmingly rural, concentrated in spaces removed from Mexico City's royal influence."[7] But blacks were not restricted to sugar plantations (*ingenios*), livestock estates (*estancias*), and mines (*minas*). They occupied the peripheries, hinterlands, and frontiers of existing commercial zones. Mobility, as we shall see, enabled rural blacks, some slaves included, to create productive and social lives beyond the circumscribed world of the estates.[8]

In the commercial zones, on the frontiers, and in the areas in between, blacks, who lived next to Indians, poor Spaniards, and small-scale slave-owners, eked out a meager existence that rarely went beyond subsistence. But steadily expanding numbers and increasing social stability enabled rural blacks to forge a social existence around their domestic arrangements. At the core of this social world was a sensibility about private lives. In the inquisitorial proceedings from the provinces of Morelos and El Fresnillo we glimpse the contours of a black interior. The incidents this historical record yield show blacks telling stories about family, neighbors, and friends, discursively reflecting a black interiority that existed in marketplaces, at work, and in their homes. The stories convey details about rural work, home life, and physical mobility, bringing into relief the presences of a Christian conscience among rural blacks and mulattos. Though refracted through Christian regulation, this conscience enabled individuals to voice claims as Christians and

7. Patrick J. Carroll, "Review of *Africans in Colonial Mexico: Absolutism, Christianity, and Afro-Creole Consciousness, 1570–1640*," *Colonial Latin American Review* 14 (June 2005): 147.

8. AGN, Inquisición 310, expediente 3, folios 87–118, 17 March 1615, "Información de Melchor, negro esclavo del convento y monejas de Santa Inés de México," Cuautla de las Amilpas; AGN, Inquisición 310, expediente 5, folios 232–258, 29 March 1618, "Información de Gracía Hernández, negra libre, que fue de Alonso Hernández Talavera," El Fresnillo; AGN, Inquisición 310, expediente 5, folios 232–258, 29 April 1618, "Información de Juan, moreno, casado, esclavo de Diego de Salazar," El Fresnillo.

exhibit lives—private lives—beyond work, subsistence, or the alleged anomie that alarmed Viceroy Villamanrique.

Tales from the Countryside

In 1611, the free mulatto Juan Luís, a laborer in the small town of Iguala in the province of Morelos, was incarcerated for allegedly stealing a steer. On 9 February 1611, days after arriving in jail, Juan Luís composed a petition (*instancia*) addressed to Father Benito Bocarro. Though he was sick and in jail, Juan Luís wanted to marry Juana Agustína, an Indian woman. He had "come from a pueblo without a notary" for that purpose because he "want[ed] to do good work and service God Our Lord." He also admitted that he had been "incarcerated for other crimes."[9]

The Indian mayor (*indio alcalde*) of Iguala, Don Juan Jeronimo, was aware of the impending marriage and knew that days before Juan Luís had been imprisoned, the couple had presented their witnesses before Alejo de Salas, the ecclesiastical assistant there. Juan Jeronimo later recalled that Father Bocarro "in his presence married (*desposo*) and veiled (*velo*) the couple in the church of this pueblo," afterward saying the nuptial mass (*misa nupcial*).[10]

Documentation from Father Bocarro confirmed this account. His record of Juan Luís and Juana Agustína's petition for a marriage license noted that they had presented witnesses who vouched that they lacked impediments.[11] When the couple's sponsors, Francisco López and Catalina Rodríguez, had presented their testimony to Alejo de Salas on 3 February 1611, it had become clear that they had known one or both of them for a long time. Francisco, a 35-year-old free mulatto, had known Juan for six years while they worked together on various estates in Amilpas and in the jurisdiction of the Cortés family known as the *marquesado del valle*. Francisco had been confident that Juan Luís lacked impediments. "I would know if he had," he had remarked. "I have had a lot of interaction with him."[12] Catalina, a 50-year-old free black woman, had demonstrated similar confidence

9. AGN, Inquisición 310, expediente 3, folios 87–118, 9 February 1611, "Instancia ante Benito Bocarro, vicario de Iguala de Juan Luís, mulato libre para que se le reciba información de ser libre y soltero para casarse con una india llamada Juana," Iguala.

10. AGN, Inquisición 310, expediente 3, folios 87–105, 3 April 1611, "Denuncia"; AGN, Inquisición 310, expediente 3, folios 87–118, 30 December 1614, "Información de Don Juan Jerónimo, indio alcalde del pueblo de Iguala."

11. AGN, Inquisición 310, expediente 3, folios 87–118, 9 February 1611, "Instancia ante Benito Bocarro, vicario de Iguala de Juan Luís, mulato libre para que se le reciba información de ser libre y soltero para casarse con una india llamada Juana," Iguala. Don Juan Jerónimo later described the proceedings: "Juan Luís arrived at the church where I was the *fiscal* and there and then Juan Luís gave the *información* about his lack of impediments to the *teniente* Alejo de Salas." AGN, Inquisición 310, expediente 3, folios 87–118, 30 December 1614, "Información de Don Juan Jerónimo, indio alcalde del pueblo de Iguala."

12. AGN, Inquisición 310, expediente 3, folios 87–118, 17 March 1615, "Información de Francisco Domínguez."

that there were no impediments, since she had known Juan Luís "as an infant" (*criado*). Persuaded by the propriety of the proceedings and convinced that Juan Luís's illness created urgency, Father Bocarro had dispensed with the banns and administered the sacraments the next day.[13]

Shortly after this, Juan Luís broke out of prison and took off with his new wife for the southern coast. The prison break and the alleged theft that had landed him in prison in the first place did not concern church officials, nor did the fact that Juan in effect deprived the hacienda owner of his labor as he hastily relocated. What concerned religious officials was the possibility that Jan Luís's new marriage might be bigamous. Father Francisco Rangel had visited the livestock and sugar estates owned by the Dominican Order in Morelos during holy week (*semana santa*). There he had heard rumors from Juan Rodríguez, the steward (*mayordomo*) of the livestock estate of Nochipan, that Juan Luís had contracted a bigamous marriage.[14] On 3 April 1611, two months after the marriage took place, Father Rangel, who did not know Juan Luís, gathered three other members of the clergy as well Juan Rodríguez and Alonso Gil, another steward of a livestock estate, and entered the chambers of the Inquisition tribunal in Mexico City, intent on revealing the existence of an illicit act. Concern that Juan Rodríguez may have neglected his Christian duty in not telling what he knew right away prompted Father Rangel himself to level the denunciation (*denuncia*). With this conscience-clearing gesture, Father Rangel observed that he had no further information to offer.[15] But he had acted as a good Catholic by bringing the allegations to the inquisitors' attention.

In this example, an allegation that an obscure free mulatto had engaged in improper acts fueled a conversation among a gathering of clerics and Spanish authorities who represented the regional patriarchs of one of the New World's most dynamic commercial areas. By the first half of the seventeenth century, Morelos's plantation economy was a key nexus in New Spain's slave society, whose geographical core extended from Veracruz in the east to Acapulco in the west, Michoacan in the north and Guerrero in the south. Plantations were enclaves in a vast landscape that relied on the productive and commercial activities of African slaves, Indian tributaries, free blacks, *mestizos,* and poor Spaniards in a variety of ways. The rise of the plantation economy fueled the introduction of enslaved Africans into Morelos. Initially, Indian tributaries worked alongside enslaved Africans before the latter population grew to be the largest group in the plantation labor force. By the third decade of the seventeenth century, Morelos had one of the largest African labor

13. AGN, Inquisición 310, expediente 3, folios 87–118, 30 December 1614, "Información de Don Juan Jerónimo, indio alcalde del pueblo de Iguala."

14. AGN, Inquisición 310, expediente 3, folios 87–118, 3 February 1611, "Información de la soltería de Juan Luís, Francisco López, mulato," Iguala.

15. AGN, Inquisición 310, expediente 3, folios 87–105, 3 April 1611, "Denuncia."

forces in the world. For a brief time, it was one of the dominant centers of sugar production in the Americas.[16] But even as African slave labor dominated, Indians, Spaniards, and free blacks filled important roles on Morelos's plantations.

In Mexico City, Juan Rodríguez's statements about the rural laborer Juan Luís turned the attention of the proceedings to an errant soul who in the eyes of the gathering was a thief and a rootless free black. In the proceedings that followed the *denuncia*, Juan Luís and his exploits appear memorable to blacks (both slave and free), Spaniards, and Indians alike. In its infinite confidence, the tribunal took its time. It was not until 1614, three years after Father Rangel's formal denunciation in Mexico City, that officials sent a letter to its local representative in Tasco requesting a formal statement from Juan Rodríguez, Father Rangel's source. They also sent a letter to the commissary of Tepoztlán, where Juan Luís had married the first time, asking him to verify the marriage. With dogged determination, not speed, the tribunal pursued the allegations against an obscure free black man. Then the proceedings came to an abrupt halt. Although the effect of the testimony was not conclusive, it nonetheless highlights the circuit of rumor and gossip among plantation workers and rural folk.[17]

In 1614, three years after he mentioned Juan Luis's marriage to Father Rangel in a conversation, Juan Rodríguez, the Portuguese steward (*majordomo*) of Nochipan, was summoned by the commissary of the Holy Office in his area. Juan Rodríguez at first said he was not aware that someone he knew had done something wrong by Christian standards. In an era when the term "Portuguese" was synonymous with "Jew," the summons may have made Juan Rodríguez anxious.

16. Cheryl English Martin, *Rural Society in Colonial Morelos* (Albuquerque: University of New Mexico Press, 1985). In the scholarly literature, the "sugar revolution" is rarely associated with seventeenth-century Morelos. As Stuart Schwartz notes, "Forms of divided ownership and management such as sharecropping, a continual mix of free and slave labor, the use of local indigenous workers or even indentured Europeans, and a relatively unregimented work regime that used personalized quotas all had existed in various early plantation regimes. Thus authors have tended to exclude these precursor sugar economies within the framework of the sugar revolution"; *Tropical Bablyons: Sugar and the Making of the Atlantic World, 1450–1680* (Chapel Hill: The University of North Carolina Press, 2004), 7. In relying on idealized types of slave production in places such as Barbados, Jamaica, and Haiti, we lose site of the scale of slavery in other locations that would allow us to situate the plantation complex of Morelos in the framework of the sugar revolution and understand how New Spain functioned as a slave society. Such analysis is important: The dispersed nature of the slavery of New Spain's plantation complex makes it difficult for us to see the viceroyalty for the slave society that it was. Comparative figures provide us with the necessary perspective. We know that Brazil, with its African labor force of 50,000, "dominated sugar production in the Western world by 1600"; Herbert S. Klein, *African Slavery in Latin America and the Caribbean* (New York: Oxford University Press, 1986), 40. During this same period, New Spain received thousands of *bozales*, who complemented a slave population that totaled 20,000 in 1570. In the initial decades of the seventeenth century, the combination of new arrivals from Africa and the surviving slave population briefly placed New Spain in competition with Brazil and Peru as the center of New World slavery.

17. AGN, Inquisición 310, expediente 3, folios 87–118, 1615, "Proceso contra Juan Luís, mulato libre que se ha criado en el ingenio, de los padres de Santo Domingo por casado dos veces."

At first the officials asked leading questions without mentioning any names. When the commissary raised specific concerns about Juan Luís, Juan Rodríguez probably sighed with relief. Rodríguez acknowledged that he had employed Juan Luís for six years. When the "tall but slender" free mulatto fell ill, however, Juan Rodríguez had expelled him from the estate.

Two years after he had fired Juan Luís, Juan Rodríguez saw him in the pueblo of Iguala guarding cattle and he learned in conversation with Anton Martín, a resident of Tasco, that Juan Luís had recently taken a wife. This information aroused Juan Rodríguez's suspicion, since he knew from conversations with Alonso Gil, the steward of another estate near Tlaticapan and another former employer of Juan Luís, that the free mulatto was already married.[18] One week after Juan Rodríguez gave his statement, the commissary followed up on this lead and asked Antón Martín for a formal declaration. Antón recalled that Juan Luís was slender and "not very dark; almost light brown." He had last seen Juan Luís in a prison in Iguala, allegedly "for having stolen a steer." Afterward, some cowboys (*vaqueros*) had told Antón that Juan Luís and his wife had headed toward the south seacoast (*costa del mar del sur*). Antón mentioned others who could offer information about Juan Luís, but the commissary never questioned them.[19]

The commissary of Tepoztlán, Father Bernardino de Roxas, did not answer the letter of inquiry from the tribunal for several months. He apologized to his superiors in Mexico City, explaining that he had had difficulty locating both the first wife and the wedding register, since the marriage had taken place on a *hacienda* (an estate that raised livestock or cultivated agriculture). But he had found witnesses who could confirm the marriage. Fr. Tomás San Jacinto, a lay brother of the Dominican order, knew Juan Luís and provided the backstory to the events just before Juan Luís's second marriage and some details about his early life. Juan Luís had been exposed to the Catholic worldview from birth; Fr. Tomás said that he had been born a free mulatto on Quavistla, a *hacienda* of the Dominican order in Cuautla de Amilpas. For seven years, Juan Luís had worked and traveled with Fr. Tomás. In 1611, however, Juan Luís had left the Dominican estate for the *estancia* of Nichiapan in the *marquesado del valle* in the jurisdiction of Cuernavaca.

He had not left on good terms. Juan Luís had stolen an animal from the hacienda and Fr. Tomás had pursued him. While in pursuit, Fr. Tomás had learned that a woman was with Juan Luís. He told the tribunal that when he asked others about Juan Luís's whereabouts, they told him that "the said mulatto had been there with an Indian woman and in order to marry her sought out a nearby cleric."

18. AGN, Inquisición 310, expediente 3, folios 87–118, 17 November 1614, "Información de Juan Rodríguez."
19. AGN, Inquisición 310, expediente 3, folios 87–118, 26 November 1614, "Información de Antón Martín."

When Fr. Tomás finally caught up with Juan Luís, the couple had already married. Fr. Tomás knew this marriage was a sinful act. "In the time that I began to know and interact with the said Juan Luís . . . I saw that he had an Indian wife . . . and with her Juan Luís had a married life, drinking and eating together . . . near the said hacienda."[20]

Fr. Tomás was not alone in this understanding of Juan Luís's marital situation. In 1615, María de la Cruz, a 24-year-old free mulatto who knew Juan Luís, was asked for her recollections of him. She said that she had "talked and interacted with [Juan Luís] many times" and had been "together [with him] on the said hacienda." She knew Juan Luís as a married man. Until the *aguacil* had arrested Juan Luís, she had seen Juan and his first wife having "a married life together in one house." María had heard that Juan Luís had fled for the "coast having married another Indian woman."[21] Melchor, a 50-year-old slave who lived on the Dominican hacienda, had known Juan Luís as a child. As a teen, recalled Melchor, Juan Luís had worked as a domestic. In that capacity, he had met and married Ana María. Evidently Juan Luís and Ana María had moved several times, since Melchor identified three separate locations—the household of Luís de Trueba, the *estancia* of Chinameca, and the village of Ticoman—where he had interacted with the couple. In Ticoman, Melchor and Juan Luís had in fact shared a prison cell one time. After that, Melchor had lost contact with Juan Luís but had "heard from some cowboys" that he had married again.[22]

Francisco Domínguez, a 35-year-old free mulatto, also gave a statement in 1615. He had also known Juan Luís "since he was born." Francisco acknowledged that Juan Luís had married Mariana (another name for Ana María), an Indian from the pueblo of Talticapan. He identified Pedro, a black slave on a nearby hacienda, and his wife Cecilia as the couple's *padrinos*. But then, "five years ago more or less," Juan Luís had fled. With Juan Luís's departure, the lifelong acquaintances had lost touch. But rumors and gossip kept Juan Luís's memory alive. Francisco said: "I was told by Gaspar, the mulatto, and the mulatto Juan . . . cowboys on a cattle hacienda that Juan Luís was in the service of a cleric of Iguala." The cowboys also told him that Juan Luís had taken a second wife.[23]

In the absence of a marriage register that could offer proof that Juan Luís had previously contracted a marriage, Tepoztlán's commissary presented the testimony

20. AGN, Inquisición 310, expediente 3, folios 87–118, 16 March 1615, "Información de Fr. Tomás San Jacinto."

21. AGN, Inquisición 310, expediente 3, folios 87–118, 16 March 1615, "Información de María de la Cruz."

22. AGN, Inquisición 310, expediente 3, folios 87–118, 17 March 1615, "Información de Melchor."

23. AGN, Inquisición 310, expediente 3, folios 87–118, 17 March 1615, "Información de Francisco Domínguez."

of Ana María, the alleged first wife. "I am a native of Tlatiçapan in the jurisdiction of the *marquesado del valle* in the *barrio* of Teniche," began Ana María. When the commissary had asked if her if she was married, Ana María had said yes. She identified Juan Luís, the free mulatto born on the Quauistlan (Quavistla) estate, as her husband. Ana María told how a Dominican father had presided over the wedding on the Quauistlan estate. Afterward, the couple had lived in the pueblo of Amenecuilco, adjacent to the hacienda. They subsequently moved and entered the service of a new employer, but then her husband had left for Achiutla, where he had found employment with an Indian noble (*indio principal*). "He never returned [to me]," said Ana María. After a constable (*alguacil*) arrested Juan Luís in the pueblo of Amenecuilco, she saw him again and brought him food and a little money. Yet Juan Luís had fled, abandoning Ana María for a second time. She learned from the steward, Alonso Gil, that Juan Luís had married again. Ana María also said that she had heard from an Indian woman named Ana that Juana Agustína, Juan Luís's second wife, was a native of Teojila in the jurisdiction of Cuernavaca in the pueblo of Iguala.[24] The record of the case comes to an abrupt end at the conclusion of Ana's testimony.

Even in this incomplete form, the proceedings reveal much about life in the countryside. Juan Luís worked on plantations or on behalf of their owners. Because he was a free person, his life was not limited to a single estate. Juan Luís grew up on and then worked on an estate owned by the Dominican order, but he and Ana María lived in a house that was separate from his employers' domain. Juan Luís was mobile; he changed employers, lived in a variety of pueblos, and eventually completely absconded from his life. Through all his moves, Juan Luís maintained contact with individuals who had known him as a boy, as a co-worker, as a married man, and ultimately as a fugitive. Some witnesses were even acquainted with his father, a *bozal* from the Caçanga caste. Those who intimated that they knew Juan Luís well observed that his identity was rather ambiguous. The witnesses noted how "he was raised among Indians," which explained why he was not fluent in Spanish and perhaps why both wives were Indians. But his intimate acquaintances were largely persons of African descent, especially free mulattos like himself. The bigamy proceedings outline a rural community composed of free blacks, Indians, and black slaves, an impression reinforced from the information the Holy Office gathered from individuals who were known to have interacted with Juan Luís. Juan Luís's familiars testified at the tribunal about hearsay and gossip that outlines the contours of a community. In glimpsing the terrain of this community, we do not see Villamanrique's rootless *vagos*.

Viceroy Villamanrique saw "free Africans and mulattos" as being "only ca-

24. AGN, Inquisición 310, expediente 3, folios 87–118, 17 March 1615, "Información de Ana María."

pable of living as vagabonds, robbing and causing violence." It is true that Juan Luís was a thief. He allegedly stole livestock. Maybe a fierce sense of justice persuaded him to view the animals as compensation for his toil or maybe he was just a thief. Even as a thief, however, he shared in the surrounding cultural norms. He requested the sanctity of matrimony, even when that decision defined him as a bigamist. Rather than focus on Juan Luís's illicit behavior—the theft of cattle and his second marriage—let us examine the formalities that led to his bigamist marriage. Here we see the cultural acumen of a rural free mulatto who had been "raised among Indians" and reputedly spoke only limited Spanish.

Clearly, Christian proceedings—including the formal request, the presentation of witnesses, the marshaling of matrimonial godparents, the enactment of the sacrament, and the saying of mass—were carefully observed. The church required as much, but Juan Luís willingly obliged, even going to some lengths to do so. Even in a remote recess of this colonial slave society, the formalities of marriage involving free blacks, slaves, and Indians were the norm, and he and Juana Agustína had traveled from their village, which did not have a notary, to find a church authority so they could follow proper Catholic procedures for their marriage. These are not the actions of rootless and atomized individuals. Even under the duress of incarceration Juan Luís insisted on partaking in the sacrament of matrimony. Perhaps his illness brought the afterlife into relief; if that was so, it would reveal how Christianity pervaded his imagination. He clearly was not under the illusion that matrimony would offer a reprieve from jail. He married, thus becoming a bigamist, and eventually fled from jail and the Inquisition. One might say that such actions flaunted the authority of the church. In the final analysis, though, these actions attest to Juan Luís's acumen as a believer and a member of a deeply rooted local community.

Juan Luís's mobility was far from exceptional. In New Spain, countless individuals traversed the countryside in search of opportunities. For the most part, they moved within defined spheres that offered work and companionship. Blacks were no exception. When allegations of bigamy compounded the charges of theft against him, Juan opted to flee with his new wife from the territorial boundaries of his youth. Juan and Juana left the familiar landscape for the southern seacoast— then and now a frontier region on the Pacific coast where the presence of the state (previously the colonial and now the Mexican state) approached its limits. In journeying to the coast, the couple left the enforceable jurisdiction of the colonial state and thus resembled absconding slaves who opted for the life of a maroon or runaway slave (*cimarron*) in the least accessible regions of New Spain. Only then did Juan perhaps resemble Villamanrique's *vagos*.

*   *   *

Most rural blacks moved in the familiar world of family members and longtime acquaintances. In the early decades of the seventeenth century, the grasp of the church was so extensive and the world beyond the frontier so ominous that few non-Indians were willing to risk complete separation from the familiarity of the Spanish orbit. The scope and persistence of the ecclesiastical and Inquisition proceedings underscores the rigor with which the Catholic Church (and therefore the colonial state) policed colonial subjects. It was difficult, though not impossible, for individuals to step beyond the known world. In the case that follows we shall see how the free mulatto Ana María fled from her employer, from her husband, and from *depósito* (female custody). Yet the pull of the familiar always drew her back. Work, of course, shaped the patterns of mobility for free blacks, but the quest for personal liberty also determined people's movement within and beyond the orbit of the familiar.

In the middle of March 1617, some of the inhabitants of El Fresnillo, a mining town of northern New Spain, were in a stir. Ana María, a free mulatto who lived in their town, had orchestrated a dramatic escape from *depósito* after years of waiting for proceedings against her to end. She and her Indian companion, Francisco Lucas, had then returned to El Fresnillo. Ana María was a woman that people talked about. More than a decade after she first entered El Fresnillo unescorted, the light-complexioned free mulatto with a solid body and medium stature was still providing the pueblo's inhabitants with steady conversational fare.[25] Single and in her early teens when she first arrived in El Fresnillo's restricted social universe, Ana María, variously known as María or Mariana, was also the subject of speculation and gossip in San Luís Potosí, where she had lived with her first husband. Such chatter was a danger for Ana María, since the clergy and inquisitors were constantly listening for stories of illicit behavior.

A mere five days after Ana María and her companion arrived in El Fresnillo in 1617, the vicar summoned her neighbors to testify. They observed that Ana María acted rather normal.[26] Some individuals expressed surprise at the couple's reappearance; they believed that the authorities had apprehended the couple, or at least Ana María. When she encountered the couple in Gracía Hernández's house, María de Garay, a free mulatto, pointedly asked who had accompanied her on her journey to El Fresnillo. María, like the other tenants, was assuming that colonial officials were responsible for Ana María's return. Gracía Hernández, a 50-year-old free black woman, was quite explicit: "I asked, and Ana María told me that

25. AGN, Inquisición 310, expediente 5e, folios 232–258, 29 March 1618, "Ratificación de Esteban Venegas, escribano público de estas minas," El Fresnillo; AGN, Inquisición 310, expediente 5e, folios 232–258, 29 May 1618, "Ratificación de Juan, negro esclavo," El Fresnillo; AGN, Inquisición 310, expediente 5e, folios 232–258, 29 March 1618, "Ratificación de Gracía Rodríguez, negra libre," El Fresnillo.
26. AGN, Inquisición 310, expediente 5e, folios 232–258, 15 March 1617, "Información de Catalina Cecilia, india, Proceso contra Ana Maria, por casada dos veces."

'her own husband the said Lucas . . . and no other person had brought her to the mines.'" This was quite a surprise. Three years earlier, Agustín Rodríguez Pulido had come to El Fresnillo claiming Ana María as his legitimate wife. For this reason and because the couple was living in her house, Gracía insisted on knowing the truth. "He [Lucas] is my husband," replied Ana María, "since the other one [is] now dead."[27] Ana María stressed the legality of her relationship with Lucas as the explanation for why "they had returned on their own."[28]

For the ecclesiastical authorities, though, the legality of Ana María's marriage was not clear. Days after she returned to El Fresnillo with a second husband, the vicar acted on the testimony Gracía Hernández, María de Garay, and Catalina Cecilia had offered. In a brief to the royal constable, he said that María had fled from *depósito* and "now has returned to these mines in a bad state (*mal estado*) with the same indio Lucas." He wanted help from the constable "in apprehending and placing her in the public jail (*cárcel publica*) of these mines . . . until the end of the proceedings (*la cabeza del proceso*)."[29]

Despite Ana María's insistence that her relationship with Lucas was legitimate, ecclesiastical officials saw matters differently. A year after Ana María returned to El Fresnillo with Francisco Lucas, her marital affairs caught the attention of the Inquisition in the person of its commissary, Fray López Izquierdo.[30] For Ana María, this was a potentially grave turn of events. Unfortunately for us, the proceedings came to an abrupt end and we do not know the end of Ana María's story.

References to patron-client relations and work are embedded in the proceedings—at one time Ana María was employed as a servant in a convoy that provisioned the northern mines of El Charcas, and after that she served as a cook for El Fresnillo's miners. The proceedings also delineate the ecclesiastical jurisdiction and the labyrinth of Christian obligations that the Catholic Church carefully cultivated. But it was social dynamics that made the proceedings possible, and focusing on these dynamics in Ana María's proceedings brings a moral economy of obligations and rights into relief.

After Ana María was arrested, the ecclesiastical judge moved forward with the initial interrogation. Ecclesiastical authorities structured the proceedings in a man-

---

27. AGN, Inquisición 310, expediente 5e, folios 232–258, 15 March 1617, "Información de Gracía de Hernández, negra, Proceso contra Ana Maria."

28. AGN, Inquisición 310, expediente 5e, folios 232–258, 15 March 1617, "Información de María de Garay, Proceso contra Ana Maria, por casada dos veces."

29. AGN, Inquisición 310, expediente 5e, folios 232–258, 15 March 1617, "Información de Testigos contra María, mulata, hecha a petición del licenciado Juan Verdugo," El Fresnillo.

30. AGN, Inquisición 310, expediente 5e, folios 232–258, "Carta del Comisario Fr. López Izquierdo," 28 March 1618, Zacatecas; AGN, Inquisción 310, expediente 5e, folios 232–258, "Certificación de Juan Verdugo," 29 March 1618, El Fresnillo; AGN, Inquisción 310, expediente 5e, folios 232–258, 2 April 1618, "Certificación de Fr. Juan Larios, Secretario de la Provincia de San Francisco de Zacatecas," Zacatecas.

ner that sanctioned only orthodox behavior and Christian identities. Propelled by the accusation and testimony of witnesses, the interrogation (*confesión*), aimed at eliciting the truth. The word *confesión* underscores the confessional nature of the laity's encounter with the clergy.

"I am called Ana María," declared the free mulatto. Like most inhabitants of New Spain, Ana María was uncertain about her age. As was the custom, the scribe recorded his estimate of her age; he noted that she appeared to be "more than thirty years old." Ana María also said that she served "Juan Pantoja and was married to Francisco Lucas the Indian." After these biographical formalities, the ecclesiastical prosecutor launched into a series of questions related to the allegations against her. Since Agustín Rodríguez Pulido had previously claimed Ana María as his wife, ecclesiastical officials had placed her in *depósito* until they could arrive at the truth. Ana María's escape after several years in custody raised the specter of guilt. The authorities placed her in *depósito* again.

"Were you *depositada* in the house of the public scribe, Juan Venegas, by order of the vicar?" began the prosecutor. "I was *depositada*," responded Ana María, "for it was claimed and is claimed that a Franciscan friar in the convent of El Agua de El Veneda married me and Agustín Pulido." Ana María then recounted how she had "fled from *depósito*" with the assistance of a quadroon (*morisco*) called Agustín, who took her to the "estancia of Santiago," where Lucas joined her. Curious as to why she had returned to El Fresnillo, the prosecutor asked a series of questions: "Who brought you to these mines and with whom did you come, did you arrive with or were brought by Juan Pantoja?" "My husband brought me to these mines," replied Ana María.

She also stated that her employer Juan Pantoja had sent Pedro Hurtado with a message two days after they arrived at Gracía Hernández's house. Pedro told her that Juan Pantoja was in possession of "some papers" from a priest that resolved "her case." When Ana María and Lucas went to Juan Pantoja's house to get the papers, Pantoja asked Ana María to go his mines to cook for the resident Indian laborers.[31] Ana María insisted that Juan Pantoja had declared that "I am free and for this reason I went to the mine where the *alguacil mayor* found me." The prosecutor explicitly asked Ana María "if the vicar had notified her . . . not to be with Lucas, indio, until it was investigated if he was or wasn't her legitimate husband." "It is true," responded Ana María, who acknowledged that she "had been notified by the vicar of the *auto*." Ana María said that from that point she had avoided Lucas until she learned from her employer Juan Pantojo "that Agustín Pulido was dead." "For this reason," Ana concluded "I came with my husband, Lucas."[32]

31. AGN, Inquisción 310, expediente 5e, folios 232–258, 15 March 1617, "Confesión de Ana María, mulata, presa en la carcel publica," Minas de El Fresnillo.
32. Ibid.

Ana María's testimony—framed by the *provisor's* questions—focused almost exclusively on her escape from *depósito* and her subsequent decision to return to El Fresnillo with Francisco Lucas. The implicit question throughout the inquiry was "If you were innocent, why did you flee?" For the *provisor,* Ana María's behavior underscored the likelihood of guilt. Perhaps she acted guilty because she was guilty. But determining guilt was only one dimension of the *confesión.* Ana María's behavior was not in conformance with that of a pious Christian. By escaping during the proceedings, Ana María violated the church's spiritual authority. The *provisor* framed Ana María's *confesión* around her flight from *depósito* and the decision to reunite with Francisco Lucas. Had the vicar "notified her . . . not to be with Lucas?" asked the *provisor.* Of course he knew the answer. In posing this rhetorical question, the *provisor* reminded Ana María of her obligations as a Christian.

The objective of this *confesión* was only partially about the truth. The greater emphasis was on the church's ability to assert its authority. In the context of the confession, it mattered very little that the charges of Ana María's first husband, Agustín Rodriguez Pulido, were, in the words of her second husband, Francisco Lucas, "sinister" and resulted in his wife being "held like a slave the entire time . . . without being paid any stipend."[33] Though they were scrupulous in their attention to due process, the ecclesiastical authorities' primary concern was Ana María's obedience to the church after she fled *depósito* and then returned in a "bad state" with Francisco Lucas.

The "confessional moment" aside, the inquisition's purview included bigamy, and eventually the clergy directed their attention to the specific allegations of the case. Fray López Izquierdo, the commissary of the inquisition, was instrumental in this turn. He wanted to know if Ana María was a bigamist. In trying to discern the truth of the matter, he consolidated evidence that drew on the testimony of Ana María's employers, housemates, and alleged husbands.[34] The testimony underscores the ambiguity that informed the allegations against Ana María.

Agustín Rodríguez Pulido was, in fact, not dead. Asked if he knew why he had been called to testify, Agustín replied that he assumed that it related to the marriage he had contracted with Mariana. Then the 30-some-year-old *mestizo* and lifelong resident of San Luís Potosí began narrating his version of events.[35] While

33. AGN, Inquisición 310, expediente 5e, folios 232–258, 24 January 1617, "Instancia de Francisco Lucas, indio, ante el Licenciado Juan de Ortega," Zacatecas.
34. AGN, Inquisición 310, expediente 5e, folios 232–258, 20 December 1617, "Auto del Comisario del Santo Oficio en Zacatecas para que Hernando Hurtado de Mendoza, vicario de San Luís Potosí, le entregue todos los autos, recaudos y papeles en el caso de Mariana, mulata, para proceder jurídicamente," San Luís Potosí; AGN, Inquisición 310, expediente 5e, folios 232–258, 28 March 1618, "Carta del Comisario Fr. López Izquierdo," Zacatecas; AGN, Inquisición 310, expediente 5e, folios 232–258, 29 March 1618, "Certificación de Juan Verdugo," El Fresnillo; AGN, Inquisición 310, expediente 5e, folios 232–258, 2 April 1618, "Certificación de Fr. Juan Larios, Secretario de la Provincia de San Francisco de Zacatecas," Zacatecas.
35. AGN, Inquisición 310, expediente 5e, folios 232–258, 21 December 1617, "Información de Agustín Rodríguez Pulido," Pueblos de San Luís, minas de Potosí.

in the service of Baltasar Hernández "sixteen or seventeen years ago," around 1600, he had escorted a pack train and supply convoy to the silver mines of las Charcas. Among the servants accompanying the caravan was a mulatto named Mariana who "was then 10 or 12 years old." Near the pueblo of El Agua de El Venedo, Baltasar Hernández "found us in a bed together in one of the carts." As Baltasar scolded the couple, Agustín and Ana María responded that "we are like husband and wife because we want to marry." Baltasar suggested that they go to "the *padre* . . . of this pueblo" and escorted the couple to the convent of San Francisco. Baltasar Hernández initially spoke to the friar, who then asked Agustín and Mariana about their marital intentions. "We both said yes," claimed Agustín. Father Bernardino wanted assurances from Baltasar Hernández that "we were single." Agustín recalled how "without additional proceedings, warning (*amonestación*) or an *información,*" the friar "married us in the *portería* (doors of the chapel)" and said that on another trip he would veil them. After this truncated ceremony, the wedding party returned to the caravan and subsequently to San Luís Potosí, where the couple lived as husband and wife for the next two months. When Baltasar Hernández began preparations for another trip to "the said mines of las Charcas," Mariana refused to go, despite Agustín's desire "to be veiled." Mariana absconded, and Agustín left with the caravan. When Agustín returned, Mariana was living and working "in the house of the miner Juan de Zavala." Though Agustín "tried making a life" with Mariana, she declined, saying that she had not been married of "her own will" but had been forced. Mariana then said that in El Agua de El Veneda she had consented "out of fear of the said Baltasar Hernández since she did not want to be mistreated." Agustín and Mariana approached the resident vicar and *provisor,* Father Juan de Ortega, for advice. Agustín recounted how Father Ortega questioned them about the wedding formalities and declared that "as residents of this pueblo Father Bernardino should not have married you." Then Father Ortega announced that "the marriage is not valid, nor are you married and each one of you ought to marry where God assists you." Agustín said that soon after that, Mariana left San Luís Potosí for "*la tierra adentro*"—a vernacular reference to the provinces. Agustín remarked, "I heard it said that she resided in El Fresnillo and there she was married . . . [to] some Indian."

Years later, Agustín harbored doubts about Father Ortega's declaration. All this was expressed verbally, recalled Agustín, "without [Father Ortega] writing anything." But Agustín had recently consulted with the pueblo's current vicar, Father Hernando Hurtado, and obtained a written confirmation declaring the marriage void. "I am a free man," Agustín said and ended his testimony by reiterating that he "was not subject to matrimony."[36] In his testimony, Agustín appears resigned to his fate and ultimately relieved. But his actions were not entirely consistent. We

36. AGN, Inquisición 310, expediente 5e, folios 232–258, 21 December 1617, "Ratificación de Agustín Rodríguez Pulido," San Luís Potosí.

must ask what possessed Agustín to reenter Ana María's life in El Fresnillo nearly two decades after she had left San Luís Potosí and insist publicly that she was still his wife. The doubts Agustín harbored about the legality of Juan de Ortega's pronouncement surfaced far too late to be entirely credible. Why did he not pursue the matter at the moment when Father Ortega ruled that the wedding ceremony was not binding? Perhaps Agustín's doubts grew over time, possibly sparked by an event, a conversation, or a confessional experience.

Interestingly enough, Agustín had not taken another wife in the intervening years. Clearly, he harbored some resentment toward Ana María that explains his public claims in El Fresnillo. But when asked about the wedding of Agustín and Ana María and the couple's parting of ways in San Luís Potosí, neither Baltasar Hernández nor his wife, Juana Rodríguez, referred to Agustín's wounded honor. "Agustin Rodríguez has not married," testified Baltasar, though he had remained "in this pueblo, in the valley and in other parts." Baltasar spoke with certainty because he had known Agustín "for more than 20 years" and had employed him for over a decade.[37] Juana Rodríguez had known Agustín Rodríguez over twenty-five years, "for he was raised in her house." "He is single," declared Juana, noting that Agustín had "never left this jurisdiction."[38] Implicit in this testimony was an assertion of familiarity that was almost parental; the couple was signifying to the ecclesiastical authorities that Agustín was not a troublemaker. If Agustín harbored shame or simmering malice, Juana and Baltasar would have known about it. According to the Spaniards Baltasar Hernández and Juana Rodríguez, after María, as they called her, returned to San Luís Potosí, she approached Father Juan de Ortega and said that she "did not wish to ratify the marriage." Agustín evidently offered no opposition. He did not press Father Juan to uphold his masculine honor by legitimizing the marriage and according him a married life (*vida maridable*). In the final analysis, Ana María's will prevailed.

The testimony Agustín Rodríguez Pulido, Baltasar Hernández, and Juana Rodríguez offered underscores that by the age of ten or twelve, Ana María had acquired a developed sense of Christian duties and rights that she readily deployed. When she was discovered "in a bed together" with a man in El Agua de El Venedo, the young girl had said that she wanted to marry him. But back in San Luís Potosí, Ana María renounced her decision because she had been motivated "out of fear." Ana María knew that her will could not legitimately be thwarted even though she was still a young child. And she was more interested in exercising her right to freely choose a partner than she was in entering a marriage that would put right

37. AGN, Inquisición 310, expediente 5e, folios 232–258, 9 October 1617, "Información de Baltasar Hernández," San Luís Potosí.

38. AGN, Inquisición 310, expediente 5e, folios 232–258, 9 October 1617, "Información de Juana Rodríguez," San Luís Potosí.

her premarital sexual activity in the eyes of the church. The resourceful young Ana María secured new employment with Juan de Zavala and solicited adjudication about the legality of the recent ceremony. When did this "ten or twelve year old" learn about free will? How did Ana María learn of the existence of her will and the rights that it bestowed upon her? How did this young free mulatto who lived in the rural environment of New Spain's northern frontier acquire the understanding that exercising her free will would bring liberty from the bondage of an undesired marriage? Answers to these questions are elusive. But a plausible response suggests that Ana María's awareness of her rights originated in the workings of moral regulation. As the clergy taught individuals about obedience, they were also providing information about the existence of free will. The proceedings offer a glimpse of the formalities that blacks as Catholic subjects had to learn, in the process conveying a sense of their juridical identities as Christians. Ana María had learned that she had a Christian will that was hers alone to exercise. And from childhood she reserved the right to live by her free will even when she experienced intense pressure from employers and other authorities to do otherwise.

The proceedings of Ana María's case also present invaluable but fragmentary insights on the rural black experience. For instance, how, when, and why did Gracía Hernández—identified as the "slave who belonged to Alonso Hernández Talavera"—acquire her freedom? Why did this freed black woman not elect to begin a new life? One scribe noted that she appeared to be more than fifty and another described her as about age seventy; did her age play a role? Did she share enduring ties with her former owners, who had the same surname of Hernández? What significance should we attach to the fact that Gracía owned a house in El Fresnillo and took in lodgers? Could this property explain her decision to remain at the site of her enslavement? The cameo appearances of the free mulatto María de Garay and the slave Juan invite similar questions.

As the subject of the proceedings, Ana María's silhouette emerges most clearly. Indeed, Ana María's life experiences are quite notable and possibly quite typical for a free black woman. At the age of "ten or twelve," she secured employment with a Spaniard who provisioned the farthest reaches of New Spain's northern frontier. In 1600, the mining region of Charcas, actually located in the kingdom of Nueva Galicia, constituted the *chichimeca* (Indian) frontier, thus making the trek and work perilous. In the northern frontier, Spanish householders, miners, and merchants drew on an assortment of slaves, free persons, blacks, and hispanized Indians to meet chronic labor shortages—a situation that favored workers in search of optimal opportunities. Employers welcomed labor, which explains why Ana María shifted seamlessly from employer to employer. In the course of the proceedings, ecclesiastical officials associated Ana María with four employers: Baltasar Hernández, Juan de Zavala, Juan de Pantoja, and Pedro Hurtado. According to Ana María's legitimate spouse, a fifth—Esteban Venegas—should be added, since "the entire time (in *depósito*) he held her like a slave."[39] In El Fresnillo's labor-starved economy, the public scribe was quite willing to avail himself of Ana María's labor.

The search for work often generated mobility for New Spain's free blacks. But it was Ana María's desire for personal autonomy that prompted her to migrate from San Luís Potosí, the site of her first marriage. The record is silent on where she went afterward and with whom. Ana María eventually made El Fresnillo home. There she married Francisco Lucas. She was connected with other people in El Fresnillo as well. Juan, a 60-year-old black slave, said he had known Ana María in Zacatecas prior to her arrival in El Fresnillo, although he did not know about her origins. The same was true for Gracía Hernández, the 70-year-old freedwoman. She had known Ana María prior to her marriage with Francisco Lucas but did not know where she had been born. As core members of Ana María's community, both of these longtime black residents of El Fresnillo served as the couple's godparents (*padrinos*). "I always saw them together enjoying a married life (*vida maridable*)," observed Juan, professing how "I always have treated them as my godchildren (*ahijados*)."[40] Gracía Hernández also affected the role of godmother by offering the fugitives Ana María and Francisco Lucas shelter when they returned to San Luís Potosí.[41] So while work and the desire for autonomy channeled movement, some individuals developed real and symbolic ties to their new homes, especially through Christian rituals such as matrimony and godparenthood.

Bondage in seventeenth-century New Spain varied considerably from later forms of bondage in the New World. For instance, Melchor and Juan Luís demonstrated considerable personal autonomy as they defied the standard characterization of slaves and slavery.[42] Their social practices—their close-knit social ties, their mobility, and their navigation of Christian traditions—contributed to a process that steadily impacted the nature of slavery and freedom. The difference in the nature of slavery and freedom in New Spain and throughout Spanish America owes much to Christianity, which played a profound role in shaping the experiences of blacks.

Context occupies a privileged place among the fragments of rural black life

39. AGN, Inquisición 310, expediente 5e, folios 232–258, 24 January 1617, "Instancia de Francisco Lucas, indio ante el Licenciado Juan de Ortega," Zacatecas.

40. AGN, Inquisición 310, expediente 5e, folios 232–258, 29 May 1618, "Información de Juan, negro esclavo," El Fresnillo.

41. AGN, Inquisición 310, expediente 5e, folios 232–258, 15 March 1617, "Información de Gracía Hernández, negra," El Fresnillo; AGN, Inquisición 310, expediente 5e, folios 232–258, 9 May 1617, "Información de Gracía Hernández, negra libre," El Fresnillo.

42. AGN, Inquisición 310, expediente 3, folios 87–118, 16 March 1615, "Información de Melchor, negro esclavo del convento y monas de Santa Inés de México," Cuautla de las Amilpas; AGN, Inquisición 310, expediente 5e, folios 232–258, 20 May 1617, "Información de Juan . . . esclavo de Diego de Salazar," Las minas de El Fresnillo.

we see in the Inquisition proceedings. Historical anthropologists Jean and John Comaroff define context as "the wider world of power and meaning," "totalities," and "a historically determinate environment."[43] These are the elements that generate the fragments and frame the stories we see in this chapter. Spanish authority constituted one context, which overlapped with another context defined by the Christian moral order. We need to speak of contexts in the plural.

Even as we piece the fragments of black life into a narrative, the institutional process is what emerges most clearly. But the stories that emerge are not about coffles and gangs of nameless slaves or the romantic typology of rebels and *cimarrones*. The fragments give names to rural free blacks and show us episodes in their lives. They are no longer nameless, anonymous, or unknown historical figures. Francisco Lucas, Ana María's husband, captured the entangled nature of context when he noted how Ana María's employer Juan Venegas "treated her as a slave" by refusing to "pay her any stipend."[44] In voicing his frustration about Ana María's lengthy incarceration, Francisco underscored that she—though she was an offspring of slaves—was not chattel. Ana María was his wife. Although Francisco did not question the legitimacy of placing Ana María in *depósito,* he took issue with the length of her custody and the manner in which Juan Venegas tapped her labor. In this instance, Francisco Lucas expressed his views on freedom: Freedom, like slavery, constituted more than a juridical status. Freedom acquired its form and content in relationship to mastery over one's use of the body and that of one's dependents—one's wife and children. But for the church authorities, Ana María was a suspect. Irrespective of her slave heritage and status as one of Villamanrique's "pernicious free . . . mulattos," in the eyes of the clergy and the inquisitors Ana María constituted a potentially errant Christian. The regulation of morality by Christian authorities reminds us that neither slavery—as a means to organize power and labor—nor freedom—as a juridical status—fully encapsulated the meaning of "contexts."[45]

*   *   *

Let us remain with the inquisition proceedings against Ana María Hernández but also return to the free mulatto Francisco de Casteñeda, whom we introduced in chapter 1. By juxtaposing the two cases we learn that Francisco de Casteñeda and Ana María navigated similar sites, San Luís Potosí and Zacatecas, at the same time.

43. Comaroff and Comaroff, *Ethnography and the Historical Imagination*, 17.
44. AGN, Inquisición 310, expediente 5e, folios 232–258, 24 January 1617, "Instancia de Francisco Lucas, indio," Zacatecas.
45. Comaroff and Comaroff, *Ethnography and the Historical Imagination,* 9.

In making this observation I do not imply—nor can I document—that Francisco and Ana María were members of the same black community. As I illustrated earlier and will demonstrate in subsequent chapters, the black community was a decidedly local phenomenon embodied in specific relations. As historian James Sidbury observed about eighteenth-century Virginia, "the concrete ties of kinship and friendship that enslaved people created" had more valence at the local level than "the abstract and imposed quality of racial similarity."[46] To assume connections or participation in an imagined black community would not be consistent with the nuanced meaning that free mulattos Francisco de Casteñeda and Ana María Hernández attributed to the respective ties they maintained. Instead, by juxtaposing these proceedings, I point to convergences that reveal an even bigger and mobile rural black presence than is signified by the specifics of a particular Inquisition case. The composite, in the absence of a household or a colonial census, facilitates a broader perspective on black life without diminishing the salience of context.

Francisco de Casteñeda, as we recall, came to the inquisition's attention in 1609 with the confession that he had married a second time.[47] A mulatto and possibly the legitimate offspring (*hijo legitimo*) of the Spaniard Juan de Casteñeda and the free mulatto Elena de la Torre, Francisco was born and raised in the parental home in Mexico. In his initial "confession" (*primera audiencia*), Francisco acknowledged several siblings: an older brother who assumed their father's name, Juan de Casteñeda (which Francisco, in turn, bestowed on his eldest and surviving son); another older brother, a cowboy (*vaquero*) named Diego de Casteñeda, who married a mulatto with whom he had three children; and finally, their 28-year-old sister Mariana de la Niebes, who was married and lived in Zacatecas with her mulatto spouse Bernabe de Santa Clara.[48] In referring to his siblings and their offspring, Francisco did more than offer his family structure to the inquisitors. He underscored the growth of the free black population, whose numbers surpassed the number of enslaved Africans in the first half of the seventeenth century. Social reproduction was central to this process, and here Francisco's mother was a key figure.

As the mother of four children—Juan de Castañeda, Diego de Castañeda, Mariana de la Niebes, and Francisco de Castañeda—the free mulatto Elena de la Torre was a seventeenth-century matriarch of the Afro-Mexican population. Although her Spanish husband Juan de Castañeda represented the head of house-

46. Sidbury, *Ploughshares into Swords*, 15.
47. AGN, Inquisición 470, folios 309–363, 1609, "Proceso contra Francisco de Casteñeda, mulato libre, sastre, natural de la Ciudad de México, por casado dos veces," Mexico.
48. AGN, Inquisición 470, 1609, folios 309–363, "Primera Audiencia, Saturday, Jan. 16, 1610."

hold and family patriarchy, Elena's racial and maternal status trumped the Spanish identity of her husband in a society where hypergamy prevailed.

Aside from documenting Francisco de Casteñeda's extensive family ties, the proceedings highlight the workings of the labor market that structured the experiences of blacks. At the age of eleven, Francisco de Castañeda left home for San Luís Potosí, where he remained for four years with the tailor Juan Rodríguez. Afterward he departed for Zacatecas, but not before returning to Mexico and initiating a marriage with María de la Cruz. Following his stay in Zacatecas, he traveled to Queretaro and Texcoco before he returned to Mexico City. As we see in the case of Francisco de Castañeda but also in the cases of Ana María, Juan Luís, Ana Romero, Lorenza de la Cruz, Diego de Soza, Juan de la Cruz, and Nicólas de la Cruz (to name just a few), the mobility of free blacks had comparable effects to those James Sidbury described for eighteenth-century Virginia's slave population. Sidbury observed how even though slave communities were disrupted by forces they could not control in the second half of the eighteenth century, "blacks . . . control[led] the way they made sense of their changing world." These actions enabled slave communities "to expand geographically and then ideologically to include all Virginians of African descent."[49]

Sidbury, of course, focused on slaves and the ways they were used in eighteenth-century Virginia while I am referring to seventeenth-century free blacks in New Spain who moved about for distinct reasons and with considerably more latitude. Individuals drew on formative relations as they found employment and established recreational ties. But as the stories of Francisco de Castañeda, Juan Luís, and Ana María illustrate, they also forged new relationships, not just with local communities of slaves and free blacks but also with Indians and Spaniards. The core community that was established around the household of Francisco's parents was augmented by Francisco's travels to San Luís Potosí, Zacatecas, and Queretaro. When he returned to Mexico City as an adult, he married María de la Cruz and drew on the patriarchal status of his father to engage a series of Spanish patrons who attended and anchored his marriage. When he moved to Queretaro, he forged new ties. But the requirements of a Christian marriage demanded that he draw on long-standing ties with individuals he knew from Mexico City. Francisco's mobility underscores the existence of distinct pockets of black communities. When he established a relationship with his wife, Gerónima de la Cruz, he connected with blacks—both slave and free—in Queretaro, extending the geography of his ties to individual slaves and free blacks. In Queretaro, for instance, he forged ties to specific persons of African descent, including the free black Juan Pasqual; his god-

49. Sidbury, *Ploughshares into Swords*, 29.

parents, Pasqual de Salazar and his wife María de Serrano, who were free blacks; Mariana de la Concepción and Juan Rodriguez, who were slaves; and Melchora de los Reyes, an eighteen-year-old free mulatto who was the sister of his wife. These ties were local and specific, but in the context of colonialism social connections defined by race also traveled.

*   *   *

Christian discipline, as the proceedings suggest, was a firmly established reality in the first half of the seventeenth century. Christianity even regulated black life, as it did all colonial life, into the hereafter. By bestowing a Christian life and identity that persisted into the realm of death, Catholicism was a more pervasive social force in the experience of New Spain's black residents than slavery and legislated freedom. Through and within the contours of Christianity, black folk mediated key cultural forms, including community formation. Christian matrimony and its associated requirements—consent or free will, the *información matrimonial* and required sponsors, the Church-sanctioned sacrament, marital godparents, *vida maridable,* and monogamous indissoluble union—expressed this phenomenon mostly clearly. Blacks in the countryside, allegedly the least regulated population of African descent, were subject to ecclesiastical and Inquisition discipline when they failed to abide by Christian norms. Blacks, of course, steadily pushed against the boundaries of Christian orthodoxy in an effort to craft lives and social ties meaningful to them. But Christian discipline demonstrated an all-encompassing malleability that tempered the possibility that one could truly transcend its reach. Blackness, as manifest in New Spain, never truly embodied a complete form of otherness, since its genesis resided within Christianity.

FIVE

Local Blackness

In Mexico City on 6 March 1674, the free mulatto María de San Diego appeared before the ecclesiastical judge (*provisor*) intent on opposing the marriage of Manuel Figueroa and Manuela Ortiz. The announcement of the couple's banns (*amonestaciones*) compelled María to act, and her motivation was strictly personal. "In virtue of the promise of marriage," lamented María, "Manuel Figueroa took my virginity and today he is trying to marry Manuela Ortiz." María then insisted that Manuel honor his promise to her. When the *provisor* ordered Manuel Figueroa's arrest, Manuel expressed surprise. Though he conceded that they had had consensual sex Manuel denied that María was at that time a virgin or that he had promised to marry her. Such claims, he asserted are "sinister and against the truth."[1]

In the contest of words among near-whites and nonwhites, the truth would be determined by María's public decorum—a woman of virtue always acted and lived within the boundaries of virtue. For this reason, the *provisor* drew on the testimony of friends and neighbors. "He is my nephew," said Josefa de la Parada, a 40-year-old *castiza* and native of Mexico, when asked why she had known Manuel "since infancy." Her acquaintance with María was far more recent. "Two years ago María informed me that my nephew had had her virginity under the word of marriage," recalled Josepha, "but when I asked him, my nephew answered that it was false." Magdalena de los Santos, a 25-year-old free mulatto widow, had known both Manuel and María only a short while, yet recounted how "on different occasions" the latter revealed that "Manuel took her virginity under the promise of marriage." Next, the free mulatto and tanner Juan Jacinto spoke. The eighteen-year-old native of Mexico had interacted with Manuel and María frequently over the course of six years. In describing a defining moment, Juan Jacinto recalled how "about a

1. AGN, Matrimonios, Sin Referencia (estaba con un bloque de documentos de la seccion de matrimonios), 1674.

year ago while talking to Manuel in a corner of the tanner's neighborhood María de San Diego passed by and called Manuel de Figueroa and I went with him until he connected with her, when he told me to leave I did. . . . They remained at a door speaking intimately. I did not know what happened between them but heard María de San Diego say on different occasions that Manuel de Figueroa, under the promise of marriage, had taken her virginity."

Following the assertions and counter-claims, both Manuel and María responded. Manuel questioned the testimony of the Juan Jacinto and Magdalena de los Santos. "The witnesses," observed Manuel, "say what she [María] has said." María, in turn, requested the dismissal of Josefa's testimony on grounds that she was Manuel's aunt. Two months after the start of the proceedings, Manuel—though still incarcerated—pressed for his license to marry Manuela Ortiz, insisting that "they [the witnesses] are not able to prove anything." Evidently, the *provisor* concurred. He ordered Manuel released and granted him a license to marry Manuela Ortiz. In the absence of an explanation, we may assume that the testimony convinced the *provisor* that María was less than virtuous.

What are we to make of a seventeenth-century drama in which an aggrieved free mulatto alleged that she had surrendered her virginity to a male suitor under the promise of marriage? The fact that a young black woman could legitimately stake such a claim in the contours of a rapacious colonial slave society in which all women constituted objects of unbridled desire speaks to María's Christian consciousness. Christianity made possible María's understanding of her self and her body. She conceived of herself as possessing virtue, which was literally embodied in her virginity. María also possessed a will that allowed her—not her parents—to decide that Manuel was the man to whom she would surrender her virtue, with the promise of marriage. A scribe, of course, wrote down María's request to prevent Manuel and Manuela's marriage, thereby imposing a generic convention on the language of the document. But the contents of the tale reflected the testimony of the speaker. The speaker, María, was aware of the setting, audience, and structure that her story needed to assume.

María clearly miscalculated Manuel's character and intent. Having taken her virginity (or at least enjoyed illicit love, *amistad ilicita*), Manuel took refuge in a racial ideology that denied mulatto women a virtuous life. Still, the *provisor* initially upheld María's claim.[2] On the assumption that María had been a virgin when Manuel had sex with her, the *provisor* had Manuel arrested to prevent his disappearance. In his search for truth the *provisor* did not preclude the possibility that a mulatto woman could be a virgin. For the *provisor* and the Catholic Church, the

2. For similar claims in the second half of the seventeenth century, see AGN, Matrimonios 19, expediente 4, folio 109, 1673; AGN, Matrimonios 37, expediente 1, "Instancia de Josefa de Sámano," 31 May 1688.

central issue was whether María de San Diego had been a maiden (*doncella*) at the time of her initial sexual encounter with Manuel. The *provisor* decided that the answer was "no."

In New World studies of race and slavery, scholars of black women rarely depict experiences beyond their dual roles as laborers and reproducers. Reproduction, of course, necessitated sex. In light of the existing racial ideology that marked the black woman's bodies as signifiers of difference, excess, and access, coercion rather than consent framed the engagement with sex and sexuality.[3] Yet María de San Diego made and embodied a set of claims that defied the conventional tropes of laboring women. She maintained that she had been chaste until a proper suitor made a contractually binding promise to her; María remained a virgin until Manuel de Figueroa pledged marriage. Manuel would later question María's chastity, but he had to contend with the Christian ideology that made it possible for her to stake claims as a virgin. But to claim the status of a virgin required more than chaste behavior. A virgin was also the offspring of a legitimately married couple. María was, in fact, the legitimate daughter (*hija legitima*) of a married couple. In the social landscape where most persons of African descent still carried the label of illegitimates known as "natural children" (*hijos naturales*), children of unknown parentage (*hijos de padres no conocidos*), or orphan (*huerphano*), María was the legally recognized daughter of Sebastian Flores and Micaela de San Jeronimo. While historian Patricia Seed has observed that "the words 'mulatto' and 'mestizo' were synonymous through the seventeenth century with illegitimate birth,"[4] María, a mulatto, did not fit the conventional stereotype.

A perspective that accounts for demographic stability and Christian matrimony among blacks and mulattos who in turn sired legitimate children offers a more appropriate starting point for understanding María's life experiences and those of countless other black virgins. As creole births and survivals increased over the course of the seventeenth century, an ever-larger number of manumitted slaves and free-born women anchored the growth of the free population. Indeed, the concept of *hijo legitimo* is intimately linked to the growth of the free black and mulatto population. While the Catholic Church sanctioned and defended the slave's right to a *vida maridable*, ecclesiastical officials did not protect a legitimately married slave couple's right to raise their offspring. In this respect, the master's property rights triumphed over the Church's willingness to protect slave families. A *vida maridable* did not shield a *hijo legitimo* against the master's civil claims. For this reason and those associated with the sexual accessibility of the slave woman, the concept of *hijo legitimo* was not widely manifest among enslaved Africans and

3. Morgan, *Laboring Women*, 12–49.
4. Patricia Seed, *To Love, Honor and Obey in Colonial Mexico*, 146.

the initial generations of creoles. But demographic stability among creoles and the expansion of the free population fostered growing numbers of legitimate children among blacks and mulattos. As a symptom of changing demographic and social realities, the presence of legitimate children raises the following questions: How did the relative structural stability of mulatto families, of which the concept of *hijo legitimo* was merely one form, produce a new configuration of the self among the growing mulatto population? To what extent did legally sanctioned marriages among mulattos produce competing formulations of mulatto identity? Did, for instance, such designations as *doncella, huerphano, hijo natural, hijo de padre no conocido,* or *hijo legitimo* matter beyond the watchful eyes of the cleric? If so, in what ways? Such questions cannot be adequately addressed for the late seventeenth century, but the frequency with which blacks and mulattos pursued Christian marriages and the growing number of their children, who were identified as legitimate offspring, requires us to rethink how best to examine the existence of private lives in the second half of the seventeenth century.

In defying the racial characterization that equated "mulatto" with "vagrant" and "bastard," María exhibited a Christian kinship identity and family structure that was increasingly prevalent among mulattos of this time period. A legitimate child was associated explicitly with a Christian kinship identity and family structure and implicitly with the culture of honor and virtue. Yet structural similarities and ideology obscure differences in content and practice. In the church's idealized view, María's mother Micaela de San Jeronimo would have instructed her in the ways of a respectable virgin (*doncella*)—a form of virtue in which Sebastian Flores as *paterfamilias* would have shielded his daughter from predators and vile gossip so as to uphold his and his family's honor. But María strayed. When she surrendered her virginity to Manuel under the promise of marriage—if we are to believe María's claim—she acted within Christian norms and the prevailing code of honor.[5] Claims to legitimacy and virginity constituted an important feature of Spanish America's discursive landscape that, as we shall see, the descendants of Africans routinely invoked in the eighteenth century. We must locate the origin of these claims for this population in the second half of the seventeenth century, when creoles and mulattos began to make such claims regularly. In so doing, they underscored the demographic stability that had come to characterize that population.

Before attending to the forms of demographic stability creoles and mulattos exhibited, we should note that María de San Diego identified herself as a *hija legitima* and a virgin in 1674—a year that approached the midpoint of the middle colonial period (1640–1750), an era that scholarship on Spanish America has long

5. Twinam, *Public Lives, Private Secrets,* 36.

characterized as static. The frequency with which black creoles and mulattos used kinship terms, expressed legitimate birth status, and made claims to propriety as virgins and honorable men belies the notion of cultural stasis. In essence, these cultural forms support the speculative yet pioneering claims of cultural anthropologists Sidney Mintz and Richard Price, who assert that "fully formed African-American cultures developed within the earliest years of settlement in many New World colonies." Mintz and Price acknowledge that documenting these claims "involves genuine difficulties" that "stem from the general shortage of descriptive materials on slave life during the initial period."[6] The archival material in this chapter provides the "descriptive materials" Mintz and Price sought about the lives of slaves and free persons. Their conjecture is correct.

* * *

In the introduction to his remarkable study of Andean cultural history, *Idolatry and Its Enemies: Colonial Andean Religion and Extirpation, 1640–1750*, Kenneth Mills commented on the historiographical gap that characterizes the period from the second half of the seventeenth century to the middle of the eighteenth century. "The mid-colonial period has been neglected by scholars, and not only in the study of colonial religion," wrote Mills, who noted that "only relatively recently have writers identified open fields of inquiry in between the much-investigated era of the military conquest and its aftermath, on the one hand, and the period of the late colonial rebellions and the eventual Spanish defeat, on the other."[7] Given the centrality of the viceroyalty in Peru, the importance of religion there, and the paradigmatic nature of the Indian presence in colonial history, such neglect comes as a surprise. But for the African past in Peru and colonial Spanish America in general, the near-total absence of studies on this period constitutes something far more troubling than a lack of historiography. At the simplest level, the dearth represents a form of epistemological exorcism akin to social death.

Creating the historical absence of the African past was more than a passive process. It constitutes a decidedly active phenomenon whose roots lie in the colonial elites' racialist sense of order—a notion of order that also informed their framing of the past—that lingers in the present in the way modern historians write colonial historiography.[8] Melville Herskovits, the cultural anthropologist and pio-

6. Mintz and Price, *The Birth of African-American Culture*, 48.
7. Kenneth Mills, *Idolatry and Its Enemies: Colonial Andean Religion and Extirpation, 1640–1750* (Princeton, N.J.: Princeton University Press, 1997), 12.
8. Aline Helg displays an awareness of how modern historians have appropriated the historical form and content of colonial elites. See Aline Helg, *Our Rightful Share: The Afro-Cuban Struggle for Equality, 1886–1912* (Chapel Hill: University of North Carolina Press, 1995), 16–20. In a later work, she wrote, "Undoubtedly, the two-century-old tradition of presenting Colombia as a mestizo nation

neering researcher of Africans and their New World descendants, framed much of his prolific career against this practice of epistemological exorcism that sent the African in the Americas as "a man without a past."[9] Herskovits understood the political valence embedded in an ideology that suggests that a people are without history: It "validates the concept of Negro inferiority." Identifying the ideological practice as "one of the principal supports of race prejudice in this country," Herskovits claimed that the process of erasure remained "unrecognized in its efficacy" and pointed out that "it rationalizes discrimination in everyday contact between Negroes and whites, influences the shaping of policy where Negroes are concerned, and affects the trends of research by scholars whose theoretical approach, methods, and systems of thought presented to students are in harmony with it."[10]

In Spanish America, racial stereotypes compound the practice of historical neglect. Aline Helg wrote that "Andean Colombians have tended to racialize the image of their Caribbean fellow citizens, whom they commonly have described as mulattos. Until the 1970s, Andean writers and authors of textbooks often ascribed to *costeños* the contradictory psychosocial traits imputed to mulattos by pseudoscientific racism: lazy but at the same time active, brave but irresponsible, fun-loving, promiscuous, and noisy."[11] Helg's observation complimented the formidable challenge that the Latin American Subaltern Studies Group leveled against the body of Latin American scholarship. "Latin American subaltern studies," wrote one of the group's founders, Ileana Rodríguez, "aims to be a radical critique of elite cultures, of liberal bourgeois, and modern epistemologies and projects, and of their different propositions regarding representation of the subaltern."[12] The sentiments expressed in this intellectual manifesto—still a largely unfulfilled promise—inform what follows.

By focusing on persons of African descent in the middle colonial period—a

has greatly contributed to black Colombians invisibility," noting that "the Andean dominant discourse of *mestizaje,* which ultimately aims at whitening of the population and the disappearance of 'full' blacks and Indians, has severely restricted the ways in which Afro-Colombians can express their distinctiveness without excluding themselves from the nation. It has incited them to minimize their racial identity and the role of racial exclusion in national formation." Helg, *Liberty & Equality in Caribbean Colombia,* 3. Anthropologist Peter Wade has underscored the way that contemporary scholars continue to neglect the study of blacks: "The study of blacks in Colombia, despite the seminal efforts of a few dedicated researchers, is neglected relative to the ethnohistorical and anthropological study of the Indian population." Peter Wade, *Blackness and Race Mixture: The Dynamics of Racial Identity in Colombia* (Baltimore: John Hopkins University Press, 1993), 3.

9. Herskovits, *The Myth of the Negro Past,* 2.
10. Herskovits, *The Myth of the Negro Past,* 1.
11. Helg, *Liberty and Equality in Caribbean Colombia,* 4.
12. Ileana Rodríguez, ed., *The Latin American Subaltern Studies Reader* (Durham, N.C.: Duke University Press, 2001), 6.

period associated with the ascendancy of the caste society (*sociedad de castas*)—I privilege the cluster of narratives in which ecclesiastical and inquisitorial sources recorded words that illustrate what the prevailing black social and cultural practices were. I acknowledge the weight in word and deed of the dominant political and social historical discourses but elect to focus on the behavior and consciousness of persons of African descent.[13] In so doing, I am conscious of eliding the reigning narrative of the colonial past. This cannot be avoided, however, since the premise of that history—then and still today—rests on questioning the historical agency, if not the humanity, of persons of African descent.[14] For instance, the complete absence of a description and discussion of black domestic arrangements, by which I mean family structure, kinship terms and practices, and existing norms, magnifies how scholars frame and thereby question the existence of agency among Africans and their descendants. Aside from being the objects of power and the subjects of resistance, blacks seem to be, if they appear at all, detached from the social universe defined by friends and family.

The Problem of Recognition

Simply put, black and mulatto family formation has not been an issue of concern to colonial Spanish American scholars. Scholars who invoke the black family—usually by talking about marriage patterns—address matrimony as an index of *mestizaje*, a process of cultural and biological fusion whereby the category of *casta* subsumes the variety of black identities (*bozal, ladino, negro criollo, mulato, pardo,* and *coyote*).[15] For the most part, scholars view matrimony alone as the way to

13. "There was one Indian battle that Britain never won," writes Ranajit Guha, a founding member of the Subaltern Studies Group. "It was a battle for appropriation of the Indian past." Despite the radically different relationship between British rule in India and Spanish colonial rule, this variant of South Asian historiography offers conceptual promise to scholars of the New World black experiences. Ranajit Guha, *Dominance without Hegemony: History and Power in Colonial India* (Cambridge, Mass.: Harvard University Press, 1997), 1.

14. In voicing these concerns, I share the problem space of the Latin American Subaltern Studies Group. Ileana Rodríguez identifies their political project as "producing scholarship to demonstrate that in the failure to recognize the poor as active social, political, and heuristic agents reside the limits and thresholds of our present hermeneutical and political condition. . . . We were also dissatisfied with the realization that the poor had not been recorded in a history of their own, but rather had been subsumed in a narrative which was not exactly their own." Rodríguez, *The Latin American Subaltern Studies Reader*, 3. But it seems quite puzzling that race as it applies to persons of African descent remains rooted in the conventional cultural area of what Marvin Harris called the "Plantation Heritage." In other words, studying and writing about blacks remains restricted to such canonical plantation societies like Cuba, Brazil, and Haiti and is temporally confined to the eighteenth and nineteenth centuries. Marvin Harris, *Patterns of Race in the Americas* (New York: Walker and Co., 1964), 44.

15. The important exceptions tend to emerge in social histories of slavery but rarely in studies of racial formation. For the latter, see Cope, *The Limits of Racial Domination*. Examples of the former include Edgar F. Love, "Marriage Patterns of Persons of African Descent in a Colonial Mexico

discern social mobility and the nature of social stratification.[16] Cognizant of the incompleteness of this level of analysis, anthropologist Raymond T. Smith noted in relationship to the West Indian family that "it is surprising to find that little attempt has been made to pay close attention to the ideas, the concepts, of the people being studied." Smith observed that "the emphasis has been on the 'objective' data gathering (using predetermined categories) or on the premature interpretation of behaviour as motivated by rational self-interest in which subjective factors are mere secondary rationalizations."[17] Contemporary knowledge production and social science assumptions about the Afro-Mexican experience have appropriated the lens of the colonialists, conceiving of all blacks as *castas* who constituted the social order's gravest problem. Colonialists' concerns have nowadays become scholarly problems.[18] Commenting on this discursive tradition in the study of Caribbean kinship, Smith observed that "anthropological assumptions are the product, partially at least, of the ideology of colonial society itself, being close to the historically generated myths of the dominant groups."[19]

At best, what we have is the shadow of the reality of black domesticity that slave trade demographics and black marriage patterns reveal. Beyond this silhouette we know very little about the shape, content, and texture of the black presence. Aggregate numbers of Middle Passage survivors and their distribution through space have yet to be followed by "more detailed inquiry into the background" of Africans or that of their descendants.[20] In the social universe of historians, as in

City Parish," *Hispanic American Historical Review* 51, no. 1 (1971): 79–91; Palmer, *Slaves of the White God*; Bowser, *The African Slave in Colonial Peru*; and Christine Hünefeldt, *Paying the Price of Freedom: Family and Labor among Lima's Slaves, 1800–1854* (Berkeley: University of California Press, 1994).

16. Magnus Mörner, *Race Mixture in the History of Latin America* (Boston: Little, Brown and Co., 1967); Seed, *To Love, Honor, and Obey in Colonial Mexico*.

17. Raymond T. Smith, *Kinship and Class in the West Indies: A Genealogical Study of Jamaica and Guyana* (New York: Cambridge University Press, 1988), 28.

18. "Perhaps the elite commentators," hypothesized Douglas Cope, "in their disgust at the plebeians' miscegenation and lack of república, exaggerated the unity of the plebe." Cope, *The Limits of Racial Domination*, 49. Patricia Seed notes: "Intense antagonism and vicious resistance to interracial marriages characterized oppositions to interracial marriage for the duration of the century." In the guise of a scholarly problem, the race-class-caste debate merely reproduces the elites' anxieties. As Seed discerned, "Historians who have noted this increase have in general believed that the increase in intermarriage failed to erode the boundaries between racial groups, in particular the critical distinctions between the Spaniards and the castas, or persons of mixed racial origin." But then Seed herself reproduces the process of appropriation by concluding that "a careful examination of the patterns of interracial marriage and change in prenuptial disputes suggests that this was not the case." Seed, *To Love, Honor, and Obey in Colonial Mexico*, 146–147.

19. Smith, *Kinship and Class in the West Indies*, 5.

20. Klein, *African Slavery in Latin America and the Caribbean*; David Eltis, Stephen D. Behrendt, David Richardson, and Herbert S. Klein, eds., *The Trans-Atlantic Slave Trade*.

that of colonialists, the term "black presence" is a shorthand that rarely represents actual substance.

But it is not accurate to claim that an entity called the autonomous black family existed.[21] The specific nature of racial formation in New Spain tempered the development of the autonomous black subject and limited the possibility that a black family could exist as a discrete social entity.[22] Even among enslaved Angolans in the first half of the seventeenth century who mostly married other Angolans, we must acknowledge that 28 percent elected spouses with a different ethnic or racial designation. Angolans manifested a similar pattern in the process of sponsor selection. Despite the alleged fact that slavery elicited black cohesiveness, the African family was a momentary apparition rather than a socially reproducible structure. The prevailing expressions of blackness were decidedly generational and territorially specific. As we have seen, Africans established families whose structure resembled that of the families their creole offspring would form but whose cultural focus varied. Even among creoles, family forms and practices varied. At no moment were creoles able to forge a completely autonomous black existence.[23] For this reason, this narrative privileges brief glimpses of black families and their internal dynamics. It does not neglect the domestic arrangements that New Spain's other racial groupings made with persons of African descent. Such ties, as a number of scholars have pointed out, were increasingly common in the late colonial period.[24] But I am intent on depicting blacks as agents even in interracial unions.

21. The nationalist romance with compulsive heteronormativity explains why the "family" has long been a foundational trope of black letters. Such imperatives informed the concerns of the black "public sphere" and the field of Afro-American studies from its inception. See Stuckey, *Slave Culture*; Carla L. Peterson, *"Doers of the Word": African-American Women Speakers & Writers in the North (1830–1880)* (New York: Oxford University Press, 1995); and Robert F. Reid-Pharr, *Conjugal Union: The Body, the House, and the Black American* (New York: Oxford University Press, 1999). The convergence of family and nation also explains why the former, then and now, figures so prominently in the works of nationalists and the study of creolization. "The discussion of West Indian kinship had been dominated either by the cultural survival theories of M. J. Herskovits . . . or by a concern with social disorganization. . . . The same concepts dominated discussion of North American black communities," remarked Raymond T. Smith, who noted that "this debate has not diminished in intensity, nor have its terms ceased to intrude themselves into discussions driven by other theoretical concerns, but the focus of attention since the 1950s has been upon creole social forms—a focus produced by the happy conjunction of structural functional theory and the drive for national self-determination." Smith, *Kinship and Class in the West Indies*, 178.

22. The insights and caution of Cope are still essential. See *The Limits of Racial Domination*, 49–105.

23. Aline Helg persuasively argues that there is no overarching racial consciousness in the Caribbean Colombia. Despite racial sentiments and the crisis of independence, it is not accurate to group *pardos, zambos,* and *negros* as a unified racial group. Individuals in these ethnic and racial groupings manifested complex identities as people of African descent. Helg, *Liberty and Equality in Caribbean Colombia*, 149, 187, 200, 211, 212–213.

24. Seed, *To Love, Honor, and Obey in Colonial Mexico*, 146–147.

In electing to do so, my study differs from the more general body of scholarship others in which blacks often appear as passive objects of the colonial social order or as social climbers. In forming families—black or interracial—Africans and creoles, slave and free exercised agency. It is important to understand the range of possibilities in which individuals made choices. Reproducing blackness, no matter how fleeting, was one of several possibilities. Most blacks and mulattos selected persons similarly identified as spouses (see tables 2.3 and 2.4).

From the earliest days of New Spain, cultural forces such as ethnicity among Africans competed with social dynamics such as the discipline of slaves to shape the social order. From this perspective, *mestizaje* reflected the social dynamics in which creole culture was ensnared rather than a conscious striving for social mobility. Stated simply, the 72 percent of Angolans who elected to marry other Angolans could more easily have selected spouses with different racial and ethnic identities. But they did not. In the end, the motives of the majority of Angolans mattered insofar as they caution us against simply viewing their choices through the lens of race relations. The stakes over the competing vantage points—the cultural dynamics among people that Spaniards defined as similar as against social processes among elites and chattel—are rather high. "We must not only observe what people do," Raymond T. Smith insists, "but also understand what they intended their action to be." Cautious about assigning causality, Smith remarked that "this creates more problems since one must now determine the meaning as well as the exterior form of behaviour. Weber was most insistent that this did not involve psychological analysis to find out what each particular individual thinks he is up to. Instead, we must find ways to study systems of concepts . . . and the way in which they become embodied in behaviour."[25] That is precisely the analytical task the historical evidence from the ecclesiastical archives presents. At stake is our ability to see the Angolans and successive generations of black creoles on their own terms. Current scholarship still fails to recognize the variety and depth of urban black culture in New Spain.

The problem of failing to see blacks clearly remains decidedly acute in the scholarship about New Spain. Many scholars of New Spain's urban centers reduce all free blacks to "plebeians" or "*castas,*" overlooking the many nuances of racial identity among urban Africans, blacks, and mulattos. Scholars invariably turn to legislation, occupational status, residence, and marital practices in their efforts to understand the social structure of the mid- to late colonial period, generally overlooking family structure and domestic arrangements. These approaches are lim-

25. Smith, *Kinship and Class in the West Indies*, 22.

ited; they neglect forms of agency embedded in such fragmented documentation in the form of marriage petitions and Inquisition records that rarely lend themselves to a coherent narrative that links individuals in the different proceedings to each other or to a specific place and time. Similarly, if scholars begin with a focus on the presence or absence of social mobility among blacks, their methodological perspective also limits what conclusions can be reached. "The ordering of urban well-being and degradation," remarks historian Steve Stern in reference to late colonial Mexico, "fail[s] to line up clearly with ethnoracial rank or labeling."[26] The sources that have survived that were generated by middling and elite Spaniards will not be much help in our quest to understand the complexities of what Stern calls "ethnoracial rank" in New Spain's cities; for Spaniards, the world was a limited bichromatic palette of "Spaniard" and "not Spaniard." The rich spectrum of color, status, race, and ethnicity in which African-descended people lived and moved was invisible or, even worse, inconsequential to Spanish colonizers.

In rural areas a distinct pattern emerged. Stern identified the market as the source of this difference. Scholars have acknowledged that in rural areas peasants and ethnic Indians could resist or engage with the market on their terms; Stern has argued out that they could not do so in urban centers. The same analysis prevails in histories of slaves in urban colonial Latin America.[27] I would argue, however, that we need to envision the existence of a "reconstituted" urban ethnicity. In other words, we need to imagine an ethnicity that does not have roots in land, self-governance, and language. In lieu of such institutions, we may find urban ethnicity grounded in religious brotherhoods, the militia, communal autonomy, spouse and sponsor selection, and local ties.[28] The problem, therefore, may not reside with the archive but with our theoretical orientations and intellectual priorities—a problem of recognition.

26. Steve J. Stern, *The Secret History of Gender: Women, Men, & Power in Late Colonial Mexico* (Chapel Hill: University of North Carolina Press, 1995), 36.

27. For reasons related to the problem of authenticity, the earlier scholarly generation did not see urban areas as sites of ethnicity and ethnic organization in the New World. Melville Herskovits, for instance, was steadfastly reluctant to see urban inhabitants as contributors, mediators, or conveyors of ethnicity in the black New World. See Richard Price and Sally Price, *The Roots of Roots: or, How Afro-American Anthropology Got Its Start* (Chicago: Prickly Paradigm, 2003). Similar sentiments animated E. Franklin Frazier's formulation of cultural preservation in the United States; see Frazier, *The Negro Family in the United States*. Stephan Palmié challenges such views in *Wizards & Scientists*, as does Brown in *Santería Enthroned*. See also Reis, *Slave Rebellion in Brazil*; Reis, *Death Is a Festival*; Lyn Schumaker, *Africanizing Anthropology: Fieldwork, Networks, and the Making of Cultural Knowledge in Central Africa* (Durham, N.C.: Duke University Press, 2001); and Malkki, *Purity and Exile*.

28. Vinson III, *Bearing Arms for His Majesty*; Von Germeten, *Black Blood Brothers*.

Friends to Lovers

By the second half of the seventeenth century, creole networks that had been created around ties that dated back to childhood had emerged as sites of psychic comfort and conflict, cultural transmission and innovation. Most Africans lived in cities because most slaveholders lived in cities. In 1646, 41 percent of the black population lived in or adjacent to Mexico City.[29] By the first half of the seventeenth century, Mexico's ethnic Africans and their creole descendants had ventured beyond patrician households and parish boundaries to forge the social networks they wanted. During this period, Africans and creoles were highly selective about who they chose as their intimates. But after the ethnic presence waned, a new social logic began to inform family and community formation. For creoles—who were mobile and increasingly free—place of birth figured prominently in their choices.

After about 1650, black social networks began to coincide with the physical boundaries of neighborhoods. This pattern—manifest in the assertions made by thousands of potential brides, grooms, and marital sponsors—highlights the growth of and accompanying density of the creole population. Space became increasingly important, and the content of black cultural memory shifted from the geographical and linguistic symbols that characterized African ethnicity in the New World to localized symbols and referents. After 1650 or so, a smaller geographical scope shaped the choices creoles made regarding spouses and marital sponsors.

In this way, too, creole culture in New Spain was not static. By focusing on patterns of interaction—who knew whom, how long they had known each other, the symbolic importance individuals ascribed to their relationships with others, and the ways that familiarity affected spouse and sponsor selection—we bring into relief a history of rich and diverse creolization among people who were rooted in particular places.[30] Specific experiences and relationships created an emotional attachment to the street (*calle*), neighborhood (*vecindad*), parish (*parroquia*), and city (*villa*)—sites that constituted the little country (*patria chica*). This familiarity with space began with Africans and subsequent generations of creoles gave it increasing depth.

As creole adults gathered at work or during the course of their daily routine, their toddlers interacted. Later in life, the children met independently on patios, in the streets, or at their favorite spots. Early entrance into the work force limited

---

29. Aguirre Beltrán, *La población negra de Mexico,* 218–219.
30. Ida Altman, *Emigrants and Society: Extremadura and America in the Sixteenth Century* (Berkeley: University of California Press, 1989), 1, 3, 11.

their experience of adolescence, but boys and girls still enjoyed the company of peers (although this was especially difficult for girls, who often labored in isolation as domestics). Since boys invariably worked alongside members of their age cohort, it is likely that they worked with some of their friends. As they worked and played together, the children reinforced the cultural and symbolic ties that united their parents and eventually linked them together. Creole children established ties with other children through their parents' networks.

A marriage petition from 1672 reveals one of many such instances. In this case, the enslaved black creole Nicolás de Sande served as a character witness for the free mulatto Diego de los Reyes and the enslaved black creole Pascuala de los Reyes. Nicolás had known the prospective couple since he was thirteen. He was also familiar with María de la Cruz, Diego's mother, since they shared the same master. The age difference between Nicolás, Pascuala, and Diego implies that Nicolás was not a playmate of the prospective bride and groom, but time had mitigated the age discrepancy between them. A relationship that had been forged in Nicolás and María de la Cruz's shared workplace eventually became a long-standing friendship.[31]

The formative childhood ties of barrio children often constituted the core of their social networks as they became adults. Childhood friends became adult companions and *compadres*. Similarly, an individual's lover or spouse was usually well known to his or her family and friends, since many, if not most, had previously been playmates. For example in 1672, when the free mulattos Simón de los Santos and Margarita de Oñate requested a marriage license, Margarita's father, Juan de Oñate, served as their character witness. The enslaved mulatto stated that he had known Simón for ten years, although he did not elaborate on the nature of this relationship. One can surmise that Simón's parents Andrés de Andarade and María de la Encarnación were the point of connection. In 1662, they had left Guadalajara for Mexico City with their children. As the mulatto family settled into their new community, Juan de Oñate and his spouse, María de la Ascensión, welcomed them. A decade later, Simón and Margarita traced their interaction to this encounter.[32] A similar scenario informed the testimony of free mulatto Agustína Martínez. In 1680, Agustína appeared as a character witness for her sister, Juana de Torres, and Juana's fiancé, the free black creole Domingo de la Cruz. Domingo had known Agustína and Juana for fourteen years. In time, Domingo and Juana had moved from friends to lovers. The tie between the free mulattos Juan Francisco Zurita and Ana Francisca Ariocoda followed a similar pattern. Juan was nineteen and Anna sixteen when they requested a marriage license. The testimony of the

31. AGN, Matrimonios 29, expediente 6, folios 16–17, 1672.
32. AGN, Matrimonios 29, expediente 21, folios 48–49, 1672.

witnesses implied that the prospective bride and groom had known each other as children and later had become lovers.[33]

Some witnesses and couples had known each other since birth. In 1671, Pascual de los Reyes, a mulatto former slave, served as a marriage witness for Nicolasa de la Cruz and Juan de Medina. Pascual had known the two free mulattos "since they were infants." All three shared childhood experiences, and as adults they had maintained their friendship.[34] Juan de Díos, María de la Encarnación, and María de Molina had a similar history. Juan de Díos, a free mulatto, and María, an enslaved mulatto, presented the enslaved mulatto Teresa and the free mulatto María de Molina as character witnesses for their 1669 marriage. The witnesses had known the prospective bride and groom "since they were children." Based on their age, one can surmise that all four had been playmates who as adults were still friends, despite their differing legal statuses.[35] Individuals who shared a common legal status but were distinguished on the basis of their racial mixture also maintained childhood friendships. For example, the mulatto Blas de la Cruz, and two black creoles, Ana de la Encarnación and Manuel Antonio, were born into slavery. As adults, they maintained their childhood ties, forged in Mexico City's barrios, despite the differences in their racial classifications.[36]

A similar pattern linked black creoles (especially mulattos) and *mestizos*. In 1688, for example, the quadroon Dominga de la Concepción testified for the *mestiza* Ana de los Reyes and her prospective spouse, the free mulatto Antonio de los Santos. Dominga testified that the lovers had been acquainted "since childhood."[37] Similarly, Nicolás Ignacio Delgado, a *mestizo*, and the free mulatto Pascuala Francisca Zurita were childhood playmates who at the age of nineteen decided to formalize their relationship. In all likelihood, the mulatto affinity for *mestizo* spouses was rooted in residential proximity and a shared cultural heritage and ambiguous racial identity. Day-to-day contact in the context of lifelong interactions between mulattos and *mestizos* trumped potential sources of conflict.

The abundance of examples referring to lifelong interaction suggests that many (if not most) adults maintained contact with their childhood friends. In the course of the seventeenth century, creoles became more, not less, rooted. An examination of residential origins among black and mulatto spouses reveals that nearly 90 percent of the wedding parties—including the bride, the groom, and the matrimonial sponsors—shared the same birthplace, where they continued to live (see table 5.1). Even as freedom gave creoles greater mobility, they forged ever

33. AGN, Matrimonios 14, folios 377–378, 1680.
34. AGN, Matrimonios 24, expediente 29, folios 110–111, 1671.
35. AGN, Matrimonios 31, expediente 61, folios 248–249, 1669.
36. AGN, Matrimonios 31, expediente 52, folios 227–228, 1669.
37. AGN, Matrimonios 1, expediente 71, folios 332–333, 1688.

TABLE 5.1.

PLACE OF BIRTH OF AFRO-MEXICANS AND MARRIAGE WITNESSES AMONG COUPLES MARRIED IN MEXICO CITY, 1651–1750

Residential Origin	Number
Mexico	320
Puebla	7
Guatemala	3
Queretaro	2
Real de Minas Pachula	2
Tacuba	2
Tusentlapa	2
Zacatecas	2
Acambaro	1
Apizaro	1
Celaya	1
Cuango	1
Pasquaro	1
Pauthemala	1
Pueblo de la Piedad	1
Pueblo de Nuestra Senora de los Remedios	1
Real de Minas de Sombrerete	1
San Bernabe	1
Tacubaya	1
Tolvca	1
Veracruz	1
Unknown	5
Total	358

Source: Matrimonios Primera and Tercera Seria, AGN.

more exclusive ties. Space and intimacy reinforced each another. Although officials constantly complained that the viceregal capital was a city of migrants and transients, Mexico had a sedentary core; the children of the barrio often became that neighborhood's adults. By the second half of the seventeenth century, slavery's former territorial site made it possible for childhood networks to become the vehicle for creole courtships and friendships.[38] A culture that was born of dislocation had become localized.

38. The blending of space and intimacy characterized earlier creole marriages involving black or mulatto women who married Spanish males. In such instances, as we shall see, the woman worked and had been reared among Spaniards and as an adult maintained childhood connections to specific Spaniards. AGN, Matrimonios 26, expediente 11, folios 308–309, 1633; AGN, Matrimonios 28, expediente 73, folios 189–190, 1628; AGN, Matrimonios, 28, expediente 82, folios 242–243, 1628; AGN, Matrimonios 113, expediente 37, folio 95, 1629.

Local ties did not, however, translate into indiscriminate patterns of interaction with neighbors. Scholars have long ago identified the ways persons of African descent, especially creoles and the racially ambiguous mulattos, demonstrated discretion in the selection of *padrinos*. Such studies usually depict powerless individuals selecting patricians—specific masters, clergy, or powerful patrons—in order to protect their children, gain intermediaries in social relations, or facilitate access to work and land.[39] In this historiography, *padrino* selection is part of the formation of client-patron relations in a restricted social universe.

But a different logic informed who creoles chose as spouses and sponsors. The desire to establish ties with other creoles from an increasingly circumscribed geographical area underscores how blacks and mulattos refined their sphere of intimacy. Such practices delineate the silhouette of an interior space that often has been overshadowed by studies of work and power. Indeed, the best studies on the moral economy reveal how power and work—as the embodiment of the social structure—shaped and simultaneously were conditioned by these interior structures. Race relations, configured narrowly as upward social mobility, were not the only logic that guided creoles as they formed families and friendships. Though racial formation and community formation were connected, they never became synonymous. Creoles constituted themselves vis-à-vis Africans, Spaniards, and Indians. It is necessary then for us to unwrap the label *casta* instead of simply accepting it as the organizing principle a generic creole and mixed-race population. In the second half of the seventeenth century, creoles of African descent simply did not act as undifferentiated *castas*.

Community as Site of Conflict

In his insightful local study of eighteenth-century Richmond, historian James Sidbury wrote that "the peculiarities of each encounter cannot be re-created but the patterns . . . can be approached with more certainty." Sidbury observed that "it was out of encounters in specific times and places" that "enslaved Virginians came to define the boundaries of their communities and their collective identities."[40] Sidbury critiques the notion that blackness was a transcendent form of be-

---

39. Landers, *Black Society in Spanish Florida*, 107–156, esp. 118–129. Landers observed that vertical ties to godparents were central. Her conclusions differed from the patterns Schwartz and Gudeman identified for Brazil in "Cleansing Original Sin," 36–58; and Kathleen J. Higgins in *Licentious Liberty in a Brazilian Gold-Mining Region: Slavery, Gender and Social Control in Eighteenth-Century, Sabará, Minas Gerais* (University Park: Pennsylvania State University Press, 1999), 121–144, esp. 123. Landers identifies a greater emphasis on horizontal ties among marriage partners. Similarly, Cope notes that in the economy and in relation to work, *castas* relied on patricians. See Cope, *The Limits of Racial Domination*, 86–105, esp. 104. But the marriage patterns I have been discussing so far underscore a different pattern.

40. Sidbury, *Ploughshares into Swords*, 15.

ing; as the identity was formed, it took on many forms. The pattern he uncovered among the enslaved in the second half of eighteenth-century Virginia expressed itself in New Spain far earlier. Still, there are important differences in the two regions. Creoles in New Spain formed their social networks around friends and kin. This process tempered the "abstract and imposed quality of racial similarity" that characterized identity formation in all of the Americas. But specific ties did not preclude the existence of a collective black consciousness. In New Spain, blackness existed in and through specific and local ties with which individuals created community boundaries.

Conflicts about marriage formation in the second half of the seventeenth century bring the local manifestations of blackness in New Spain into stark relief. Such conflicts highlight the complex ways individuals established black social networks but simultaneously resisted the generic formulations of blackness. Blackness mattered, but it mattered in ways that were always specific. As the following cases illustrate, friends and family played a key role in the concrete ways blackness was expressed. In 1673, while in custody at the order of church officials, the free mulatto Josefa León petitioned ecclesiastical authorities to disregard the mulatto Gregorio Galindo's objection to her pending marriage to the Spaniard Ignacio Mexía. Josefa noted that Gregorio, as the *compadre* of Ignacio's mother, "had appeared maliciously before the royal judge where he voiced his impediment with the spirit of wanting to disrupt the said marriage." Josefa then stated that the authorities had placed her in *depósito* and sequestered Ignacio solely on the basis of Gregorio's statement. Now a month had passed, and though the impediment lacked merit Josepha was still in custody and unable to contract the marriage she wanted. Josefa asked the ecclesiastical judge to command the parish priest to honor the marriage license so that she could marry Ignacio.[41]

The presiding official requested proof that the couple had received a marriage license and inquired "if the *amonestaciones* (the banns) had elicited any impediments affecting the marriage." Prompted by the ecclesiastical judge, church officials located the license "in the Cathedral's marriage register for *negros, mulatos* and *mestizos,*" noting that the *provisor* (the ecclesiastical judge) had scribbled "there is an impediment" subsequent to granting the couple the license.[42] For this reason, responded a priest, "it [the marriage] did not proceed." On learning that Ignacio's mother had leveled an objection, Josepha insisted that the marriage take place since Isabel Gomez "his mother has not presented a verifiable impediment."[43] Following Josefa's accusation, the ecclesiastical judge ordered Ignacio's mother to

41. AGN, Matrimonios, tomo 19, expediente 4, folio 109, 1673, "Instancia de Josefa Leon."
42. AGN, Matrimonios, tomo 19, expediente 4, folio 109, 1673, "Auto del Provisor."
43. AGN, Matrimonios, tomo 19, expediente 4, folio 109, "Instancia de Josefa de Leon," 1673.

present her impediment. He instructed his staff to proceed with the marriage ceremony if she did not do so.

Isabel Gomez, a Spaniard, appeared promptly before the ecclesiastical authorities. She stated that her son, Ignacio, had already promised marriage ("*palabra de casamiento*") to the mulatto Micaela Tenorio. She asked the officials to ascertain the truth from Micaela and two other witnesses. The initial witness, the 42-year-old free mulatto Domingo de Moya, identified himself as a familiar of Isabel and her son Ignacio. He recounted that two months earlier, Ignacio had been in his house in the company of Micaela Tenorio, whom he had not previously known. Domingo recalled that in the presence of him and his wife, Juliana de la Cruz, Ignacio vowed to marry Micaela. Domingo testified that Ignacio had openly professed that "he would not have any other woman than Micaela Tenorio." Domingo also said that Micaela had expressed a similar commitment, proclaiming that "she would have no other husband but Ignacio Mexíca." Domingo confessed that after making this binding pledge, the couple had spent the night in his house, but in the morning they had departed for a neighboring woman's house. Domingo stated that "under the pledge of matrimony they had interacted carnally and had wanted to marry."[44]

Following Domingo's declaration, the ecclesiastical judge heard the testimony of the 32-year-old Spanish *doncella* María de León. María said that she had known Isabel; her son, Ignacio; and Micaela Tenorio for a period of six years. María recalled how "four months ago more or less" Ignacio had taken Micaela from her parental home and then hid with her in the house of his aunt, Juliana de la Cruz. On learning of her son's actions, observed María, Ignacio's mother was scandalized "by the affront to God that would result." She went to Juliana de la Cruz's house and brought Micaela to "my house." After three days "some men who said they were her [Micaela's] brothers arrived." Confronted by the angry siblings, María asked Ignacio "what was the intent of taking Micaela from her parental home?" Micaela, Ignacio responded, "is my wife." When María asked the same question of Micaela, the young mulatto stated that Ignacio "is my husband." María said that after making these declarations, the couple repeated their vows "*palabra de casamiento* (promise of marriage; lit. 'word of marriage')." Even though Micaela's brothers witnessed the exchange, they "carried Micaela Tenorio off." "The marriage never took place," concluded María.[45]

At the conclusion of Domingo and María's testimony, the ecclesiastical judge demanded that Ignacio Mexíca be brought before him. Ignacio answered questions

44. AGN, Matrimonios, tomo 19, expediente 4, folio 109, 1673, "Información de Domingo de Moya."
45. AGN, Matrimonios, tomo 19, expediente 4, folio 109, 1673, "Información de María de León."

about his relationship to Micaela and Josefa. Asked if he knew Micaela Tenorio and had given her a promise of marriage, Ignacio professed to have known her for eight months. He testified that he had promised to marry her. But Ignacio regretted not having married Micaela, as intended, because her parents removed her from Mexico City. "I always wanted to comply with the said promise," testified Ignacio, "but since she did not come to this city [Mexico City] for a very long time I tried to marry Josefa de León." Asked if he had pledged marriage to Josefa de León, Ignacio recalled initially expressing his desire to marry her during Holy Week, but only after Micaela had been absent for three months. In an effort to minimize his responsibility to Josefa, Ignacio added that "she was not a virgin nor did I violate her virginity." Next, the *provisor* again asked Ignacio why the marriage with Micaela was not contracted. Ignacio responded that he wanted to marry her "in order to discharge his conscience and so as to pay his obligation for having taken her virginity."[46] Hearing Ignacio voice his will, the ecclesiastical judge ordered that a statement be presented to Micaela and Josefa "so that they could respond."

In her response, Josefa de León continued to insist that the "impediment presented by Isabel Gómez [was] malicious." She was also adamant that Ignacio could have pursued the matter with Micaela Tenorio through proper channels. "Ignacio Mexía," declared Josefa "was intimidated by his mother and her *compadre* Gregorio Gallardo." Maintaining that Ignacio really wanted her, Josefa confessed that she was pregnant. But in a subsequent *instancia* (petition), Josefa withdrew her request to marry Ignacio, stating that he was now at liberty to marry whom he wanted.[47]

Clearly, the Spaniard Ignacio Mexía experienced the results of black agency when he confronted opposition from Micaela's family when he tried to marry her. Micaela's family was not delighted with her choice of spouse, and they physically separated the two after the couple initiated nuptial proceedings. As Micaela's brothers confronted the couple and then carried Micaela off, they demonstrated that as a woman and a daughter, Micaela, was the family's possession and the decision of who she should marry was not simply hers. The actions of Micaela's family, who were black creoles—in fact mulattos—counter the prevailing scholarly assumption that socially ambitious mulattos were only too willing to forge ties with their racial betters.

In these proceedings we also hear the voice of mulatto Josefa León as she made complex claims about honor and virtue. Josefa was astute and keenly apprised of her rights as a Christian woman. She was not easily deterred. Understandably, the stakes for Josefa, who was allegedly pregnant, were rather high. But in the final

46. AGN, Matrimonios, tomo 19, expediente 4, folio 109, 1673, "Declaración de Ignacio Mexía."
47. AGN, Matrimonios, tomo 19, expediente 4, folio 109, 1673, "Instancia de Josefa de León."

analysis Josefa did not prevail. In the end, Ignacio and presumably Micaela's will prevailed against the claims expressed by Josefa and possibly angry kinfolk. In the case of Micaela—whose family exhibited strong feelings about the strategic choices of a female kinswoman whom neighbors and strangers publicly acknowledged as a *doncella*—the clergy surely would have been keen to protect her right to exercise her free will threatening her family with excommunication if they did not return Micaela to Mexico City. If her will remained unbent, Micaela would soon be united with Ignacio in holy matrimony while the family would be left to sort out their anger and eventually their differences. Unfortunately we do not learn how this family drama in which a mulatto family objected to one of their own marrying a Spaniard ended.

On 18 October 1674, the mulattos Nicolás Gallego and María de Valverde requested a marriage license from Mexico's ecclesiastical officials.[48] The couple presented three witnesses. The 22-year-old free mulatto Francisco Gallego, Nicolás's brother, had known María for six years. The 38-year-old free mulatto José de Gamboa, a native of Mexico City, had known the prospective spouses "since they were infants." Nicolás Roman, the third witness, a free mulatto and also a native of Mexico City, had known the couple for six years. Evidently the couple received their license, but they had to wait for three consecutive feast days before the license took effect. Two days after the banns were issued the first time, the free mulatto Luís de Alcaraz raised objections to the pending marriage on grounds that María had previously pledged to marry him. In his petition, Luís claimed that three years earlier María had promised to marry him but her family had objected and "had sequestered her." Now Luís implored the ecclesiastical officials to question María about her intent. Luís's request makes it clear that he was aware that Catholic authorities respected personal will as the basis for contracting a marriage.

In support of his case, Luís marshaled a battery of witnesses who testified that on several occasions María was in his company, often in circumstances suggesting that they were *novios*. Pedro de Medina, a 40-year-old free mulatto and native of Mexico, said that Antonio Patino, Luís's father, had confided in him that his son had exchanged marital promises with María. Pedro noted that he was on intimate terms with Luís and María and had known "both for a long time."[49] The eighteen-year-old free mulatto carpenter Bernabe Lopez was even more adamant. After noting that he had known both individuals "for six years," Bernabe recalled that in the course of a conversation Luís had informed him of his pending marriage to María. Bernabe had then turned to María, whom he claimed was present

48. AGN, Matrimonios 2, expediente 10, folios 99–123, 1674.
49. AGN, Matrimonios 2, expediente 10, folios 99–123, 22 October 1674, "Información de Pedro de Medina."

during this conversation, to ask if this was the couple's intent. María had said yes. Soon thereafter Bernabe had questioned María de Santa Teresa, María's mother, during a chance encountered in the neighborhood. She too, said Bernabe, had affirmed the news.[50] The final witness, José de la Cruz, a 23-year-old black creole slave, had known the couple for years; all three "grew up together." He recalled an incident three months earlier when Luís had accosted María, who was conversing with an unknown *mestizo*. Luís, José stated, wanted "to hit" María. "Fearing a fight in which they would hurt each other," José "separated them." When José asked Luís for an explanation, he told him that he wanted to marry María and she him. Luís then said "that he had the permission of her mother" (*que se habia de casar con el qusto de su madre*).[51]

Following this testimony, the ecclesiastical officials placed María in *depósito* in the house of Don Andres del Rosal. Evidently the authorities needed time to mull over matters and wanted to ensure that María was shielded from individuals who sought to thwart her will. Two days later, Nicolás petitioned for María's removal from Don Andres's care. "Her mother," Nicolás claimed, "wielded much influence in that house" (*por tener la dicha su madre mucha cabida en aquella casa*). Nicolás then charged María de Santa Teresa and Luís with conspiring to "disrupt the marriage that both [Nicolás and María] desired." "Ask María de Valverde," pleaded Nicolás, "if she wants to marry me or not."[52] Nicolás's petition had the intended effect. Church officials removed María from the care of Don Andrés and placed her in the female penitentiary, the Recogimiento de Santa María Magdalena.

As the case unfolded over the next several weeks, María's mother, María de Santa Teresa, emerged as a manipulating parent intent on thwarting her daughter's desire to marry Nicolás. Here a mother conspired to shape the specific form blackness should assume by choosing a particular black person as a spouse for her daughter. María de Santa Teresa wanted María to marry in accordance with her desires, and she prompted Luís de Alcaraz to "disrupt" the couples' plans. Adamant in her objection to Nicolás, María attempted to obstruct her daughter's will even after church officials placed María in custody. Why she did so remains a mystery. Had she wanted her daughter to forge a family alliance with a more prosperous suitor? Did María's objections stem from personal considerations? Was Nicolás simply trouble?

In a petition dated 31 October—two weeks after the couple requested a mar-

50. AGN, Matrimonios 2, expediente 10, folios 99–123, 22 October 1674, "Información de Bernable López."
51. AGN, Matrimonios 2, expediente 10, folios 99–123, 22 October 1674, "Información de José de la Cruz."
52. AGN, Matrimonios 2, expediente 10, folios 99–123, 25 October 1674, "Petición de Nicolás Gallego."

riage license—Nicolás insinuated that personal motives prompted María's objections. "María de Santa Teresa instigated and orchestrated the impediment," Nicolás stated, "solely because she opposed me."[53] Nicolás then questioned the veracity of the testimony of Luís's witnesses, alleging that their testimony constituted merely rumors and hearsay. Insistent on marrying María, Nicolás observed that the testimony could not impede María's will to marry him instead of Luís (*no es acto suficiente, ni con los requisitos prevenidos por derecho para quedar ligado a no poder retractor su voluntad*). Displaying concern for María, who languished in the women's penitentiary, Nicolás asked that she be lodged in the house of Doña Nicolasa de la Parra. The ecclesiastical officials modified Nicolás's request, placing María instead in the custody of Don Andrés and telling him that "under no circumstances should Tomasa [María] de Santa Teresa be permitted to abuse or verbally threaten her daughter." In a subsequent *audiencia* with ecclesiastical officials, María expressed her wish to marry Nicolás. On 16 November 1673, Luís withdrew his objections. In the final act, Church officials granted Nicolás and María a marriage license.

Clearly, Nicolás and María and María's mother, María de Santa Teresa, had agency. They expressed their will about what they wanted to happen and persuaded authorities to hear them and take actions based on their words. But a number of neighbors took sides in what likely was a domestic dispute between mother and daughter over an acceptable spouse. Some neighbors expressed their opinions by serving as matrimonial sponsors for Luís and María. On the basis that they had known Luís and María "six years," "a long time," or "since they grew up together," several neighbors testified that both members of the couple were single. These declarations were tantamount to supporting María de Santa Teresa. What consequences flowed from their actions? Would it result in lifelong animosity with María de Santa Teresa? Would they heal the breach by claiming to have been unaware or duped? Indeed, if they were duped would Pedro de Medina, Bernabe Lopez, or José de la Cruz have words with the instigators? What effect did this conflict have on local ties? Answers to these questions are elusive. Nonetheless, Nicolás and María's marriage petition and the conflict surrounding the couple underscore the complexity of black private life. This community, as the mother-daughter relationship between María and María de Santa Teresa illustrates, involved more than cohesiveness and consensus.

In the sixteenth century, the Church invariably accepted the expression of free will of lovers as sufficient reason to proceed with a marriage. But this began to change in the last decades of the seventeenth century. Historian Patricia Seed found that

53. AGN, Matrimonios 2, expediente 10, folios 99–123, 31 October 1674, "Petición de Nicolás Gallego."

"whereas in the seventeenth century marrying for love, as an expression of personal will, was widely esteemed," in the eighteenth century parents began to argue successfully against the legitimacy of such a motive for marriage."[54] A transformation in Church-state relations accompanied the change in parental behavior, a phenomenon with dire consequences for the ability of *novios* to express their personal will. "In the final decades of the seventeenth century a subtle shift began to take place in Mexican church-state relations," observed Seed. The change originated "not in high-level political debates about the relationship of the two but rather on a more practical, day-to-day level."[55] Seed argues that by the end of the eighteenth century the Church had withdrawn its respect for the free will of children and had begun to side with parents in an effort to shore up paternal authority. The Church's retreat from aggressive intervention on behalf of couples reflected the shifting alliance whereby the state and the Catholic Church joined elites in a growing concern about the *casta* population and its members' desire to contract marriages with Spaniards. "The increasing occurrence of this sort of marriage—Spaniards, both male and female, marrying mulattos, mestizos, or castes," concluded Seed, "presented potentially catastrophic consequences for a social structure primarily organized on the basis of racial distinctions."[56] Accordingly, parents and patriarchy prevailed in the eighteenth century.

Whether the Church aligned itself with parents or lovers, conflicts over marriage were endemic in New Spain. In all societies but especially in colonial societies, conflicts over family formation are an enduring theme. In an effort to regulate racial authenticity, New Spain's elites limited access to Spanish women. The attitude of elites toward interracial sex for Spanish men was more lax, but marriages across races were frowned upon. The Church monitored illicit sex, often disciplining offenders. Both parties accorded greater vigilance to protecting the sacrament of marriage. Illicit sex invited gossip and censure, but since matrimony engendered legitimacy, it posed the gravest threat to parental authority, family genealogies, and the racialized social order. For these reasons, family members expressed serious interest in who their kin married, often mounting opposition when a union did not meet their approval. But conflicts over marriage did not always emanate from a dominant perspective, as we saw in the case of Nicolás and María. In cases involving blacks and mulattos, there were other motives for conflicts. Conflicts often emanated from the authority of parents who were divorced from access to resources and existing kinship patterns. In the process of forging ever-denser networks, creoles increasingly manifested conflicts for reasons that

54. Seed, *To Love, Honor, and Obey in Colonial Mexico*, 122.
55. Ibid., 161.
56. Ibid., 146.

had little to do with upward social mobility. As we shall see in the remaining chapters, conflicts were sparked by claims that touched on promises, personal virtue, and family honor. In all such instances, black creoles displayed agency.

*   *   *

In the preceding pages, domesticity emerges as a critical component of the multifaceted cultural process that was affected by and generated by peoples of African descent. Survivors of the Middle Passage employed Christianity to claim social selves as New World ethnics, a process that tempered the effects of social death. As Angolans drew on friendships and long-standing familiarity to establish urban ethnic networks, the creole population engaged in a similar process. But as New World natives, creoles drew on far more expansive ties to forge families and delineate the boundaries of their communities. Demographic evolution among creoles, a black but increasingly mulatto population, prompted a shift from African cultural formation to an elaborate social process of creole cultural formation. It would be misleading, however, to think of this as a linear dynamic. Just as free mulattos overlapped and mingled with black slaves, creoles and Angolans coexisted, fusing in some instances. Many black cultures flourished throughout and at any one time in seventeenth-century New Spain. Christianity—by sanctioning the metaphysics of life among slaves—permitted successive generations of Africans and their creole descendants to channel social and cultural agency into elaborate kinship genealogies. As we shall see, by the end of the seventeenth century creole genealogies exhibited a formidable complexity, embedded in new domestic idioms and novel kinship practices for the descendants of slaves increasingly removed from an experience with bondage.

SIX

Narrating Freedom

In the conventional characterization of Mexican history, including social histories, seventeenth-century New Spain slept.[1] In these narratives of Mexican history, social and cultural quiescence defined the middle period, a contrast to the tumult of conquest and the era of independence. These scholars view colonialism through conventional formulations of politics and economics. They argue that societal stasis was compounded by the contraction of New Spain's economy, which led to a period of imperial neglect. The decline of the mining economy—a problem of inadequate production and a steep decline in the indigenous population—restricted social and cultural possibilities. Scholars interested in the Atlantic economy have recently started to question such claims of stasis. Economic historian David Eltis suggests that far from slumbering, the economy of colonial Mexico during this period was awake and active. He writes that "the question of the relative size of the export sector in the Spanish Americas is poorly understood."[2]

The need for a reappraisal of the colonial slumber becomes even more pressing when we consider the extent of the growth of the creole population over the course of the seventeenth century. Both the volume of the slave trade and the subsequent process of cultural formation require us to reassess the standards we use to assess the middle colonial period. The slave trade brought an unprecedented number of ethnic Africans into the viceroyalty in the first half of the seventeenth century, bringing the slave population to its apogee. While the slave population

1. D. A. Brading, *Miners & Merchants in Bourbon Mexico: 1763–1810* (New York: Cambridge University Press, 1971), 8–14; Louisa Schell Hoberman, *Mexico's Merchant Elite, 1590–1660: Silver, State, and Society* (Durham, N.C.: Duke University Press, 1991).

2. David Eltis observed that "while coerced Indian labor was the mainstay of the silver mines, the number of free and mita laborers employed in the production of silver in New Spain and Peru even at peak export periods was small compared to the number of slaves that were employed on sugar plantations." David Eltis, *The Rise of African Slavery in the Americas* (New York: Cambridge University Press, 1999), 25.

grew rapidly, the number of free blacks grew even faster. Among the creole population, free mulattos were steadily moving toward numerical ascendancy.

The growth of the free black population in the seventeenth century raises numerous questions about the nature and meaning of freedom in the Atlantic world. Scholars of slavery typically situate freedom in relation to the economy. They overlook the link between sexuality and freedom. In the Atlantic, freedom initially emerged from sexual contact between free and enslaved people. If Spaniards sought to stave off the growth of the free black population (a goal they acknowledged), they needed to regulate sexuality. Yet the Spanish Crown never prohibited interracial contact or punished slaves for having sex with free persons. Though the clergy punished sinners, the legal status of the offending parties was not the issue for the Church. If free blacks posed a threat to Mexican society, as so many have claimed, why did Spanish settlers, the Spanish monarchy, and the Catholic Church choose not to restrict sexual relations between black male slaves and Indian women? Such relations likely played a key role in fostering the growth of the free black population.

In the New World, freedom did not emerge as an abstraction. In the wake of the Spanish conquests and the slave trade, freedom was above all a lived experience. Freedom was a social practice, something people learned in and through their relationships with others long before early modern theologians and modern philosophers upheld it as an abstraction and ideal. Enslaved Africans and creoles made it abundantly clear that the freedom they experienced cannot be equated with the ideologies of liberty formulated during the Age of Revolutions. New Spain's black population conceived of freedom in and through the encumbrance of slave status. This chapter offers a contextualized understanding of first freedom in New Spain—an emerging social practice in the New World among human chattel whose existence defined the meaning of freedom for the modern world. Africans in Spanish America forged this freedom through their lived experience as slaves who nonetheless could stake claims as Christians to social selves. As we have seen, individuals of African descent channeled many of their life experiences through Christianity, and their understanding of freedom is no exception; Africans and creoles linked Christianity, sexuality, and freedom. The words and actions of slaves and free persons clearly indicate that for them, sexuality and Christianity offered routes to freedom. Private lives, in other words, were instrumental in charting first freedom.

Before examining how Africans and creoles used their private lives to effect an early modern culture of freedom, we must acknowledge the ways that intimacy among slaves complicates our understanding of slavery. We need more subtle understandings of slavery than the standard narratives offer. The formative depictions of slavery—which introduced the subject as a line of scholarly inquiry—rested on historical abstractions that were formulated around the number of Africans and the structure of slavery.[3] The anthropologist David Scott has written brilliantly about the ways the present demands different questions, reformulated engagements, and distinct strategies of representation in order to speak to the pressing needs of our time. "How . . . and with what conceptual resources," asks Scott "do we begin to extract a new yield, a new horizon of possibilities, from within the contours of our postcolonial present?"[4]

Scholars of colonial Latin American slavery must risk questioning the works of the pioneers who brought the black experience into relief. Thirty years ago, historian Colin A. Palmer could write:

> The third major racial component of society, the African slaves, also possessed some degree of internal social differentiation. Taken as a group, the social divisions among the slaves were not as clearly marked as those existing within the other two groups. The realities of slavery were not conducive to the emergence, development, and maintenance of a well-defined social structure among the slave population. Slaves were not like free people; their status as human chattel defined and limited their individual potential and subjected them to the will and caprice of the master. It is apparent, nevertheless, that they did not all perceive themselves as belonging to a socially undifferentiated mass of people. There were at least two principal groups within the slave population: the elite and the non-elite.[5]

For Palmer, the slave embodied the black experience. His perspective did not take into account the salience of ethnicity or the presence of a rapidly growing free black population. Palmer wrote during a time when the Mexican public and other scholars denied the very existence of an African presence in colonial Mexico, and he felt compelled to demonstrate the worst of slavery in his efforts to demonstrate its existence. "The rigors of the ingenio, the sweatshop conditions of the obraje, and the physical hell of the silver mines," writes Palmer, "represented the worst aspects of Mexican slavery."[6] But even on estates, Africans and their descendants did not exist as mere forces of production in the form of slaves and freedmen. To

---

3. Aguirre Beltrán, *La poblacion negra de México*; Palmer, *Slaves of the White God*; Carroll, *Blacks in Colonial Veracruz*.

4. David Scott, *Refashioning Futures: Criticism after Postcoloniality* (Princeton, N.J.: Princeton University Press, 1999), 3; Scott extends his brilliant engagement with historical representation in *Conscripts of Modernity: The Tragedy of Colonial Enlightenment* (Durham, N.C.: Duke University Press, 2004), which examines the shifting representational strategies employed by C. L. R. James in *The Black Jacobins*.

5. Palmer, *Slaves of the White God*, 36–37, 44, 59–61; quote on 37.

6. Ibid., 83.

what extent did these industries shape the slave and larger black experience?

Shifts in political context enable us to ask different questions than those posed by Palmer and his generation. Decades after struggling to have scholars and the public acknowledge the African and black past, Palmer's concerns have been vindicated since the central issue no longer revolves around a brutalized yet simplified slave experience. Of course, brutality defined the slave and various black experiences, but in the wake of Third World independence and civil rights movements, respectively characterized as the postcolonial and post-civil rights eras, new questions have arisen. The current questions—animated by the unfulfilled promises of decolonization and the struggle for racial equality—push against the limits of independence and political enfranchisement. Yet within the historical profession, these questions do more than highlight the unfulfilled promises of sovereignty and freedom. They attend to the complexities that inform colonial and racial social formations and the attendant subjectivities among the colonized and racially oppressed.

In the clusters of estates that constituted the core of the commercial economy, patriarchal social relationships governed the presence and experiences of Africans and their descendants.[7] In the typical archival record, Spaniards, as masters, employers, or ecclesiastical authorities, recount an event or series of events in which a particular person of African descent appears as a named individual with a specific story. These stories provide evidence of an individual's distinct connections to other inhabitants of a particular locale, his or her noteworthy features or experiences.[8] Despite persistent references to social status formulated around race, occupation, and juridical identity, the testimony of masters, employers, and ecclesiastical authorities brings to light their familiarity with an individual—even a slave, underscoring the personal nature of social interaction in this colonial and

7. Such practices, according to the anthropologist Igor Kopytoff, reveal the outline of a moral economy. Kopytoff noted that "the same thing may be treated as a commodity at one time and not at another. And . . . the same thing may, at the same time, be seen as a commodity by one person and as something else by another. Such shifts and differences in whether and when a thing is a commodity reveal a moral economy that stands behind the objective economy of visible transactions." Igor Kopytoff, "The Cultural Biography of Things: Commodification as Process," in *The Social Life of Things: Commodities in Cultural Perspective,* ed. Arjun Appadurai (New York: Cambridge University Press, 1986), 64.

8. Among the countless examples, see Inquisición 310, expediente 3, folios 87–118, 1616, "Proceso contra Juan Luís mulato libre que se ha criado en el ingenio de los padres de Santo Domingo por casado dos veces"; Inquisición 310, expediente 5e, folios 232–258, 1618, "Proceso contra Ana Maria, mulata, por casada dos veces"; Inquisición 582, expediente 6, folios 505–524, 1641, "Proceso contra Pedro Romero, negro esclavo de Capitan Francisco de Ribas, vecino de Ciudad de Leon en Nicaragua, por casada dos veces"; Inquisición 470, folios 309–363, 1609, "Proceso contra Francisco de Castaneda, mulato libre, sastre, natural de la Cd de Mexico, por casado dos veces"; Inquisición 539, expediente 8, folios 72–79, no date (1690s). All in AGN.

bourgeoning capitalist environment.[9] Because the stories are largely formulated around transgressions, family histories and particular experiences emerge as the subjects of rumors and gossip. The Spanish elite and commoners alike shared such knowledge about individuals, though each group offered particular inflections as they told their stories. The fragments these stories represent have highlighted the informal interactions of blacks in the colonial landscape and provide us with a particularistic rather than a stylized understanding of the social and culture formation of this people.

When we shift from a patriarchal to a horizontal perspective we glimpse how people of African descent forged and maintained deep ties (measured by length of time but also by biological ties to a father, mother, brother, sister, grandparent, aunt, uncle, or cousin) that also acquired breadth (the geographical scope that ranged across a wide swath of territory throughout the Atlantic world and in New Spain). But in most instances people were rooted in a particular space, acquiring meaning through the memory of kin and familiars that gave a place emotional appeal. (It was not the plot of land but the experiences associated with that land that people identify as their *patria chica*.) The choices people made were shaped by community dynamics (which sometimes included conflict), gender conventions, sexual norms, modification of Christian mores, and the ability to narrate experiences in the context of village customs and in the face of periodic vigilance of the Church. The language people mobilized in order to frame the self and rationalize their deeds—though it illustrates the Church's authority and its culture of power— underscores the complexity of the various black experiences.

Colonial Spanish slavery enabled the enslaved to define themselves as social beings who were legally entitled to contract marriages and maintain a family. This ambiguity made the growth of the free black population possible. It also meant that the possibility of freedom loomed in the consciousness of most Africans or that of their descendants. For slaves, the presence of and daily interaction with free blacks served as an example that they too could be free. Yet throughout the seventeenth century, rather than striving for freedom by fleeing or resisting, many Africans and even more creoles came to experience freedom as the product of legal proceedings or as their birth legacy.[10]

The urban nature of slavery in New Spain in which African women and sub-

9. For an understanding how such talk related to the disciplinary function that defined the early modern state see, Silverblatt, *Modern Inquisitions*, 3–27, 37.

10. In her magisterial study of freedom in colonial Cuba, María Elena Díaz insists that freedom constituted a distinct possibility for the royal slaves of El Cobre, an expectation that tempered their lives as slaves. María Elena Díaz, *The Virgin, the King, and the Royal Slaves of El Cobre: Negotiating Freedom in Colonial Cuba, 1670–1780* (Stanford, Calif.: Stanford University Press, 2000), 93.

sequently mulattos engaged in illicit interracial sex led to the emergence of free blacks. But the urban mulatto population in the late sixteenth and early seventeenth centuries developed after the initial nucleus of free blacks emerged from unions between African and black men and Indians and mestizos after the sixteenth-century conquest. Social reproduction among African, black, and especially free mulatto women was important for the growth of the free population. Newborn children, of course, followed the status of their mothers. Still, we should not underestimate the importance of a Christian conscience that generated social claims among people of African descent and eventually encouraged some slaves to sue for their or their children's freedom. An awareness of rights was not, however, restricted to slaves with a Christian conscience. Slaves filed numerous suits for freedom, grounding their claims in an understanding of the master's legal will.[11] Some daring souls even appeared before the authorities to insist that the abuse they or their children had suffered constituted a breach in the master-slave relationship that entitled them to freedom.[12] In making claims, challenging their legal status, and negotiating over freedom, the enslaved contrasted their social status as persons with rights and their legal identity as property and pressed for the primacy of the former. As individuals argued publicly over their enslavement, countless other slaves learned about their potential rights and nurtured the possibility of freedom. Though thousands of individuals in New Spain spent their lives as slaves, a steady stream of people navigated and even widened the avenues to freedom.

When they were removed from the constraints slavery imposed on their freedom, most descendants of Africans participated in the colonial economy and polity as marginal figures. From this marginalized position, persons of African descent created lives, communities, consciousness, and cultures that we need to define and understand. Though this population originated in bondage, the narrative that privileges slavery followed by freedom is not sufficient for discussing the larger Afro-Mexican experience. The experiences of most seventeenth-century Afro-Mexicans cannot be reduced to the analytical categories derived Haiti, Jamaica, and the United States in the Age of Revolution, even though they were the offspring of chattel living in a society in which slavery still flourished.

According to classic notions of political economy inspired by Enlightenment thought, freedom was an ideal and ideology that projected a rational self-interested individual engaged in commercial activities secured by the contract. Unencumbered by the state or the will of others, a free man was an individual fully

11. AGN, Bienes Nacionales 1158, expediente 16, 1604; AGN, Inquisición 503, folios 17–44, 1649; AGN, Bienes Nacionales 131, expediente 6, 1656; AGN, Bienes Nacionales 79, expediente 12, 1664; AGN, Matrimonios 36, expediente 45, folios 181–183, 1682.

12. AGN, Inquisición 419, folios 320–364, 1649; AGN, Bienes Nacionales 79, expediente 12, 1664; AGN, Bienes Nacionales 79, expediente 14, 1664.

capable of pursuing his will in the larger society. In Haiti, Jamaica, and the United States, the contract between possessive individuals (the planter) guaranteed that property relations (the dynamic between master and slave) were sacrosanct and productivity (slavery) constituted the foundation of the social order. As Haitian, Jamaican, and American slaves made claims to freedom in the nineteenth century, their meanings of the concept challenged those of colonial and national elites but also bore the burden of the social order of which the slave societies were a constitutive part. In defining freedom they understandably emphasized their complete autonomy from the control of others. But to the enslaved in New Spain, complete autonomy was a thoroughly alien notion that if enacted would have resulted in a form of social death. For Africans in the Old World and New Spain, vertical and horizontal ties were critical to their concept of life and their sense of freedom. In staking claims to private lives and freedom, New Spain's enslaved relied on access to the clergy and royal officials. They could do so because in New Spain, slaves constituted both chattel and legally recognized persons who had rights beyond those that the master bestowed.

For similar reasons, the concepts and terms of slavery in the eighteenth and nineteenth centuries need to be used with care when thinking about slavery and freedom in New Spain. Using such labor categories as field hand, slave artisan, house slave, proto-peasants, and plantation laborer risks both overdetermining and simplifying slavery and freedom. Treating Afro-Mexicans as unemancipated objects of historical analysis shackles them in ways slavery in New Spain never seemed capable of achieving. María Elena Díaz, a historian of slavery in colonial Cuba, underscores the notion that historical representations of Africans and their descendents have invariably constituted an analytical prisonhouse. She suggests that "rather than enslaving people in the past and in our texts to an overdetermining category of 'slavery,'" we explore "the ways in which their lives overlapped . . . with those of other sectors of society, particularly other free but subordinate groups of colonial society."[13]

Afro-Mexicans, of course, confronted the problem of freedom. They entered freedom lacking the economic and political resources that could sustained a fully autonomous life. But as they struggled to give meaning to their lives, they did not face a class of slaveholders intent on denying them employment or dispossessing them of land or other means of subsistence. In this respect, the experience of seventeenth-century Afro-Mexicans differed from that of other descendants of Africans in the Atlantic world's plantation zone. Their experience resembled that of New Spain's *mestizos*, Indians who left the customary communities, and impoverished Spaniards. Because enslaved Africans and the initial generations of creoles

---

13. Díaz, *The Virgin, the King, and the Royal Slaves of El Cobre,* 14.

could legally form families, subsequent generations of creoles did not enter the state of freedom frantically searching for loved ones. Afro-Mexicans entered freedom as persons with diverse kinship structures that gained depth and complexity during the seventeenth century and beyond. In the second half of the seventeenth century, Afro-Mexican gender and domestic conventions were increasingly characterized by fewer residues of slavery. Creoles, as we have seen, found it easier to stay together and live in one place as families while maintaining kinship ties. This domestic stability, a phenomenon of both African and creole desire, was the result of the rights accorded to Christians regardless of status.

The cultural practices of Afro-Mexicans underscored that population's familiarity with Christian orthodoxy and the degree to which Christian norms were in play among persons of African descent. Freedom allowed individual Afro-Mexicans to act in accordance with their desires to be either good or errant Christians, and it gave them much more. As we have seen throughout, Christianity involved much more than social discipline. In this chapter, we shall hear stories that illustrate how Afro-Mexicans took from Christian tenets principles of justice and morality that they used to push against the authority of the state and employers as they constructed private and community life. For this population, the meaning of freedom was mediated through Christian tropes about domesticity.

In weighing individual tales drawn from slaves and free blacks in seventeenth-century New Spain, we must constantly be aware of the issue of significance. What stories defined the seventeenth-century social history of Africans, especially that of creoles?[14] Our representational strategy must privilege the utterances of the creolized population captured by the colonial archive. This strategy provides glimpses into how slaves, former slaves, and descendants of slaves emerged as black and mulatto plebeians and a "reconstituted" black and mulatto peasantry—formulations that move our understanding of freedom beyond the juridical.[15] But above all else, we see how claims to a private life among slaves and their offspring enabled them to enjoy a vibrant social existence as people. If we are willing to see Africans, blacks, and mulattos, and their descendants as more than slaves and examine their lives beyond the moment when they obtained freedom, we can actually hear them narrate the meanings they ascribed to freedom and their lives. By listening to those we have neglected to see, we can discern the social and cultural logic of formerly commodified beings. As we shall see, freedom emerged for this population

14. Michel-Rolph Trouillot, *Silencing the Past: Power and the Production of History* (Boston: Beacon, 1995).

15. By using the term "peasant" to refer to slaves in colonial Cuba, Díaz underscores that this "is not a standard story of slavery." *The Virgin, the King, and the Royal Slaves of El Cobre*, 9.

as a gendered process. Freedom meant the ability to act in accordance with one's identity as a Christian man or woman.

Representing freedom demands that historians do more than understand the process of manumission for persons of African descent. The way Africans and their descendants acquired freedom is a critical story, but that story should not be limited to the important shift in status. Freedom, like slavery, was more than a juridical status. Freedom resulted from particular social experiences—relations to family, kin, and friends—that were accompanied by specific social practices constituted through the Afro-Mexicans' status as both subjects of the king and persons with souls. Freedom also acquired its form and content in relationship to mastery over one's use of the body. For men, freedom meant having authority over one's dependent wife and children. For women, freedom entailed the ability to control their children. In the stories that individuals told about themselves and each other we discern the meanings of the freedom that persons of African descent steadily forged.

The Narrative of a Non-event

On 8 May 1688, as the 57-year-old Spanish widow Doña Ana de Colmenares stood before Mexico City's ecclesiastical judge, she seemed visibly nervous. Yet after the routine formalities, Ana de Colmenares regained her composure and humbly informed the *provisor* that the previous night her mulatto slave, Salvador Antonio, had married a quadroon (*morisca*) freedwoman Josefa de Sámano, whom she also employed in her house. Since Josefa was on the verge of death, the priest had dispensed with the required banns (*amonestaciones*) and married the couple. But after this hastily arranged ceremony, Ana suddenly recalled that the spiritual kinship tie that bound Salvador and Josefa constituted a legitimate impediment to their marriage: The slightly older Josefa had been Salvador's godmother at his confirmation. In the eyes of the Catholic Church, the newlyweds had contracted an incestuous marriage. As she concluded her confession, Doña Ana implied that as a contrite and devout Christian she simply wanted this egregious act to be known "so that his mercy can arrange what he pleases."[16]

Alarmed by this incestuous breach, the *provisor* called for an immediate investigation into Ana's allegations and ordered her to keep the newlyweds apart. Two days later and before the ecclesiastical investigation had begun, the *provisor* received a petition (*instancia*) from María de Marradón, a young Spanish woman

16. AGN, Matrimonios (tercera seria), tomo 37, expediente 1, 8 May 1688, "Denuncia ante el Juez Provisor del Arzobispado," Mexico City.

who was Ana's niece. María beseeched the ecclesiastical judge to act on her behalf. In her petition, María revealed that Salvador, her aunt's mulatto slave, "had ravished and impregnated her" after giving her a "verbal promise of marriage" (*palabra de casamiento*; lit. "word of marriage" or "promise of marriage"). Ana, who opposed the union, had orchestrated the wedding between Salvador and Josefa. María insisted that that marriage was void since Josefa had "taken ill and lost reason," and because, more important, Josefa was Salvador's godmother (*madrina*). Convinced that Doña Ana had coerced Salvador into marrying Josefa and deliberately sought to misinform "your excellency," María asked the *provisor* to call on Salvador, who "under oath would confirm the content in this letter." María also requested that the hastily arranged marriage be declared void, "since Salvador Antonio is my husband and the banns had not been publicized but made secretly and with the fraud that Josefa de Sámano had lost reason."[17]

The *provisor* wasted no time in ordering Salvador Antonio to appear before him, along with María. On the same day that he issued his order (*auto*), he also interrogated María about her allegations. But the ecclesiastical judge seemed more interested in María's relationship with Salvador and her desire to marry a slave than in the charges of conspiracy she had leveled against her aunt. From the beginning, the *provisor* wanted to know how long María had known Salvador Antonio, how long they had been in a "bad state" (*mal estado*), and whether she really wanted to marry him of her own free will (*de su libre voluntad*). María responded that she had known Salvador for a long time "since he was the slave of Doña Ana de Colmenares." She could not recall how long "she had been in a bad state with the so said" but noted that he had "taken her virginity under the promise of marriage and now she found herself impregnated by the so said (and) therefore wanted to marry him of her own free will." The *provisor* asked "if she knew the so said is a slave" and added, "being that he was, did she know that as his wife she was obligated to go wherever his master wants to send or sell him?" The judge also wanted to know if María understood that Salvador was not obligated to support her or "give her what is necessary." Evidently, the *provisor* struck a responsive chord with this point, since María noted that "she had been told" that if they married "his mistress has an obligation to free him and with his occupation as a tallow maker he would be able to sustain her." María reiterated her desire to marry Salvador of her own free will. The ecclesiastical judge manifested little interest in María's desire and proceeded to correct her false impressions. Even if they married, he informed her, Salvador could not request his freedom, nor could he give her what he earned, "for it was as if it were of the said his mistress." "Without her consent,"

17. AGN, Matrimonios (tercera seria), tomo 37, expediente 1, 10 May 1688, Instancia, Mexico City.

the *provisor* concluded, "[Salvador] would not be able to give her anything." These remarks clearly caught María by surprise, and she responded that she "had been told" that Salvador would be freed if they married and said that on that basis "she had made the petition." "But if he were not free," María concluded, "I do not want to marry him."

After a few more questions, the *provisor* ended the interrogation. María, in turn, made a sworn deposition in which she formally rescinded her marriage petition.[18] Afterward, the ecclesiastical judge placed her into *depósito* where she would have time to reflect on her sudden change of mind.[19] A week later, on the basis that Salvador would remain a slave, María formally requested that her verbal promise be rescinded. In the letter, she petitioned for release into her mother's custody and demanded that "silence be imposed on Salvador Antonio." Although María still had to contend with her pregnancy, as far as her family was concerned the matter was closed.[20] Once María terminated her pregnancy or gave birth in secret, her relatives could ward off idle rumors about lost honor. In the absence of tangible proof that their chaste young kinswomen (*doncella*) and a mulatto slave had been romantically involved, María's relatives could dismiss the allegations as spurious and vile gossip.

This proceeding illustrates, among other themes, a slave conducting a private life. For Salvador, private life with elites carried ambiguous valences. On the one hand, his location in the household of an elite Spanish woman enabled him to form a sexual (and one would presume emotional) bond with a young Spanish women. Yet Salvador's Christian social existence as a godson, which the Church intended to bring him benefits, prohibited him from forming intimate relationships with Josefa, any of her immediate relatives, or his unborn child, who would be legally recognized.

The proceedings also illustrate how freedom was a valuable individual possession. The presence or absence thereof could shape personal relations in a slave society. As we shall see, claims to a private life fueled the household drama that

18. María swore that "no one has forced me to desist from the marriage" and said that she had done it "on her free will." AGN, Matrimonios (tercera seria), tomo 37, expediente 1, 10 May 1688, "Declaración ante el Provisor de María de Marradón," Mexico City.

19. Ecclesiastical officials sought to shield the woman from being influenced one way or the other by interested parties. AGN, Matrimonios (tercera seria), tomo 37, expediente 1, 10 May 1688, "Auto del Provisor," Mexico City. María spent the first night in a room of the bailiff's house in the "company of his wife." The next day, the *provisor* ordered that she be moved to the house of Don Pedro Espejo under the conditions that "she not be allowed to speak to any one who would induce or counsel her against the marriage." AGN, Matrimonios (tercera seria), tomo 37, expediente 1, 11 May 1688, "Auto del Provisor," Mexico City.

20. See Ann Twinam, "Honor, Sexuality, and Illegitimacy in Colonial Spanish America," in *Sexuality and Marriage in Colonial Latin America,* ed. Asunción Lavrin (Lincoln: University of Nebraska Press, 1989), 118–155. See also Twinam, *Public Lives, Private Secrets.*

brought the possibility of Salvador's freedom into relief. We glean how private lives—in this case consensual and illicit sex—raised the possibility of freedom. In the case of María and Salvador, a love affair that resulted in a pregnancy between unequal partners sustained the expectation of freedom. María expected that her lover, the father of her unborn child, and (in her eyes) her "husband" would be freed through marriage to her. She hoped that once he had his freedom, "he would be able to sustain her." When she learned that marriage would not affect Salvador's status as a slave, María ended the romance.

We can only surmise how María acquired this fiction of freedom. Perhaps Salvador courted her with promises of love, protection, and sustenance. As Salvador seduced the niece of his mistress, he may have hoped that their marriage would free him. But rather than view María as the seducer's victim, we may profit from seeing her, or both her and Salvador, as instigators. A pregnancy might be a fait accompli with which even the most honor-bound family would have to contend. María knew her aunt and mother in ways that Salvador could not. Family honor mattered. In protecting it, Doña Ana de Colmenares displayed a cunning that brought Salvador judicial scrutiny. In the economy of honor, the mistress Doña Ana de Colmenares embodied the state.

In the proceedings, freedom emerges as the site of possibilities. Like María, the growing creole population—a population that included Salvador—could hope for freedom. Salvador hoped, plotted, and ultimately failed. But through his failure we glimpse the expectations that slaves nurtured in New Spain. Over the course of the seventeenth century, a cultural sea change occurred. Freedom began to characterize the status and daily reality of most descendants of Africans. Yet for contemporary chroniclers and their modern heirs—historians—the emerging culture of freedom and its narratives constitute an unremarkable event and an uneventful history.[21] Africans and their descendants did not view freedom as a non-event. As this episode underscores, even in the absence of massive manumission, an abolition decree, or general emancipation, freedom was a real possibility and defined the experiences of black creoles in the seventeenth century.

21. Trouillot, *Silencing the Past*. Scholars' inability to see free individuals also poses a problem in the well-studied slave society of Brazil. "Free women of color have seldom been the subject of specific historical research in the otherwise large and growing literature about women in colonial and nineteenth-century Brazil," observe B. J. Barickman and Martha Few, noting that "the general lack of such research may be due in part to difficulties in identifying free non-'white' women in the sources. It may also reflect the fact that, until recently, historical research on Brazil has tended to focus on either race or gender rather than on the intersection of the two." B. J. Barickman and Martha Few, "Ana Paulinha de Queirós, Joaquina da Costa, and Their Neighbors: Free Women of Color as Household Heads in Rural Bahia (Brazil), 1835," in *Beyond Bondage: Free Women of Color in the Americas*, ed. David Barry Gaspar and Darlene Clark Hine (Urbana: University of Illinois Press, 2004).

Christian Time and Being

After releasing María de Marradón into her mother's custody, the ecclesiastical judge turned his attention to Doña Ana de Colmenares's allegations and the relationship between Salvador Antonio and Josefa de Sámano, who respectively were identified as a mulatto and a quadroon. On May 31, eleven days after Salvador's arrest, the *provisor* received written correspondence from Josefa. Identifying herself as a Spaniard and a resident of Mexico, Josefa recounted the circumstances that had led to her recent marriage. She recalled how Salvador "ravished me and took my virginity" and said that therefore when "near death I married him." Josefa acknowledged that the priest had disregarded the required procedure due to the severity of her illness, but she blamed herself "for being a woman of little capacity and no understanding of similar matters." "I never stated," Josefa confessed, that "Salvador was my godson. . . . . This impediment would legitimately prevent the contracting of a marriage according to the mandates of our holy mother the Roman Catholic Church." By highlighting her Christian consciousness in this manner, Josefa sought to emphasize the extent to which she was "outside of my full senses and memory (*fuera de mi entero juicio y acuerdo*) when the marriage took place."

Despite her rhetorical willingness to assume responsibility, Josefa accused Salvador of complicity and maliciousness. Josefa recalled that "during this time inside the same house," Salvador Antonio had "ravished and deflowered another Spanish virgin to whom he gave a verbal promise of marriage." "For this reason as much as for all the others expressed," Josefa asked "to remain free and liberated from said slavery" (*quedaria libre y horro de dicha esclavitud*)—that is, the slavery of her marriage to Salvador. Aware that her request could be construed as a demand, Josefa did not rule out the possibility that the ecclesiastical judge would decree their marriage to be valid. She assured the *provisor* that if he validated the union, "my husband would be able to use my person and to dominate me for whatever purpose" (*mi marido . . . pudiera usar de mi persona y dominar para cualquiera parte*). But again Josefa pleaded with the *provisor* to annul the marriage. Josefa insisted that since she had regained her senses, "I have not been together with the said Salvador Antonio."[22]

Six weeks after Josefa's testimony, the ecclesiastical officials finally interrogated Salvador Antonio. Salvador identified himself as a 20-year-old native of Mexico who initially had been owned by Esteban del Campo. After del Campo's death fifteen years earlier, Doña Ana de Colmenares had purchased Salvador when he

---

22. AGN, Matrimonios (tercera seria), tomo 37, expediente 1, 31 May 1688, "Instancia de Josefa de Sámano," Mexico City.

was five years old. The prosecutor (*fiscal*) wanted to know if Salvador knew the freed *morisca* Josefa, how long they had known each other, and what the nature of their relationship was. Salvador acknowledged that he had known Josefa since he had entered Ana de Colmenares's household but said that he had not been aware of their kinship tie until after the incestuous marriage had taken place. "Did you have illicit interaction with the said Josefa de Sámano?" the *fiscal* asked. "For a year more or less," responded Salvador, "I have interacted carnally (*tratado carnalmente*) with Josefa and took her virginity." (That is why the priest married them when Josefa fell ill.) The prosecutor asked Salvador if he had "interacted carnally" with Josefa after the marriage and "how many times did he ascend her." Salvador denied that he had had carnal contact with Josefa after their wedding. According to Salvador, they had abstained from sexual relations after Doña Ana had informed him of his spiritual kinship tie with Josefa.

Evidently, the *fiscal* doubted Salvador's claims that he did not know he was Josefa's godson, because he pointedly asked "why did he not know nor remember being the godson of Josefa if, when they joked or played, María de Sámano, the said Josefa de Sámano's sister, instructed him to show her respect because she was his godmother." Salvador, however, denied that such an exchange had ever taken place. "Why do you deny remembering that the said Josefa de Sámano was your godmother?" the *fiscal* demanded. Salvador answered that Doña Ana had purchased him at such a young age that he could not recall the confirmation or where it had taken place, nor could he recognize the truth in what he heard Doña Ana and others say.

After Salvador's declaration of innocence, the *fiscal* asked the young mulatto if he had known María Marradón, how long he had known her, and why he had known her. Salvador replied that he had known María for seven years, "which is the time the so said lived in the house of her aunt Doña Ana de Colmenares." Salvador also acknowledged that he had "taken her virginity and [given] her a verbal promise of marriage two years ago." But, Salvador said, when Doña Ana learned about this relationship, she had tried to thwart her niece's marriage to a slave by entreating Salvador to marry Josefa. Salvador said that Doña Ana had promised him his freedom and said that she would assist him "in search of his livelihood" if he married Josefa. On the other hand, Doña Ana warned Salvador that "if he tried to marry her niece, she would send him to a stone grave." "Out of fear of what had been proposed," Salvador married Josefa. But he noted that his intentions (*ánimo*) always had been to marry María Marradón.[23] Though he was a slave, as a Christian Salvador knew that his ability to exercise his own free will (*ánimo*) mattered.

23. AGN, Matrimonios (tercera seria), tomo 37, expediente 1, 30 June 1688, "Confesión de Salvador Antonio," Mexico City.

On August 25, three months after Ana de Colmenares had denounced Salvador and Josefa, the *fiscal* requested that the couple's marriage be declared void and asked the judge to have them punished. The *fiscal* based his opinion on the longevity of their "illicit love." He maintained that Josefa and Salvador had disregarded their kinship ties. Although the *fiscal* remarked that "ignorance does not excuse the gravity of the sin," he was not convinced that ignorance had been a factor. He told his superior that Josefa and Salvador had deliberately maintained a two-year illicit relationship and had willfully contracted an incestuous marriage.[24] The ecclesiastical judge concurred with the *fiscal*.

Even after he was presented with the formal charges, Salvador insisted on his innocence. He reiterated that he had been confirmed "within the time of my infancy" and therefore could not even recall that the event had taken place. Salvador also raised a more intriguing objection to the charges. He observed how "prior to contracting the marriage . . . no one from the household warned him that Josefa had been my godmother until after celebrating the said marriage." Salvador placed the blame on Ana de Colmenares, whom he called "sinister." Salvador concluded his defense by questioning the testimony of the witness who had allegedly heard Josefa's sister, Maria de Sámano, remind him not to disrespect his godmother. Salvador, through his legal defendant, dismissed this as uncorroborated evidence. After all, Salvador pointed out, "this was a single witness."[25] But his words fell on deaf ears. The *fiscal* issued his final and unchanged brief.

The judge delayed ruling on this case for more than a month while waiting for Josefa to recover from her illness. According to her physician, Josefa's death was imminent. Concerned that Josefa would die without being having been properly condemned and sentenced, the judge issued his ruling. He annulled the marriage and sentenced Salvador to ten years of exile at a distance of ten leagues from Mexico City. He instructed Ana de Colmenares to sell Salvador, her slave, to "someone who did not live with ten leagues of Mexico City." The judge threatened the loss of "the slave" if she did not comply, but in the event that Salvador failed to acquiesce he would be sent to the Philippines. Ana consented by renting, rather than selling, Salvador Antonio to the owner of an *ingenio* (sugar mill) in Pantitlán. Although Doña Ana de Colmenares accomplished her goal, she did not do so as a mistress wielding absolute authority over her chattel. Salvador had been disciplined as a Christian and, by implication, as a royal subject. With the conclusion of the proceedings Salvador Antonio, like thousands of Afro-Mexicans, faded from view.

24. AGN, Matrimonios (tercera seria), tomo 37, expediente 1, 25 August 1688, "Informe del Fiscal," Mexico City.
25. AGN, Matrimonios (tercera seria), tomo 37, expediente 1, 31 August 1688, "Instancia de Salvador Antonio," Mexico City.

Striving for Freedom

In their quest for freedom, enslaved individuals like Salvador Antonio deployed specific tactics learned in the context of master-slave relations and the structure of slavery. But they also drew on their strategic consciousness and those of intimates. The resulting matrix underscores the idiosyncrasies of the paths toward freedom in the seventeenth century. Salvador Antonio's strategy emerged from the relaxed atmosphere in Doña Ana de Colmenares's household that permitted a slave to have repeated personal contact and sustained privacy with María de Marradon, the owner's niece. Enslaved persons who did not have such opportunities used other ways to seek freedom. Countless slaves ran away. In some instances, such efforts resulted in the formation of maroon communities like Yanga or Amapa.[26] A less dramatic form of flight—perhaps the most typical—involved an individual absconding to some distant region and then assuming an identity as a free person.[27] Such efforts magnify both how the enslaved challenged their servile condition and the peculiarities of social control of slaves in New Spain. In both instances, we discern a politics involving domesticity and the absolutist state.

The story of Diego Bran illustrates the strategy of fleeing to a new identity of freedom. In 1654, more than twelve years after fleeing from his mistress, the Countess de Peñalba, the slave Diego Bran found himself incarcerated and under intense scrutiny. After he fled from the countess, thereby also leaving his first wife, Diego Bran chose not to join other runaway slaves who formed maroon communities. Instead he adopted the name Gabriel and claimed to be free. He gained employment as sugar master (*maestro de azúcar*) on the estate of Doña Catalina de Avila Manrique in the province of Chiapas. Gabriel married for a second time, an act that eventually brought him to the attention of the Inquisition. Although the *alcalde* of the Santa Hermandad apprehended him on suspicion of being a runaway, Gabriel's greater crime was that he had become a bigamist. As a result, the inquisitors showed great interest in this runaway slave.[28]

In striving for freedom, Diego Bran fled, but in constituting his freedom he formed a second marriage. As a new man, Diego equated freedom with the ability create a new social existence. Mobility and passing as free enabled him to do this. Many bigamists used mobility to their own advantage as they constructed two unions, and slaves were able to use this strategy as well. The fact that some

26. David M. Davidson, "Negro Slave Control and Resistance in Colonial Mexico, 1519–1650," in *Maroon Societies*, 92–98.

27. Richard Boyer's work on bigamists offers a critical starting point for rethinking the question of slave flight and identity transformation in the decidedly fluid social environment of New Spain. See Boyer, *Lives of the Bigamists*.

28. AGN, Inquisición 434, 1654, expediente 13, folios 65–75.

slaves achieved mobility underscores the porous nature of slavery in seventeenth-century New Spain. It took the authorities over twelve years to apprehend Diego. The proceedings suggest that in the hierarchy of transgressions, bigamy prevailed over absconding from slavery. What does that say about the institution of slavery and the mechanisms of social control of slaves? Posed differently, why was the slave Diego Bran not simply returned to the authority of his mistress?

Historian Stephanie Camp has noted that in the southern plantations of the United States, "space mattered," adding that "places, boundaries, and movement were central to how slavery was organized and to how it was resisted." For Camp, containing slaves in space was the essence of slavery. She writes that "more than any other slave activity—such as trading, learning to read, consuming alcohol, acquiring poisoning techniques or plotting rebellions—slave movement was limited, monitored, and criminalized."[29] But in early modern New Spain and in the proceedings against Diego Bran, mobility was a lesser threat than bigamy. Diego could simply claim a new name and status as a free person and then use that identity to find gainful employment. In this process, perhaps his cultural versatility and occupational skills played a key role. In a slave society with an African slave population, Diego Bran—whose surname suggests that he was a directly from Africa—distinguished himself.

The fact that slaves and free blacks were not contained in space in colonial New Spain suggests that physical restraint was not the social order's most pressing problem. According to scholars of slavery, the early modern state's inability to regulate slaves illustrated the limits of its power. But as the proceedings against Diego Bran and Salvador Antonio highlight, some masters were often reluctant—if not unwilling—to use "their private power of discipline"—the owner's ability to whip individuals, torture bodies, and incarcerate slaves. Why was this so? Perhaps the answer lies in the specific nature of slavery under absolutism.

Efforts to regulate slaves involved contradictory impulses. As property, slaves were subject to their masters' power. Masters could act with physical abandon; they could punish and torture their slaves. Many did. In the seventeenth-century archive, evidence of the injured body is rampant. Yet such displays of raw power seem remarkable in light of the restraint numerous masters manifested and their deference to ecclesiastical authorities and the inquisitors. What prevented Doña Ana de Colmenares from venting her wrath on her slave Salvador's body before bringing him to the attention of the ecclesiastical judge? At best, the authorities could admonish an owner for excessive punishment. When the authorities acted in response to owner violence, they usually did so in cases involving repeated abuse,

29. Stephanie M. H. Camp, *Closer to Freedom: Enslaved Women and Everyday Resistance in the Plantation South* (Chapel Hill: University of North Carolina Press, 2004), 6, 15.

and then they acted reluctantly. Even in those cases, they rarely acted to separate the slave from the owner but instead counseled restraint. What would prevent an owner from punishing her slave before subjecting him to Catholic discipline? One explanation might be that owners rarely indulged in the excessive punishment that might cost them the life of a slave.

In addition, and this is important, in New Spain, slaves could level charges of abuse against their owners. This speaks to more than jurisdictional conflict between elites, royal authorities, and church officials. As slaves and free persons pressed claims for various reasons, they were caught up in the shifting practices of power expressed through the modality of Catholic modernity. Inadvertently, their exercise of their rights bolstered the state bureaucracy's authority over individuals, thereby rationalizing Spanish rule.

Slaves and free persons operated with ease inside Christianity's boundaries, but some individuals, including persons who normally abided by Christian mores, transgressed the boundaries. Yet even as they did so, they mobilized a Christian discourse of justice. Lorenza de la Cruz was such a person. Lorenza thought that she had acted justly by absconding after suffering at the hands of an abusive spouse. But Lorenza married again, thus becoming a bigamist. In her statements during the bigamy proceedings, we see glimpses of Lorenza's sense of justice, a moral code that was inextricably linked to her sense of personal liberty.

"I am Lorenza de la Cruz, a free mulatto native of Amenecuilco in the jurisdiction of Cuernavaca in the archdiocese of Mexico, thirty years old more or less and a cook," testified the accused bigamist.[30] Lorenza then recounted that she had married the free mulatto Geronimo de San Juan "thirteen or fourteen years" ago, a union that had produced a daughter named Manuela. After she gave this biographical information, an official interjected that "this criminal left her husband for another mulatto and went to the pueblo of San Juan Periban in the diocese of Michoácan and being there for more than a period of six years then went to the city of Guadalajara where she had a illicit affair (*mala amistad*) with the free mulatto Diego de Soza alias Guaracha, a native of San Juan Periban."

In Guadalajara, civil authorities arrested both Diego de Soza and Lorenza on suspicion of being runaway slaves. Concerned about their fate, possibly fearing the loss of their liberty, Lorenza and Diego contracted a marriage on 27 March 1691. In marrying, the couple probably were attempting to forestall a sale or separation by invoking the rights associated with married life (*vida maridable*). While this strategy makes clear that the couple was familiar with the Christian moral universe, it also illustrates that they were not averse to unscrupulous methods; they

---

30. AGN, Inquisición 539, expediente 8, folios 72–79, "Proceso del Santo Oficio contra Lorenza de la Cruz, mulata libre, por Bigamia."

persuaded two inmates to offer false testimony on Lorenza's behalf. Lorenza in fact lied to the *provisor* when she said that she "had never been married." Colonial authority had already touched her life in many ways, and this second marriage brought Lorenza additional scrutiny. She had been married by ecclesiastical officials, then arrested by civil authorities. The Inquisition entered her life when its officials ordered Lorenza arrested on 30 January 1692, ten months after the wedding ceremony. It had taken Inquisition officials almost three months to find her. Finally they located her in Cuernavaca with Diego de Soza. The authorities placed her in the Inquisition's "secret cells."

On 23 April 1692, four days after her incarceration, Lorenza de la Cruz gave the first of three *audiencias*. Lorenza stated that her relatives and parents were "casta and generations of negros and slaves, indios and mulattos." She acknowledged that she was a "baptized and confirmed Christian" who frequently attended mass, confessed regularly, and partook in communion. Lorenza then demonstrated her ability to make the sign of the cross while "saying the four orations, the commands of God's law, those of the Church and the sacraments." Following this demonstration of competence with the rituals of the church, Lorenza testified that she and her first husband, Geronimo de San Juan, had had a *vida maridable* for six years. But Geronimo's physical abuse had been insufferable. "He gave me a very bad life (*muy mala vida*) and mistreated me," said Lorenza. When she was unable to endure any more, she had fled.

In this instance we hear Lorenza telling the inquisitor that the unjust nature of the abuse warranted her departure. She was Geronimo's wife, not his slave, and as a free woman she could fulfill her desire for a better life. Lorenza defined freedom as the ability to mitigate, if not end, the abuse she suffered. Lorenza had forged an understanding of personal liberty through the Christian discourse of justice. For this mulatto, freedom was much more than a juridical category. Freedom touched on the quality and nature of her domestic life. As a woman, Lorenza played to the masculine sentiments of the inquisitors. She had previously claimed that a resident of Amilpas had told her that Geronimo was dead; now she admitted to the inquisitors that this falsehood was not right in the eyes of the church. But she insisted that the greater sin was Geronimo's, for he had given her a *mala vida*.

Lorenza used a rhetorical strategy widely employed by women in the mature colonial period. Mulattos were no exception. Countless mulattos expressed their dissatisfaction with an abusive spouse by fighting back or fleeing. Christian justice established the norms of marriage, and violation of those norms made it thinkable for women to seek redress if not claim freedom from abuse. A sense of justice

---

31. Richard Boyer, "Women, *La Mala Vida*, and the Politics of Marriage," in *Sexuality and Marriage in Colonial Latin America*, ed. Asunción Lavrin (Lincoln: University of Nebraska Press, 1989), 252–286.

framed what Richard Boyer referred to as the "politics of marriage," which also informed the concept of freedom.[31]

Freedom was not merely an abstraction to these women; it assumed meaning in the context of the intimacies of daily life. We have already seen in the case of Salvador Antonio how freedom acquired its meaning in and through domestic relations. These stories illuminate how freedom emerged as an expression and constituent element of family life. Among the descendants of slaves, this concept of freedom acquired its meaning in relation to abusive masters and subsequently in relation to husbands. The paterfamilias—the master or the husband—played a significant role linking justice to freedom. Christianity made possible a discourse of justice and defined the nature of freedom. Lorenza understood that the injustice she experienced justified her decision to be free from Geronimo's abuse. Just as the relentless brutality of the master-slave dynamic elicited the desire for freedom, domestic abuse was reason for many women to seek a better life, as Lorenza insisted.

After Lorenza offered her version of events, the *fiscal* sought to discern if she was a heretic. "Being a woman legitimately married with a man," queried the *fiscal* "ought you to marry another man while the first lives?" Lorenza agreed that marriage was inviolable but then observed that she had been "under the assumption that her husband Geronimo de San Juan was dead" when she married for a second time. When the *fiscal* pressed Lorenza for the "discourse of her life," She simply responded that "I have always interacted and communicated with persons of my strata and was fearful of god." Following additional questions about knowledge of others who had committed "*delictos*" (sins), the *fiscal* remanded Lorenza back into custody. Lorenza appeared at two more *audiencias,* then languished in the inquisition's dungeon for two years before being sentenced to an *auto de fe* during which she received 100 lashes. She was also banned from Guadalajara for a decade. Before her exile began, however, Lorenza was sentenced to serve three years in the Hospital of Jesus Nazareno in Mexico City. In this instance, the inquisitors curtailed Lorenza de la Cruz's freedom because she had violated Christian boundaries.

In bringing our discussion to a close let us turn again to enslaved persons, individuals deprived of liberty and freedom's most ardent advocates. Yet even among slaves, freedom assumed meaning in relationship to their social existence as persons and kinfolk.

On 12 May 1767, Don Fernandez de Otanes, the *alcade mayor* of the province of Teutila, brought into relief the tensions among maroons in the province of Veracruz. According to the *alcalde,* tensions over strategy among runaway slaves had recently erupted into armed conflict, resulting in Diego Macute's incarceration. Led by Fernando Manuel, their "Capitan," a contingent of creole runaways wanted peace with the planters and were keen to establish a settlement in which they would be joined by their still-enslaved family members. This group fought the faction led by Diego Macute who wanted freedom and were not willing to compromise. The victorious creole contingent delivered Diego Macute and his allies to the Spanish authorities as an expression of good faith. Beyond handing over the recalcitrant Diego Macute and his defeated allies, Don Andres Fernandez de Otañes also informed his superiors that the erstwhile maroons had formed themselves into a militia company under the command of their "Sergeant" Fernando Manuel. In light of the invaluable service this black militia company offered the king of Spain, Don Andres endorsed the maroons' appeal for a permanent settlement.[32]

As the news traveled and individuals assigned it different meanings, both excitement and concern filled the air. In the town of Cordoba and on the plantations in its immediate vicinity, slaves and free persons traded information, gossip, and interpretations of recent events. Few could recall a more momentous affair since the revolt or rumored slave revolt of 1735. Those with a deeper historical sensibility recalled the periodic exodus of slaves who then formed maroon communities, *palenques,* which in 1609 had prompted the founding of Cordoba but did little to stem the tide of runaway slaves. The reaction among plantation slaves was mixed. Some anticipated that the latest developments would affect their lives and the lives of their children. Others merely saw the avenue to freedom becoming increasingly tenuous. Most planters did not share this view. Alarmed by the escalating breach, the majority saw recent events as an affront to their authority and, by implication, the social order. Some planters, a number of military authorities, and several royal officials, including Don Fernandez de Otañes, offered a different view. The circulating chatter underscored both the political nature of recent events and the way that conversations in a colonial social order acquired a political nature. This was especially true since runaway slaves, maroons, were the protagonists in recent events.

At this moment, 1769, runaway slaves (*cimarrones*) in Veracruz—colonial Mexico's remaining center of plantation slavery—vividly demonstrated how ideological differences among them, which reflected specific social, cultural, and historical circumstances, overshadowed the Spanish-imposed political beliefs and practices shaping the New World. After years of barely preserving their hard-earned freedom, the fugitives' endurance was strained by periodic pursuits by the local militia and the rigors of mountain life. The psychic toll extracted for their precarious liberty eventually sapped some of their resilience, leading a number of them to question the viability of marronage. Fernando Manuel represented those

32. AGN, Tierras 3543, expediente 1, folio 1.

who wanted peace and a permanent settlement. But the maroon leader, Diego Antonio Macute, saw these injudicious sentiments as a threat to his leadership. A battle ensued. Fernando Manuel's supporters gravely wounded Macute and condemned the vanquished to a life of slavery with the former masters. As Diego Antonio Macute and his fifteen followers languished in prison in Cordoba waiting for their erstwhile masters to reclaim them as slaves, their former compatriots engaged the local elite and the Spanish Crown for the terms of their hard-won freedom.

As leader of the maroons, Fernando Manuel voiced his and his compatriots' desire to "establish a permanent settlement" (*forma Población fixa*) and "be instructed in the Christian doctrine . . . so as to arrange our conscience and attain the salvation of our souls." By constituting a village under Christian tutelage, Fernando Manuel expressed confidence that the maroons would cease their long-standing lawlessness and sinful behavior. But the former *capitan* and now sergeant of the black militia attributed their illicit behavior to the extreme treatment the former slaves had received at the hands of the planters. "We deserted the sugar mills of Cordoba, where we were slaves, as a result of the harshness with which they treated us," stated Fernando Manuel, noting how "we fled for the most inaccessible mountains of this jurisdiction and that of Mazathiopia to form palenques . . . which we inhabited for more than forty years." A life of "toil, hunger and inconveniences" posed a challenge equal to slavery. In light of their privations, Fernando Manuel and his allies expressed a willingness to abandon life as maroons.

Although the proceedings were ostensibly about freedom, they also contain evidence of the social and cultural practices that informed the decision of Fernando Manuel and his supporters. Though the records are replete with details about slave resistance—a rebellion and massive and individual flight and a chronicle of maroon life dating back to the sixteenth century—they also document the existence of families and the engagement of maroons with Christianity while enslaved. In discussing their families, Fernando Manuel and other maroons used Christian terminology to describe their kinship ties with individuals who were still enslaved on various estates. In their masters' eyes, the individuals who were named were slaves. But for the maroons they were a wife, a parent, or a child. Fernando Manuel and his supporters waged war to sue for a freedom in which their still-enslaved kin would be manumitted and united with them in an autonomous political settlement. In a social universe where even the brutalized plantation slave made family ties possible, freedom acquired its valence in relationship to kinfolk. By the middle of the eighteenth century, as we shall see in the next chapter, the overlapping worlds of slaves and free persons were replete with complex kinship idioms and practices, thus highlighting why even maroons interpreted peace with the freedom to be with kinfolk.

SEVEN

Sin

In 1740, a local priest informed his superiors that he was granting the free mulattos Joseph Antonio de Ochoa and Veronica de Guerra a special dispensation to marry.[1] "Joseph," observed the priest, "had violated Veronica de Guerra's virginity under the faith and promise of marriage and was in habit of knowing her carnally." In the eyes of the church, their relationship was incestuous; Joseph and Veronica were second cousins (*primos segundos*). "Both had ignored the impediments," observed the priest.[2] He had to justify granting the cousins an ecclesiastical dispensation. Joseph had requested the dispensation so as to "honor . . . Veronica de Guerra." He also spoke of the looming danger if "a marriage were not effected (*no efectuandose el matrimonio*)." "Veronica's father and brother," warned Joseph "are men of base action and resolution." In defending their claims to honor such men would quickly resort to violence.[3] It is not clear if the threat of rampaging men affected the priest's decision to grant the cousins a dispensation. But grant it he did, and thus the ecclesiastical proceedings came to an abrupt end. We never learn what prompted the threat. Was it the loss of Veronica's virtue? Did the shame associated with an incestuous affair ignite the family drama? Perhaps the violation of trust and honor by a kinsman stoked the family ire. The dispensation merely settled matters in the ecclesiastical realm. If Joseph did, in fact, tell the truth, the cousins still had to resolve tensions with family and kin over undeclared claims of and affronts to honor.

---

1. Archivo Casa Morelos (Morelia) (hereafter ACM), Negocios Diversos (siglo XVIII), legajo 158.

2. Goody, *The Development of the Family and Marriage in Europe*; Twinam, *Public Lives, Private Secrets*, 128, 130, 233–235.

3. Stern, *The Secret History of Gender*.

By the eighteenth century, mulattos regularly employed terms and exhibited behavior that indicated their participation in a culture of family honor. Building on seventeenth-century patterns whereby ethnic Africans, black creoles, and mulattos defined their relations through such sentiments as: "forever" (*desde siempre*), "as little ones" (*desde pequenos*), "since he was born" (*desde que era criatura*), and "since he could reason" (*desde tiene razon*), eighteenth-century mulattos consistently invoked ties of kinship (*parentesco*), such as mother (*madre*), father (*padre*), brother and sister (*hermano/a*), grandfather and grandmother (*abuelo/a*), and the ubiquitous cousin (*primo/a*).[4] Assertions of legitimacy accompanied these ties. As eighteenth-century mulattos—a term the colonial elite associated with illicit love and social disorder—stood before ecclesiastical officials, they frequently identified themselves as legitimate sons or daughters (*hijo/a legitimo/a*).[5] In addition to terms associated with birth status (*hijo legitimo, hijo natural,* or *padre de no concosido* [unknown father]), mulattos drew on kinship ties (*parentesco*), sexual status (*virginidad, doncella, soltera*), and verbal pledges (*palabra de casamiento*) to justify these actions and claim legitimacy. As the vocabulary of family honor, these terms ascribed virtue and its loss. Parents routinely staked claims around these labels, expressing interest in the spouse selection of their offspring or the virtue of female kin. It would be misleading, however, to conclude that mulattos merely replicated the elite culture of honor. Since their ancestors had been denied honor, eighteenth-century mulattos manifested novel and therefore modified social practices.[6]

The prevalence of this terminology speaks to much more than family stability and Catholic legitimacy. Individuals used legitimate son or daughter (*hijo/a legitimo/a*) as a juxtaposition that signified moral status. Embedded in this notion of virtue—which in its idealized form featured a desiring man "fragile and miserable violat[ing] the virginity" (*fragil y miserable violo la virginidad*) of a respectable woman—we hear mulattos expressing sentiments about gender and sexual norms.

4. Nicole von Germeten comes to a similar observation, based on an extensive examination of baptismal records from the diocese of Michoacán. See *Black Blood Brothers*, 124–137.

5. For Mexico City, see, for instance, Matrimonios (Primera Seria) 1, expediente 65, folios 303–305, 1754; Matrimonios (Primera Seria) 1, expediente 66, folios 306–309, 1754; Matrimonios (Primera Seria) 4, expediente 11, folios 48–49, 1758; Matrimonios (Primera Seria) 14, expediente 106, folios 324–326, 1754; Matrimonios (Primera Seria) 23, expediente 9, folios 35–39, 1772; Matrimonios (Primera Seria) 23, expediente 32, folios 161–163, 1772; Matrimonios (Primera Seria) 23, expediente 37, folios 185–189, 1772; Matrimonios (Primera Seria) 25, expediente 46, folios 248–251, 1749. All in AGN.

6. Historian Bianco Premo has written: "In both criminal and civil legal cases over their slave sons and daughters, mothers and fathers used the cultural mores associated with legitimacy to suggest that their authority, too, was legitimate, and thus worthy of legal consideration. At times, when slave parents referred to themselves as the legitimate mother or legitimate father of a child, they were referring to the fact that they had been married in the church. In many other cases, however, references to marriage were absent. 'Legitimacy' might mean that they had been baptized their children, or it might simply indicate that they had recognized and raised the child as their own. This could be true of fathers as well as mothers." Bianca Premo, *Children of the Father King: Youth, Authority, and Legal Minority in Colonial Lima* (Chapel Hill: University of North Carolina Press, 2005), 226–227.

Of course, this Christian terminology reflected the Catholic Church's influence and claims of cultural dominance. Well after Mexican Independence (1821), Christian precepts and terms defined the self. In this discursive context, mulattos, like others, relied on Christian forms of being. In order to claim publicly a specific Christian status, however, an individual needed the appropriate family history and decorum. Christian terms required a basis in fact. For instance, the legitimate daughter (*hija legitima*) of a formally married couple who alleged that she had surrendered her virginity to a first cousin (*primo hermano*) was expected to have exhibited modesty as a maiden (*doncella*). To claim a status completely detached from reality could engender a public rebuke. In an anxious social order, individuals perennially challenged the moral status and claims of others, tacitly and explicitly questioning which persons exhibited honor and virtue.

This chapter explores the claims made by mulattos in the eighteenth century who petitioned for a marriage license in the diocese of Michoácan. In voicing requests, testifying on behalf of a couple, or contesting a marriage, individuals brought social claims, kinship ties, and love affairs into relief. As individuals described themselves or another person, they identified ties of kinship and invoked the network of relatives that surrounded a couple. Often this network reached back generations. Individuals frequently recited genealogies of relatives and friends that included grandparents (*abuelos*) and even great-grandparents (*bisabuelos*). These kinship ties and the accompanying claims were novel expressions for the mulatto population; the social memories of their elders and seventeenth-century ancestors were far shallower.[7] In this dense landscape composed of kin, claims to female virtue and individual honor appear alongside assertions of sexual violations and illicit affairs.

The most prominent claims mulattos expressed—most notably ties of kinship—are the subject of the following pages.[8] By consciously jumping into the

7. Von Germeten, *Black Blood Brothers,* 124.

8. Obviously, any analysis of social reproduction among mulattos requires qualifications. Over the course of the seventeenth century, the concept "mulatto" had lost much of its original meaning as the offspring of a Spaniard and an African. But it still meant someone who was descended from an African. In reflecting on the racial nomenclature of eighteenth-century New Spain, Irish merchant, antiquarian, and frequent visitor to New Spain Don Pedro Alonso O'Crouley highlighted the prevalence of racial mixing and the European population's obsession with racial classification. "From the union of a Spaniard and a Negro," noted O'Crouley, "the mixed-blood retains the stigma for generations without losing the original quality of a *mulato.*" O'Crouley observed:

> Because it is agreed that from a Spaniard and a Negro a *mulato* is born; from a *mulato* and a Spaniard, a *morisco;* from a *morisco* and a Spaniard, a *torna atrás;* and from a *torn atrás* and a Spaniard, a *tente en el aire,* which is the same as a *mulato,* it is said, and with reason, that a *mulato* can never leave his condition of mixed blood, but rather it is the Spanish element that is lost and absorbed into the condition of a Negro, or a little less, which is that of a *mulato.* The same thing happens from the union of Negro and Indian, the descent being as follows: Negro and Indian produce a *lobo; lobo* and Indian, a *chino;* and *chino* and Indian, an *albarazado;* all of which incline toward the *mulato.*

A Description of the Kingdom of New Spain by Señor Don Pedro Alonso O'Crouley 1774, trans. and ed. Seán Galvin (London: John Howell Books), 20.

middle of the eighteenth century, I explore the late colonial manifestations of family and kinship practices, the same issues that captured our attention in the seventeenth century when Angolans experienced their transformation into slaves. In an effort to make audible sentiments voiced by the eighteenth-century black population—mostly mulattos—I take issue with those scholars who have framed the social history of this population around upward social mobility, thereby losing sight of the crucial role that family dramas assumed. As the resulting and obviously provisional snapshot illustrates, the population composed of mulattos and blacks flourished in a dense social grid that illustrates much more than social mobility. As the reading of several hundred marriage petitions reveals, parents lamented the loss of a daughter's virtue and the shame it brought to their family's honor. Mothers and fathers challenged the choices that their offspring made in selecting a domestic partner or electing to have children out of wedlock. Parents sanctioned the desire of their offspring to marry kinfolk but demanded that they request an ecclesiastical dispensation. Such behavior reveals how far the norms and customs among the descendants of Africans had evolved in a little more than a century. Mulattoes valued virtue and honor for reasons that were particular to their experiences as a recently constituted people. Scholars of colonial Mexico have focused narrowly on upward social mobility and framed their eighteenth-century social history exclusively in relation to the Bourbon Reforms; this perspective loses sight of how mulattos, like the other segments of New Spain's population, channeled their experiences and history through their private lives.

Ecclesiastical archives are replete with family dramas. Through glimpses of individuals navigating the Christian life cycle from baptism to death, these sources bring the family and some of its dramas into relief. In what follows, I rely on ecclesiastical marriage records from the diocese of Michoacán classified as *negocios diversos* from the middle to late eighteenth century (1740–1790). These proceedings grant us momentary sightings of mulattos forging communities that were far more extensive than the networks seventeenth-century Africans and creoles were able to create.

Michoácan's eighteenth-century ecclesiastical records delineate a layered and complex mulatto interiority forged around elaborate kinship ties and genealogical memory. Relatives and neighbors memorialized kinship in marriage proceedings through the act of reciting genealogies. As individuals recalled family genealogies in the course of testifying on behalf of a couple, they also referenced acts of deflowering, consensual intercourse, procreation, and years of common-law marriage. Such details, which are rarely present in histories of slavery and freedom, demand a new conceptual horizon in which to situate this material.[9] The request for

9. "For more than twenty years," writes Ann Twinam in her marvelous study of gender, honor, and sexuality, "demographers and historians have designated the eighteenth century as the century

an ecclesiastical dispensation that framed the opening of this chapter requires far more nuance than our existing cultural theories afford. Joseph Antonio de Ochoa's request requires a perspective that brings kinship, honor, and desire into a single frame.

As Michoacán's eighteenth-century black population worked on haciendas and isolated ranchos, they largely restricted their social life to the kinfolk that constituted the surrounding free mulatto population.[10] Cousin marriages proliferated in the eighteenth-century landscape, reflecting the natural rate of growth among mulattos that, in turn, fostered an expanded genealogical memory. Joseph Antonio and Veronica—*hijos legitimos,* the legitimate offspring of formally married couples—knew that they were second cousins. In their kin-based community, the cousins' desire precipitated conflict and a threat of violence principally directed at members of the same village.

Other couples were not as brazen as Joseph Antonio and Veronica. Some couples alleged that they had learned of their kin ties only after a relationship had been well established. On 8 January 1740, in the jurisdiction of Santa Ana Iracapu (Izacapu), the *mestizo* Juan Francisco Vega and Rita Melchora, his free mulatto *novia* (bride), requested a marriage petition. A widower since the death of the mulatto Rita Antonia, Juan's first wife, Juan now sought to marry another mulatto named Rita. But in the clergy's eyes this marriage petition was not a routine affair. After formalities that included the testimony of three witnesses (*testigos*), Juan Francisco revealed how in the course of requesting permission from Rita's parents he had learned that he, Rita, and his deceased wife shared kinship ties. By defini-

---

of illegitimacy." After reviewing the historical literature on Europe in this time period, Twinam asked "To what extent was the illegitimacy of Don Gabriel Muñoz, or the 244 applications for *gracias al sacar,* or eighteenth-century rates of illegitimacy in Spanish America any part of this trend?" Twinam, *Public Lives, Private Secrets,* 7–16. Profound Eurocentricism informs the framing of the "century of illegitimacy," a concept that focuses on how customary and traditional stability was disrupted by the structural changes associated with industrialization and urbanization. Why make this ahistorical argument the starting place in discussions of Spanish America and its subjugated populations of Indians and Africans?

10. The growth of the Afro-Mexican population made possible a dense clustering of kinship ties in the eighteenth century. Changes in the demographic structure were closely related to economic shifts. In the late sixteenth and early seventeenth centuries, sugar and livestock haciendas dominated the landscape. But as the seventeenth-century economic crisis swept Spain and the Spanish Atlantic, Michoacán's agricultural producers and livestock cultivators shifted their attention inward to local and regional markets. The commercial estates, far from Atlantic markets, operated on the practice of autarky, which produced an economy that was more attuned to local demands in villages, towns, and cities along with the isolated mining center. Since estates tied their fortunes to local and regional markets, the eighteenth-century population booms had tremendous implications for their economic viability. Though slavery persisted in Michoacán, the region's black population was increasingly comprised of free people. Largely free from the structural constraints of slavery, the expanding mulatto population generally toiled as day laborers (*labradores*) on the commercial estates that at one time had relied on the slave labor of their parents and ancestors. Many more eked out a subsistence existence on the margins of the rural commercial estates or in the vast expanse of uncontested land. See von Germeten, *Black Blood Brothers,* 205.

tion Juan was related (a quarter in the third degree [*en quarto de tercer grado*]) to the *hija legitima* of his prospective in-laws. In order to contract a marriage, the couple needed an ecclesiastical dispensation to circumvent the obstacle their kinship ties presented.[11]

In requesting the dispensation, Juan Francisco claimed that he had "violated [Rita's] virginity with words of marriage" (*aver violado la virginidad de la dicha con palabra trato de casamiento*) before he knew of their kinship ties. But he also acknowledged that after learning of their ties, they did not stop having sex. Now, two months after the alleged revelation, the couple was still in the habit of "knowing each other as husband and wife." Juan Francisco concluded his request for a marriage license by invoking the "indignation of [Rita's] parents." By alluding to the animosity of Rita's parents in light of their legitimate daughter's shame, Juan Francisco raised the specter of honor. What respectable groom, asked Juan Francisco would contract marriage with a woman "defrauded of her honor?"

As Rita corroborated Juan's testimony, she disavowed that she had ties to Juan Francisco's first wife, Rita Antonia. But the couple's marriage witnesses knew of these ties. Two unnamed Spaniards acknowledged the affinity ties that joined the couple. A third witness dated his familiarity with the couple back to "their infancy." This unknown Spaniard implied that the couple frequented the same social space—a space defined by specific ties and shared local knowledge. Far from being strangers until they caught sight of one another, Juan Francisco and Rita moved in the same social universe, shared acquaintances, and frequented a similar circuit of rumors and gossip. Interestingly enough, the priest never pressed Rita or Juan Francisco about their assertions of ignorance and innocence. For that matter, ecclesiastical officials in the eighteenth century rarely questioned supplicants in marriage petitions about their claims as long as they expressed contrition in their request for a dispensation. In contrast to the actions of the seventeenth-century clergy, the eighteenth-century clergy in the diocese of Michoacan regularly offered ecclesiastical dispensations to parishioners who had contracted incestuous ties.

Concerned that gossip would erode Rita's honor and foster conflict with Rita's parents, Juan Francisco pleaded for an absolution and a dispensation for a sin born of ignorance. But what are we to make of the silence of Rita's parents? When did they learn of their daughter's interest in Juan Francisco? Was the relationship presented as a fait accompli after their daughter had surrendered her virginity to their kinsman? How should we interpret Juan Francisco's claim about their "indignation?" If they expressed such sentiments, were they born of a concern about their daughter's (and her family's) loss of honor? In the elite social universe where "mulatto" was a synonym for "illegitimate and rootless," Rita embodied the op-

11. ACM, Negocios Diversos (siglo XVIII), legajo 158, 8 January 1740.

posite. Rita Melchora was a *hija legitima* whose parents' formal marriage bestowed legitimacy and a modicum of respectability on their offspring, a free mulatto. Yet under what circumstances did she escape the watchful eyes of her parents and find herself in the arms of a kinsman?

What are we to make of the declaration that Rita Melchora's parents had informed the couple of their kinship tie? Juan Francisco said that he had sought the blessing of Rita's parents. Did Rita return home for a blessing as a prodigal daughter keen on showing her parents her ability to earn a livelihood and secure a husband? Perhaps Juan and Rita had learned the truth when they conferred with their prospective in-laws. We must ask why their familiars, especially the *testigos,* did not raise the issue earlier. Perhaps they did but the couple chose to ignore the moral implications.

Answers to these questions are elusive, but through this petition we glimpse how important a Christian-sanctioned marriage was in the eighteenth century, as it had been in the seventeenth. Even after learning of their error, the couple requested Christian nuptials. In applying for an ecclesiastical dispensation, they demonstrated their understanding of Church norms. Christianity clearly played some role in Rita and Juan Francisco's lives, even if only discursively. Juan pledged to marry Rita before consuming her virginity. In Spain and Spanish America, such gestures were tantamount to a marriage. In keeping with the code of honor and Christian norms, the clergy and neighbors expected a couple to sanction their union in the church. In its Western European incarnation and its eighteenth-century expression, honor in New Spain was inextricably bound to Christianity and the Christian community. In expressing a desire to marry Rita, thereby honoring his pledge, Juan Francisco conformed to both the popular and local codes of honor. Even if this act was a rhetorical gesture to convince Rita to have sex with him or a fabrication intended to evince the clergy's sympathy, the ability to orchestrate this performance highlights the sophistication of Juan Francisco and Rita's consciousness of Christian norms.

Scribes, of course, crafted the *informaciones matrimoniales,* thereby imposing a generic convention on the document. But the contents of the narrative reflected the testimony of the speaker. The speakers knew the setting, the audience, and how to structure their stories for maximum effect. The speakers, as the following case illustrates, exhibited a consciousness immersed in both Christian terminology and local lore. On 27 May 1740, in his petition to marry the free mulatto Phelipa de la Cruz, Alejandro de la Cruz—an Indian and the legitimate son of Juan Ruíz and Magdalena de la Cruz—appealed to ecclesiastical authorities to help him overcome parental opposition to the proposed marriage on the grounds that he was kin to Phelipa. Alejandro told the presiding ecclesiastical official that "as a fragile and miserable man he violated the virginity of Phelipa de la Cruz under the promise of marriage" (*como hombre fragil y miserable violo la virginidad de Phelipa de la Cruz . . . debejo de la palabra de casamiento*). Intent on exonerating himself, Alejandro performed the role of the contrite man who had succumbed to carnal lust and now wanted to honor his word and the virtue of a legitimate daughter. Though it is unclear which set of parents objected to the marriage on grounds of the kinship ties, Alejandro's father served as the couple's matrimonial sponsor. Identifying himself as an Indian noble (*indio principal*), Juan de la Ruíz testified that the "mother of Luisa de la Cruz was the sister of Antonia Truxillo, the mother of Salvador Truxillo who is the father of Phelipa Truxillo." A subsequent witness simplified matters. Juan de la Ruíz and Salvador Truxillo were paternal cousins (*primos hermanos*), and this fact precluded their respective children—Alejandro and Phelipa—from marrying without a dispensation from church authorities. We do not know if the clergy granted the dispensation, but based on the observable pattern the couple likely wed after the routine formalities.[12]

Though it is unclear where, when, and why the objection originated, Alejandro's carefully worded request was intended to counteract the ties that bound the couple and their respective families, Indians and mulattos. Through the performance of contrition and the invocation of honor, the couple sought to circumnavigate parental objections rooted in their overlapping genealogies. Since the memory of kin, the discourse of contrition, and the idiom of honor flowed from Christian discourse, the various parties knew how to fashion their strategy in compliance with Christianity and the teachings of the clergy. Though the clergy was only periodically present in this rural diocese and thus had only a fleeting presence in the lives of its residents, Christianity was always discursively present.[13]

Before proceeding, we might again want to ask under what circumstances the couple was able to circumvent the watchful eye of their parents to court each other and then consummate their desire. In his testimony, Alejandro stated that Phelipa's parents, Salvador Truxillo and Rita Michaela, were residents of the *pueblito* in which the *novios* began their illicit affair. The presence of family in a small village clearly made their courtship a public affair. This raises another question: If the affair was public knowledge, why did the parents ultimately object to a marriage? Because Alejandro and Phelipa were *hijos legitimas,* their parents probably were interested in having their legitimate offspring marry, just as they had. In short, the parents had probably been privy to the affair of Alejandro and Phelipa from the outset. As honorable Christians and the parents of legitimate offspring, Juan Ruíz,

12. ACM, Negocios Diversos (siglo XVIII), legajo 158, 27 May 1740.
13. Nancy M. Farriss, *Crown and Clergy in Colonial Mexico, 1759–1821: The Crisis of Ecclesiastical Privilege* (London: Athlone, 1968); D. A. Brading, *Church and State in Bourbon Mexico: The Diocese of Michoacán 1749–1810* (New York: Cambridge University Press, 1994); William B. Taylor, *Magistrates of the Sacred: Priests and Parishioners in Eighteenth-Century Mexico* (Stanford, Calif.: Stanford University, 1996).

Magdalena de la Cruz, Salvador Truxillo, and Rita Michaela may have simply desired an ecclesiastical dispensation.

Legitimacy mattered. But the timing of a marriage petition and the request for an ecclesiastical dispensation suggest that legitimacy was not the primary goal of all new couples. For the free mulattos Joseph Antonio Sanchez and Gregoria de Jesus, legitimacy became an issue only after they had produced two children. As natives (*naturales*) and residents (*vecinos*) of San Nicolas, Joseph Antonio and Gregoria had had a long-term and public illicit love (*amistad ilicita*).[14] A free mulatto and resident of the Soledad hacienda testified that he had known both Joseph Antonio and Gregoria "since they were little children." Another free mulatto and resident of the Soledad hacienda dated his long-term interaction with the couple by declaring that he had known their parents and grandparents. He said that Joseph's mother was Gregoria's second cousin. A third witness, a free mulatto, certified that he had known the couple "since they were little children" and had also known their grandparents and parents. Collectively, the testimony suggested that Joseph Antonio and Gregoria had been born and raised in an extensive community of kin and familiars who lived and worked in San Nicolas and the adjacent Soledad hacienda. For years the couple, who were related in the "third degree," did not and could not hide their relationship. In a social universe defined by kin and familiars, the couple began and sustained their *amistad ilicita* until unknown circumstances convinced them to legitimize their family life. Evidently, an illicit affair that produced illegitimate children in a small community in which a preponderance of kin resided did not result in ostracism.[15] Even though they were bound by kinship ties, the couple raised their offspring in a public manner and evidently in the absence of

14. ACM, Negocios Diversos (siglo XVIII), legajo 158, "Pueblo de San Nicolas de los Hueros, 1740."

15. For "*amistad ilicta*" in Mexico City, see Matrimonios (Primera Seria) 4, expediente 31, folios 111–116, 1758; Matrimonios (Primera Seria) 4, expediente 37, folios 132–133, 1758; Matrimonios (Primera Seria) 4, expediente 81, folios 265–268, 1758; Matrimonios (Primera Seria) 4, expediente 88, folios 289–293, 1758; Matrimonios (Primera Seria) 7, expediente 109, folios 373–377, 1764; Matrimonios (Primera Seria) 12, expediente 11, folios 37–40, 1755; Matrimonios (Primera Seria) 13, expediente 45, folios 228–231, 1749; Matrimonios (Primera Seria) 16, expediente 34, folios 131–135, 1764; Matrimonios (Primera Seria) 23, expediente 38, folios 190–194, 1772; Matrimonios (Primera Seria) 25, expediente 46, folios 248–251, 1749; Matrimonios (Primera Seria) 26, expediente 17, folios 321–326, 1760; Matrimonios (Primera Seria) 26, expediente 34, folios 377–381, 1760; Matrimonios (Primera Seria) 25, expediente 63, folios 325–329, 1752; Matrimonios (Primera Seria) 29, expediente 119, folios 372–378, 1773; Matrimonios (Primera Seria) 51, expediente 18, folios 66–70, 1743; Matrimonios (Primera Seria) 54, expediente 39, folios 173–177, 1763; Matrimonios (Primera Seria) 56, expediente 53, 1744; Matrimonios (Tercera Seria) 71, expediente 27, 4 folios, 1750; Matrimonios (Tercera Seria) 71, expediente 28, 5 folios, 1750; Matrimonios (Tercera Seria) 72, expediente 8, 4 folios, 1743; Matrimonios (Tercera Seria) 157, expediente 15, 1762; Matrimonios (Tercera Seria) 163, expediente 66, 1764; Matrimonios (Tercera Seria) 174, expediente 78, 1774; Matrimonios (Tercera Seria) 221, expediente 44, 1751; Matrimonios (Tercera Seria) 224, expediente 48, 1751; Matrimonios (Tercera Seria) 227, expediente 81, 1743. All in AGN.

disapprobation. Defining their love as "illicit" was merely a discursive description generated in the context of the ecclesiastical proceedings. Ultimately, the cousins opted to legitimize their union and the birth status of their offspring.

The issue of legitimacy took on different meanings when a couple had known each other for decades, if not as children. In 1740 in the pueblo of Tlaxsalca, María Josepha de Villaseñor and Leonardo Lopes replicated the pattern whereby cousins who had shared a life together as children entered adulthood only to become lovers. In requesting a marriage license, Leonardo, a free mulatto, a legitimate son and a native of Tlaxsalca, confessed to having "violated the virginity of María Josepha de Villaseñor." María—a free mulatto, a legitimate daughter, and a resident of the same pueblo—acknowledged that she had been morally indiscrete with her cousin, to whom she was related "in the third degree by blood on her maternal and paternal side." How egregious was this offense? Although the cousins required an ecclesiastical dispensation in order to contract a formal marriage, beyond this formality the case invited little attention. Indeed, since the details emerged in the routine formalities of an *informacíon matrimonial* as opposed to the proceedings of an ecclesiastical judge or the inquisition's commissary, we can surmise that María Josepha and Leonardo's behavior was less than extraordinary.

Also in 1740, the free mulattos Gregoria de la Trinidad and Cristobal Joseph stood before an ecclesiastical official intent on receiving a marriage license. Gregorio identified herself as a legitimate daughter, a native of San Luís Potosí, and for the previous fourteen years a resident of the *rancho de los Melchores*. Cristobal described himself as a native (*originario*) and resident of the same rancho. Cristobal confessed that he had "desired Gregoria" due to his "fragile" nature. Gregoria was even more explicit. "We cohabited for a period of ten years," said Gregoria, "engaging in illicit love with the intent of marrying." But formal matrimony never occurred because of their kinship ties (kinship ties in the third degree and a quarter with consanguinity [*parentesco de tercero con quarto de consanguinidad*]).[16] Inhabitants of the rancho were familiar with those ties. Indeed, the matrimonial sponsors—both of whom also lived on the rancho—intimated that they were familiar with the family genealogy. Since Gregoria shared blood ties with Cristobal but was a native of San Luís Potosí, we can only speculate about their family tie. In light of Gregoria's migration from a city to a rancho—which reversed the pattern for mulatto women—we might surmise that Gregoria's family had deep roots in the vicinity of the rancho. When she arrived at the rancho in 1726, Gregoria may have returned to the ancestral landscape in search of a livelihood. This explanation—one of several possibilities—brings into relief the decade-long illicit affair. In a social landscape where their ties were well known, the two rela-

16. ACM, Negocios Diversos (siglo XVIII), legajo 158, 1740.

tives could not easily contract a marriage, since at all times they were under the watchful eyes of family and familiars. Cohabiting illicitly, though a sin, was not as egregious as willfully marrying a relative. Neighbors and kin tolerated the former behavior—even a ten-year common-law marriage—but formal matrimony was another matter entirely. In rural Michoacán, friends, neighbors and kin consented to long-term cohabitation, even when it produced children, a social more that stood at odds with ecclesiastical policy.

On 6 December 1740, as an ecclesiastical official received requests for a marriage license in the congregation of Nuestra Señora de los Dolores, he learned of matters that contravened the teachings of the church. Pablo Victorino, a free mulatto native and resident of the settlement, confessed to being "fragile," for he had been "cohabiting for more than a year with" the free mulatto María Josepha. In her declaration, the native and resident of San Joseph de las Palmas admitted that she had had an "illicit love with Pablo Victorino for more than a year." Now the couple wanted to formalize their relationship. Pablo alleged that "in attempting to contract a marriage," he had recently discovered the kinship tie that bound him by blood to María Josepha's deceased husband. Before a marriage could take place, the priest needed to grant the couple an ecclesiastical dispensation. While Pablo's professed innocence seems questionable in light of testimony that acknowledged that María Josepha's deceased husband, Julio Joseph, was Pablo's second cousin, the community's indifference to this relationship is of greater interest. The witnesses conveyed little concern about the common-law arrangement among spiritual relatives. All three unnamed free mulattos had known the couple "since childhood" and noted that "Pablo Victorino is the son of Geronimo Calletan who was the second cousin of Julio Joseph de la Cruz." For the community to which Pablo and María Josepha belonged, little stood out as extraordinary. As the couple requested their marriage petition, a performance of contrition swayed the priest to grant a dispensation to the couple, who promptly returned to their life as it had been for over a year.[17]

In the available evidence, we see the eighteenth-century clergy accepting as a fait accompli many permutations of mulatto relationships. But the clergy also had its limits. As we shall see in the case of Joseph Mateo Aviles and María Antonia Aviles, the union of first cousins called for more scrutiny. Perhaps a local cleric observed the formalities in light of a local family drama in which a resourceful if not affluent mulatto opposed his daughter's selection of a spouse. In this instance, the cleric may have been careful to attend to the existing formalities in order to protect himself from allegations of having acted improperly. The prevailing pattern suggests that most priests rarely pressed couples about their illicit relations and routinely granted couples ecclesiastical dispensations.

17. ACM, Negocios Diversos (siglo XVIII), legajo 158, 6 December 1740, La congregación de Nuestra Señora de los Dolores.

Some individuals voiced objections to a pending union that were not related to the issue of legitimacy. On 24 February 1777, Joseph Mateo Aviles confessed that as a result of his "fragility he had engaged in a morally shameful act." Joseph claimed responsibility for having "violated" the virginity of his cousin María Antonia Aviles and habitually "violating her integrity." Both Joseph and María identified themselves as *hijos legitimos*. Compelled by his Christian conscience and love for María, Joseph requested a marriage license to keep his soul "on course for salvation."[18] María, who accompanied Joseph, also attributed her lapse to "fragility" and the couple's close proximity on the Xanipes hacienda in the diocese of Michoacán. Since Joseph and his family were "miserable people . . . who are only able to earn *real* daily in order to eat," María told the priest that her "wealthy and well situated" parents would oppose the marriage. After hearing their confessions, the priest placed María in *depósito* and Joseph in jail. He then questioned their witnesses, who testified that the mulattos were first cousins because their respective fathers, Eusebio Aviles and Hilario Aviles, were brothers. The following day, the priest informed María's parents of their daughter's confession and her desire to marry Joseph. As María predicted, her parents objected because of the poverty of Joseph and his family. This did not deter the priest; after granting Joseph and María a dispensation, he united them in holy matrimony.[19]

To what extent did María's parents' behavior represent a form of endogamy? As an ideal, endogamy is premised on value and scarcity—it acquires valence through its function in a sharply delineated social landscape—in this case, the constellation of symbols that informed a slave and colonial society. But formulations of endogamy in the New World have invariably examined it—and its related social phenomena of marriage, property, gender, honor, and virtue—from an elite perspective. And when scholars extended their analysis to peoples of African descent, Spanish practices were the baseline against which they assessed the behavior of those groups. At what point in the historical development of a formerly natally alienated population did the notion of endogamy come into existence? And if endogamy did indeed emerge, was it configured in a manner akin to how it was manifest among the Indian or Spanish population?

Perhaps we need a modified version of endogamy. In light of the general impoverishment of the mulatto population, the bulk of which had concrete ties to slavery in previous generations, the accumulation of wealth was unusual. By substituting the idea of value for the concept of property (in its most basic formulation that which people esteemed) we might be closer to understanding how a modified configuration of endogamy was in play among the mulatto population. The definition of endogamy among the descendents of Africans in New Spain might

18. Twinam, *Public Lives, Private Secrets,* 93.
19. ACM, Negocios Diversos, legajo 489, 1777.

not hinge on the relationship between kinship and property. As a body of scholarly work on slave and colonial societies in the New World shows, even among whites endogamy was never exclusively defined as the preservation of wealth.[20] "In Spanish America," Ann Twinam has observed, "stable and decreased illegitimacy rates suggested a social and racial consolidation as the colony passed through a third century."[21] We might benefit by thinking how endogamous practices in the New World might be related to the ideological effects of slavery and colonialism. For the descendants of Africans, this touched on the very thing that slavery as a form of social death denied: kinship. In this respect, marriage was the vehicle for an "endogamy of conscience" whereby successive incarnations of blacks—Africans, black creoles, and mulattos—valued family and other social ties for the relative autonomy they provided in a socially oppressive landscape.

Another instance of marriage opposition was manifest on August 22, 1777, in the pueblo of San Francisco, when Josef Jacinto Fragozo dictated an *instancia* from jail to the ecclesiastical authorities. Josef Jacinto Fragozo identified himself as a slave and said he was a native and resident of the hacienda of Orocutin. He was also the legitimate son (*hijo legitimo*) of Juan Fragozo and the deceased Feliciana Alexandria. Josef's legitimacy, though of interest, was not the most memorable aspect of the brief. Joseph had been incarcerated for "the sin (*el Delicto*) of having continued in the illicit commerce with Antonia Sebastiana, a slave of the said hacienda, the legitimate daughter of the deceased Antonio Silberi and Juana Gertrudis." He was convinced that Antonia's mother had conspired with their owners to oppose his marriage because: "Sebastiana is my niece (*sobrina*) in the third with four degrees (*tercero con quarto grado*)." Josef said that while the administrator of the hacienda, Don Antonio Solorzano, had consented to a marriage petition, Juana Gertrudis opposed the union. When he received the *instancia,* the vicar took declarations from both Josef and Antonia Sebastiana. Both claimed that they were willfully unaware of their blood ties and confessed to having had "carnal knowledge" of each other. The vicar was content with the confession and the admission of guilt, and he granted them a dispensation.

Then Josef and Antonia presented their matrimonial witnesses. The 60-year-old slave Francisco Xavier Mendoza, who lived on the same estate, declared that "they are relatives . . . for he is the second cousin by blood of her mother." Another

---

20. Martínez-Alier, *Marriage, Class and Colour in Nineteenth-Century Cuba.*
21. Twinam, *Public Lives, Private Secrets,* 11. Here then we might view the practice of mulatto *hijo/a legitimos* marrying other kin as a process of racial consolidation in the context of increasing racial consolidation among Spanish whites. Another way of thinking about this phenomenon is to see the process of state consolidation and the discursive frequency of the language of race—*mala raza*—as having a corollary among the black population. They were increasingly likely to marry among themselves as a reflection of the things they valued—autonomy from the gaze and encroachment of Spanish strangers, a presence that was accompanied by state and market discipline.

slave from the same estate, 80-year-old Pablo de la Cruz, acknowledged that he knew that "Josef Jacinto and Feliciana Alexandra were second cousins by blood [and that] as a result he [Josef] is her uncle in three-quarter degrees." The scribe attached a sketch of the family tree to the record of the proceedings:[22]

Siblings (hermanos) in the first degree
Juana Antonia and Pedro Benito
Fraternal cousins (primos hermanos) in the second degree
Feliciana Alexandra and Monica
Second cousins (primos segundos) in the third degree
Josef Jacinto Fragoso and Juana Gertrudis
Fourth degree
Antonia Sebastiana (22)

Individuals used a family tree in a slightly different manner in the petition of José Nicolas Rallas. On 12 July 1777, the free mulatto José Nicolas Rallas addressed himself to the ecclesiastical judge. "For a year," said José, "I have tried to contract matrimony with the *mestiza* Maria Roxelia." He also acknowledged that as a "weak man (*hombre fragil*) . . . I violated her integrity (*violé su integridad*)." He informed the *provisor* that his conquest had been accompanied by the promise of marriage. "Obligated to honor my word," José recounted how he had "asked her mother." But she rejected the proposed union on the basis of family ties. José observed that when he had previously "frequented the house to see [María]," "they never told me." José was suspicious about María's mother's motives. "Her mother," declared José "does not want this marriage." As he stood before the ecclesiastical authorities expressing his desire to save "my soul and conscience (*mi anímo*)," Jose petitioned for a dispensation so he could marry María. María Roxelia Qames, the legitimate daughter of the deceased Geraldo Qames and Guadalalupe Gusan, spoke next. She said that they had ignored "to the present the kinship ties between them." "Under the promise of marriage (*palabar de casamiento*) more than a year ago," conceded María, "we knew each other carnally." She too claimed that her mother "did not want the said marriage."

After the marital witnesses presented their testimony on behalf of the couple, the *provisor* agreed to receive a formal request for dispensation. All three witnesses offered similar testimony, including that fact that they had known both members of the prospective couple for a lifetime. They detailed their intimate knowledge of the family history. "I have known them since they were born," declared the 80-year-old free mulatto Lucas de Alviles. He then rehearsed their family genealogy.

22. ACM, Negocios Diversos, legajo 488, 22 August 1777.

Siblings (hermanos) in the first degree
Josepha de Santiago and Lorenzo de Santiago

2nd degree: Mother of	**Father of**
Isabel de Abiles	Melchora de Santiago
3rd degree: Mother of	**Mother of**
Manuela Maldonado	Geraldo Qames
4th degree: Mother of	**Father of**
Joseph Nicolas Rallas	María Roxelia Qames

"They are third cousins," said Lucas, "within the fourth degree." In addition, Lucas noted that they both were poor. "Jose Nicolas Rallas is an orphan without any faculties . . . maintaining himself with his personal work," reported Lucas, while "María is equally poor . . . and in the shadow of her mother." The *provisor* had heard enough. He granted José the dispensation for reasons of "honor."[23]

A final example of contestation illustrates that opposition to proposed marriages among mulattos could assume various forms. When mulatto Juan Jose Moreno, who some people said was still a slave, asked the ecclesiastical judge to grant him and the free mulatto María Remigio Maciel a marriage license, he faced stiff resistance from his *novia*'s parents. He offered the judge a description of his life from birth to the present, a journey that took him from slavery to a contested freedom. Juan José began by identifying himself as the mulatto son of Manuela de Figueroa and "an unknown slave father" (*padre no conocido esclavo*). As a result of "his necessities," Don Luís Maciel, Juan's first owner, had sold him to Don José de Estrada of the same pueblo, who, in turn, had passed him on to Don Pedro Navarro Cavadas of Zamora. "All three are dead," reported Juan José. In the company of his last owner, he had made his way to Mexico City via Queretaro, where he stayed briefly in the house of Don Antonio de Solar. In Mexico, he entered the service of a priest, Fray Vicente Aranjo, but then was sent to the *obraje* of Escando. He had fled from the *obraje,* making his way to Oaxaca, where he remained for a year. In Oaxaca, he had enlisted for "ten years in the Fifth Regiment of the Americas and more in the Marine Battalion," serving in the "diverse Kingdoms of Castile, the Kingdom of Naples." Juan José alleged that for his heroic service, the king had granted him liberty. Now, however, "Doña Antonia Isabel de Alarcon, Don Pedro Navarro Cavados's widow," questioned his freedom. With this description of a vivid and adventurous life, the 28-year-old Juan José asked the *provisor* for a marriage license.

María Remigio Maciel, the free mulatto and legitimate daughter of Diego Maciel and Juana Sandoval, was "in *depósito* as a result of her parents' resistance." The *provisor* questioned María about her decision to marry a slave. "I know he

23. ACM, Negocios Diversos, legajo 488, 1777.

is a slave," replied the seventeen-year-old, but "I want to marry him of my own free will" (*de su propria voluntad*). María's expression of her will was sufficient for the *provisor,* who, in the absence of impediments, allowed the couple's witnesses to testify in order to complete the *información matrimonial.* Three respected Spaniards—they all bore the title "don"—spoke on the couple's behalf. Though ten years separated the birth of Juan José from that of María Remigio Maciel, all acknowledged that they had known both members of the prospective couple from birth. They also recalled Juan José's successive owners and confirmed Juan José's lengthy absence from the pueblo while he "traveled to diverse countries."[24] The *provisor* granted the license.

In the cases cited above we see the eighteenth-century clergy siding with mulatto couples despite parental opposition. Earlier I noted historian Patricia Seed's observation that in the late seventeenth century the Catholic Church began to withdraw its unconditional support of individual will and increasingly side with parental authority.[25] In the instances cited here and in chapter five the clergy maintained its defense of individual will in the face of parental opposition. Perhaps location explains these divergent patterns. In urban areas, as the colonial state withdrew from its alliance with the Catholic Church, the clergy may have been interested in cultivating support among elite patricians. In rural areas—especially zones with large black, Indian, mulatto, and mestizo populations—the clergy may have felt that preserving a social order premised on Christian matrimony was a more pressing problem. This might explain why the clergy in eighteenth-century Michoacan supported individual will in the face of parental opposition. Additional research centered on the clergy's diverse objectives in urban and rural locations and the racial classification of the prevailing population could result in more definitive conclusions.

To what extent did financial constraints determine whether a couple cohabited or entered common-law marriages? What did a Church wedding cost? Wedding expenses went beyond ecclesiastical fees. Elaborate fiestas attended by family, kin, and neighbors accompanied nuptials. For laborers struggling to make ends meet, the expense of a formal wedding could be a substantial (if not inconceivable) burden. Ecclesiastical sources do not reveal the actual extent that poverty played in forming common-law rather than formalized arrangements, but individuals frequently remarked that their dire circumstances had prevented them from fulfilling their Christian obligations. "He is a poor man" (*es un probre*), declared a witness speaking on behalf of the free mulatto José Feliciana Perez, who was requesting a license to marry the free mulatto María Petina Silva, who was also his cousin. Despite the fact that José Feliciano had sired two children with María Petina, the

24. Ibid.
25. Seed, *To Love, Honor and Obey in Colonial Mexico,* 161–204.

witness stated that José was a "good son" for supporting his widowed mother "in his company."[26] In the marital witness's eyes, José was a "poor man" and a "good son" who deserved an ecclesiastical dispensation so he could legitimize his union with María.

José Feliciano's relationship with his mother as a topic in the testimony of witnesses was not unique. A dutiful child's relationships with an aging parent sometimes took prominence over the words of family and friends in marital proceedings. A priest brought up the issue of loyalty to parents in the course of the marriage proceedings of *mestizo* Juan Martín Gomez and free mulatto María Prudencía Castro. The priest noted that at age thirty-eight, María Prudencia was ever loyal to her mother, who was "very advanced in age." María faced few prospects of "encountering another marriage." The aging *hija legitima* was a "poor orphan of a well-known father" who lived "in great poverty." In this case, the priest reasoned that her poverty and her family status were not reason enough to refuse her a dispensation to marry her beau, even though he was her younger cousin, Juan Martín Gomez.[27]

Poverty was a determining factor in another case where a couple requested a marriage license. Since the death of her father, eighteen-year-old free mulatto María Albina Ribera had confronted circumstances resembling those that María Prudencía faced. Though María Alibina's mother was still robust, she was caring for three other children. The family of five was without a male breadwinner, and María's job at the *tortillera* (tortilla shop) was not enough to support them. Less than a month after entering a state of concubinage with 24-year-old free mulatto José Victoriano Hernández, María confessed her shame and guilt so she could receive a marriage license. In pleading their case, the bride and groom invoked María's dire poverty. In the absence of an impediment and aware that a delay could result in the birth of an *hijo natural* as opposed to a *hijo legitimo*, the priest granted the couple a wedding license, even without the customary testimony of witnesses.[28] The priest rationalized his actions on grounds of María's poverty and the absence of a father.

In numerous eighteenth-century cases involving women and girls accused of illicit behavior, neighbors and friends invoked the trope of "poor orphan" whose father was absent. Women like María Prudencía and María Albina were poor woman in households without fathers who could not keep masculine predators at bay. In the absence of a father, virile brothers, or vigilant uncles, who would protect the family's honor? The threat of violence made honor a decidedly masculine prerogative. A woman's fall from honor would often be framed using the language "the poor orphan" (*pobre huerfana*) to describe a young woman who

26. ACM, Negocios Diversos (siglo XVIII), legajo 641, 1790.
27. ACM, Negocios Diversos (siglo XVIII), legajo 579, 1786, Villa de San Sebastián de Leon.
28. ACM, Negocios Diversos (siglo XVIII), legajo 579, 1786, Pueblo de Santiago Indameco[?].

had lost her parents, especially her father. The Spaniard Antonio de Herrera y Arriaga clearly expressed such sentiments when he testified as a marriage witness on behalf of the free mulatto and *hija legitima* María Margarita Ramírez. "She is a poor orphan without father and mother and with a recently born baby (*criatura*)," declared Antonio, who had known the 22-year-old since birth. The child's father, the *mestizo* Antonio Maximo Aguilar, was not the prospective groom. Antonio de Herrera insisted that María would find "it very difficult to attain another marriage." Implicit in the testimony of both men was a strong sense that María's orphan status explained this legitimate daughter's descent from honor. Her last resort was marriage to her cousin, 20-year-old free mulatto Jose Estanislao de la Luz Ramírez. The priest concurred, granting the couple a marital dispensation.[29]

In another case in which poverty was invoked, Lorenzo Luciano García, a free mulatto cowboy (*vaquero*), spoke in his own defense. "For more than two years I have had illicit love (*amistad ilicita*) and since then have wanted to marry her [but] due to my poverty I could not do so." The prospective bride, 20-year-old *mestiza* María Guadalupe Guerrero testified that "as a result of the notorious poverty of the said" they could not marry. But she also confessed that they were cousins: "Marcel Guerrero and Isabel Francisca were siblings; Antonio Guerrero came from the former and me from him [Antonio]. María Favrana came from Isabel Francisca and from her Lorenzo Luciano García." Hoping to sway the vicar's sentiments in her favor so that the cousins could receive an ecclesiastical dispensation, María acknowledged the presence of a baby (*criatura*). Evidently, this strategy worked. After the testimony of three witnesses—a Spaniard and two free mulattos, including Lorenzo's nephew Jose Ramon García—the vicar granted the couple a marriage license.[30]

In another instance of the bride or groom invoking poverty, the free mulatto Bartolomé de Anaya initiated the request for a license. "I am a poor man," remarked Bartolomé de Anaya, "with limited intelligence." In voicing these sentiments, Bartolomé, a native and resident of the pueblo of Tangantigo, tried to explain why he had had an illicit relationship with the free mulatto Rita Mundoz. "As a fragile man," noted Bartolomé, "I have had illicit love" with her. But poverty prevented Bartolomé from marrying his kinswoman (in the Catholic taxonomy they were cousins in the third degree). Clearly the cousins had known each other since birth. All the matrimonial witnesses—who were residents of the same pueblo and were acquainted with the couple's genealogy—emphasized Rita and Bartolomé's lifelong interaction. As cousins and playmates, Bartolomé and Rita entered adulthood and sexual awareness together. Bartolomé conceded that he had deflowered his cousin Rita years earlier under the promise of marriage. Still unmarried years

29. ACM, Negocios Diversos (siglo XVIII), legajo 641, 1790, La Congregación de Silao[?].
30. ACM, Negocios Diversos (siglo XVIII), legajo 579, 1785, Villa de San Felipe.

later, the cousins claimed to lack the resources to legitimize their union. Was it possible that the expense of a dispensation made the prospect of a marriage even costlier?[31]

What are we to make of the relationship to the Church of the individuals whose lives we have glimpsed? Clearly the communities of mulattos that proliferated in rural Michoacán simultaneously appropriated and modified Christian practices. In adopting Christian practices, they illustrated a degree of conformity to Catholic (and Spanish) norms. Yet in utilizing Christianity, mulattos subjected its institutional practices to different ends than the designers had intended. It seems clear that the clergy granted dispensations to marry to individuals engaged in illicit relationships more often than not. Complicit acceptance from family, friends, and neighbors was widespread, as was premarital sex, common-law marriages, and marriage between cousins, highlighting a culture of tacit dissent that nonetheless defined itself as Christian.

Even the clergy responsible for regulating their flocks expressed little concern about the frequency of what the Catholic Church defined as incestuous relations. The perfunctory nature of such arrangements can be seen in how the ecclesiastical authorities processed them. All of the cases described were administered and archived as routine *informaciones matrimoniales*. Practices that threatened Christian orthodoxy were classified as a separate category and were often forwarded to the authorities in Mexico City, including the Holy Office of the Inquisition. This did not happen when couples had engaged in premarital sex, entered long-term common-law arrangements, and or wanted to marry their cousins.

The Royal Pragmática and Beyond

Until the mid-eighteenth century, the Church regulated marriage. But in the late eighteenth century, against the backdrop of the Bourbon ascension and the contest for power between church and state, the Crown began to intervene in the regulation of marriage. In an attempt to preserve the economic resources and bloodlines of Spaniards in the New World, Charles III issued a royal order in 1776 known as the Real Pragmática, which was designed to prevent marriages among unequal individuals. The Pragmática required children to obtain permission from their parents before marrying; if they did not, parents were within their right to disinherit

---

31. ACM, Negocios Diversos (siglo XVIII), legajo 158, 1740, Tangandiguaro. For additional references to poverty, see ACM, Negocios Diversos (siglo XVIII), legajo 641, 1790, Pueblo de Santa Anna Furicatto; ACM, Negocios Diversos (siglo XVIII), legajo 579, 1785, Villa de San Felipe; ACM, Negocios Diversos (siglo XVIII), legajo 579, 1786, Pueblo de Santiago Indameco; ACM, Negocios Diversos (siglo XVIII), legajo 579, 1786, Villa de San Sebastian de Leon; ACM, Negocios Diversos (siglo XVIII), legajo 579, 1786, Pueblo de Taretan, Hacienda de Taretan.

them. Families could also thwart marriages if the prospective partner did not meet acceptable standards regarding wealth, race, or reputation. Thus, in the colonial epic, the ascension of Charles III was a critical moment in Spanish American history and historiography.

But the reforms that accompanied the dynamic transition from Hapsburg to Bourbon rule were a colonial drama that had few repercussions in the lives of the rural inhabitants in this chapter. Within the mulatto community, children continued to use the tenets of Catholicism to embark upon marriage with the partners they chose, even when parents or other family members objected. The Real Pragmática did not significantly affect the course of their lives. That is not to say that their lives were not changing. Throughout the eighteenth century, the dramas of family and friendship persisted as the dominant narrative in the private lives of ordinary black subjects in the villages of Mexico.

In 1777, the free mulatto Joseph Ignacio Zarate and the Spaniard María Manuel Espanola requested a marriage license. Though a native (*originario*) of Salvatierra, Joseph, a *hijo legitimo,* had lived in the pueblo of Indaparapeo for eleven years, perhaps explaining why the priest did not ask for a dispensation for vagrancy. Joseph's ability to marshal witnesses with whom he shared kinship ties by marriage from the surrounding haciendas offered the presiding priest additional guarantees. The bride, a *hija legitima,* and Joseph's brother-in-law, another witness, were native to the region. Building on the precedent set by seventeenth-century Afro-Mexicans, blacks and mulattos maintained deep ties to their place of birth. Space mattered, and it anchored family ties and friendships. All the witnesses had known the couple for a substantial period of time. One 50-year-old unnamed mulatto had known the couple fifteen years. Another mulatto, a 38-year-old native and resident of the Hacienda de los Naranjos, said that Joseph was his brother-in-law (*cuñado*). A 36-year-old Indian native of the parish of Salvatierra (*cura de Salvatierra*) who lived at the Hacienda de los Naranjos also identified himself as Joseph's brother-in-law, noting that he had known the groom "since birth" (*desde manzebo*) and the bride "since she was a little child" (*desde mui niña*). Evidently, the slightly older Joseph had known María since she was a child as well. Arriving eleven years previously, perhaps to join a relative who had preceded him to Indaparapeo region, Joseph had probably first laid eyes on María when she was a child of four.[32]

In the marriage petition involving the Spaniard Ana Rita la Trinidad Zamudio and the free mulatto Francisco Antonio Mantiner, kinship ties and long-standing friendship ties were even more explicitly delineated. A 40-year-old *mestizo,* a native of Acambaro and resident of Zinapequaro, had known both the bride and groom but emphasized his connections to their respective parents. For five years

32. ACM, Negocios Diversos, legajo 488, 1777.

"I have interacted and communicated with [Francisco's] parents," with whom "I have not ceased my friendship." For that reason (*por esta razon*), the *mestizo* said he had known Francisco as a youth. His familiarity with Ana Rita and her parents was even more impressive. He observed that he had known her "since a little child" on the Rancho Viejo near Acambaro, where he "said also friends with her parents." Similarly, a Spaniard testified that he had known Francisco since twelve years earlier, when as a boy "[Francisco] was [at] the side of his parents (*el lado de sus Padres*)." He dated his familiarity with Ana Rita "since she was a little girl on the Rancho Viejo," where he had maintained a "friendship" with her parents. The 48-year-old Spaniard José Zamudio simply identified himself as Ana Rita's uncle. As natives of the hacienda of Santa Clara Jose Zamudio and the *hijo legitimo* Francisco had interacted since the latter was born.[33]

What drama is manifest in these marriage petitions? I would say the drama of the African descended—the descendants of slaves—acting and loving each other as other colonial subjects did. In short, in the eighteenth century the mulatto population attended to their lives and domestic arrangements—dramas in their own right—in the midst of the Bourbon reforms. In examining the marriage petitions after the promulgation of the Royal Pragmatic, we learn how disconnected the social reality manifest among the mulatto population was from the fantasy that black exogamy was curtailing intraracial unions.

In 1777, a 40-year-old Spaniard and resident of the San Luís hacienda in the vicinity of the pueblo of Tecpan, sought to contract a marriage in 1777. The widower did not search far in selecting a second wife, choosing the free mulatto and *hija legitima* María Magdalena Baldobinos. But as the couple petitioned for their marriage license, the witnesses observed that Juan Galiana had had a long-standing affair with Maria's *prima hermana* (fraternal cousin) that had produced a child. Juan had an "affinity for having had *versado yligitamente . . . con una prima hermana de la pretensa* (illicit communication with a maternal cousin of the supplicant)," testified the 66-year-old Spaniard Don Marcelo but then observed that Juan had been punished for his illicit behavior. Juan Joseph Mendoza, a 55-year-old who had known the prospective bride and groom "since they were children," offered a similar statement. Aside from the ties of affinity binding the couple, he conceded that the daughter of the previous affair "is a single woman . . . *espuesta a cometer* (that commits) many offenses against God."[34]

The marriage petition involving the free mulatto María Guadalupe Salinas and the *mestizo* Josef María García underscores how couples drew on those who lived and worked in proximity to one another when they selected a spouse. In this instance the *hijos legitimos*, though they lived on separate ranchos in the district

33. Ibid.
34. Ibid.

(*partido*) of the pueblo of Santa María Tzinitziquara, probably had had a lifetime of interaction that built on the interactions of members of their families before deciding to marry. But the couple shared more than proximity. According to all three witnesses, the couple was related by blood (*consanguinidad*) "in the fourth degree (*grado*)." The scribe concluded the proceedings by attaching a sketch of their connections showing how Josef and María were third cousins:[35]

Hermanas (sisters)
Clara Barrera and Bernarda Barrera
***Primas hermanas* (first cousins)**
Beatriz Sota and Paula Polonia Chaves
***Primos segundos* (second cousins)**
Josefa de Soto and German Salinas
***Primos tercer* (third cousins)**
Josef María García and María Guadalupe de Salinas

As members of local communities, individuals shared a cultural memory that included knowledge of family dramas and existing kinship ties. Individuals from such communities who engaged in spiritual incest did so quite knowingly.

In 1777, the free mulattos Diego Toledo and Nicolasa Benites were asked for a deposition as part of their marriage petition to explain years of illicit conduct. "It is certain," began the 36-year-old widow Nicolasa, that "I have *versado inhonestamente*" with Diego Toledo. Nicolasa declared that the relationship had produced two daughters. She also acknowledged that the authorities had warned them to separate, an order with which they complied for eight years. In the last six months, however, she and Diego had revived their "*mala amistad.*" Diego professed similar guilt. Because of "my great fragility," observed Diego "I returned . . . to my ancient guilt (*antigua culpa*)." As inhabitants of the pueblo of Pungarauato and as the parents of two daughters, Diego and Nicolasa constantly confronted their "ancient guilt." As far as the Church was concerned, the issue was neither the "illicit commerce" nor the children that it produced. The matter that needed to be resolved before Diego and Nicolasa could legitimately marry was the existence of spiritual kinship between the free mulattos. In the language of the church, the couple shared ties of "affinity of the second to third degree (*parentesco de afinidad de Segundo a tercero grado*)." In layman's terms, Diego first wife, Marcela Gutierres, was a first cousin to Nicolasa's father, Agustín Benites.

Siblings (*hermanos*) in the first degree
Manuel Gutierres and María Gutierres
Cousins (*primos hermanos*) in the second degree
Marcela Gutierres and Agustín Benites

35. Ibid.

Cousins (*primos hermanas*) in the third degree
Marcela Gutierres (wife of Diego Toledo) and Nicolasa Benites

A clerical dispensation was needed to surmount the marital impediment posed by the threat of spiritual incest.[36] The request for dispensation was a part of the couple's proceedings for a marriage license. Interestingly enough, their witnesses—all residents of Pungarauato—did not allude to the impediment, though they said they had "[known] them since their initial years." But the existence of extensive family ties raises another question. In selecting their marital sponsors, why did Diego and Nicolasa not rely on their kinfolk? As I have demonstrated throughout this book, the selection of *testigos* was of paramount importance, and as kin became available, blacks and mulattos relied on them to sanction their unions. For this reason, we may surmise that a hidden history of conflict may explain the absence of kin as sponsors.

In 1777, an anguished appeal reached ecclesiastical officials in the archdiocese of Michoacan. "The mulato Anastacio Morales," began the *loba* María Albina Gama "has violated my virginity . . . with words of marriage." María acknowledged the compelling role that "love" played when she consented to the "violation." But now María lamented the fact that the promise had not been fulfilled. Anastacio, in turned, admitted that he had committed the transgression. He claimed, however, that since they were related, the marriage could not be consecrated. María implored the priest for a dispensation so that a marriage could take place, thereby enabling a return home. Unfortunately, the record ended abruptly without detailing how the case concluded.[37]

The free mulattos and *hijos legitimos* María Salome and Crispin Anastación also petitioned for a marriage license that year. The testimony of Crispin's uncle, a free mulatto and a resident of the Hacienda de Otates Jose Manuel de Quixco, illustrates the ways in which family memory held sway in the rural communities of New Spain. The 73-year-old Jose observed that he knew of no *parentesco* (kinship tie) between María and Crispin other than a blood tie in the third degree. He then narrated the followed genealogy: "Bernarda and Jose Guzman, were siblings who had children . . . the first Francisca Guzman and the second Nicolasa Guzman, Francisca also produced her daughter María Nicolas . . . and Gregoria Rocha had for his daughter the supplicant Maria." Jose Manuel recounted four generations of a black family.

Siblings (*hermanas*) in the first degree
Bernarda Guzman and Josefa Guzman

36. Ibid.
37. Ibid.

First cousins (*primas hermanas*)
Francisca Guzman and Nicolasa Guzman
Second cousins (*primos segundos*)
María Nicolas and Gregoria Rocha
Third cousins (*primas tercera*)
Crispin Anastacio and María Salome

Uncle Jose Manuel evidently offered a pared-down version of the family tree since he did not include himself or María's uncle Jose Francisco de Vargas. Tio Jose Francisco, a free mulatto of more than seventy years, said that he had seen Crispin and María being born. He also observed that the couple had not "mixed carnally but immediately [after] he [Crispin] took her from her house, and brought her to his house which is near." As a result "he [Crispin] has lost her parents' grace," while María found herself confined at home. "He is a poor *jornalero* (day worker)," declared Tio Jose Francisco, "who lives from his work and remains punished by the excess that he had committed." With little delay the priest granted the couple a dispensation and a marriage license.[38]

In a petition from jail, the free mulatto widow and muleteer Antonio Cervantes wrote: "I would like to marry the free mulatto Juana Manuela de Torres with whom to the present I have interacted . . . and lived with *incontinensia* for a long time." Conceding that the ecclesiastical authorities had incarcerated him for *amancebamiento,* Antonio pointed to the affinity ties that until now had prevented a marriage. Juana Manuela, observed Antonio, was related to his deceased wife, Antonio, by blood. In order to marry, the couple would require an ecclesiastical dispensation. Though contrition informed his petition Antonio Servantes explained his "domestic love [*amor domestico*]" as the result of a search for someone "to care for his kids." But now this prolonged "*versacion*" had convinced Juana to marry him.

Residents of the pueblo were well aware of Antonio and Juana's transgression. Indeed, they seemed resigned, if not accepting, of the couple's long-standing relationship. "Since Antonia died," testified the 57-year-old free mulatto Jose Gutierrez, "she [Juana has] lived in his [Antonio's] house, caring for and educating his kids." He then narrated Juana and Antonio's genealogy.

Siblings (*hermanas*) in the first degree
Juana de Cardenas and María de Cardenas
First cousins (*primos hermanos*) in the second degree
Geronima and Pedro
Second cousins (*primos segundos*) in the third degree
Antonia Miranda (deceased wife of Antonio Servantes) and
Juana Manuella de Torres

38. Ibid.

Asencio Mendez, a 60-year-old free mulatto, also spoke on behalf of the couple. He insinuated that Juana Manuela was compelled by duty to enter Antonio's household. "She lived with her parents," remarked Asencio, "then when they died about five years ago she went to live with the said Antonio." The 50-year-old free mulatto Agustín Ruíz offered a similar testimony, concluding that "it will be difficult for her to marry with another as I have said they are poor."[39]

Despite the prevalence of *hijos legitimos,* not all free mulattos who appear in the sample from the diocese of Michoacan knew their fathers.[40] In 1777 in the pueblo of Cuisio de la Lagua, the 20-year-old free mulato Juan Antonio Arroyo from the Pauraurio Hacienda identified his mother, Josepha Encarnación, in his marriage petition but acknowledged he did not know his father. Similarly, his *novia,* the 17-year-old free mulatto Juana Manuela was unaware of the identity of her father but named Pascuala de la Trinidad as her mother. Their witnesses—the Indian Domingo Flores, the free mulatto Juan Antonio Mendez, and the Indian Joseph Miguel Ortiz—had known the *novios* "since they were children." Perhaps in their collective knowledge, these elder natives of the Pauraurio Hacienda had some idea about the identities of the unnamed fathers, but in the specific instance of a marriage petition, this information would be relevant only if the father of both *novios* was one and the same. In such a case, the priest would have expected Domingo, Juan, or Joseph to voice objections to the marriage.[41]

On 29 July 1777, notary Francisco Sanchez recorded the following statement from the free mulatto Joseph Manuel Morales:

> In order to better serve God and save his soul he has tried to contract marriage with Luciana Michaela, a free mulatto, native [*orginario*] and resident [*vecino*] of this jurisdiction, and the legitimate daughter of Gabriel Sotelo and Juana Maria. . . . It is true that he had illicit conversation with the mentioned Lucian with the knowledge of having heard it said that she was his relative without distinguishing the degree because only his mother had heard and no one else and the said kinship tie [*parentesco*] had proceeded from Maria Antonia Orosco and Antonio Orosco who were brother and sister and from María Antonia Orosco came the daughter Casilda his mother and from Antonio Orosco came the daughter Margarita not by marriage . . . but she was known as the daughter of the said Antonio Orosco. From this referenced Margarita came the daughter María, mother of Luciana.

This passage acknowledges the uncertainty of genealogy. The rehearsing of

39. Ibid.
40. Von Germeten, *Black Blood Brothers,* 134–138.
41. ACM, Negocios Diversos, legajo 488, 1777, Pueblo de Cuisio de la Laguna[?]

family connections for the ecclesiastical archive lends the utterances the impression of certainty. This impression should be questioned. Joseph Manuel Morales said that "it is said that she was his relative." Joseph, of course, was defending having had "illicit conversation" with Lucian, whom he now wanted to marry. But he rightfully observed the limits of knowing based on rumor and gossip. Since illicit sex was far more pervasive than a formal marriage, one could never truly be certain about an individual's paternity.[42] Though family members, neighbors, and community elders spoke with certainty about kinship ties, they daily encountered the elusive nature of illicit sex, even in the smallest of villages.

Casilda Guadalupe, Joseph Manuel's mother, captured the undercurrent of illicit sexuality as she testified on behalf of her son's union with Lucian Michaela. "It is certain that my uncle and my mother's brother Antonio Orosco always recognized Margarita as his daughter and her as my cousin," observed Casilda, alluding to conception beyond the sanctity of marriage, "but I have also heard that the mother of the said Margarita was married to another and I do not know if at the time of her birth her husband was alive." Despite insinuating that Margarita's paternity was uncertain, Casilda concluded by noting "I am certain that she was the daughter of Antonio Orosco her uncle," thereby linking Margarita to the family by blood. Joseph Morales, Joseph Manuel's uncle and baptismal sponsor (*padrino de baptismo*) framed the matter succinctly for the ecclesiastical officials. "If you do not marry them," declared Uncle Joseph, "it will be seriously difficult for Luciana to [contract] another marriage for the defect of having to relive the violation of the virginity for which she remains in danger of *incontinencia.*" In his mind there was no doubt that Margarita was Antonio Orosco's daughter, but he hoped to persuade ecclesiastical officials of the practicality of his opinion. "They are," he noted after all, "both very poor." Evidently the clergy saw the matter in similar terms and granted Joseph Manuel Morales and Lucian Michaela a dispensation in order to marry.[43]

In the course of the eighteenth century the discursive requirements increased considerably from the initial half of the seventeenth century, when the age of the witness and the length of time that a matrimonial sponsor was familiar with the bride, the groom, or both were sufficient. The requirements mounted, in part, because the stakes in Bourbon Mexico had increased over the course of the eighteenth century. But in many respects, the discursive creation of genealogy illustrates the complexity of a social landscape in which mulattos figured prominently. Despite the stakes in the centers of power and authority, the free mulatto Joseph Antonio de la Zerda probably voiced the prevailing sentiment in New Spain's vil-

42. Twinam, *Public Lives, Private Secrets.*
43. ACM, Negocios Diversos, legajo 489, 29 July 1777, Pueblo de Santa Anna.

lage communities and plebeian neighborhoods when declaring that these "miserable poor people . . . do not have any goods (*bienes ningunos*)."[44]

In many respects, the family practices described in this chapter invite our attention for their distinctiveness in New World slave societies. A social landscape populated by great-grandparents and grandparents (or the memory thereof), cousins, and cousin marriages is a largely unacknowledged phenomenon in the historiography of Afro-Latin America.[45] The usual kinship configuration invoked in discussions of the ties of Africans, slaves, and blacks in colonial Latin America typically includes a mother, might refer to a father, and sometimes points to siblings that an individual grew up with.

For imperial policymakers and the Spanish elite, it was simply inconceivable that blacks and mulattos constituted legitimate offspring with developed sentiments about kinship. But the life experiences of mulattos—individuals whom the Spanish elite saw as bastards and the source of illicit sex—suggest otherwise. The demographic and cultural dynamic that took hold among blacks and mulattos in the second half of the seventeenth century ensured that eighteenth-century mulattos manifested a formidable sense of kinship accompanied by notions of legitimacy, female virtue, and masculine honor. In the century when many Western European countries experienced the "illegitimacy explosion," the mulattos inhabiting the least supervised rural villages placed considerable value on their formal kinship ties and their status as respectable virgins and honorable men.

As a growing number of *hijos legitimos* navigated the social landscape of sex, gender, and honor, they made decisions that elicited tension with their neighbors, their family members, and their Christian selves. Years later, some couples sought to rectify earlier choices—often made in a moment of passion. Cousins petitioned for ecclesiastical dispensations to circumvent existing impediments to a formal marriage. Individuals in longstanding common-law unions pled for absolution and a marriage license, thereby sanctioning their ties and bestowing legitimacy on their offspring. The resulting depositions, which number in the thousands in the diocese of Michoacan alone, uncover genealogies rarely associated with blacks and mulattos, slave or free prior to nineteenth-century emancipations. These genealogies reveal that in eighteenth-century New Spain, mulattos came into the world with deep roots already established that allowed them to venture through adulthood enhancing the kinship ideologies at the center of the late colonial manifestation of blackness.

44. ACM, Negocios Diversos, legajo 489, 12 August 1777, Pueblo de Penramo.
45. Norman E. Whitten Jr., *Class, Kinship, and Power in an Ecuadorian Town: The Negroes of San Lorenzo* (Stanford, Calif.: Stanford University Press, 1965), 114–147.

Colonial Blackness?

In recent years, one of the most insightful intellectual interventions among Latin Americanists has focused on postcolonial studies and its relevance for discerning the realities of the region. In surveying the engagement with "postcolonial theory" and "postcolonial studies," anthropologist and historian Mark Thurner identified among Latin Americanists an explicit critique of the "noticeable geographical and historical homogenization of the history of colonialism," whose effect was "the subalternization (read as: marginalization) of Latin America's colonial and postco-lonial pasts." For this reason, observed Thurner, "in the Latin American historical field . . . questions about the postcolonial were often formulated in more or less re-active ways: 'How and on what basis can we establish links between Latin America and other colonized regions?' and 'Can a word such as "colonialism" really refer to the historical experience of Latin America?"'[1]

In delineating the historiographical terrain of this debate, Thurner singled out the anthropologist Jorge Klor de Alva as offering the most searing critique of the idea of a "colonial" and "postcolonial" Latin America. For Klor de Alva, "neither term (colonialism nor postcolonialism) is applicable to the set of poli-cies and practices that defined the historical experience of nonindigenous Latin or Anglo America."[2] But the political practices directed at Indians, including the usurpation of their territory and wholesale cultural disruption, were in fact co-lonial. Extending this logic forward in time, Klor de Alva insisted that the lack of an indigenous vanguard during the nineteenth-century Wars of Independence

---

1. Mark Thurner, "After Spanish Rule: Writing Another After," in *After Spanish Rule: Postcolonial Predicaments of the Americas*, ed. Mark Thurner and Andrés Guerrero (Durham, N.C.: Duke University Press, 2003), 19–20.
2. Klor de Alva, "The Postcolonization of the (Latin) American Experience," 241.

precluded Latin America's entrance into the postcolonial era. On the grounds that Indians continue to be subjugated, Klor de Alva disavowed the relevance of post-colonialism for studies on Latin America, a sentiment that Thurner noted was "fairly common in the Latin American literature."[3] Critics felt that the term and concept would not be applicable until Native Americans had reclaimed their territory.

Here, without seeking to rehearse this wide-ranging, distinguished, and politically charged exchange, I simply note that this vibrant debate glossed over the African experience. Irrespective of a professed intention to question contemporary formulations of colonialism, the participants in the postcolonial studies debate largely disavowed diasporic formations and the black presence and its complexity as they theorized about Latin America and Latin Americans. In configuring Latin America without an African heritage, all sides in the debate contributed to the epistemic violence that has for centuries denied peoples of African descent a place in the colonial past and the nationalist present. If Africans are invoked, they are referred to "slaves" or *cimarrones*, tropes for cultural resilience. Beyond a static invocation of "the slave," blacks and mulattos appear as the amorphous *castas* that in Klor de Alva's alchemy turns them into subalterns—a term that includes such radically distinct social groups as the descendants of slaves and the offspring of Spanish masters. The extant yet fleeting references in the writings of Latin Americanists to black creoles and mulattos characterized them as permanent aliens detached from the social landscape whose very culture ensnared them in limbo awaiting the imminent return to a distant homeland. By representing peoples of African descent in this manner, Latin Americanists perpetuated a practice I labeled as epistemological exorcism, thereby fueling the very critique that inspired the writing of *Colonial Blackness*.

The pervasiveness of Latin American ideologies that either eviscerate the black experiences or flatten its complexity partially explains why Klor de Alva's definition of the colonial subject invited scant attention.[4] Klor de Alva wrote, "From a modernist perspective the term is a misnomer because the postcolonial condition has yet to occur among those who became colonial subjects of the empire and, later, of the nation-state: the tribute-paying indigenous peoples who remain in corporate 'Indian' communities."[5] In Klor de Alva's formulation, *castas* never

---

3. Thurner, "After Spanish Rule: Writing Another After," 20.
4. Carl N. Degler, *Neither Black Nor White: Slavery and Race Relations in Brazil and the United States* (Madison: University of Wisconsin Press, 1971, reprint 1986); Winthrop B. Wright, *Café con Leche: Race, Class and National Image in Venezuela* (Austin: University of Texas Press, 1990); Helg, *Liberty and Equality in Caribbean Colombia*, 2–13, 237–242; Sibylle Fischer, *Modernity Disavowed: Haiti and the Cultures of Slavery in the Age of Revolution* (Durham, N.C.: Duke University Press, 2004).
5. Klor de Alva, "The Postcolonization of the (Latin) American Experience," 244.

constituted colonial subjects: "The racial mixed *castas,* or castes, many of whose members identified with (and were part of) the *gente de razón*—the elites who triumphed in the wars of independence—although they were mainly subalterns, were never colonial subjects . . . In effect, one of the main points I would like to suggest is that a subaltern condition, rather than a postcolonial one, best describes the nineteenth- and twentieth-century subjectivity of both the indigenes who did not reside in indigenous communities and the non-elite racially mixed groups."[6] By framing the black presence in this way—if they frame it at all—the participants in the post-colonial debate missed an opportunity to participate in an inclusive intellectual project intent on generating "the history and theory of Spanish America's postcolonial predicaments."[7]

Let us briefly focus on the social logic that led Klor de Alva to posit a subaltern status for those descended from Africans. These assertions, which are still shared by most scholars of Spanish America, rest on static and profoundly outdated notions of slavery as well as a myopic conceptualization of hybridity. As a result, this representational strategy denies black creoles a juridical place as colonized subjects in the colonial and national order. In the minds of royal officials and now most Mexicanists, the deep and profound cultural disruption that transformed Africans into slaves was a distinct political process from the analogous process that Native Americans experienced. At the core of this distinction is a limited conceptualization of slavery that defines it narrowly as a labor system. Africans in this formulation appear as slaves and as persons capable of cultural resilience, but writers rarely acknowledge the range of experiences that defined black life, a ranged that included an acknowledged legal status with the accompanying obligations and rights. Yet scholars do recognize Indians as juridical subjects with defined rights and obligations that competed with their status as tributaries and Christians. In essence, the experiences of Africans and Indians are framed differently on the basis of a largely unquestioned sociological distinction—derived from traditions in Western philosophy and European political thought—in which the centrality accorded land and territoriality played a substantial role in characterizing the history of conquest and colonization.[8]

Under Spanish absolutism, polities rather than property occupied a prominent position. As inhabitants of polities, Amerindians acquired political representation and visibility as nations, in contrast to enslaved Africans. In this formulation, which mimes Klor de Alva's distinction between subaltern and colonial sub-

---

6. Ibid., 244–245.

7. Thurner, "After Spanish Rule: Writing Another After," 13.

8. Pagden, *The Fall of Natural Man.* For a dissenting perspective, see Patricia Seed, *Ceremonies of Possession in Europe's Conquest of the New World, 1492–1640* (New York: Cambridge University Press, 1995).

jects, Africans acquired freedom while the territorially dispossessed Indians still await their independence. In the maelstrom surrounding the quincentenary commemorating Columbus's momentous voyage, scholars seamlessly reproduced this distinction on the basis that nations were decidedly absent among the enslaved. As the following vignette illustrates, the erasure resulted from the fact that many modern scholars of Spanish America still allow Spanish chroniclers and national elites to serve as their cognitive guides, thereby confining the complex nature of the black presence to the subject of slavery.

As the Nahua-speaking emissaries sent by Moctezuma gathered intelligence about the new arrivals from the East, they noticed the obvious, the existence of varying phenotypes. In assessing the new arrivals' presence, their strength, and the nature of their mission, the Nahuas characterized all arrivals as gods, *teutiles,* yet particularized the black strangers as soiled gods. Though the Nahuas quickly corrected their misperception of the Spaniards and blacks, the initial observation underscores the presence of Africans in the earliest phase of the Spanish *entrada* (entrance), revealing a reality that still remains largely ignored. For the Spaniards and their historians, this presence was neither noteworthy nor the subject of historical inquiry, thus fading from memory except for references to the institution of slavery. In victory and in history, the Spaniards narrated their *entrada* as an encounter between the New and Old Worlds, denying the complexity that characterized the initial ethnography of the Nahua. In Spanish eyes, slaves did not merit any reference nor was that presence accorded any significance beyond the slave's service on behalf of his master and the Castilian sovereign.

In the rich scholarly exchange framed around, the encounter between Old and New Worlds in which the concept of the Other occupied a privileged position, modern observers have also theorized freely without substantively engaging with the African presence. Subsequently, the many works published in the context of quincentenary of Columbus's voyage replicated the epistemic violence that depicted the colonial divide as formulated around Spaniards and Indians.[9] After a half a millennium, the hermeneutics of the Spanish chroniclers still prevailed: early modern theologians and natural law theorists asserted that the absence of sovereignty made some inhabitants of Guinea into chattel, thus denying that slaves had a juridical status associated with a perceived polity. In the imperial configuration, this made them, as property, invisible.[10] Spanish absolutism posited a relationship between polity and *nación,* but as we have seen, juridical status and political representation were not contingent solely on the political equation that enabled

9. Stephen Greenblatt, *Marvelous Possessions: The Wonder of the New World* (Chicago: University of Chicago Press, 1991).
10. Pagden, *The Fall of Natural Man.*

Spanish chroniclers and now modern-day observers to frame the conquest and the subsequent colonization of Spanish America as an exclusively Spanish-Indian affair revolving around the issue of territory and its possession.

By juxtaposing "hybrid" and "colonial"—a formulation that equates authentic native to mythologized (primordial) ties to the land—the various sides in the postcolonial studies debate ignore the Afro-Latin American experience beyond the rural plantation slave. In some respects the indifference to the black experience also rests on a notion that conflates the black subject with a slave who in his cultural memory and customary practices nurtured an all-consuming engagement with the African past. From this vantage point, Africans obviously lacked the status of New World natives (*naturales*), but after centuries, officials still described *negros, mulatos, pardos, lobos,* and *coyotes* as rootless and de-territorialized individuals even though the variously defined black creoles appropriated identities as *vecinos, naturales, criollos,* and *hijos legitimos* that were associated with space and place. For royal officials, nineteenth-century statesmen, and now analysts like Klor de Alva, the diaspora made blacks and mulattos perpetual cultural aliens akin to Villamanrique's *vago.* But as we have seen, existential exile and slavery were but two states that the black experience assumed in colonial Mexico. Indeed, numerous social forces shaped the meaning and expression of blackness.

Blackness, as it appeared in the preceding pages, was both a form of identification and a strategic means of representation. By using the term "blackness," I registered my intellectual frustration with the ways that scholars of Latin America—beyond the canonical sites of black cultural formation in Brazil and Cuba—referenced Africans and their descendants as slaves and servants, *castas* and hybrids but rarely acknowledged that as persons they brought a perspective, a way of seeing, if you will, to the historical experience. Of course, peoples of African descent left few records in which they actually voiced their perspectives. But even if such records existed it would be specious to argue for an authentic perspective. "To claim to pass through the looking glass," writes the anthropologist Serge Gruzinski with regard to native Mexicans, "to grasp the Indians apart from the western European influence, is a perilous and often impracticable and illusory exercise . . . There remains, however, a still considerable field: indigenous reactions to models of behaviour and thought introduced by the Europeans; analysis of their perception of the new world established by the colonial domination in violence and chaos."[11] In an effort to discern such "reactions" among the African descended as they appear in the colonial sources, I have concentrated on behavioral practices and routine patterns. Archival sources highlight a far more complex social experience than does the standard narrative associated with slavery and freedom.

11. Gruzinski, *The Conquest of Mexico,* 5.

Individuals "from the land of Angola" alongside *negros criollos* and mulatos constantly expressed the importance they placed on personal autonomy and liberty through their behavior, thereby leaving voluminous evidence of an elaborate social existence that belies the existential shorthand ascribed to slaves by all but a few scholars of Mexican history.

In conventional histories the formative African experience (the story of slaves) gives way to the numerical ascendancy of mulattos (the storyline of *castas*). To a certain extent this is, in fact, what happened: Creoles replaced Africans as free mulattos outnumbered the slave population. Widespread *mestizaje* fueled complications for the elite and subalterns who tried to adhere to the colonial script. Many more individuals experienced *mestizaje* as a daily reality or as a form of emancipation. Eventually, the cultural divide between the descendants of Africans, Indians, and Spaniards diminished, but the elaborate and layered ideology of colonial difference bolstered existing social cleavages. Elite and metropolitan anxieties about the profusion of difference resulted in a fantasy of racial exogamy in which the alleged authenticity of Indians and Spaniards was steadily besieged by Africans, their offspring (blacks and mulattos), and the colonial hybrids (*mestizos*) that issued from unions of Spaniards and Indians. In voicing their anxieties, the elite and metropolitan authorities invariably invoked the specter of *castas*. Spaniards thus transformed their fabricated fantasy, the desires and practices of an elite minority, into an alleged reality. Another elite anxiety—the desire and penchant for order— led diverse metropolitan authorities to imagine that by naming and categorizing differences they could impose their will on the social reality that constituted the colonial order. Elaborate racial taxonomies fueled this conceit.[12]

The unwillingness of creolized hybrids (mulattos and *mestizos*) to characterize themselves generically as *castas,* especially during transactions that marked significant events in the Christian lifecycle (baptism, confirmation, and matrimony) should not be seen as a simple discursive imposition enforced by the clergy. Such practices also signified the particular ways that hybrids identified themselves. Identification among creolized hybrids resembled what historian R. Douglas Cope called the limits of racial domination. Cope convincingly illustrated how physical proximity and shared material conditions bridged ideological cleavages among ethnically and racially distinct plebeians. Class clearly bridged ideological cleavages, but as I have suggested, another social process was also operative. Again, I am not arguing for an authentic or pure space devoid of European contamination. We need, however, to acknowledge that the collective behavior of *negros* and *mulatos* routinely challenged the elite fantasy of racial exogamy and its projection of a profusion of grasping *castas* intent on acquiring whiteness at all costs. At the

12. Ibid.

core of the identification process is an assumption that some social phenomenon sanctioned the actions of those who claimed the labels *negro, negros criollo,* and *mulato,* those who colonial authorities labeled as *castas.*

A premise on which I stake significant theoretical claims is the belief that not all social practices, even those of the descendants of slaves, were engendered by resistance. Of course, the support for this argument resides in the ecclesiastical records that are my principal sources. The intimate nature of these sources, which focus on baptism, confirmation, matrimony, and extreme unction—life and death—come as close to personhood as any surviving record in the black Atlantic archives can. I am firmly convinced that the practices I have been at great pains to have the reader see and hear again and again in their truncated and fragmented state speak to a cultural vitality—not cultural resistance—that scholars and the public are quite keen on moving beyond and rather quickly. Rarely do we perceive of domesticity as the heroic stuff of history when writing about the descendants of the enslaved who made valiant efforts to define themselves by staking claims to a family life and kinship ties.

Bibliography

Alberro, Solange. *Inquisición y Sociedad en México, 1571–1700.* México: El Fondo de Cultura Económica, 1988.

Altman, Ida. *Emigrants and Society: Extremadura and America in the Sixteenth Century.* Berkeley: University of California Press, 1989.

———. *Transatlantic Ties in the Spanish Empire: Brihuega, Spain, and Puebla, Mexico, 1560–1620.* Stanford, Calif.: Stanford University Press, 2000.

Andrews, George Reid. *Afro-Latin America, 1800–2000.* New York: Oxford University Press, 2004.

Asad, Talal. *Genealogies of Religion: Discipline and Reasons of Power in Christianity and Islam.* Baltimore: Johns Hopkins University Press, 1993.

Bastide, Roger. *African Civilisations in the New World.* Trans. Peter Green with a foreword by Geoffrey Parrinder. New York: Harper & Row, Publishers, 1971.

———. *The African Religions of Brazil: Toward a Sociology of the Interpenetration of Civilizations.* Trans. Helen Sebba. Baltimore: Johns Hopkins University Press, 1978.

Bennett, Herman L. *Africans in Colonial Mexico: Absolutism, Christianity, and Afro-Creole Consciousness, 1570–1640.* Bloomington: Indiana University Press, 2003.

Benton, Lauren. *Law and Colonial Cultures: Legal Regimes in World History, 1400–1900.* New York: Cambridge University Press, 2002.

Berlin, Ira. *Many Thousands Gone: The First Two Centuries of Slavery in North America.* Cambridge, Mass.: Belknap Press of Harvard University Press, 1998.

———. *Generations of Captivity: A History of African-American Slaves.* Cambridge, Mass.: Belknap Press of Harvard University Press, 2003.

Best, Stephen M. *The Fugitive's Properties: Law and the Poetics of Possession.* Chicago: University of Chicago Press, 2009.

Bilby, Kenneth M. *True-Born Maroons.* Gainesville: University Press of Florida, 2005.

Blackburn, Robin. *The Making of New World Slavery: From the Baroque to the Modern, 1492–1800.* New York: Verso, 1997.

Bowser, Frederick P. *The African Slave in Colonial Peru, 1524–1650.* Stanford, Calif.: Stanford University Press, 1974.

Boyer, Richard. *Lives of the Bigamists: Marriage, Family, and Community in Colonial Mexico.* Albuquerque: University of New Mexico Press, 1995.

Brading, D. A. *Church and State in Bourbon Mexico: The Diocese of Michoacán, 1749–1810.* New York: Cambridge University Press, 1994.

———. *Haciendas and Ranchos in the Mexican Bajío, León, 1700–1860.* New York: Cambridge University Press, 1978.

———. *Miners & Merchants in Bourbon Mexico, 1763–1810.* New York: Cambridge University Press, 1971.

Brooks, James F. *Captives and Cousins: Slavery, Kinship and Community in the Southwest Borderlands.* Chapel Hill: University of North Carolina Press, 2002.

Brundage, James A. *Law, Sex, and Christian Society in Medieval Europe.* Chicago: University of Chicago Press, 1987.

———. *Medieval Canon Law.* New York: Longman Group Limited, 1995.

———. "Playing by the Rules: Sexual Behaviour and Legal Norms in Medieval Europe." In *Desire and Discipline: Sex and Sexuality in the Premodern West,* ed. Jacqueline

Murray and Konrad Eisenbichler, 23–41. Toronto: University of Toronto Press, 1996.

Burnard, Trevor. "'Do Thou in Gentle Phibia Smile': Scenes from an Interracial Marriage, Jamaica, 1754–86." In *Beyond Bondage: Free Women of Color in the Americas,* ed. David Barry Gaspar and Darlene Clark Hine, 82–105. Urbana: University of Illinois Press, 2004.

Canclini, Néstor García. *Hybrid Cultures: Strategies for Entering and Leaving Modernity.* Trans. Christopher L. Chiappari and Silvia L. López. Minneapolis: University of Minnesota Press, 1995.

Carroll, Patrick J. *Blacks in Colonial Veracruz: Race, Ethnicity, and Regional Development.* Austin: University of Texas Press, 1991.

Caulfield, Sueann. *In Defense of Honor: Sexual Morality, Modernity, and Nation in Early-Twentieth-Century Brazil.* Durham, N.C.: Duke University Press, 2000.

Chakrabarty, Dipesh. *Provincializing Europe: Postcolonial Thought and Historical Difference.* Princeton, N.J.: Princeton University Press, 2000.

Chatterjee, Partha. *The Nation and Its Fragments: Colonial and Postcolonial Histories.* Princeton, N.J.: Princeton University Press, 1993.

Christian, William A., Jr. *Local Religion in Sixteenth-Century Spain.* Princeton, N.J.: Princeton University Press, 1981.

Comaroff, Jean. *Body of Power, Spirit of Resistance: The Culture and History of a South African People.* Chicago: University of Chicago Press, 1985.

Comaroff, John, and Jean Comaroff. *Ethnography and the Historical Imagination.* Boulder, Colo.: Westview Press, 1992.

Cope, R. Douglas. *The Limits of Racial Domination: Plebeian Society in Colonial Mexico City, 1660–1720.* Madison: University of Wisconsin Press, 1994.

Dayan, Joan. *Haiti, History, and the Gods.* Berkeley: University of California Press, 1995.

De la Cadena, Marisol. *Indigenous Mestizos: The Politics of Race and Culture in Cuzco, Peru, 1919–1991.* Durham, N.C.: Duke University Press, 2000.

De La Santidad a la Perversión: O de porqué no se cumplía la ley de Dios en la sociedad novohispana. Ed. Sergio Ortega. México: Editorial Grijalbo, S. A., 1986.

Díaz, María Elena. *The Virgin, the King and the Royal Slaves of El Cobre: Negotiating Freedom in Colonial Cuba, 1670–1780.* Stanford, Calif.: Stanford University Press, 2000.

Edwards, Brent Hayes. *The Practice of Diaspora: Literature, Translation, and the Rise of Black Internationalism.* Cambridge, Mass.: Harvard University Press, 2003.

Eire, Carlos M. N. *From Madrid to Purgatory: The Art and Craft of Dying in Sixteenth-Century Spain.* New York: Cambridge University Press, 1995.

Elbl, Ivana. "'Men without Wives': Sexual Arrangements in the Early Portuguese Expansion in West Africa." In *Desire and Discipline: Sex and Sexuality in the Premodern West,* ed. Jacqueline Murray and Konrad Eisenbichler, 61–86. Toronto: University of Toronto Press, 1996.

Eley, Geoff. *A Crooked Line: From Cultural History to the History of Society.* Ann Arbor: University of Michigan Press, 2005.

Elias, Norbert. *The Civilizing Process: Sociogenetic and Psychogenetic Investigations.* Trans. Edmund Jephcott. London: Blackwell, 1994.

Eltis, David. *The Rise of African Slavery in the Americas.* New York: Cambridge University Press, 2000.

Ely, Melvin Patrick. *Israel on the Appomattox: A Southern Experiment in Black Freedom from the 1790s through the Civil War.* New York: Alfred A. Knopf, 2004.

Familia y Poder en Nueva España: Memoria del Tercer Simposio de Historia de las Mentalidades: Seminario de Historia de las Mentalidades. México: Instituto Nacional de Antropología e Historia, 1991.

Familia y Sexualidad en Nueva España: Memoria del Primer Simposio de Historia de las Mentalidades: Familia, Matrimonio y Sexualidad en Nueva España. México: El Fondo de Cultura Económica, 1982.

Familias Novohispanas, Siglos XVI al XIX: Seminario de Historia de la Familia Centro de Estudios Históricos. México: El Colegio de México, 1991.

Farris, Nancy M. *Crown and Clergy in Colonial Mexico 1759–1821: The Crisis of Ecclesiastical Privilege.* London: Athlone, 1968.

———. *Maya Society under Colonial Rule: The Collective Enterprise of Survival.* Princeton, N.J.: Princeton University Press, 1984.

Few, Martha. *Women Who Live Evil Lives: Gender, Religion, and the Politics of Power in Colonial Guatemala.* Austin: University of Texas Press, 2002.

Fischer, Kirsten. *Suspect Relations: Sex, Race, and Resistance in Colonial North Carolina.* Chapel Hill: University of North Carolina Press, 2002.

Fischer, Sibylle. *Modernity Disavowed: Haiti and the Cultures of Slavery in the Age of Revolution.* Durham, N.C.: Duke University Press, 2004.

Foucault, Michel. "Governmentality." In *The Foucault Effect: Studies in Governmentality,* ed. Graham Burchell, Colin Gordon, and Peter Miller, 87–104. Chicago: University of Chicago Press, 1991.

———. *The History of Sexuality, Vol. 1: An Introduction.* New York: Vintage, 1990.

Gerhard, Peter. *A Guide to the Historical Geography of New Spain.* Cambridge: Cambridge University Press, 1972.

Gibson, Charles. *The Aztecs under Spanish Rule: A History of the Indians of the Valley of Mexico, 1519–1810.* Stanford, Calif.: Stanford University Press, 1964.

Gomez, Michael A. *Exchanging Our Country Marks: The Transformation of African Identities in the Colonial and Antebellum South.* Chapel Hill: University of North Carolina Press, 1998.

Goody, Jack. *The Development of the Family and Marriage in Europe.* New York: Cambridge University Press, 1983.

Greenblatt, Stephen. *Marvelous Possessions: The Wonder of the New World.* Chicago: University of Chicago Press, 1991.

Gruzinski, Serge. *The Conquest of Mexico: The Incorporation of Indian Societies into the Western World, 16th–18th Centuries.* Trans. Eileen Corrigan. Cambridge, Mass.: Polity, 1993.

———. *The Mestizo Mind: The Intellectual Dynamics of Colonization and Globalization.* Trans. Deke Dusinberre. New York: Routledge, 2002.

Guardino, Peter F. *Peasants, Politics, and the Formation of Mexico's National State.* Stanford, Calif.: Stanford University Press, 1996.

———. *The Time of Liberty: Popular Political Culture in Oaxaca, 1750–1850.* Durham, N.C.: Duke University Press, 2005.

———. *Dominance without Hegemony: History and Power in Colonial India.* Cambridge, Mass.: Harvard University Press, 1998.

Guha, Ranajit. *Elementary Aspects of Peasant Insurgency in Colonial India.* Durham, N.C.: Duke University Press, 1999.

Gutiérrez, Ramón A. *When Jesus Came, the Corn Mothers Went Away: Marriage, Sexuality, and Power in New Mexico, 1500–1846.* Stanford, Calif.: Stanford University Press, 1991.

Gutman, Herbert G. *The Black Family in Slavery and Freedom, 1750–1925.* New York: Vintage Books, 1976.

Hahn, Steven. *A Nation under Our Feet: Black Political Struggles in the Rural South from Slavery to the Great Migration.* Cambridge, Mass.: Belknap Press of Harvard University Press, 2003.

Hall, Gwendolyn Midlo. *Slavery and African Ethnicities in the Americas: Restoring the*

Links. Chapel Hill: University of North Carolina Press, 2005.

Hanger, Kimberly S. *Bounded Lives, Bounded Places: Free Black Society in Colonial New Orleans, 1769–1803.* Durham, N.C.: Duke University Press, 1997.

Harding, Rachel E. *A Refuge in Thunder: Candomblé and Alternative Spaces of Blackness.* Bloomington: Indiana University Press, 2000.

Hardwick, Julie. *The Practice of Patriarchy: Gender and the Politics of Household Authority in Early Modern France.* University Park: Pennsylvania State University Press, 1998.

Hartman, Saidiya. *Lose Your Mother: A Journey along the Atlantic Slave Route.* New York: Farrar, Straus and Giroux, 2007.

Hartman, Saidiya V. *Scenes of Subjection: Terror, Slavery, and Self-Making in Nineteenth-Century America.* New York: Oxford University Press, 1997.

Helg, Aline. *Liberty and Equality in Caribbean Colombia, 1770–1835.* Chapel Hill: University of North Carolina Press, 2004.

———. *Our Rightful Share: The Afro-Cuban Struggle for Equality, 1886–1912.* Chapel Hill: University of North Carolina Press, 1995.

Herrera, Robinson A. *Natives, Europeans and Africans in Sixteenth-Century Santiago de Guatemala.* Austin: University of Texas Press, 2003.

Herskovits, Melville J. *The Myth of Negro Past.* Boston: Beacon, 1990.

Herzog, Tamar. *Defining Nations: Immigrants and Citizens in Early Modern Spain and Spanish America.* New Haven, Conn.: Yale University Press, 2003.

Higgins, Kathleen. *"Licentious Liberty" in a Brazilian Gold-Mining Region: Slavery, Gender, and Social Control in Eighteenth-Century Sabará, Minas Gerais.* University Park: Pennsylvania State University Press, 1999.

Hoberman, Louisa Schell. *Mexico's Merchant Elite, 1590–1660: Silver, State, and Society.* Durham, N.C.: Duke University Press, 1991.

Hsia, R. Po-Chia. *The World of Catholic Renewal, 1540–1770.* New York: Cambridge University Press, 1998.

Hulme, Peter. *Colonial Encounters: Europe and the Native Caribbean, 1492–1797.* New York: Routledge, 1986.

Hünefeldt, Christine. *Paying the Price of Freedom: Family and Labor among Lima's Slaves, 1800–1854.* Berkeley: University of California Press, 1994.

Hsia, R. Po-Chia. *The World of Catholic Renewal, 1540–1770.* New York: Cambridge University Press, 1998.

Johnson, Walter. *Soul by Soul: Life inside the Antebellum Slave Market.* Cambridge, Mass.: Harvard University Press, 1999.

Kale, Madhavi. *Fragments of Empire: Capital, Slavery, and Indian Indentured Labor in the British Caribbean.* Philadelphia: University of Pennsylvania Press, 1998.

Kazanjan, David. *The Colonizing Trick: National Culture and Imperial Citizenship in Early America.* Minneapolis: University of Minnesota Press, 2003.

Klein, Herbert S. *African Slavery in the Latin America and the Caribbean.* New York: Oxford University Press, 1986.

———. *Slavery in the Americas: A Comparative Study of Virginia and Cuba.* Chicago: Elephant Paperbacks, 1989.

———. *The Atlantic Slave Trade.* New York: Cambridge University Press, 1999.

Koselleck, Reinhart. *Futures Past: On the Semantics of Historical Time.* Translated and with an introduction by Keith Tribe. New York: Columbia University, 2004.

Landers, Jane. *Black Society in Spanish Florida.* Foreword by Peter H. Wood. Urbana: University of Illinois Press, 1999.

Larson, Brooke. *Colonialism and Agrarian Transformation in Bolivia: Cochabamba, 1550–1900.* Princeton, N.J.: Princeton University Press, 1988.

Laslett, Peter. *Family Life and Illicit Love in Earlier Generations: Essays in Historical Sociology.* New York: Cambridge University Press, 1977.

Lewis, Laura A. *Hall of Mirrors: Power, Witchcraft, and Caste in Colonial Mexico*. Durham, N.C.: Duke University Press, 2003.

Lockhart, James. *Of Things of the Indies: Essays Old and New in Early Latin American History*. Stanford, Calif.: Stanford University Press, 1999.

Lomnitz, Claudio. *Death and the Idea of Mexico*. New York: Zone Books, 2008.

———. *Deep Mexico, Silent Mexico: Anthropology of Nationalism*. Minneapolis: University of Minnesota Press, 2001.

Lomnitz-Adler, Claudio. *Exists from the Labyrinth: Culture and Ideology in the Mexican National Space*. Berkeley: University of California Press, 1992.

Lovejoy, Paul E. "Identifying Enslaved Africans in the African Diaspora." In *Identity in the Shadow of Slavery*, ed. Paul E. Lovejoy, 1–29. New York: Continuum, 2000.

———. *Transformations in Slavery: A History of Slavery in Africa*. New York: Cambridge University Press, 1983.

Mahmood, Saba. *Politics of Piety: The Islamic Revival and the Feminist Subject*. Princeton, N.J.: Princeton University Press, 2005.

Martin, Cheryl English. *Rural Society in Colonial Morelos*. Albuquerque: University of New Mexico Press, 1985.

Martínez, María Elena. "The Black Blood of New Spain: Limpieza de Sangre, Racial Violence, and Gendered Power in Early Colonial Mexico." *William and Mary Quarterly* 61 (July 2004): 479–520.

Martínez-Alier, Verena. *Marriage, Class and Colour in Nineteenth-Century Cuba: A Study of Racial Attitudes and Sexual Values in a Slave Society*. New York: Cambridge University Press, 1974.

Matory, J. Lorand. *Black Atlantic Religion: Tradition, Transnationalism, and Matriarchy in the Afro-Brazilian Candomblé*. Princeton, N.J.: Princeton University Press, 2005.

Mattoso, Katia M. de Queirós. *To Be a Slave in Brazil: 1550–1888*. Trans. Arthur Goldhammer. New Brunswick: Rutgers University Press, 1986.

McKnight, Kathryn Joy. "'En su tierra lo aprendió': An African Curandero's Defense before the Cartagena Inquisition." *Colonial Latin American Review* 12, 1 (2003): 63–84.

Metcalf, Alida C. *Family and Frontier in Colonial Brazil: Santana de Parnaíba, 1580–1822*. Berkeley: University of California Press, 1992.

Métraux, Alfred. *Voodoo in Haiti*. Trans. Hugo Charteris with an introduction by Sidney W. Mintz. New York: Schocken Books, 1972.

Miller, Joseph C. *Way of Death: Merchant Capitalism and the Angolan Slave Trade, 1730–1830*. Madison: University of Wisconsin Press, 1988.

Miller, Nicola. *In the Shadow of the State: Intellectuals and the Quest for National Identity in Twentieth-Century Spanish America*. New York: Verso, 1999.

Mills, Kenneth. *Idolatry and Its Enemies: Colonial Andean Religion and Extirpation, 1640–1750*. Princeton, N.J.: Princeton University Press, 1997.

Morgan, Jennifer L. *Laboring Women: Reproduction and Gender in New World Slavery*. Philadelphia: University of Pennsylvania Press, 2004.

Morgan, Philip D. *Slave Counterpoint: Black Culture in the Eighteenth-Century Chesapeake & Lowcountry*. Chapel Hill: University of North Carolina Press, 1998.

Morin, Claude. *Michoacán en la Nueva España del Siglo XVIII: Crecimiento y desigualdad en una economía colonial*. México: Fondo de Cultura Económica, 1979.

Moten, Fred. *In the Break: The Aesthetics of the Black Radical Tradition*. Minneapolis: University of Minnesota Press, 2003.

Murray, Jacqueline. "Introduction." In *Desire and Discipline: Sex and Sexuality in the Premodern West*, ed. Jacqueline Murray and Konrad Eisenbichler, ix–xxviii. Toronto: University of Toronto Press, 1996.

Nadar, Helen. *Liberty in Absolutist Spain: The Habsburg Sale of Towns, 1516–1700*. Baltimore: Johns Hopkins University Press, 1900.

Nalle, Sara T. *God in La Mancha: Religious Reform and the People of Cuenca, 1500–1650.* Baltimore: Johns Hopkins University Press, 1992.

Oestreich, Gerhard. *Geist und Gestalt des frühmodernen Staates: Ausgewählte Aufsätze.* Berlin: Duncker & Humblot, 1969.

Palmer, Colin A. *Slaves of the White God: Blacks in Mexico, 1570–1650.* Cambridge, Mass.: Harvard University Press, 1976.

Palmié, Stephan. *Wizards & Scientists: Explorations in Afro-Cuban Modernity & Tradition.* Durham, N.C.: Duke University Press, 2002.

Penningroth, Dylan C. *The Claims of Kinfolk: African American Property and Community in the Nineteenth-Century South.* Chapel Hill: University of North Carolina Press, 2003.

Pescador, Juan Javier. *De Bautizados a Fieles Difuntos: Familia y mentalidades en un parroquia urbana: Santa Catarina de México, 1568–1820.* México: El Colegio de México, 1992.

Phelan, John Leddy. *The People and the King: The Comunero Revolution in Columbia, 1781.* Madison: University of Wisconsin Press, 1978.

Premo, Bianca. *Children of the Father King: Youth, Authority, and Legal Minority in Colonial Lima.* Chapel Hill: University of North Carolina Press, 2005.

Proctor, Frank T., III. "Slavery, Identity, and Culture: An Afro-Mexican Counterpoint, 1640–1763." Ph. diss., Emory University, 2003.

Rabasa, José. *Writing Violence on the Northern Frontier: The Historiography of Sixteenth-Century New Mexico and Florida and the Legacy of the Conquest.* Durham, N.C.: Duke University Press, 2000.

Reis, João José. *Death Is a Festival: Funeral Rites and Rebellion in Nineteenth-Century Brazil.* Trans. H. Sabrina Gledhill. Chapel Hill: University of North Carolina Press, 1991.

———. *Slave Rebellion in Brazil: The Muslim Uprising of 1835 in Bahia.* Trans. Arthur Brakel. Baltimore: Johns Hopkins University Press, 1993.

Ricard, Robert. *The Spiritual Conquest of Mexico: An Essay on the Apostolate and the Evangelizing Methods of the Mendicant Orders in New Spain, 1523–1572.* Berkeley: University of California Press, 1966.

Russell-Wood, A. J. R. *Slavery and Freedom in Colonial Brazil.* Oxford: Oneworld Publications, 2002.

Saldaña-Portillo, María Josefina. *The Revolutionary Imagination in the Americas and the Age of Development.* Durham, N.C.: Duke University Press, 2003.

Sánchez, Isabel González. *El Obispado de Michoacán en 1756.* México: Comite Editorial del Gobierno de Michoacán, 1985.

Schmidt-Nowara, Christopher. *The Conquest of History: Spanish Colonialism and National Histories in the Nineteenth Century.* Pittsburgh: University of Pittsburgh Press, 2006.

Schumaker, Lyn. *Africanizing Anthropology: Fieldwork, Networks, and the Making of Cultural Knowledge in Central Africa.* Durham, N.C.: Duke University Press, 2001.

Schwartz, Stuart B. Slaves, *Peasants, and Rebels: Reconsidering Brazilian Slavery.* Urbana: University of Illinois Press, 1992.

Scott, David. *Conscripts of Modernity: The Tragedy of Colonial Enlightenment.* Durham, N.C.: Duke University Press, 2004.

———. *Refashioning Futures: Criticism after Postcoloniality.* Princeton, N.J.: Princeton University Press, 1999.

Scott, Rebecca J. *Degrees of Freedom: Louisiana and Cuba after Slavery.* Cambridge, Mass.: Belknap Press of Harvard University Press, 2005.

———. *Slave Emancipation in Cuba: The Transition to Free Labor, 1860–1899.* Princeton, N.J.: Princeton University Press, 1985.

Seed, Patricia. *Ceremonies of Possession in Europe's Conquest of the New World, 1492–1640.* New York: Cambridge University Press, 1995.

————. *To Love, Honor, and Obey in Colonial Mexico: Conflicts over Marriage Choice, 1574–1821.* Stanford, Calif.: Stanford University Press, 1988.

Seminario de Historia de las Mentalidades: El Placer de Pecar y el Afán de Normar. México: Instituto Nacional de Antropología e Historia, 1987.

Sensbach, Jon F. *A Separate Canaan: The Making of an Afro-Moravian World in North Carolina, 1763–1840.* Chapel Hill: University of North Carolina Press, 1998.

————. *Rebecca's Revival: Creating Christianity in the Atlantic World.* Cambridge, Mass.: Harvard University Press, 2005.

Sidbury, James. *Ploughshares into Swords: Race, Rebellion, and Identity in Gabriel's Virginia, 1730–1810.* New York: Cambridge University Press, 1997.

Smith, Raymond T. *Kinship and Class in the West Indies: A Genealogical Study of Jamaica and Guyana.* New York: Cambridge University Press, 1988.

Spalding, Karen. *Huarochirí: An Andean Society under Inca and Spanish Rule.* Stanford, Calif.: Stanford University Press, 1984.

Stern, Steve J. *The Secret History of Gender: Women, Men, and Power in Latin Colonial Mexico.* Chapel Hill: University of North Carolina Press, 1995.

Stuckey, Sterling. *Slave Culture: Nationalist Theory and the Foundations of Black America.* New York: Oxford University Press, 1987.

Sweet, James H. *Recreating Africa: Culture, Kinship, and Religion in the African-Portuguese World, 1441–1770.* Chapel Hill: University of North Carolina Press, 2003.

Taussig, Michael T. *The Devil and Commodity Fetishism in South America.* Chapel Hill: University of North Carolina Press, 1980.

Taylor, William B. *Drinking, Homicide, and Rebellion in Colonial Villages.* Stanford, Calif.: Stanford University Press. 1979.

————. *Magistrates of the Sacred: Priests and Parishioners in Eighteenth-Century Mexico.* Stanford, Calif.: Stanford University, 1996.

Telles, Edward E. *Race in Another America: The Significance of Skin Color in Brazil.* Princeton, N.J.: Princeton University Press, 2004.

Thomas, Deborah A. *Modern Blackness: Nationalism, Globalization, and the Politics of Culture in Jamaica.* Durham, N.C.: Duke University Press, 2004.

Thurner, Mark, and Andres Guerrero, eds. *After Spanish Rule: Postcolonial Predicaments of the Americas.* Durham, N.C.: Duke University Press, 2003.

Trouillot, Michel-Rolph. *Silencing the Past: Power and the Production of History.* Boston: Beacon, 1995.

Turner, Victor. *Dramas, Fields, and Metaphors: Symbolic Action in Human Society.* Ithaca, N.Y.: Cornell University Press, 1974.

————. *The Ritual Process: Structure and Anti-Structure.* Ithaca, N.Y.: Cornell University Press, 1969.

————. *Schism and Continuity in an African Society: A Study of Ndembu Village Life.* Oxford: Berg, 1957.

Twinam, Ann. *Public Lives, Private Secrets: Gender, Honor, Sexuality, and Illegitimacy in Colonial Spanish America.* Stanford, Calif.: Stanford University Press, 1999.

Vaughan, Meghan. *Creating the Creole Island: Slavery in Eighteenth-Century Mauritius.* Durham, N.C.: Duke University Press, 2005.

Vinson, Ben, III. *Bearing Arms for His Majesty: The Free-Colored Militia in Colonial Mexico.* Stanford, Calif.: Stanford University Press, 2001.

Von Germeten, Nicole. *Black Blood Brothers: Confraternities and Social Mobility for Afro-Mexicans.* Gainesville: University Press of Florida, 2006.

Wade, Peter. *Blackness and Race Mixture: The Dynamics of Racial Identity in Colombia.* Baltimore: Johns Hopkins University Press, 1993.

Walker, Charles F. *Smoldering Ashes: Cuzco and the Creation of Republican Peru, 1780–1840.* Durham, N.C.: Duke University Press, 1999.

Wallerstein, Immanuel. *The Modern World-System I: Capitalist Agriculture and the Origins*

of the European World-Economy in the Sixteenth Century. New York: Academic
   Press, 1974.
Weisner-Hanks, Merry E. *Christianity and Sexuality in the Early Modern World: Regulating
   Desire, Reforming Practice.* New York: Routledge, 2000.
Whitten, Norman E., Jr. *Class, Kinship, and Power in an Ecuadorian Town: The Negroes of
   San Lorenzo.* Stanford, Calif.: Stanford University Press, 1965.
Young, Robert. *White Mythologies: Writing History and the West.* New York: Routledge,
   1990.

Index

HERMAN L. BENNETT is a professor of history at the CUNY Graduate Center and author of *Africans in Colonial Mexico: Absolutism, Christianity, and Afro-Creole Consciousness, 1570–1640* (Indiana University Press, 2003).